EARLY ROMAN OCCUPATION AT CIRENCESTER

Aerial photograph of Cirencester, looking north-west.

CIRENCESTER EXCAVATIONS I

EARLY ROMAN OCCUPATION AT CIRENCESTER

J.S. Wacher, B.Sc., F.S.A. and A.D. McWhirr, B.Sc., M.A., F.S.A.
(University of Leicester)   (Leicester Polytechnic)

WITH AN INTRODUCTION BY

Professor S.S. Frere, C.B.E., D.Litt., Litt.D., F.B.A., F.S.A.

AND CONTRIBUTIONS FROM

P.D.C. Brown, Dorothy Charlesworth, Ann Connolly, Brenda Dickinson, S.S. Frere, B.R. Hartley, Katharine F. Hartley, M.W.C. Hassall, D.F. Mackreth, G.C. Morgan, P.J. Osborne, R.M. Reece, Valery Rigby, Clare Thawley, H.S. Torrens, Linda Viner, G.A. Webster, D.F. Williams

Published by Cirencester Excavation Committee
Corinium Museum, Cirencester, England
1982

© Cirencester Excavation Committee

ISBN 0 9507722 0 8

Produced by Alan Sutton Publishing Limited,
17a Brunswick Road, Gloucester.
Printed in Great Britain by
Page Bros (Norwich) Ltd.

CONTENTS

LIST OF PLATES

LIST OF FIGURES

LIST OF TABLES

Acknowledgements (JSW and ADMcW)

As always on excavations covering such a scale many people gave their services, and money was received from a large number of sources. First among the latter should be recorded the then Ministry of Public Building and Works, who undoubtedly shouldered the largest financial burden, both of the excavations and of the post-excavation work. Secondly, the help of the Society of Antiquaries of London, who sponsored the formation of the excavation committee as one of its major research projects, must be gratefully recorded. Other grants were received from time to time from: the British Academy, the Gulbenkian Foundation, the Royal Archaeological Institue, the Haverfield Bequest and the Craven Fund of the University of Oxford, the University of Leicester, Cirencester Urban District Council, the Bristol and Gloucestershire Archaeological Society, the Cirencester Archaeological and Historical Society, the Association for Cultural Exchange and the Cotswold District Council. Help in kind was provided by Gloucestershire County Council, Cirencester Urban District Council and Mr. Harry Pitts, while the Royal Agricultural College provided a dark-room on a number of occasions and the University of Leicester made laboratory accommodation available for all the conservation work. Thanks must also go to the very many people who contributed money towards the excavations through the site collecting boxes.

It is impossible to acknowledge individually the help of everyone. The site supervisors shouldered the main burden of recording: Elizabeth Dowman, Rosalind Dunnett, Brian Gill, Mark Hassall, Sheelagh Johnson, Christine Mahany, Alan McWhirr, T.J. O'Leary, Alan Perkins, Tony Poole, Mary Rennie, S.P. Roskams, Sarah Smith, Anna Wacher. Tony Pacitto, Gillian Jones, R.A. Fagence, C. Birchell, R. Rumens and Colin Shuttleworth have, at various times, served as photographers. In charge of the finds shed, on different occasions, were Marion Owers and Helen McWhirr. During the preparation of the reports, J. Thawley and Ann Woods successively acted as conservators at Leicester University. Also engaged on the post-excavation work have been Valery Rigby, and Linda Viner; whilst Peter Wright, Nick Griffiths and Tony McCormick have been responsible for the drawing of plans, sections and illustrations. Cheryl McCormick and Phyl Muir have shared the task of typing the manuscript.

Besides the authors of the separate specialist reports, several experts commented on various types of pottery from the early occupation for this report. Mrs. K.F. Hartley examined all the mortaria. Dr. K.T. Greene had already discussed elsewhere the main group of imported glazed and colour-coated wares from the area of the Leaholme fort ditches; he has also examined the sherds from the subsequent excavations. Dr. D.P.S. Peacock examined the amphorae, and Dr. D.F. Williams the Iron Age pottery. In addition, help has been received from Ms M. Darling, Mrs. V.S. Swan, Mr. P. Arthur, Ms J. Wills, Mr. W.J. Britnell, Mr. P.V. Webster, and Mr. A. Vince. Thanks must be extended to the staff of all the museums visited, in particular the Corinium Museum, Stroud Museum, Cheltenham Museum and Art Gallery, Bristol City Museum and Art Gallery and the Ashmolean Museum, Oxford.

In the field of non-ceramic studies, thanks for assistance in the preparation of notes are recorded to Mr. Leo Biek, Dr. R.J. King, Dr. Morna Macgregor, Dr. Margaret Roxan, and the late Mr. M.R. Hull.

For fifteen years Miss D.M. Radway organised an invaluable service of guides from the Cirencester Historical and Archaeological Society, with great advantage to the public. The late Instructor Capt. H.S. Gracie, C.B., F.S.A., R.N. (Retd.) was, for many years, secretary to the Excavation Committee; later Miss Joyce Barker, F.S.A., as local secretary, shouldered many of the administrative burdens, which latterly were assumed by Mr. K. Povah. Foremost among local supporters was Mr. John Jefferies, sometime Chairman of the Cirencester Urban District Council; his interest, untiring support and ready cooperation can never be adequately recompensed. Mr. Derek Waring, Chief Executive of Cotswold District Council, has rendered much help, as have also Mr. T. Ridge as Planning Officer and Mr. David Viner as curator of the Corinium Museum. Before him, Mr. John Real, as custodian of the museum, provided help on many occasions. Many local residents and business firms allowed access to premises or gave help in kind. Latterly, Professor S.S. Frere, C.B.E., D.Litt., Litt.D., F.B.A., F.S.A., Chairman of the Committee since 1966, has given valuable advice.

Tribute must also be paid to helpers now deceased; Mrs. Petty and Miss Eleanor Waite successively took charge of the finds shed; Mr. H.J.M. Petty, F.S.A., and Mr. W. Blythe acted as site accountants from 1961-63 and 1964-66 respectively; Professor Donald Atkinson, F.S.A., sometime Honorary Curator of Cirencester Museum, provided museum services and made preliminary identifications of the coins; Mr. J.W. Elliott, sometime Engineer and Surveyor to the Urban District Council, contributed much help and information. Finally we must record the untiring support and wise advice of the late Professor Sir Ian Richmond, C.B.E., F.B.A., P.S.A., founder and first Chairman of the Committee.

Thanks are also due to the property owners or their agents who permitted excavations to take place: Cirencester Urban District Council, Gloucestershire County Council, Mr. Keen of Messrs. Van Gelder and Keen, the Post Office, and Eric Coles and Partners. Our thanks are also expressed to the University of Leicester and Leicester Polytechnic for active encouragement of the authors in their research.

INTRODUCTION
By Professor S.S. Frere, C.B.E., D.Litt., Litt.D., F.B.A., F.S.A.

Urban archaeology in recent years has become a fashionable and growing practice, and there is no doubt that both its difficulties and its achievements make it an exacting but rewarding school. Those who have learnt to unravel the complex stratification, and to recognise the sometimes almost invisible complications introduced by dark pits cut into equally dark deposits, which are normal in city sites long occupied, may be held to be at the top of their profession. In the growth of this new and enthralling discipline the excavations at Cirencester have played an influential role. In 1960 when they began, the post-war excavations at Canterbury and at Verulamium were over, the others not yet started. A great opportunity was available both to volunteers and to the directing staff. In those far-off days large excavations were still run with volunteer labour and by directors who in real life held other jobs. Large numbers of people who have since made their names in one or another branch of archaeology received their early training thus. The experience was usually enjoyable; the strains were felt only later, when the great bulk of material, amassed year after year from the maintained impetus of what may now be called the proto-rescue phase, proved an excessive burden on the part-time archaeologists in charge. Nevertheless the devotion of those in charge, year after year devoting their holiday seasons to the project, deserves our grateful recognition. The Cirencester excavations have continued annually for eighteen years, and perhaps only the increased assistance latterly provided by the State to further the research on finds, and to get them processed and drawn, has made possible the appearance of a report so soon. Long past are the days when it was possible to toss off a superficial final report on an important site in only a year or eighteen months after the spade was laid aside; the standard of information nowadays looked for in reports calls for much more detail to be made available, and in far greater variety, than used to be thought necessary. Thus the authors of this first volume on the Cirencester excavations are to be congratulated.

The present volume deals with the military remains. The division has the advantage of being not only thematic but also chronological, for, like the majority of cities and other large settlements in Roman Britain, Cirencester owed its origin and choice of site to the first-century Roman army. Nineteenth-century discovery of two military tombstones had already suggested that there once had been a garrison at Cirencester; but Mommsen had dated them stylistically to the late first or even to the early second century. In 1917 Haverfield prophetically wrote: "If the whole area could be minutely excavated, a skilful excavator might, no doubt, detect the fort by its ditch, or even by the post-holes of its wooden buildings. Nothing of the sort has yet been noted, and, even if found, such traces would form only a temporary feature of the site in its earlier days. Cirencester remained, then, like most of Southern Britain, civilian, and free from the incubus of a garrison". Half a century later skilful excavation has provided some of the answers. We now know the context of the tombstones and have a better understanding of the complex processes whereby the site of a fort became the administrative centre of a civitas. We may even question the use of the word 'incubus'.

But urban archaeology and rescue excavation have their limitations; a living town cannot be stripped nor 'the whole area minutely excavated', and it continues to guard important secrets. In this volume a great advance of knowledge is revealed, and we have a basis of proven fact from which to watch the future. Vigilance is indeed required, for only excavation at the right spot, when fleeting opportunity offers the chance, will pierce the uncertainties which still surround the extent and character of the various military establishments now proved to exist beneath the Roman city. In the circumstances of modern development it is fatally easy for apathy, ignorance or plain absence of resources to miss these opportunities, and the task is made no easier by the great depth below the modern surface at which these earliest vestiges are often stratified; any excavation has to be sizeable to be worth while, and correspondingly expensive.

The publication of a great series of excavations may excusably be thought to mark an epoch, to be followed by a period of rest and contemplation, and perhaps by the switch of scarce resources elsewhere. This comfortable point of view must be resisted, if only because the tide of destruction caused by modern building-construction does not similarly take a siesta. The process of archaeological discovery can never be complete, for fresh facts and new outlooks continue to raise questions which were not, and perhaps even could not be, posed before, just as new techniques offer better opportunities of recovering a broader spectrum of historical or environmental information.

Fortunately Cirencester possesses a first-class museum professionally staffed, and the local authority has long shown enlightened interest in the archaeology of the town. Nor is local interest in archaeology confined to official circles. All this augurs well for future work. Meanwhile we eagerly await the further volumes of this important excavation report.

25 January 1978

EDITORS' NOTE

The principal contents of this volume were completed six years ago. In order to forestall criticism from those people who are all too ready to draw attention to lengthy delays in the publication of rescue excavations, let it be made clear that the delays in this were entirely beyond the control of the joint writers and editors. They were due solely to the fact that two successive publishers were unable to reach decisions within a reasonable time, on whether to accept the manuscript. Neither can any blame be attached to the Department of the Environment. In both cases, officers of the Department and of the Excavation Committee were always ready to propose and accept reasonable compromises in order to try to break deadlocks: but to no avail.

J.S.W.
A.D.McW.

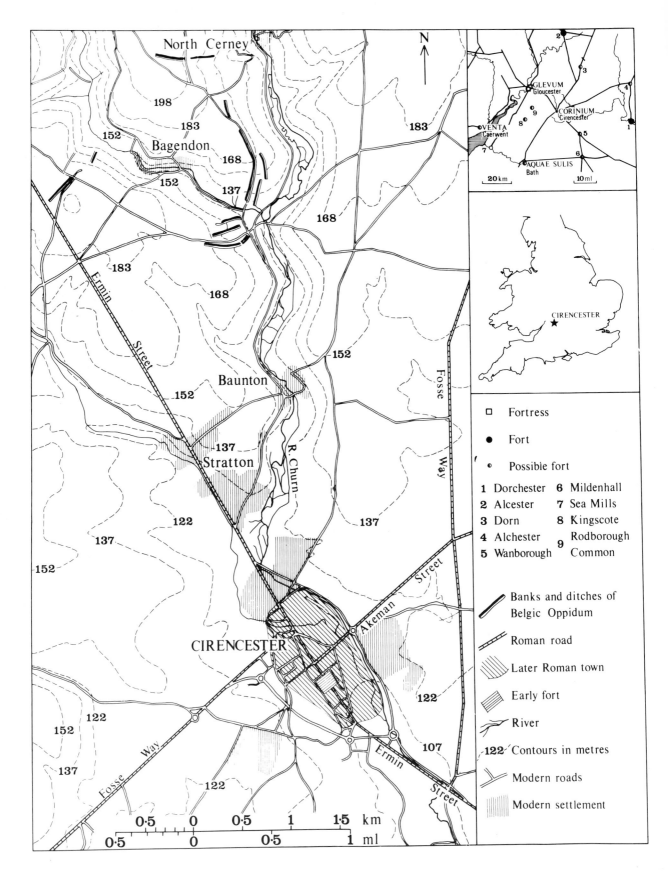

Fig. 1.   Cirencester and district

SITE CODING SYSTEM

The recording system used during excavations has been retained in this report. Pottery and small finds were labelled in a similar way beginning with site and year reference (e.g. CIR 61). This was followed by a trench or area number in Roman numerals and a layer number in arabic script contained in a circle; the circle has been omitted in this report. Further catalogue numbers were added for small finds, but these are omitted here. To save space the first part of the recording system has been condensed to a letter so that, for example, CIR 61 becomes A. Sites excavated by the Committee between 1960 and 1976 are listed in the following table which provides a key to fig. 2. Of particular relevance to discussions in this volume are nos. 21, 23, 28-32, 36 and 41.

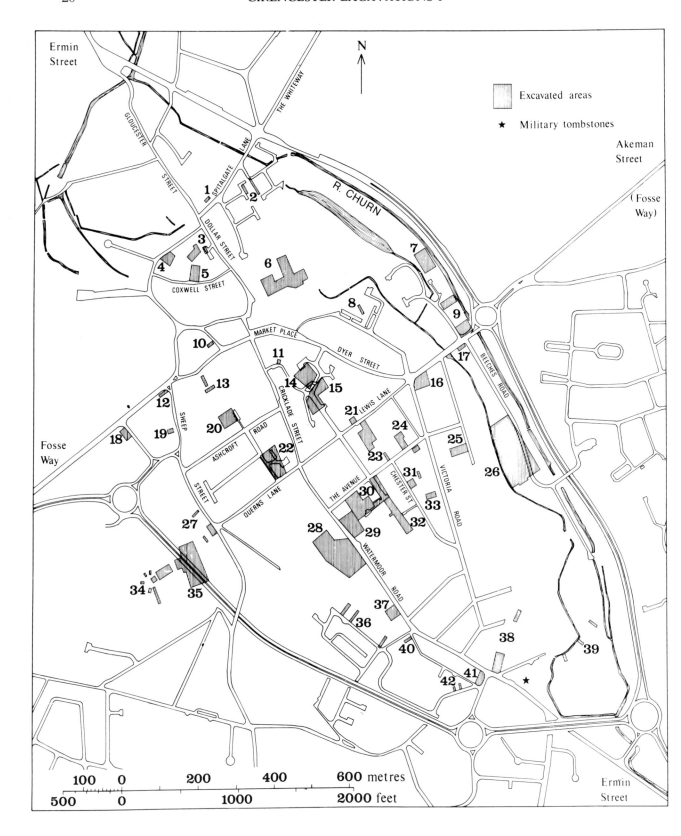

Fig. 2.   Cirencester, showing positions of excavated areas between 1960–76

TABLE 1: Sites excavated 1960-1976, to accompany fig. 2.

1.	St. John's Hospital	CW	1971 and 1976
2.	Northern Defences	BQ, BR	1965
3.	Dollar St.	BW	1966
4.	Thomas St.	BS	1966
5.	Coxwell St.	AP	1962
6.	The Abbey	BG-BP, BT, BV	1964-66
7.	North-East Defences		1966
8.	The Waterloo	CK	1968
9.	North-East Defences and Verulamium Gate	AA-AC	1960
10.	Lloyds Bank	BF	1964
11.	King's Head Yard	AZ	1963
12.	Town Station Yard	CF	1967
13.	Bridges Garage	CR	1970
14.	Police Station	AS	1962
15.	Police Station	AR	1962
16.	Gaumont Cinema	BD	1964
17.	London Road	DC	1973
18.	Oakley Cottage, Bridges Garage observations		1960, 1975
19.	Town Station Yard	CN	1967
20.	Ashcroft		1951, 1961
21.	Telephone Exchange	BB	1963
22.	Ashcroft House	BE	1964
23.	Forum between Lewis Lane and The Avenue	AY	1963
24.	17 The Avenue	AH	1968
25.	Purley Road	DB	1972
26.	The Beeches	CQ, CX, CY, DE, DF	1970-1973
27.	The Bath Gate	DX	1975
28.	Parsonage Field, and Health Centre	AX	1958-9, 1963
29.	Price's Row	DA	1972
30.	Leaholme Garden	AD-AH, AK-AM	1961
31.	Chester Mews	BC	1964
32.	St. Michael's Field	DG-DN, DQ	1974-76
33.	Victoria Road	CJ	1968
34.	Amphitheatre	AN, AU, CA	1962-3, 1966
35.	Cemetery and Extra-mural building	CS, CT	1969-1975
36.	Watermoor Hospital Gardens	AW	1963
37.	Watermoor School	CC	1967
38.	South Gate	DP	1974
39.	City Bank	AQ	1962
40.	Midland Road	BY	1967
41.	The Sands	BZ, BG	1966-7
42.	36 Stepstairs Lane	CV	1971

In the finds section of this report the site, trench and layer number are quoted when describing pottery and small finds. For example, DK I 81 refers to excavations carried out in 1974 at St. Michael's Field, I is the trench number and 81 the layer number. Correlation tables are provided on pp. 80–3 in advance of the individual reports on the finds, and show the significant contents of each layer, which are commented upon in this volume.

CHRONOLOGICAL SUMMARY (JSW)

The excavations have established the existence of a fort at Cirencester in the decades following the invasion of A.D. 43. Although at least three phases of military occupation are indicated, the evidence is too circumscribed to permit more than the basic outlines of chronology and structure to be established. Most was revealed about the second fort (Period II B); it has proved possible to suggest its boundaries and something of its internal arrangements. In the text the following chronological sequence has been adopted:

Period I   :   Native, pre-Roman occupation.

Period II A :   First fort, established *c.* A.D. 45.

Period II B :   Second fort, established *c.* A.D. 50.

Period II C :   Replanning, probably within the boundaries of the second fort, *c.* A.D. 60.

Period II D :   Abandonment and general evacuation of military forces, *c.* A.D. 75.

THE EXCAVATIONS

GENERAL INTRODUCTION (JSW and ADMcW)

For many years, the existence of a Roman fort at Cirencester had been suspected from casual finds of tombstones, coins and military equipment. It was not, however, until 1961 that structural remains of military occupation were discovered during work on the basilica. Thereafter, further information has been won; but the full picture of military occupation at Cirencester remains unfortunately obscure in many details, and the conclusions given in this report must still be considered provisional. Further work will not be easy because of the complexity of the timber buildings already uncovered, the disturbances caused by later Roman building construction, and the great depth of the stratified deposits. Indeed, it was only by deciding to use a bull-dozer to cut through later buildings, which had been only partly excavated, that the small, but significant area of military timber structures in the Leaholme Garden was uncovered. Shortages of time and money would otherwise have prevented these discoveries.

Further information was gained in 1973. In that year Gloucestershire County Council announced plans to develop St. Michael's Field with the construction of a school and an old people's day centre. At the same time Cotswold District Council revealed plans for a road to link The Avenue with King Street, affecting the north-east side of St. Michael's Field and a disused garden in the north corner, known locally as Admiral's Walk. Confronted with a threat to 3 ha. (7½ acres) close to the centre of the Roman town, the Excavation Committee proposed to organize excavations in those parts of the site to which access could be gained. The major part of the field was at the time in use as football pitches and thus escaped development. Excavations were accordingly confined to the area threatened by the link road; they produced military levels but very little structural evidence.

In this account of the excavations, the title of each section is followed by the initials of the writer.

THE LEAHOLME FORT (JSW)

In 1961, opportunity arose to examine a large area of private gardens lying between Tower Street and the Watermoor Old People's Home. The principal objective was the south-west end of the basilica, first excavated in 1898 by Mr. Wilfrid Cripps (Cripps, 1898, 70; 1897-99, 201). During the course of these excavations in the Easter season, subsidence cracks were noted in certain of the basilica's walls, following a line along its long axis. Unfortunately, owing to lack of time and to one of the wettest springs for many years, it was only possible to show then that a pair of parallel ditches were running beneath the south-eastern rooms and colonnade of the building. The ditches appeared to be some 2.5 m. (8 ft.) wide and were separated by a ridge

23

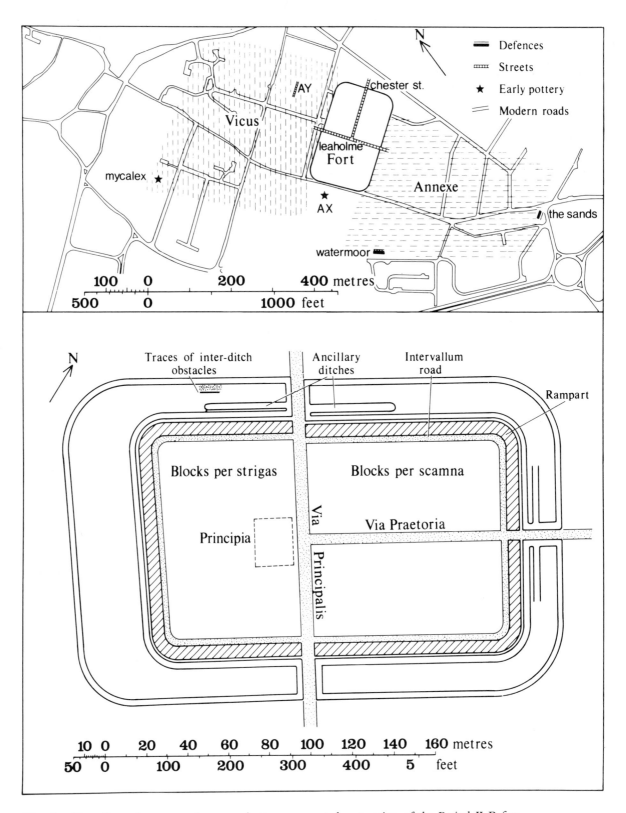

Fig. 3. Top: fort, *vicus* area and annexe; bottom: suggested restoration of the Period II B fort

1.   General view of the excavations in Leaholme Gardens.

2.   St. Michael's Field during the dry summer of 1976, showing the site of Admiral's Walk in the bottom left
hand corner. Leaholme adjoins at the bottom of the plate.

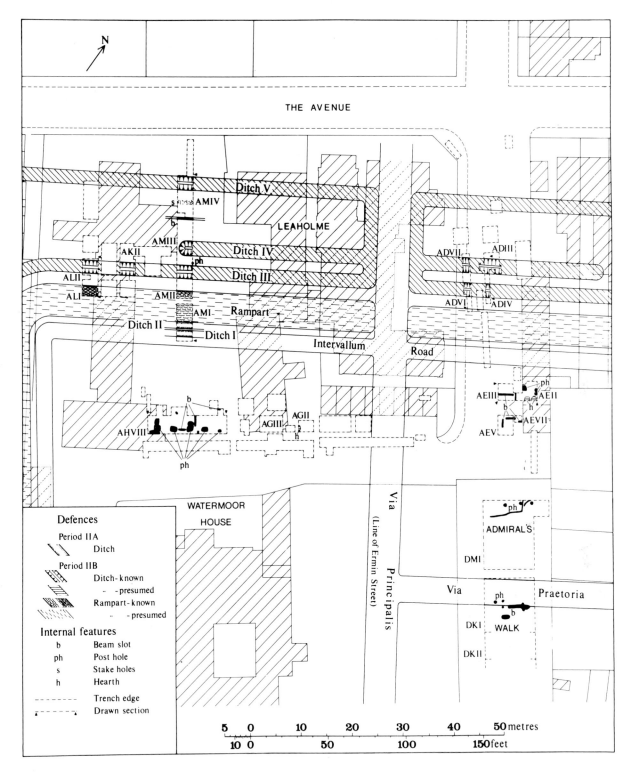

Fig. 4. Site and trench plan of Leaholme and Admiral's Walk

about 1 m. (3 ft. 4 in.) wide. They were, however, the first indication of early military works to be revealed at Cirencester, and enabled plans to be made for the ensuing summer season, when a complete section, 3 m. (10 ft.) wide, was cut across the fortifications in an adjacent garden, showing that this was the north-west side of the fort. With the aid of mechanical excavation, and the sacrifice of some later Roman levels, an area within the fort was also cleared, measuring 15.24 m. (50 ft.) by 3.0 m. (10 ft.), so enabling three phases of timber structures to be identified.

In 1964, a trench in Chester Mews, to establish the line of one of the town streets, fortunately also revealed evidence for two underlying ditches, so providing a line for the north-east side of the fort, while in 1962 observation of a sewer trench between the Leaholme site and Watermoor Road, followed by excavation at Price's Row in 1972/3, suggested the line of the western corner and south-west side respectively. Finally, excavations at Admiral's Walk, adjacent to and south-east of the Leaholme site, in 1974 revealed further evidence of internal streets and buildings. It should be added that a magnetometer survey was kindly carried out in 1961 by Mr. Michael Tite, of the Oxford Research Laboratory for Art and Archaeology, in St. Michael's Field, in an attempt to locate the ditches of the south-east side. While some linear anomalies were traced, they were insufficiently emphatic for any reliance to be placed upon them, and doubt remains about this boundary of the fort, although reasons of symmetry and overall size would suggest its position as shown.

PRE-ROMAN OCCUPATION (PERIOD I) (JSW)

There is evidence to show that the valley of the river Churn was occupied during the pre-Roman Iron Age (p. 66).

In AH VIII this was demonstrated by the discovery of a stake circle, 2.43 m. (8ft. 0 in.) in diameter, together with other random post- and stake-holes at the level of undisturbed clay, associated with several scraps of soft, exceedingly friable, red pottery. It is unlikely that this feature belonged to the Roman military occupation and it has, therefore, been assigned a pre-Roman date. The circle was made up of 17 stake-holes, each varying in diameter from 2.5 cm. (1 in.) to 7.5 cm. (3 in.). (Fig. 12).

THE DEFENCES (PERIOD II A)

The earliest defensive system consisted of a pair of parallel ditches, situated immediately behind the later rampart, and apparently running on the same line, at the south-east end of AM I (figs. 4 and 6). Unfortunately the trench could not be extended to confirm the existence of a contemporary rampart.

The ditches had been cut through the covering layer of undisturbed brown clay into the underlying gravel. They were approximately 0.65 m. (2 ft.) deep and 1.25 m. (4 ft.) across, although Ditch I had been quarried at its eastern end. Originally they appear to have been V-shaped, but weathering had rendered them partly bowl-shaped. Most of the early pottery from Ditch II was found in the weathered, primary silt at the bottom, and was demonstrably earlier than that in the main, or secondary, filling. Ultimately they had been filled with reddish-brown clay, inter-leaved in places with bands of gravel (AM I 61) and Ditch II appears to have been superficially recut at a later date, perhaps to act as a roadside ditch for the intervallum road of the later (Period II B) fort.

Although the ditches are small for those of a fort, it is unlikely that they belonged to a marching camp; twin ditches are virtually unknown in such installations. Nevertheless, as indicated above, some trouble was later encountered by the Roman army in digging larger and deeper ditches, owing to the high water-table and loose nature of the gravel, so it may have been decided that small ditches would suffice at first.

Nothing was found to indicate the date of construction of these fortifications, although on stratigraphical grounds they must precede those of Period II B. Below the filling of the ditches (AM I 61) however, were found some scraps of coarse wares, mainly in the primary silt, which could be dated as early as A.D. 45, and probably represent the ditches in use.

3.   Early ditches, (Period II A?) behind the rampart of the Period II B fort in trench AM I.

4.   Base of Period II B rampart in AM I with the earlier ditches to the rear and the urban street above.

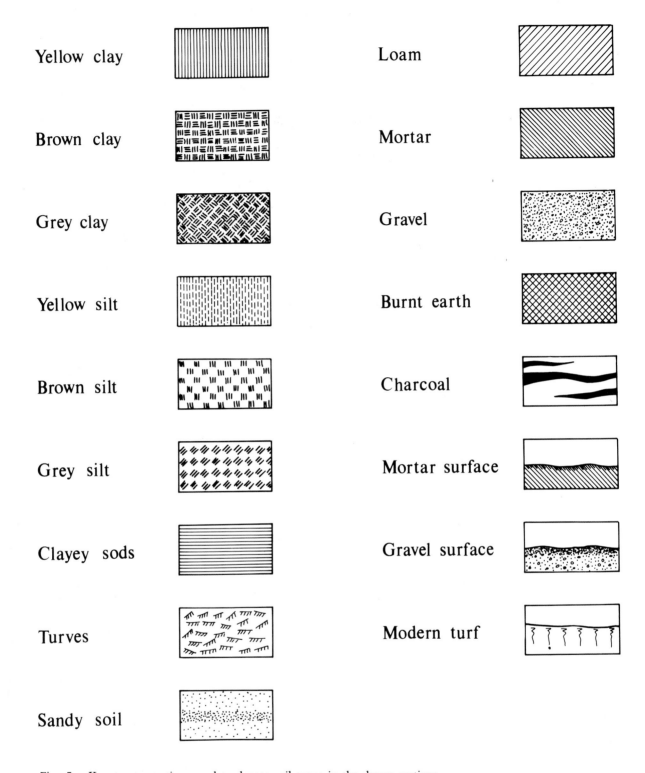

Fig. 5. Key to conventions used to denote soil types in the drawn sections

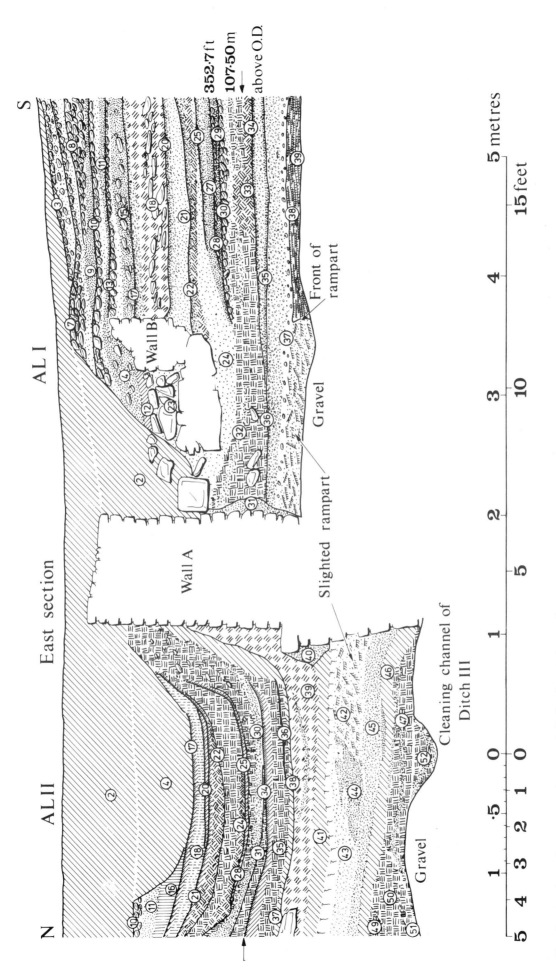

Fig. 8. Section of rampart and quarried ditch of Period II B fort, AL I–II

5.   Compressed turf of Period II B rampart in AM I.

6.   Median ditch of Period II B fort as first discovered beneath the basilica in AD III. The subsidence crack should be noted in the wall above.

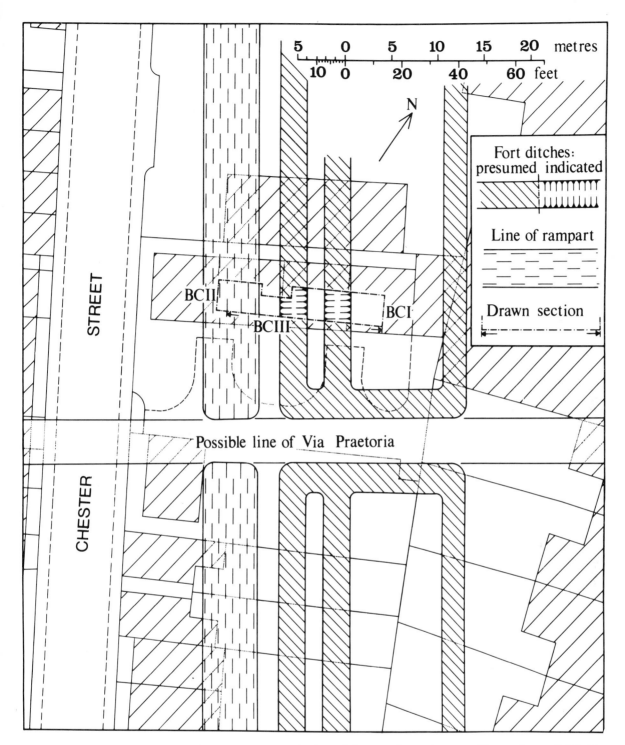

Fig. 9. Plan showing position of the north-eastern ditches of the Period II B fort near Chester Street, BC I–III

THE DEFENCES (PERIOD II B)

Substantial traces (AM I 63) of a turf rampart, 6 m. (19 ft. 6 in.) wide at the base, were found immediately north-west of the ditches referred to in the preceding section. Its line had been readopted for one of the town streets, and the weight of the overlying aggregate had compressed some six layers of turf into a thickness of *c.* 20 cm. (8 in.). Nevertheless the turf layers were clearly visible in section, as was the underlying old ground surface which had not been stripped. No trace of timber lacing beneath the rampart or of revetments at either the back or front were observed, and it should be assumed that the breast-work was mounted directly on top of the stacked turf. The front of the rampart, with a vertical face at its lowest level, was also readily distinguished from the jumbled turves which had been deposited in front when it was dismantled. The rear face was not so obvious and it is not impossible that the rampart continued over Ditch II, into which it had subsided, for a further 1.4 m. (4 ft. 7 in.), although this would have made it abnormally wide.[1] It is more likely, therefore, that the turf observed over the south-eastern lip of Ditch II and sealed by the edge of the intervallum road (AM I 57), but cut by a ditch (AM I 60) of the early town street, was spilt during the construction.

The front of the rampart was again revealed in AL I and II (layers 38, 39). Some seven superimposed layers of turves were counted, compressed to a thickness of 15 cm. (6 in.) while in front lay a jumbled mass, doubtless formed during the demolition.

The lip of the contemporary inner ditch (Ditch III) lay 2.25 m. (7 ft. 4 in.) beyond the front face of the rampart. The ditch was 2.5 m. (8 ft. 2 in.) wide, with a total depth to the bottom of the cleaning channel of 1.2 m. (3 ft. 10 in.); the cleaning channel itself was placed centrally in the bottom of the ditch, and was 0.55 m. (1 ft. 10 in.) wide and 0.22 m. (9 in.) deep. In AM II, however, its course ran slightly diagonally across the bottom. The ditch was cut through the surface cover of brown clay into the underlying gravel, and when excavated the bottom, somewhat flat, was found to coincide with the level of the water-table. It had clearly been scoured a number of times; the loose gravel sides would have weathered easily and both ditch and cleaning channel had assumed bowl-shaped proportions. It is not impossible that the sides had been "clayed-up" to prevent weathering, as brown clay mixed with pebbles was found in the bottom levels (AM II 65 and 67).

This same ditch was also located in AL II, but there both original edges had been completely removed by later quarrying, and only the cleaning channel (AL II 52), 0.53 m. (1 ft. 9 in.) wide and 0.20 m. (8 in.) deep, survived to indicate its line.

The outer ditch (Ditch V) could not be completely excavated, but its presence was shown by subsidence in two juxtaposed later walls running parallel with it. The outer lip was, however, located in trench AM VI and appeared to show that a ditch with approximately the same dimensions as Ditch III existed on that line. If so, it would have been separated from Ditch III by a space 13.8 m. (45 ft.) wide.

However, the butt-end of yet another ditch (Ditch IV) was found only 1.9 m. (6 ft.) forward of the outer lip of Ditch III in trench AM III. This ditch would appear to correspond with Ditch IV on site AD under the south-eastern edge of the basilica. It could not be fully excavated in AM III because of the water-table, but it certainly exceeded 1.25 m. (4 ft.) in depth and was consequently deeper than Ditch III. It was approximately 2.8 m. (9 ft.) wide, but the inner lip could not be precisely located, since it was obscured by a later wall.

Since Ditch IV was obviously not a continuous feature surrounding the whole fort, it may be suggested that it, together with its companion on site AD, formed part of extra defensive works in the immediate neighbourhood of a gate, which may be postulated as lying where Ermin Street strikes the north-western side of the fort. Short sections of ancillary ditch set to give extra protection to points of weakness are not unknown in forts of the Claudio-Neronian period and can be seen at Hod Hill (Richmond, 1968, 68 and fig. 62), and apparently also at

---

1.   Compare Longthorpe, where the rampart was postulated as being 6.1 m. (20 ft.) (Frere and St. Joseph, 1974, 11), and Hod Hill where it was only 3 m. (10 ft.) wide.

7.	Inner ditch of Period II B fort in AM II, showing the cleaning channel at the bottom. It was this section which produced the mass of pottery.

8.	Inner ditch of Period II B fort in AL II, where the sides had been quarried for gravel, leaving only the cleaning channel below.

Great Casterton (Todd, 1968, 17, and fig. 2). Consequently the ditch-system of the fort seems to be in close accord with others of known Claudian date, with a wide "target area" between inner and outer ditches. The purpose of such an area has been described with great perspicuity by the late Sir Ian Richmond in his account of the Hod Hill excavations, and need not be repeated here (Richmond, 1968, 68-9), but it is worth comparing the overall distance of 21.1 m. (69 ft.) between the front of the Cirencester rampart and the outer lip of the furthermost ditch with the equivalent space at Hod Hill of 27.43 m. (90 ft.) and that at Great Casterton of 16 m. (52½ ft.).

However, unlike Hod Hill and Great Casterton, the space at Cirencester was beset with additional obstacles comprising three separate elements. At a distance of 50 cm. (1 ft. 8 in.) from the outer lip of Ditch III, a post-hole 38 cm. (1 ft. 3 in.) wide and 30 cm. (1 ft.) deep was found in the north-eastern face of AM II, while 8.35 m. (27 ft. 2 in.) further out, a beam-slot, parallel with the ditches, 20 cm. (8 in.) deep and approximately 27 cm. (11 in.) wide, ran across AM IV. Both these features were cut into the undisturbed clay. Beyond the beam-slot at a distance of 2.95 m. (6 ft. 5 in.) was a turfy ridge (AM IV 42) at least 1.1 m. (3 ft. 7 in.) wide and about 10.2 cm. (4 in.) high, in which were a number of randomly-placed, but comparatively shallow, stake-holes. The maximum diameter of the holes was c. 7.6 cm. (3 in.) and the minimum little more than 2.5 cm. (1 in.). These stake-holes may have been produced by inserting branches of some prickly shrub, such as blackthorn, into the original turf, which had elsewhere been stripped from the area between the ditches. Since the turf from this area had undoubtedly been used for the construction of the rampart, it might imply that this particular obstacle had been erected first, perhaps to provide limited protection before the rampart was completed. The loose fixing of the branches in the ground, apparent from the shallowness of the impressions, would give an added advantage, for the thorns would have attached themselves to the clothing of an assailant charging through the barrier, so that he would have found himself wedded to an uncomfortable embarrassment. Inter-ditch obstacles of this nature have been observed in the Tiberian legionary fortress at Strasbourg (Hatt, 1953), in the temporary camps at Neuss (Petrikovits, 1961) and also at Inchtuthil (Anon. *J. Roman Stud.* xliii, 1953, 104), and are indicated at Brough-on-Humber, Coelbren, Slack and Metchley, while Trawscoed II appears to have had obstacles and no ditches, (Jones, 1975, 113, 132, 167, 176, 179).

In 1964, excavations (trenches BC I, II) in Chester Mews, then a garden lying behind a house fronting Victoria Road, revealed two ditches running approximately north-west to south-east and consequently at right angles to those revealed at Leaholme. The inner ditch had been extensively quarried at a later date, and neither of the original edges survived, but it was thought to have been some 1.2 m. (4 ft.) deep and cannot have been more than 5.1 m. (16 ft. 6 in.) wide. The outer edge was 1.5 m. (4 ft. 11 in.) from the lip of another ditch, 3.1 m. (10 ft. 4 in.) wide and 1.3 m. (4 ft. 4 in.) deep. The latter had a suspected cleaning channel at the bottom, which had been much mutilated when a later wall-foundation was sunk to the bottom of the ditch.

The relative positions of these two ditches appear to reflect those of Ditches III and IV on the Leaholme site. It is likely, therefore, that the Chester Mews excavation lies within some 40 m. (130 ft.) of a gate, and that the outer ditch, corresponding to Ditch V on the Leaholme site, lay north-east, beyond the limits of the excavation.

No trace of any rampart material was found associated with these ditches, for the old ground surface had not survived in the area where it might have been expected. On the surface of the undisturbed clay was a layer (BC II 37) made up of sandy rubble and many roof-tile fragments. Overlying it was a layer (BC II 34) of compact brown clay, which had itself been cut by the quarried edge of the inner ditch.

INTERNAL BUILDINGS (JSW)

Internal buildings of the fort were disclosed in AH VIII, AE II, III, V and VII at Leaholme, and also in Admiral's Walk (see below, p. 42). Unfortunately, at no point was sufficient of the plans recovered for certainty about the buildings' functions. In AH VIII, three phases of structures were observed, but no more than two can be proved in the other two areas. Neither was it

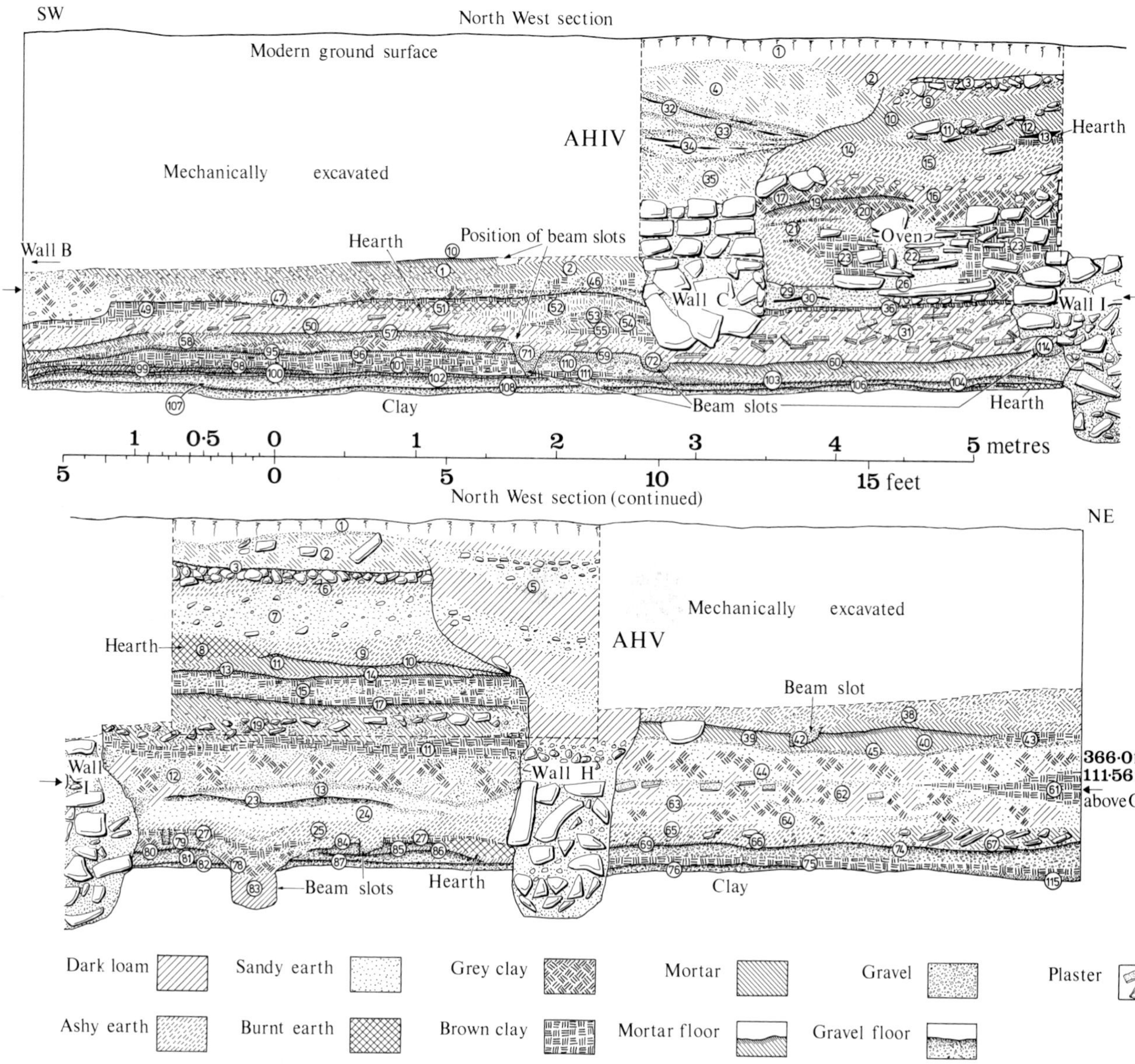

Fig. 11 Section through military buildings in AH VIII (= AH IV and V at upper levels)

9.	Butt end of median ditch of Period II B fort in AM III. A temporary hearth had been constructed in it, when the filling had been only half completed.

10.	Indentations and stake-holes of obstacles erected between the median and outer ditches in AM IV.

11.   Fourth-century wall subsiding over the inner lip of the outer ditch in AM IV.

12.   Post-holes and slots of successive military buildings in AH VIII.

possible stratigraphically to equate the three sites, and consequently we cannot say with certainty which phase in AH VIII was precisely equivalent with phases elsewhere. It may be, perhaps, that not all buildings in the fort were reconstructed at the same time. However, even allowing for this, problems are still presented by AE and Admiral's Walk, as it seems likely that structures of the earlier phases had largely been planed off during later reconstruction. Alternatively, it might be considered that the Period II A fort, represented by the small pair of ditches (p. 28) above, did not extend north-east of the line of Ermin Street; but this solution would raise additional problems, which are discussed more fully below.

In AH VIII, two different methods of construction were observed. In the two earliest phases, probably corresponding to Periods II A and II B, the building was erected around posts set in individual pits. In the typical manner of the Roman army, each pit, no matter the size of the post, which here cannot have been large, was of dimensions that allowed the digger to stand in the bottom and shovel out the earth. Consequently a fair amount of wasted labour was involved using this method. It is hardly surprising, therefore, that in the third, and last, phase, probably corresponding to Period II C, a change was made to intermittent foundation-trenches. This alteration may reflect more general changes in the army's logistics. When it first arrived in Britain, stocks of timber for building will not have existed, and each fort would have been built of newly-cut green wood, (Richmond, 1968, 120), perhaps generating a somewhat piecemeal and individualistic approach to construction. By the 60s, however, adequate stocks of seasoned timber would have been available, and some degree of standardisation and even, possibly, prefabrication introduced, so rendering the change to linear foundation-trenches more feasible.

The change from individual posts to foundation-trenches was also observed in AE and in Admiral's Walk, but on both these sites only one phase of individual post-construction existed.

BUILDINGS IN AH VIII

Phase I (probably Period II A). The key to the building-sequence in this trench is provided partly by the intersection of P.H.3 by P.H.4 and partly by the relationship of the foundation-trench (AH VIII 83) to the latest floors (AH VIII 70 and 84). These relationships suggest that P.H.s 3 and 5 belong to Phase I, together with the gravel floor AH VIII 76/82/87/106/108. This floor terminated on a line across the trench 1.97 m. (6 ft. 6 in.) from the north-east end. There was then a gap of 0.61 m. (2 ft.), in which undisturbed clay was exposed, before a sand floor (AH VIII 115) was reached, which continued beyond the north-eastern limits of excavation. The gravel floor was of variable thickness, ranging from 7.6 cm. (3 in.) to 2.5 cm. (1 in.), and the sand was 2.5 cm. (1 in.) at its thickest, dying out to nothing on its south-western edge. In places a thin, dirty layer of mud (AH VIII 81 and 107) had accumulated on the floor, while, in the north-west section, a small hearth, 0.69 m. (2 ft. 3 in.) across, appeared.

The post-pits, all of which tended to be subrectangular in shape with rounded corners, had the following dimensions and fillings:

P.H.3 was 1.14 m. (3 ft. 9 in.) in one direction and must have exceeded 1.52 m. (4 ft. 3 in.) in the other where it had been cut by P.H.4. Its depth was 0.86 m. (2 ft. 10 in.) below the surface of the undisturbed clay. No sign of a post-socket was observed in the filling, nor was there an impression in the underlying gravel at the bottom; consequently the post was probably dug out and the filling of the pit must represent that ultimate disturbance. The filling was a general mixture of clay and gravel, and contained a rosette brooch (fig. 24, 6).

P.H. 5 measured 1.27 m. (4 ft. 2 in.) by 1.04 m. (3 ft. 5 in.) and its depth and filling were approximately the same as for P.H.3.

Phase II (probably Period II B). This consisted of the main sequence of posts: P.H.s 1, 2, 4, 6, 7, together with the gravel floors represented by layers AH VIII 80/86/102/104, and probably AH VIII 92. It was unfortunate that the posts and floors of this phase had been badly mutilated by the foundations of a later wall (Wall G), which, not only ran along the same line as the posts, but also made it impossible directly to equate the layers to the north-west with those to the south-east of the line. It should also be noted that AH VIII 86 terminated at a point 4.27 m. (14 ft.) from the north-eastern end of the trench and, therefore, against P.H.2. Again, considerable

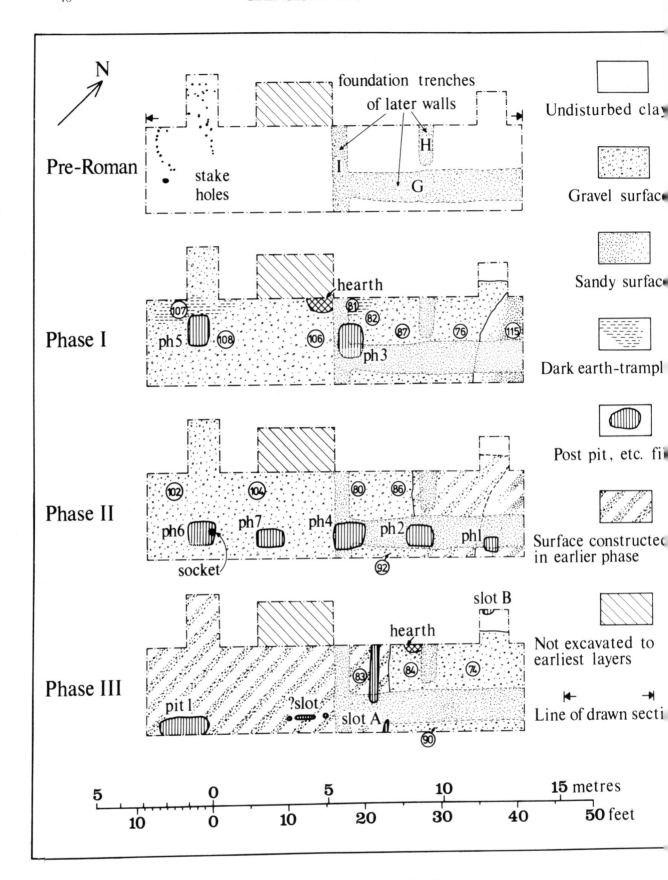

Fig. 12.   Phase plan of successive military buildings at Leaholme, AH VIII

variation in thickness of the floors was noted, ranging from 2.5 cm. (1 in.) to 10.2 cm. (4 in.).

The post-pits had the following dimensions and fillings:

P.H.1 was unusual in being smaller and more circular than the remainder, measuring 0.91 m. (3 ft.) in diameter and 0.89 m. (2 ft. 11 in.) deep. It was filled with a mixture of clay and pebbles and also contained larger stones, presumably used originally to pack the post.

P.H.2 measured 1.22 m. (4 ft.) by 1.36 m. (4 ft. 6 in.) and was 0.84 m. (2 ft. 9 in.) deep. The filling was similar to P.H.1.

P.H.4 was more irregular in shape than any other, measuring 1.14 m. (3 ft. 9 in.) by 1.36 m. (4 ft. 6 in.) and was 0.86 m. (2 ft. 10 in.) deep. The filling resembled that of the two above.

P.H.6 measured approximately 0.91 m. (3 ft.) each way and had a similar depth and filling to those already described. However, against the north–east edge, the socket of a circular post was observed, 0.17 m. (7 in.) in diameter, and penetrating the underlying gravel for a depth of some 0.15 m. (6 in.).

P.H.7 measured 0.86 m. (2 ft. 10 in.) by 1.22 m. (4 ft.) and was 0.91 m. (3 ft.) deep. It was filled with a mixture of clay and gravel.

Except in P.H.6 no evidence was obtained for the posts which these pits must have contained, and it must be concluded that, as in Phase I, they had been dug out and the packing material replaced in the pits; so their contents represent the demolition of the building and not its construction.

Its demolition was also probably represented by the clayey layers, AH VIII 75 and 85, formed from the fallen daub which had originally covered the walls.

Phase III (probably Period II C). In this phase the change was made in methods of construction from individual posts set in pits to intermittent foundation-trenches. Two short lengths of such trenches (AH VIII 83 and AH VIII Slot A) together with more ephemeral indications of a third were found in the main part of AH VIII, while an extension to the north-west near the north-eastern end indicated the end of a fourth (AH VIII Slot B). These foundation-trenches were associated with gravel floors AH VIII 74, 84 and 90. Layers 74 and 84 did not extend to the south-west of AH VIII 83, while an edge to layer 74 was established in the north-western extension of AH VIII, 0.3 m. (1 ft.) in from the section face. A small hearth had existed on the floor, 1.14 m. (3 ft. 9 in.) north-east of AH VIII 83. Its full dimensions could not be determined since it lay partly in the north-west section and had been partly destroyed by the foundation-trench of the later Wall H.

The foundation-trenches had the following characteristics:

AH VIII 83 was 0.33 m. (1 ft. 1 in.) wide and was 0.36 m. (1 ft. 2 in.) deep below the surface of AH VIII 86, from which level it was cut. It extended out from the north-western face of AH VIII, but ended in the area disturbed by the foundation of Wall G. It was filled with brown loam, mixed with charcoal flecks, probably derived, as possibly also was layer AH VIII 78, from the demolition of the daub walls.

AH VIII Slot A (0.13 m. (5 in.) wide and 0.3 m. (1 ft.) deep, with a rounded end) projected outwards from the south-eastern side of AH VIII for a distance of 0.53 m. (1 ft. 9 in.) and did not coincide with the line of AH VIII 83, there being a discrepancy of some 0.23 m. (9 in.) between them. Its filling was similar to AH VIII 83.

AH VIII Slot B projected only 0.15 m. (6 in.) into the extension to AH VIII. It was 0.43 m. (1 ft. 5 in.) wide and 0.3 m. (1 ft.) deep.

A further possible foundation-trench may be represented by a shallow depression in the surface of the underlying clay between P.H.s 4 and 7. It was 0.76 m. (2 ft. 6 in.) long and 0.23 m. (9 in.) wide, and at each end were impressions of standing posts.

Also to be equated with this period is AH VIII Pit I, which cut the backfill of P.H.6, and must, therefore, be later than the removal of the post. The pit was roughly oval in shape and approximately 1.82 m. (6 ft.) by 0.91 m. (3 ft.) and 0.91 m. (3 ft.) deep. It was filled with many large stones, some clay, and gravel, and the sides and contents were heavily stained with iron. It was possibly a latrine pit.

It is exceedingly difficult to envisage the shape of the building belonging to this phase. The only new floors were laid north-east of AH VIII 83, which might, therefore, be interpreted as an outside wall, unless the earlier floors to its south-west were reused. It must be admitted, therefore, that no great sense can be made of these results.

BUILDINGS IN AE II, III, V AND VII

The interpretation of these structures was rendered almost impossible by their scanty nature and by the fact that all the contemporary floor-levels had been disturbed or removed after the evacuation of the fort. Nevertheless, some post-pits and foundation-trenches were found, but these can only be loosely related to the structural sequence established for AH VIII.

The following were observed:

In **AE II**, a single large post-pit, 0.99 m. (3 ft. 3 in.) in diameter, together with two smaller ones each about 0.61 m. (2 ft.) in diameter. Also, in the south-east side of the trench was an extensive area of heavy burning on the surface of the undisturbed clay, which had been worked into a slight depression, clearly to contain the fires.

In **AE III** and its extension, there were two foundation-trenches (AE III 22, 23) at right angles to one another but not joined, 0.18 m. (7 in.) and 0.36 m. (1 ft. 2 in.) wide respectively.

In **AE V**, two further lengths of foundation-trench were found, again at right angles to each other. AE V 19 was 1.47 m. (4 ft. 10 in.) long, 0.25 m. (10 in.) wide and 0.3 m. (1 ft.) deep. AE V 20 was 1.22 m. (4 ft.) long and just extended into AE VII; it was 0.46 m. (1 ft. 6 in.) wide.

In **AE VII**, in addition to the continuation of AE VII 20, was a further stretch of indeterminate length and breadth in the south-east corner of the trench.

CONTEMPORARY LEVELS IN AG II AND III

These two trenches were the only ones on site AG to be sunk to undisturbed clay, and between them covered a very limited area. Nevertheless in AG II three superimposed floor-levels and two small hearths were encountered, from which it might be supposed that they lay within a building. But it has not been possible to equate these levels with particular phases of building-activity.

ADMIRAL'S WALK (ADMcW)

The construction of the link road through the north-east side of St. Michael's Field was likely to cause damage to structures within a metre of modern ground level; accordingly as large an area as possible was opened up. Large trees and high dry-stone boundary-walls limited the area available for excavation, but even so a trench measuring 90 m. by 10 m. (295 ft. by 33 ft.) was examined to varying depths. This narrow strip was divided into five sites, DH, DK, DL, DM and DQ. Details of the excavation of the upper levels will be described elsewhere; only two sites, DK and DM, were excavated to natural, and discussion is limited to those two. Site DK was divided into two areas, I and II, whereas site DM was treated as one area, I.

It was decided to excavate sites DK and DM completely in order to learn more about the internal buildings of the fort for site AE (see fig. 4) was only about 5 metres north-west of site DM. During the excavation of the upper Roman levels, the wall of a large public building standing in the corner of insula VI was found to follow the south-western edge of sites DK and DM and to have disturbed earlier levels. The disturbance caused by these wall-foundations and the presence of a second-century timber building made it necessary to reduce the width of site DK from 10 to 8 metres at the lower levels.

Phase I

The earliest recognisable signs of occupation on sites DK and DM were small patches of trampled mud consisting of clay and gravel resting directly upon the natural red-brown clay. Those in DK produced no finds, but DM I 133 contained Neronian samian and a small group of coarse wares, some of which appear to be Neronian or early Flavian.

The first definite surfaces were of well-laid gravel, smooth and hard, placed directly upon the natural clay, except where the earlier trample survived. The main area of gravel, DK I 111,

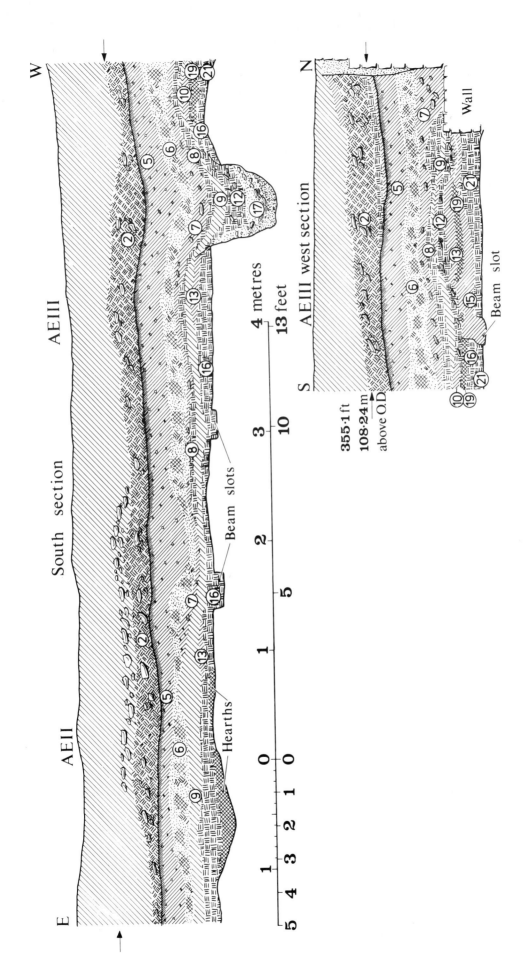

Fig. 13. Sections through military buildings in AE II, III

13.   General view of Admiral's Walk from the south. Sites DK and DM are at the far end; the parish church is in the distance.

14.   Site DM, Admiral's Walk, from the north in 1974. Site DK can be seen beyond the baulk. The circular feature in the foreground is DM I 134, 136.

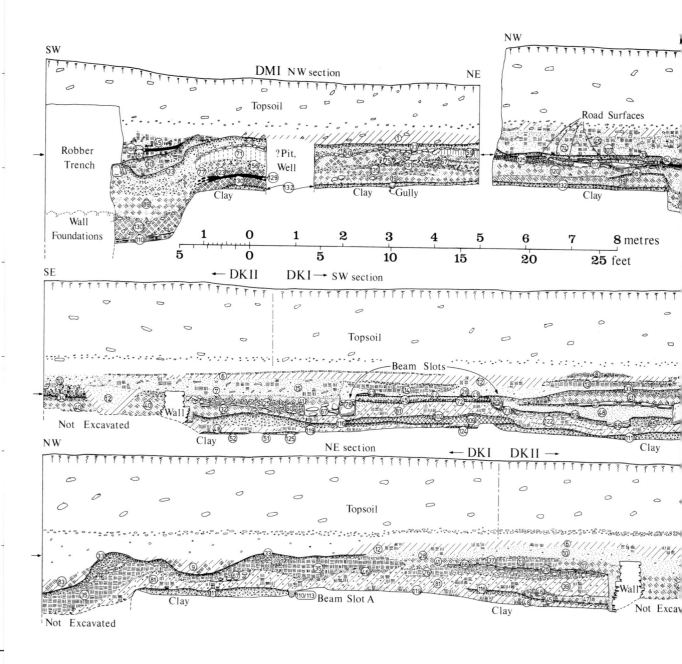

Fig. 15. Sections through military buildings in DM I, and DK I and II

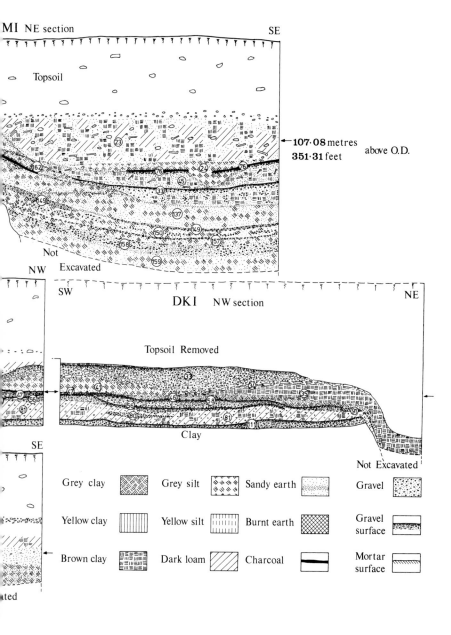

MI NE section

SE

Topsoil

← **107·08** metres   above O.D.
     351·31 feet

Not Excavated

NW

SW   DKI   NW section   NE

Topsoil Removed

Clay

Not Excavated

SE

Grey clay		Grey silt		Sandy earth		Gravel
Yellow clay		Yellow silt		Burnt earth		Gravel surface
Brown clay		Dark loam		Charcoal		Mortar surface

extended over the whole of the northern part of site DK and had a maximum thickness of 18 cm. (7 in.). It reached site DM (DM I 144) and can be seen as a relatively flat surface on all three sections (fig. 15).

The south-eastern limit of DK I 111 was marked by an almost straight north-west to south-east line across the site. In the eastern area of DK I this line was defined by a trench cut into the natural subsoil, and regular in shape, 2 m. (6 ft. 7 in.) long, 70 cm. (2 ft. 4 in.) wide and on average 20 cm. (8 in.) deep (plan see fig. 14). As it approached the east section it narrowed to 15-20 cm. (6-8 in.). On either side, two small projections 10 cm. (4 in.) deep and c. 50 cm. (1ft. 8in.) long had been cut at right angles to, and joining, the main trench. There was no way of telling whether these projections were original or later additions. The fill of both the trench and projections was similar to the silty layer which sealed them, but included more burnt material. In the bottom of the trench were three post-holes, P.H.4, 5 and 6 (fig. 14) all c. 25 cm. (10 in.) in diameter and 60 cm. (2 ft.) deep below the bottom of the trench. They contained no stone packing.

In the south-western part of DK I, layer 111 coincided with the edge of slot A and so DK I 111 ended in an almost straight line across the whole of DK I. Post-hole 3 was also in this part of the site, and appeared to be associated with DK I 111 and in line with P.H.s 4 and 5.

The south-eastern limit of DK I 111 was marked in the west of the site by a ridge of natural clay which itself formed an almost straight line against the layer to the south-east, DK I 124.

Slot A, P.H.3 and the two straight edges to the gravel surfaces DK I 111 and DK I 124 appear to mark the line of a timber partition dividing these surfaces to the north-west (DK I 111, DM I 144) from those to the south-east (DK I 124 and 125, DK II 51, 52 and 53).

The remaining P.H.s 1 and 2 were different from the rest and not in line with them. They were shallower and had a packing of small stones. The offset placing of two posts in this way might suggest an entrance leading from a gravel surface outside (DK I 111) into a timber building floored with gravel, only patches of which survive; for the absence of post-holes or wall trenches elsewhere in DK I 111 could indicate that this was an outside surface, possibly a street or alleyway between buildings. There were no signs of wear on DK I 111 which could be associated with vehicular traffic. Whether this was the *via praetoria* of the fort is discussed later (page 59).

South-east of the partition there were several gravel patches (DK I 124 and 125, DK II 51, 52 and 53), which might have been part of a more extensive surface over the site. None contained any finds which could show whether they were contemporary with DK I 111 or not, but as they all lay on natural subsoil, it seems most likely that they belonged to the earliest phase of occupation. DK I 124 was 6 cm. (2 in.) thick, of loose gravel with no hard surface, DK I 125 (equivalent to DK II 51) was similar, and DK II 52 and 53 were patches of yellow gravel 5-8 cm. (2-3 in.) thick. Also lying on natural subsoil in this part of site DK was a small area of limestone slabs 10 cm. (4 in.) thick (DK I 121) which were laid flat and showed no signs of burning, presumably forming some kind of base.

The earliest gravel surface on site DM was DM I 144, which was equivalent to DK I 111, but was present only in the south-east corner of the trench. There were no traces of any timber structures which could be associated either with those found on DK or with a building on the other side of the street.

The only sherd from DK I 111 is similar to material from the Leaholme site in equivalent levels and could even be pre-Conquest in date. Material from DM I 144 is totally different; the samian is Neronian or early Flavian while the coarse wares include vessels which appear to be Flavian and post-date the group from the filling of Ditch III on Leaholme. However, matches with sherds found in pit DM I 145/154 suggest that DM I 144 was contaminated when the pit was filled.

Overlying the gravel patches in the south-east of DK was a very mixed layer of grey silt heavily flecked with charcoal and including occasional patches of brown clay (DK I 119 = DK II 48). Where the patches were absent, DK I 119 rested directly on the natural clay, and was up to 20 cm. (8 in.) thick (figs. 14, 15). As it respected the line of the post-holes and wall-trench, it is evident that the timber partition existed before layer DK I 119 accumulated. The way the

15.   Site DK, Admiral's Walk, from the south-west showing the earliest layers and beam-slot extending beneath the ranging pole.

natural clay forms a ridge in line with the post-holes, and its slope away from the line, suggests that it was protected in some way when the successive surfaces either side were laid, again supporting the hypothesis that the timber partition still existed when DK I 119 was put down (see section fig. 15). According to the samian and coarse wares, this was in the Neronian or early Flavian period. No equivalent layer existed in the north-west of DK nor over the whole of site DM (i.e. over DK I 111 or DM I 144).

Phase II

Over much of site DM there was a second substantial gravel surface DM I 132, very compact and giving the impression of having been grouted with mortar. It was on average 5-7 cm. (2-3 in.) thick, but in places reached 20 cm. (8 in.), and it is clear that great efforts were made to create a firm and well-laid surface. Cut into the surface in the north-west of it were a series of shallow, V-shaped gullies and three post-holes nos. 7, 8 and 9. Post-hole 7 was 20 cm. in diameter and packed with three stones. Post-holes 8 and 9 were 40 and 50 cm. (16 in. and 20 in.) in diameter respectively, and again stone-packed.

Layer 132 became less pronounced towards the south-east of DM, and at the borders of the patches of stones, DM I 148, it became indistinct. The substantial gravel layer that existed over most of DM certainly did not seal DM I 143/8, but isolated small patches of gravel existed over parts. DM I 143/8 was a very mixed deposit of stones, silt and gravel apparently put down to fill a subsidence into the pit (145/154) below.

Pit 145/154 contained a relatively large group of pottery, with an unusually high proportion

16. Stone features and pit on site DK. See plan fig. 14.

of samian. Most of the latter is pre-Flavian, but there were 10 definitely Flavian pieces, coming from all levels in the pit. Among the coarse wares there are only a few sherds which are obviously residual, but there is a marked absence of parallels with the material from the filling of Leaholme Ditch III. A mortarium, fig. 51, 68 is dated c. A.D. 80-120, while the majority of the coarse wares are Flavian or possibly Flavian-Trajanic, and are closely paralleled in the thick silty layers which seal the early occupation and this pit itself. The group must have accumulated after both the filling of Ditch III and the backfilling of the quarried stretches of the defences on the Leaholme site; the final deposition cannot have taken place before c. A.D. 80 at the earliest, c. A.D. 100 being a more likely date.

Although in the north-west of DK and most of DM only one phase of gravel surface existed (DK I 111 and DK I 144), the sequence of layers south-east of the timber division was different, for immediately over the grey silt layer DK I 119, which lay in part directly on natural subsoil, was a layer of gravel with a firm compacted surface, DK I 116 (= DK II 45) which varied in thickness from 10 to 25 cm. (4 in. to 10 in.). It was not possible to define stratigraphically the relationship between DK I 111 and 116; they could have been contemporary but separated by the timber partition. The fairly small group of pottery from DK I 116 includes samian of

18. Beam-slot and post-holes on site DK after the excavations of the latter. Compare with plate 17.

17. Beam-slot and post-holes.

Neronian or early Flavian date and coarse wares which are different from those in the early occupation layers on the Leaholme site and, with the exception of one jar, fig. 52, 94, also from those in the filling of Ditch III; it appears therefore that the group is Neronian to early Flavian.

That there was more than one period of timber building is suggested by the discovery of the post-holes in the bottom of the trench, implying a change from a building using posts to one using horizontal beams sunk in the ground. The plan and profile of the trench, DK I 110/113, fits an interpretation as a bedding trench for a horizontal beam which must have cut through the post-holes when it was placed in the ground. No datable material came from the post-holes, but samian from the filling of the trench shows that it went out of use after c. A.D. 55, while the coarse ware suggests a date after c. A.D. 65/70. The presence of layer DK I 105 also implies two periods associated with the timberwork. Layer 105 is a patch of gravel 12 cm. (5 in.) thick resting directly upon DK I 111 and respecting the wall trench on its south-eastern edge; it could be either a repair to DK I 111 or the remains of a much more extensive surface, representing a second phase contemporary with the change from post-holes to timber beams. The coarse wares from DK I 105 are Neronian or early Flavian.

There were other features belonging to this phase including an irregular surface of flat stones and a possible post-hole (DK I 108); one stone had been burnt before reuse in this layer. Layer DK I 109, with DK I 108 was the first to extend over the timber division on this site. DK I 109 was a layer of heavily burnt material which contained much animal bone, iron slag, and pottery of Neronian-Flavian date. It varied in thickness from 5 to 15 cm. (2 in. to 6 in.) but existed only in the western part of DK where it lay directly on DK I 111 and DK I 116 (see south-west section fig. 15). There was no evidence that the burning took place in situ; the presence of slag suggests that DK I 109 was a dump of industrial waste.

Cutting through layer DK I 116 was a circular pit 1.25 m. (4 ft. 1 in.) in diameter. The layers filling it (DK I 106, 107, 114 and 115) yielded a considerable group of pottery which shows that the pit went out of use after A.D. 70. To the west of the pit was a group of stones (DK I 120) (see plan fig. 14) which on the south-east side were pitched vertically, while those to the north-west were laid flat; it is difficult to suggest an interpretation.

Phase III

The layers and features in this phase are those which appeared when the various sealing layers of silt were removed. By this time some of the post-holes in DK were not in use. Post-holes 4, 5 and 6 had been disturbed by the wall-trench, and P.H. 3 was covered by layers DK I 102 and 103; this suggests that the timber partition was no longer standing. If the building did survive into this phase, then its plan and function seem to have changed.

There were a number of isolated patches of grey clay flecked with charcoal, DK I 103, 112, 117 and DK II 43, and several patches of gravel, DK I 97 and DK II 44 and 46. Details of the datable material recorded in these layers can be found later (p. 80–3) but in general they cover the years A.D. 50–70; the latest material was Flavian and came from DK I 97.

Associated with layer DK I 103, and perhaps even with the later surface DK I 102, was an almost rectangular pit with vertical sides which contained layers of grey loam and gravel (DK I 99, 100, 101 and 104); it resembled a tank. Only a few coarse-ware sherds were recovered; they are of Claudio-Neronian date. Overlying the tank was an elongated feature 3 m. (9 ft. 10 in.) long (fig. 14) composed of brown loam, DK I 90, in which lay irregularly-shaped and vertically-sided wedges of clay (DK I 87, 88 and 89). DK I 90 itself had nearly vertical edges and was up to 15 cm. (6 in.) thick and yielded animal bones and iron slag. This too may represent a tank. Much of the pottery was residual, but it contained some Flavian pieces. A shallow pit (DK II 42) cut from the surface DK II 45 was also contemporary. It measured 2 m. by 1.5 m. (6 ft. 7 in. by 5 ft.) and was between 25 and 30 cm. (10-12 in.) deep, with a filling mainly of grey silt, but it also contained some burnt clay, charcoal flecks and a group of pottery including Neronian samian and Neronian-Flavian coarse wares.

On site DM there were relatively few features that could be equated to this phase. A large pit in the east corner extended into the north corner of DK and appeared early in the excavation. Later layers dipped dramatically over it, some becoming vertical rather than horizontal. As so

19. Large pit on site DM showing the subsidence of later layers into the pit.

little of this pit occurred on site DK, excavation was impossible there.

On site DM where there was room for excavation, the pit was excavated to below the water-table. It cut through layers DM I 144 and 132 and had been filled with alternate layers of green grey silt and gravel, DM I 137, 149, 150, 157, 158 and 159. At the western edge the pit was 1 m. (3 ft. 3 in.) deep below the level of DM I 132, but this increased to 2 m. (6 ft. 7 in.) further east. The pit had cut through the capping of natural clay into the clean white gravel and a considerable quantity of gravel must have been extracted. The profile of the pit suggests that once it had been dug it was either backfilled immediately or supported with timber, for in places it had almost vertical sides which would not have survived for long exposed. No evidence of timber was found, but there was a layer of stones at the edge of the pit which may have formed some form of lining. Excavation was difficult since the stones were under water.

Without obtaining the complete outline and cross-section of the pit, it is difficult to offer any explanation for its use. The most likely interpretation is that it was a lined water-tank, but it may have been no more than a quarry for gravel, as seen on other sites. Pottery from the pit shows that it was beginning to be backfilled sometime after *c.* A.D. 70.

Over both sites and sealing the phases just described, there was a thick layer reaching a depth in places of 40 cm. (1 ft. 4 in.). Its composition was not homogeneous, but on the whole it was silt-like and gave the impression of deliberate dumping as well as natural accumulation. Everywhere there were considerable quantities of animal bone, pottery, oyster shells and iron slag. Most of the small finds discussed from this site came from these layers and there was plenty of pottery, much of which was residual, all supporting the view that this layer represented the deposition of considerable quantities of rubbish.

Among the residual pottery was a particularly large quantity of pre-Flavian samian, and there was one coin of Tiberius and five of Claudius. It is suggested that the layers accumulated over a period of time up to about A.D. 100-110 (although not necessarily *in situ*); there were coins of Vespasian and Domitian, Flavian samian and Flavian-Trajanic coarse wares. In addition there was a small group of Antonine material, a coin of Antoninus Pius and two sherds of Antonine samian and some sherds of black-burnished ware. The occurrence of this Antonine material is conspicuous, but the study of the upper levels of the silt suggests that it is intrusive. The coin was certainly from the top of the silt.

We may conclude that the material in these layers, which covers both sites DK and DM, accumulated during the period A.D. 80 to 100-110, with the possibility that some additions were still being made as late as A.D. 140. It forms a distinct division between the first-century occupation and the subsequent buildings which were to be erected later in the second century.

THE ANNEXE(S)

RAMPART IN WATERMOOR HOSPITAL GARDEN (JSW)

In cutting a routine section across the town defences on a part of the circuit just south of Watermoor Hospital, an earlier rampart was found encapsulated within them, which could not be explained within the established sequence of the urban fortifications.

The rampart consisted of a turfy-clay core (AW I 76) overlying a sand and cobble base (AW I 77 and 80) and was backed by a clay cheek, into which an oven had been inserted. The surviving height of this rampart was 0.58 m. (1 ft. 11 in.). Its front had not survived the construction of the later town wall, but the overall width must have exceeded 3.65 m. (12 ft.). No sign of a contemporary ditch was encountered, which here would have needed excavating into solid rock.

To the rear of the rampart, however, was a metalled road 3.35 m. (11 ft.) wide, made up of a gravelly surface (AW I 72) overlying larger stones packed into the surface of the thin cover of undisturbed clay (AW I 78). On the edge away from the rampart the road was bounded by a ditch 0.71 m. (2 ft. 4 in.) wide and 0.38 cm. (1 ft. 3 in.) deep, filled with loamy brown clay (AW I 79).

The oven appears to have been roughly square or rectangular in shape, recessed 0.76 m. (2 ft. 6 in.) into the rampart, but its full dimensions could not be obtained within the excavated trench. It was lined with stone, of which three courses survived on the side against the rampart cheek, while the floor, set in a shallow excavation in the undisturbed clay and rock, was of baked clay.

RAMPART AND DITCH AT THE SANDS, WATERMOOR (ADMcW and PDCB)

A small plot of land at the junction of Watermoor Road and Chesteron Lane (fig. 19) was excavated in 1966. The unexpected and important nature of the discoveries caused a further season of excavations to be carried out in 1967, supervised by P.D.C. Brown.

The site, known locally as The Sands, was previously occupied by cottages numbered 89-95 Chesterton Lane. Since 1967 the construction of the ring road has caused slight variations in road alignments in this part of the town and the plot has been landscaped. The cottages, which were demolished in 1963, had cellars which restricted the area of the excavations.

The initial clearance was carried out by machine and the layout of the trenches in 1966 (trenches I and II) was dictated by the discovery of the cottage walls and cellars. In 1967 the trenches (III and IV) were placed so as to section the features found in 1966 and in areas which had not been disturbed in that year. Roman levels were encountered at a surprisingly high level, some 0.6 m. (2 ft.) above the pavement of Watermoor Road. Presumably the level of Watermoor Road, the main road leading south from Cirencester, was lowered when the railway bridge was constructed in 1882 for the Midland and South Western Junction Railway. It was at that time that large foundations were reported to have been found. Although no details of the discoveries have survived, these, no doubt, belonged to the Silchester Gate.

Certain difficulties were encountered during the 1966 excavations when differences between

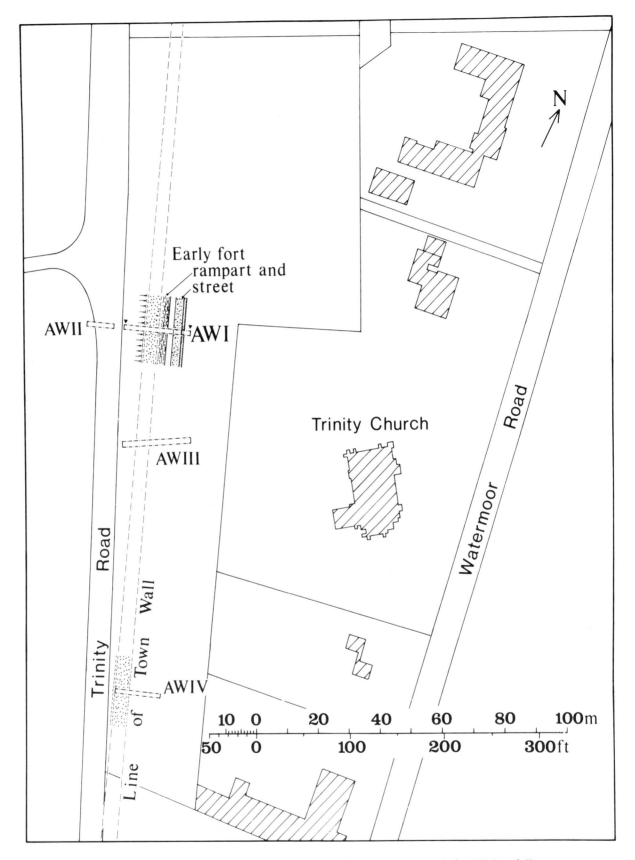

Fig. 16.   Plan showing annexe (?) defences in the grounds of Watermoor Hospital, AW I and II

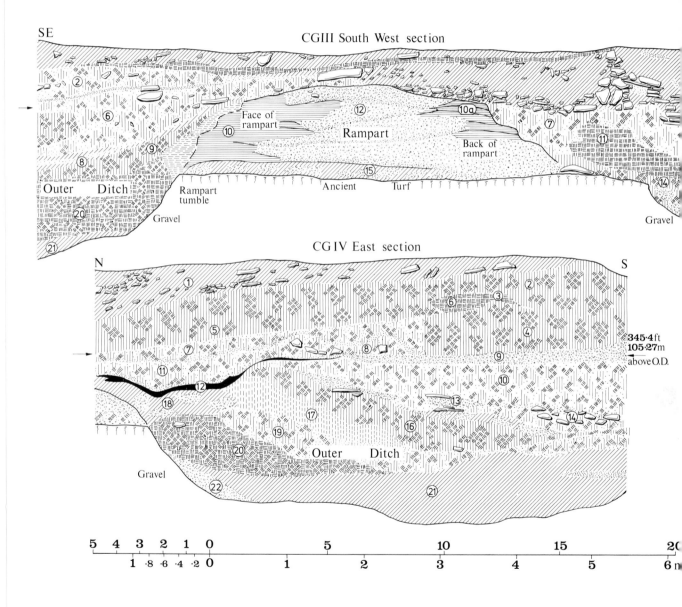

Fig. 18. Section through annexe (?) defences in CG III and IV

NW

itch

feet

tres

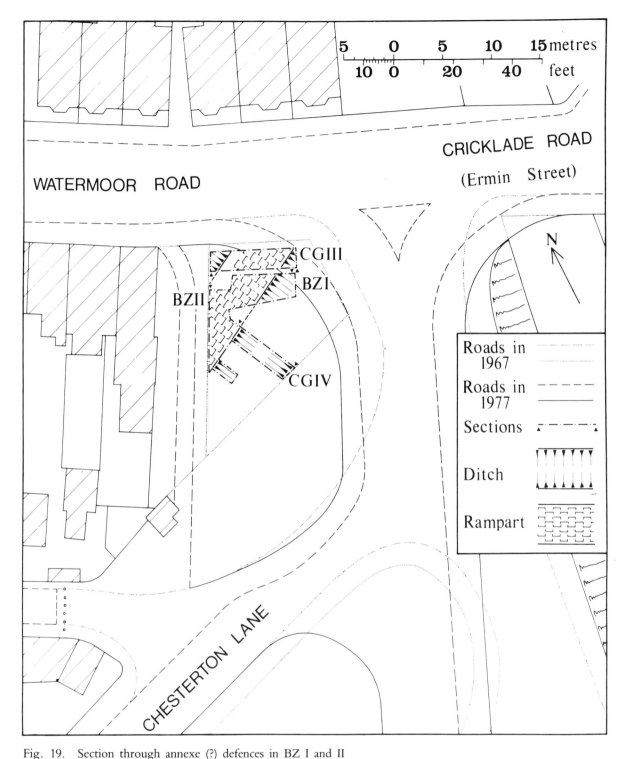

Fig. 19.   Section through annexe (?) defences in BZ I and II

20.   The Sands: section through the rampart.

the collapse from the rampart and the rampart itself were not noticed and so the 1967 excavations were aimed at recovering material which, with the help of information gained in 1966, could give dates for the construction and collapse of the rampart. The opportunity was also taken in 1967 to section the ditch in front of the rampart. In 1966 the site code was Z (in this report BZ) and the trenches numbered I and II; in 1967 the code letter was G, (here CG), with trenches numbered III and IV (fig. 19).

   The rampart which was sectioned in both years' excavations was built of sandy gravel with turf checks back and front; it stood upon a rammed gravel base (sections, figs. 18 and 20). The rampart was 5 m. (16 ft.) wide and survived to a height of 1.5 m. (5 ft.) in places. The faint outline of individual turves could just about be made out in the front cheek, but nowhere was it possible to obtain measurements for a complete sod. Immediately in front of the rampart was a ditch of somewhat irregular profile (fig. 18) which had perhaps been dictated by the high water-table in this part of the town. To the rear of the rampart were found the beginnings of another ditch which could not be fully investigated in the space available for excavation.

The filling of the outer ditch, in trench IV, was of clay (layer 16) and mixtures of sand and clay (layer CG IV 17), not unlike material from the rampart. There are in fact some probable matches of pottery from the core of the rampart and from layers in the ditch which lend strength to the suggestion that they represent collapsed rampart. These matches occur in layers CG III 12 and CG III 11, with a further possible match in the ditch fill to the rear of the rampart, CG III 6. Above these supposed layers of collapsed rampart was a layer of gravel CG IV 9 on which rested a broad wedge of clay CG IV 2, 4, 5 and 7. The surface of this clay sloped upwards towards the south, that is, towards the postulated position of the town wall, and it seems probable that it represents the tail of the rampart behind the town wall. The dating evidence depends on an assessment of the pottery and this is fully discussed on p. 195. The conclusion reached from both samian and coarse pottery is that the rampart was constructed after c. A.D. 70 and that it had collapsed by c. A.D. 125 at the latest.

Reference has already been made to problems of stratification encountered during the 1966 excavations; the provenance of some of the pottery found in trenches BZ I and II is doubtful, and it is to the pottery from the 1967 excavations that we must turn for reliably stratified evidence (trenches CG III and IV).

Although the quantity of samian noted from the rampart, CG III 12, is very small and cannot in itself provide firm dating evidence, the position of these sherds was individually recorded at the time they were discovered. One piece, is dated to after A.D. 70; the other is of indeterminate first-century date. The group of coarse ware is larger but more difficult to date precisely; the most significant fact about it is the lack of black-burnished wares and of local wares which are usually common in the Flavian-Trajanic period.

None of the small-finds recovered from this site helps with the dating of the rampart or has any particular military associations. The evidence, scanty though it is, indicates that the rampart and ditch were probably constructed after c. A.D. 70. Material from over the rampart and from in the ditch indicates that by c. A.D. 125 the rampart had collapsed.

The use of turf cheeks at back and front of The Sands rampart and the rammed gravel base are reminiscent of a number of excavated military ramparts. At Gloucester, during the excavations in King's School gardens, a clay rampart was found with an outer cheek of turves (O'Neil, 1965, 20 and fig. 2); M.J. Jones notes this as a frequent method of construction by the army, (Jones, 1975, 68). The rampart therefore is of military character and presumably surrounded a fortress, a fort or an annexe to one of these. The ditch outside the rampart does not have a characteristic military profile, but the problems with the high water-table in this area may have necessitated a different shape.

The small section of rampart found under the civilian defences in the grounds of Watermoor Hospital (discussed above on page 51) is of a similar method of construction, consisting of a turfy clay core with clay turf cheek at the rear. The front was not found but the core of the rampart rested on a rammed stone base. The rampart was found only in one of the trenches (AW I, fig. 16) as quarrying had destroyed the evidence in the other two. Consequently its alignment could not be closely established.

In view of the similarity of construction of these two ramparts there is a possibility that they both belong to the same structure, the variable fill of the core between the turf cheeks reflecting the local changes in geology (cf. Brough, Wacher, 1969). A sufficient length of The Sands rampart was recovered to give a clear indication of its direction, and although trial excavations in a garden in Stepstairs Lane failed in the time available to find The Sands rampart extending that far, yet if it had extended to the north-west and if a line were drawn at right angles to it to pass through the Watermoor Hospital rampart, two sides of a possible fort or fortress would be suggested.

Two further pieces of evidence can be cited to give support to the suggestion that The Sands rampart and ditch belonged to a military installation. First, at the point where Ermin Street meets the projected line of the rampart, the road changes direction as it might well do at a gate in the defensive circuit. Secondly, in the nineteenth century two cavalry tombstones (RIB 108 and 109) were found beside Ermin Street, south of The Sands; assuming that they were in their original positions when found, it is more reasonable to associate them with a fort or annexe in

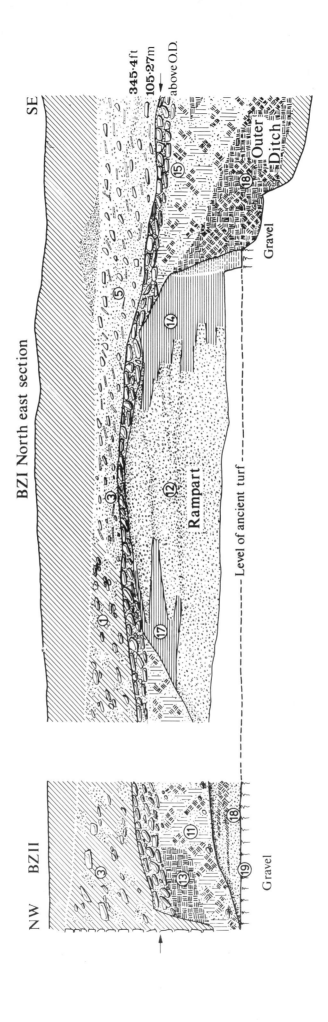

Fig. 20.   Section through annexe (?) defences in BZ I and II

the southern part of Cirencester rather than with the 'Leaholme' fort further north.

If this rampart and ditch are accepted as belonging to a military installation, the question of its place in the military history of Cirencester arises. The dating evidence suggests that the rampart was built between A.D. 60 and 85, perhaps *c.* A.D. 70, at a time when troop movements are known to have been taking place in the region with the establishment of the legionary fortress at Gloucester.

Finally the possibility arises that these defences may not be military and that they belong to a first-century civilian defensive circuit for which, at present, there is no other evidence.

DATING AND DISCUSSION OF THE FORTS AND ANNEXE (JSW)

The dates of the principal periods and phases have already been indicated (p. 22) and it only remains to summarise the key dating layers and their contents.

PERIOD II A, includes the pair of small ditches in AM I, the structures of Phase I in AH VIII and sundry levels in AG II and III.

In the primary silt of Ditch II, and below AM I 61, were coarse wares (p. 179) which could be Claudian, but might be as late as A.D. 85. In view of their position, an early date is to be preferred.

In AG II a thin sandy layer (AG II 49) overlay the undisturbed clay; it could equate with AH VIII 115. Above this was a small hearth AG II 48, set on a thin layer of clay; which contained coarse pottery (p. 163) of possible Claudian date.

In AH VIII, pressed into the surface of the undisturbed clay or included in the layers immediately above (AH VIII 76, 82, 87, 106, 108, 109, 116) were several coarse-ware fragments (p. 161), which could be Claudian, and need not be later than *c.* A.D. 55-60. There was also Claudian samian (p. 124), and again for stratigraphical reasons the earlier date is to be preferred for the coarse wares. Altogether, therefore, a date for Period II A of not much earlier than *c.* A.D. 45 but probably before *c.* A.D. 50 (in view of the limits imposed by Period II B) is most likely.

PERIOD II B, includes the main defences of the Leaholme fort, the structures of Phase II in AH VIII, a pit in AD III, and undated structures in AE II, III, V, VII, and DK I.

In the main rampart core (AM I 63) were coarse wares (p. 161) with a date range of *c.* A.D. 40-70.

The slot (AM II 66) which had probably contained an obstacle beyond Ditch III, had later been filled with material containing coarse wares (p. 206) with a date after *c.* A.D. 65. The obstacle is likely, therefore, to have belonged to this period.

In AH VIII, material (p. 162) dating to *c.* A.D. 45-55 came from the filling of P.H.4 but this is probably residual and included with the backfilling of the pit, after removal of the post.

The floors, and associated levels in AH VIII, which can be attributed to this period, are layers 75, 80, 81, 85, 86, 92, 102, 104 and 107; they contained pre-Flavian samian (p. 124) and coarse wares with a general date range of *c.* A.D. 45 to 60 or 65 (pp. 162, 204).

A pit (AG III 49) cut through AG III 48, into undisturbed clay, may date to this period; it contained samian which was possibly pre-Flavian (p. 125) and coarse wares dating to A.D. 50 to 70 (p. 163).

The earliest levels in AE dated to the Flavian or Trajanic periods, notably AE III 16, which lay directly on undisturbed clay and sealed the hearths in AE II; a layer near the bottom of the pit (AE III 17) was Trajanic (p. 125). But the post-holes in AE II contained pre-Flavian samian and coarse wares ranging from *c.* A.D. 45 to 80 (p. 165).

Unfortunately no dating evidence was obtained from the post-holes in DK I. The street, DK I 111, can be dated to *c.* A.D. 45, but its comparable layer in DM I 144 is unlikely to have been laid before the Neronian times.

It would appear, therefore, that although there are similarities, and indeed overlaps, between the evidence of Period II A and II B, that of the latter tends to be generally later. A starting date for Period II B of *c.* A.D. 50 would not, therefore, be inappropriate.

PERIOD II C shows little change in the arrangements of the fortifications, although it may have seen the contruction of the annexe; internally it is represented by the foundation-trenches of Phase III in AH VIII, together with those in AE II, III, V and VII and those in DK I.

In AH VIII, the associated gravel floor (layer 70) yielded a coin of Nero (A.D. 64–68) from its surface (p. 86).

In AE II, the post-holes contained pre-Flavian samian (p. 125) and coarse wares ranging from *c.* A.D. 45 to 100. Since the fillings represent the destruction of Period II B, they must reflect the construction of Period II C. For reasons already given above, other levels in AE were useless for dating this period.

In the cleaning channel in the bottom of Ditch III (AM II 67) was a pre-Flavian mortarium (p. 181) and coarse wares with a date range of *c.* A.D. 65 to 70, which must be contemporary with continued use of the ditch.

But the most cogent reason for dating the start of this Period to A.D. 60–65 is the large group of unused samian vessels (p. 133), closely dated *c.* A.D. 60–65, a mortarium dated *c.* A.D. 55–85 (p. 182) and coarse wares ranging from *c.* A.D. 65 to 70 in the main filling of Ditch III (AM II 59). It is interesting that the coarse wares reflect a slightly later date than the samian. It might be that they suffered a rather brisker turn-over in the stores from which the whole group of vessels probably came and, therefore, had a shorter shelf-life. If, as has been argued above, they represent new stock taken in when a change of unit dictated reconstruction work, then they must also reflect the date of that change.

If the evidence for this period is, therefore, taken as a whole, it can be seen that it largely reflects a late Neronian date, probably starting *c.* A.D. 60–65.

The construction of the annexe is probably best considered to fall within this period; the rampart (AW I 76) in the Watermoor Hospital garden contained samian (p. 119) dating to *c.* A.D. 45–60, while the associated street (AW I 72) contained samian of Claudio-Neronian date (p. 143). Nevertheless, the rampart at The Sands produced a piece of early Flavian samian from beneath it, and it must be acknowledged that more than one annexe may have existed. Generally, the pottery from The Sands was later in date than the Leaholme fort.

PERIOD II D relates to the final abandonment and destruction of the fort, as represented by the fillings of foundation trenches in AH VIII and the layers of clay and gravelly-clay overlying the upper floor surfaces in that area, which were probably derived from the demolition of daub walls. Similar evidence comes from AE and DK. It must also include the lower levels of the unquarried ditches in AM and AL, and the layers sealing the levelled rampart in the same areas.

In AH VIII, relevant layers are 27, 67, 69, 78, 79, 96, 98, 99, 100, 101, 103, 110 and 111, together with the contents of the two foundation-trenches AH VIII 83 and Slot A. The overwhelming mass of samian (p. 124) and coarse wares (p. 161) from these levels dates to the early Flavian period, with a slight overlap backwards into the 60s.

AE III 22, the filling of a foundation-trench yielded Neronian samian while in that of AE VII were early Flavian coarse wares (p. 167). More important, however, was the filling of the trench AE III 19, which contained coarse wares possibly as late as *c.* A.D. 85. The general run of sealing levels in AE where, as already noted, contemporary fort levels had largely been removed, ranged in the Flavian-Trajanic period (pp. 165–167) and included coins of Vespasian (A.D. 72), and of Hadrian (A.D. 118).

AL II, the filling of the quarried inner ditch contained samian and coarse wares (p. 142) with an early Flavian bias. The mass of material in the same ditch in AM II has already been considered.

The slot filling, DK I 110/113, was at the earliest Neronian, but could be as late as A.D. 80, and the general run of sealing layers in Admiral's Walk date from *c.* A.D. 80 to 110.

The ditch of the annexe at The Sands contained Flavian pottery in the bottom, and nothing much later than A.D. 100–125 in the remainder of the fill.

From all this evidence it can be seen that the fort can hardly have continued in existence for long after A.D. 70, since the material in the destruction-levels should represent that in use during the closing years.

Attention should be drawn at this point to Dr. Reece's report on the coins (p. 85). He has noted the paucity of the numismatic evidence and has given his opinion on what it represents in terms of a military occupation, when compared with similar sites. But it should also be pointed out that the sites he quotes in comparison have all been much more extensively excavated, whereas the sample from Cirencester has been derived from no more than about 400 sq. m. of exposed, contemporary levels. It must be emphasised, therefore, that the conclusions which have been drawn above about the fort at Cirencester rely more heavily on other evidence than on the coins.

Although little more can usefully be said about the fort of Period II A, enough evidence is available for that of the two subsequent periods to be considered further.

With two sides of the Leaholme fort established beyond reasonable doubt and with a third indicated by the lip of a ditch to the north-east of Price's Row (Site DA, fig. 2, no. 29), it is possible to make some estimate of the overall size of the fort. In the first place the Price's Row ditch must represent the inner ditch (equivalent to Ditch III, Site AM). Had it been the outer ditch, then the curve of the inner would have been observed within the confines of Leaholme; it was not. Consequently, it is possible to ascribe a north-east/south-west dimension for the fort, over the ramparts, of approximately 165 m. (540 ft.).

If it is also assumed that the line of Ermin Street indicates one of the main axes, with a likely gate situated on its line between Sites AD and AM at Leaholme, then it must be decided whether it represents the *via principalis* or *via praetoria*. Reference has also been made above (p. 36) to the probability that another gate lies just south-east of the Chester Mews site (BC), to coincide with the penultimate alignment of the Fosse Way approaching from the north-east. It is interesting, therefore, that the gravelled surface in DK I in Admiral's Walk, if interpreted as a street and extended to the north-east fortification, would strike them at approximately the same point. This street therefore may be assumed to represent the other main axis.

It is also important to record that the fort does not appear to be symmetrically placed about Ermin Street. Although we cannot be precise about the earliest line of the road it would, nevertheless, have had to pass through Sites AE, DK and DM for symmetry to be achieved; it did not do so. Consequently, its line probably represents the *via principalis*, and the probable street revealed in DK I should be taken as the *via praetoria*. On these assumptions the fourth side of the fort can be restored, with a length of 110 m. (360 ft.), from south-east to north-west, bisected by the *via praetoria*.

These measurements give a fort of 1.8 ha. (4½ acres) facing east. It must be admitted that this is on the small side for a garrison composed of a full *ala*. Yet these overall dimensions are to some extent supported by the sizes of the *praetentura* and *retentura* so formed. Each half of the former, allowing for an intervallum road of some 3 m. (10 ft.), would measure 41.4 m. (136 ft.) by approximately 91 m. (300 ft.). Barrack-blocks of the Claudio-Neronian period range from 30 m. (100 ft.) to 54.8 m. (180 ft.)[2], so that the most likely placing of barracks in the *praetentura* at Cirencester would be *per scamna*, with lengths of approximately 40 m. (131 ft.). But regularity of buildings was not observed, for, although the timber building foundations in DK I (Admiral's Walk) might represent the decurion's end of a barrack, whose long sides could just have lain outside the excavated area, it is not matched by a similar building on the opposite, north-western, side of the *via praetoria*.

In the rear of the fort, which must have been dominated by the *principia* and *praetorium*, the barracks were probably reduced in length, if *per scamna*, but it is more likely that they would have been placed *per strigas*, to take advantage of the longer dimension, 64 m. (210 ft.) between rear rampart and *via principalis*.

---

2.   Compare 36.6 m. (120 ft.) at Hod Hill; 39.8 m. (131 ft.) and 54.8 m. (180 ft.) at Valkenburg; 48.8 m. (160 ft.) and 30.5 m. (100 ft.) at the Lunt, postulated sizes of 45.7 m. (150 ft.) at Great Casterton and 54.8 m. (180 ft.) for the *ala* barracks at Longthorpe.

A quingenary *ala* at full strength would normally require some sixteen full-sized barracks, and probably nearly as many stable-blocks. If barracks and stables were packed cheek-by-jowl in the *praetentura* there would, if average widths are considered, have been room for some ten barracks and eight stables. But the buildings were clearly not so closely spaced, so this figure should undoubtedly be reduced. But even if it is accepted, there is unlikely to have been room in the *retentura* for another six barracks and possibly as many stables, in addition to the administrative and support buildings.

It might be suggested, therefore, that the garrison at Cirencester, if ostensibly a quingenary *ala*, was not at full strength, or else consisted, as at Hod Hill, (Richmond, 1968, 122), of a composite force of part of an *ala* with some legionary centuries. In this respect, it is as well to remember that, although Hod Hill occupies some 4.05 ha. (10 acres) within its ramparts, the area taken up by the buildings is little more than 1.62 ha. (4 acres), making it more nearly equivalent to Cirencester.

THE VICUS (JSW)

It was apparent from excavations north-west of the Leaholme fort that a civilian *vicus* had developed during the later years of the military occupation.

The most telling evidence for its existence came from a site (AY) lying between the Avenue and Lewis Lane and south-west of the cinema. There, in trench AY I, traces of the foundations for a timber building together with a well-metalled street were found beneath the piazza of the later forum. A foundation-trench (AY I 20) ran parallel with the north-east side of AY I for a distance of 1.52 m. (5 ft.) before turning through a right-angle to the south-west for a distance of 0.3 m. (1 ft.). The full widths of these two arms could not be determined, since one lay beneath the baulk and the other beneath a later wall, but both were 0.25 m. (10 in.) deep. A single post-hole lay 0.76 m. (2 ft. 6in.) north-west of the longer arm, while some 1.22 m. (4 ft.) south-east of the shorter arm, but again partly obscured by the later wall, were two parallel, adjacent scoops in the undisturbed gravel, each 0.20 m. (8 in.) deep and no less than 1.02 m. (3 ft. 4 in.) in length. All these features were filled with a uniform mixture of brown clay and gravel, and no post positions were revealed. Immediately south-east of the two scoops was a declivity in the surface of the undisturbed clay which appeared to run at right angles to the line of AY I, and in the centre there was a shallow, V-shaped gully, 1.47 m. (4ft. 10in.) wide and 0.25 m. (10 in.) deep, filled with stiff brown clay and turf (AY I 27). All these features were sealed by layers (AY I 18 and 26) of varying thickness of mixed red and grey clays, loams and gravel, and therefore must antedate the street, which lay above AY I 27.

The street was made up of a layer (AY I 25) of rubble set in clay 0.15 m. (6 in.) thick, and topped with a thin screed of yellowish mortar (AY I 24), 5 cm. (2 in.) thick. It was cambered downwards to the north-west and appeared to be running approximately at right angles to the line of AY I, and consequently parallel with the Leaholme fort's north-western defences. Its south-eastern limit could not be ascertained, but the street was probably about 3.35 m. (11 ft.) wide.

The dating for these features is provided by AY I 26, beneath the street, which contained little material earlier than A.D. 60, and by AY I 18, which sealed the foundation trench at the north-east end, and which contained nothing earlier than A.D. 70.

In considering evidence which is extra-mural to the fort, it is worth including that from a single trench (BB I) 4.23 m. (14 ft.) by 3.05 m. (10 ft.), dug in 1963 in the front garden of the G.P.O. Telephone Exchange in Lewis Lane, since it throws light on yet another street, which may be considered as the main line of the Fosse Way, running north-east to south-west and lying north-west of the fort. In this trench, gravel street-surfaces were found directly overlying the undisturbed subsoil. At least two superimposed gravel surfaces, (BB I 30, 33), separated by a thick layer of silt (BB I 31) were recorded, together with a side ditch (BB I 32) for BB I 33.

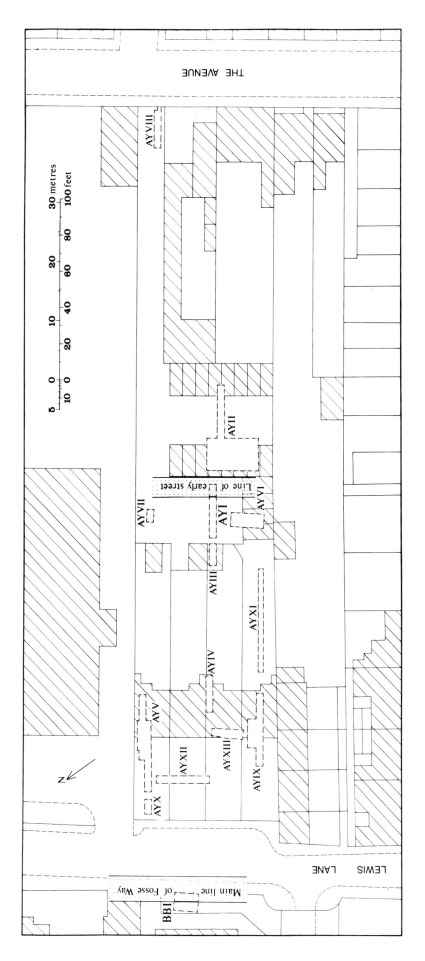

Fig. 21. Streets in the *viœ* below the forum piazza. BB I and AY

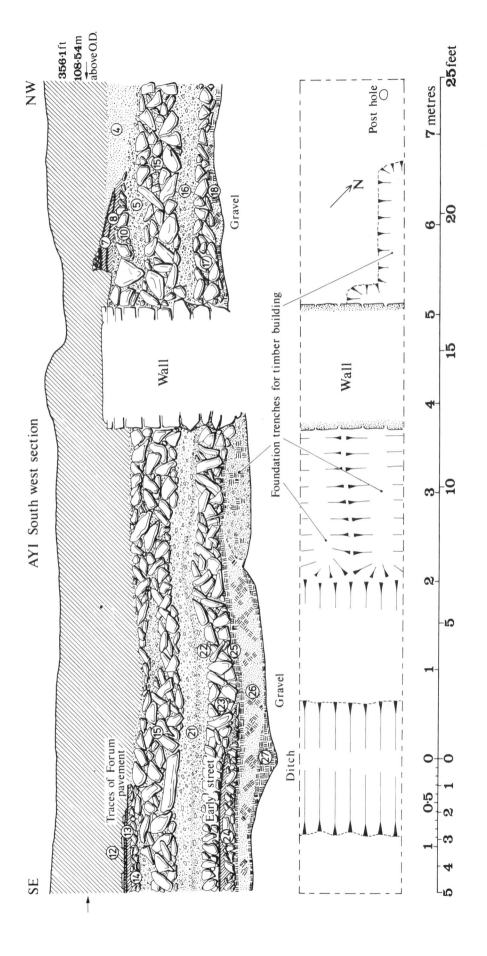

Fig. 22. Section through street and buildings in the *vicus*, AY I

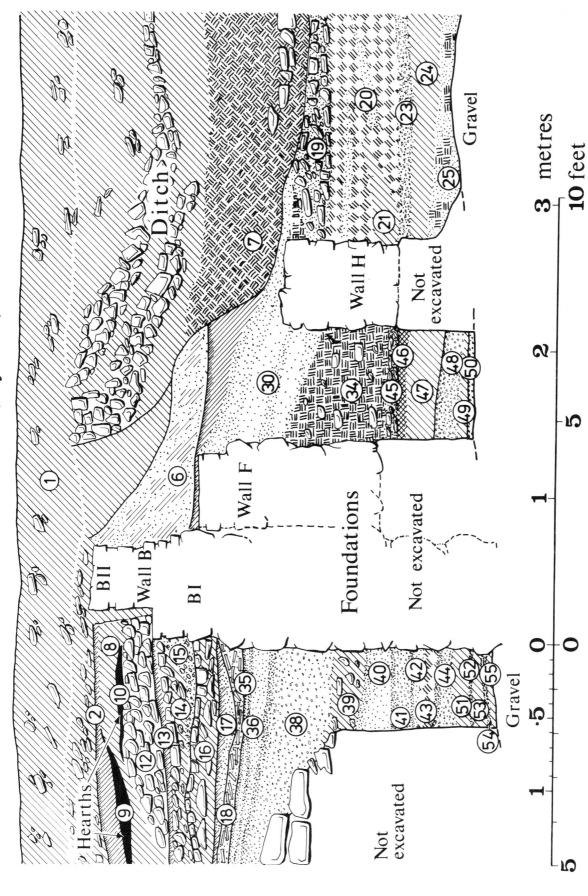

Ashcroft Road (Mycalex)

Fig. 23. Section through early (vicus?) layers at the Mycalex site, near Ascroft Road

Nothing later than A.D. 55 was found in the ditch, while BB I 31 contained nothing later than A.D. 60. The silt (BB I 29) overlying the upper surface, contained coarse pottery dating as late as A.D. 80.

Other early, extra-mural features were also recorded from the Mycalex site in Ashcroft Road (Reece, 1977, 92) and from Site AX beside the Health Centre in Watermoor Road. A large and deep pit (AX II 58) at the latter site produced pottery of the Claudio-Neronian period, but there is nothing to show that the pit was not originally dug by the army. At least three other levels, however, (AX II 45, 47 and AX V 33) produced pottery of the same general date range in addition to some native, Iron Age fabrics.

CIRENCESTER IN THE EARLY MILITARY PERIOD (JSW)

The fort established at Cirencester was one of a number designed to hold the earliest frontier of Roman Britain. It lay in the territory of the Dobunni at the meeting of three major roads, Akeman Street, the Fosse Way and Ermin Street, where the two former joined and crossed the river Churn. It lay only 4.8 km. (3 miles) from Bagendon *(Corinion)* (Wacher, 1975, 293), the contemporary native capital of the Dobunni, whose attitude towards the Roman advance has frequently been discussed (Hawkes, 1961, 43-67, and Wacher, 1975, 289-93).

Unfortunately, on present evidence, it is not possible to be certain precisely when the Roman army arrived at Cirencester. Undated structural features, from the period before the principal fort was founded *c.* A.D. 49, were uncovered in the course of the excavations, and suggest that an establishment existed before that date. Among them were two small, parallel ditches, earlier than, and behind, the rampart of the Leaholme fort.

If these belong to a fort founded within a year or two of the invasion, it was but one of a number in the area. Others may be envisaged at Bath *(RIB* 159) and Wanborough (Anderson, 1977, 155); while a third has been suggested on Rodborough Common, near Stroud (Rennie, 1959, 24-43). To the east and north-east further forts are known, or may be expected, e.g. at Alcester, Alchester and Dorchester (Oxon.), and perhaps at Dorn or Chesterton. Uncertainty still surrounds the date of the placing of a fort at Kingsholm, near Gloucester, (Garrod and Hurst, 1975). It has often been assumed that a fort for a part-mounted cohort *(Coh. VI Thracum RIB* 121) preceded the legionary base, thought to have been built *c.* A.D. 49. It is also usually assumed that Legio XX was transferred in its entirety from Colchester to Gloucester in that year, but it is still possible that a vexillation fortress may have been the first establishment at Gloucester, garrisoned jointly by a legionary detachment and *Coh. VI Thracum.* If so, an earlier fort at Cirencester would have been in an important pivotal position, commanding the main approach from the south-east to the Severn crossing and south Wales, where Caractacus was still entrenched.

At one stage during the investigations at Cirencester, it was, indeed, suggested (Wacher, 1975, 30 and 294) that a vexillation fortress might have existed there before A.D. 49 and before the establishment of the fort (see also p. 55). However, this interpretation has not stood up to a rigorous examination of the evidence, and the theory must be discarded.

As things stand at present, we can recognise a probable military presence at Cirencester soon after the invasion, followed by the foundation of a cavalry fort (referred to hereafter as the Leaholme fort) *c.* A.D. 49. The fort lay on a terrace of oolitic gravels masked by a thin cover of brown clay, on the south-western bank of the river Churn, (see p. 72). The north-west and north-east defences have been positively identified, but the other two are less certainly located. Evidence cited on p. 59 suggests a perimeter measuring approximately 165 m. by 110 m. (540 ft. by 360 ft.), giving an area of some 1.8 ha. (4½ acres).

Tombstones attest the presumably successive presence at Cirencester of two quingenary *alae* (*RIB* 108 and 109 and page 67 below), but three phases of military buildings have been shown to exist within the fort. Consequently it is not impossible that an unidentified unit also served there. Nothing is known of later possible expansions or reductions in the fort's size. But it must be remembered that many early military installations in Britain do not conform readily to later, more standardised patterns, and the complexity of the better known sites is only now beginning to be realised. That being so, it is possible to postulate the existence of joint garrisons of legionaries and cavalry, as at Hod Hill (Richmond, 1968, 122), or Great Casterton (Todd, 1968, 36), although a major objection is the lack of any finds of a specifically legionary nature from Cirencester.

The army movements which took place *c*. A.D. 49, in which both Cirencester and Gloucester were seemingly involved, were undoubtedly to tighten the net more securely around Caractacus and his allies, the Silures. Two years earlier they had raided the province (Tacitus, *Annales*, XII, 31), possibly attacking territory of the Dobunni. Consequently, it was sound tactics to station an *ala* at Cirencester, where the radiating roads offered a mobile force the ability to strike in any direction.

Further extensive troop movements followed in the decade after the Boudiccan rebellion. It is likely that a change in garrison occurred at Cirencester, although present evidence allows various interpretations.

(1) The ramparts discovered at both the Sands and Watermoor Hospital post-date the Leaholme fort rampart. It is not impossible, therefore, that a wholly new site, south of the existing fort, was selected for the third phase of military occupation. This suggestion, however, imposes problems if the third-phase buildings at Leaholme have to be included within this fort, since it would give it an unusually large area of some 12 ha. or more, so equating more with the size of a vexillation fortress.

(2) The large mass of pottery found in the filling of the inner ditch at Leaholme seems at first sight to support (1). The samian, in particular, from this layer may be closely dated to A.D. 60-65, and the obvious conclusion to be drawn is that the ditch, together with the rest of the north-west fortifications, went out of commission by that date. From this it might be deemed that a fort on a different site replaced, or was partly built over, the Leaholme fort. But there are additional complications. The accumulated evidence of all sites implies that the Leaholme fort was not finally closed down until the early to mid 70s, although it is not impossible that the north-west side was earlier re-positioned. However, the samian vessels from the ditch had clearly never been used and some were of types not likely to have been in great demand by soldiers. The evidence suggests, therefore, that it was probably discarded direct from a store for disposal in the ditch, and had never been issued. How long it had gathered dust on a remote shelf in the quartermaster's store cannot be assessed, but it may well have remained there until the fort was abandoned in the early or mid 70s. We might also suggest that the vessels were the sole survivors of a consignment of new stock taken into the stores during the early 60s, and such restocking could well equate with a change of unit. By 65, it may be added, Period II B buildings might have been showing signs of decrepitude after a life of some 15 years, so requiring replacements or repair, and giving rise to the Period II C internal reconstructions.

(3) If the proposals in (2) are accepted as the most likely explanation, the two outlying sections of fortification at the Sands and Watermoor Hospital have still to be explained. It seems most probable, in view of their later date, that they formed part of a large fortified annexe to the Leaholme fort. Several Claudio-Neronian forts are now known with annexes attached, often of a size larger than the parent fort, as at Thorpe-by-Newark, Notts. (Wilson D.R., 1966, 203). The likely purpose of these annexes at this period was for the stock-piling of strategic materials, such as timber possibly already cut for building use. Such stocks may well have existed by the early Flavian period to allow for the massive programme of fort construction then carried out so rapidly. Idle soldiers are discontented soldiers and a major programme of tree-felling in the non-campaigning, winter seasons would have provided work for many hands, at the most appropriate time, when the sap was down in the trees. (But see Hanson, 1978).

It is suggested, therefore, that the Leaholme fort was the principal fort at Cirencester, lasting from *c*. A.D. 49 to the early or mid 70s. The course of the main roads seems to add substance to this conclusion, although a good deal of uncertainty still obtains over the early alignments of Ermin Street, south-east of the site, and the Fosse Way to the south-west. The known direction of that part of Ermin Street seems to aim at a point to the west of the fort so as, perhaps, to bypass it. But the last main course of the Fosse Way, before it changes direction to the south some 3 km. (1¾ miles) north of the town, clearly points towards a gate in the north-eastern side of the fort and not far from the excavations in Chester Street, where peculiarities in the ditch spacings might indicate its presence, and where it would meet the street emerging from the fort, whose traces were found in Admiral's Walk. Equally clearly the north-western line of Ermin Street from Gloucester is extended by the street which strikes a gate of the fort lying in the area unavailable for excavation between the two main excavated arms of the Leaholme site. The slight difference in alignments of the lengths of ditches which can be observed in these two areas, strongly suggests an interruption at that point.

We may, therefore, tentatively postulate the following sequence:

(1)   Ermin Street reaches Cirencester from the south-east, probably representing the line of the initial military advance.

(2)   A fort was established in the general area of the Leaholme fort, but probably not coinciding precisely with it. The fort did not embrace the already positioned line of Ermin Street (south-east).

(3)   The Fosse Way from the north was sited on the north-east gate of the fort. It is still difficult to work out the relationship of the Fosse Way (south-west) with the fort, and much more information is required, as indeed also for the line of Akeman Street.

(4)   Ermin Street (north-west) was extended from Cirencester to Gloucester, starting as a projection of one of the principal streets in the fort.

It is suggested, therefore, that construction of a fort must have preceded the laying-out of the Fosse Way and the extension of Ermin Street to Gloucester, (Margary, 1973). But it is not yet possible to explain what would then have to be subsequent radical changes in these road alignments.

As already indicated, the final abandonment of the fort probably fell within the decade A.D. 70-80; together with others in the area the garrison was removed, presumably by either Julius Frontinus or Cn. Julius Agricola in preparation for their campaigns in Wales or the north. Evacuation involved much clearing up and demolition. The ramparts of the Leaholme fort and of the annexe appear to have been mostly levelled, the material being thrown into the inner ditch, together with much rubbish. The lines of the ditches must, nevertheless, have been still visible a few years later, for they were in places used as gravel quarries to provide aggregate for the new streets of the civil town. Indeed, much of the filling of post-pits and ditches was carried out in a superficial way, so that considerable subsidence occured over them in later years.

There is a growing mass of evidence that some Iron Age farms, or a minor settlement (Period I), were already in existence in the Churn valley at the time of arrival of the Roman army, in addition to the major centre at Bagendon. But in the post-Boudiccan period a military *vicus* developed on the land immediately north-west of the Leaholme fort. At least one street of this settlement, running parallel to the defences on that side of the fort, was found beneath the later forum piazza, and was flanked by a timber-framed building on the edge away from the fort. The nature and position of the street suggest that a degree of official recognition was accorded. The connection between the growing *vicus* and the abandonment of the native capital at Bagendon has been discussed by this writer elsewhere (Wacher, 1975, 30). Here it is worth noting that a process of migration, which may have been proceeding gradually for some years, was apparently hastened by the events of the early 60s. Whether this was the result of coercion on the part of the military, of official persuasion, or of economic forces, we cannot say. Certainly the economic, to say nothing of the protective, advantages of settling nearer to the fort than at Bagendon would have been apparent to most members of the community.

It will be seen from the foregoing account that most of the evidence for this period at Cirencester is of a fragmentary and often-uncoordinated nature; the historical implications, however, are not without importance.

EPIGRAPHIC EVIDENCE FOR THE AUXILIARY GARRISON AT CIRENCESTER
by
Mark Hassall

Two well-known tombstones found at Cirencester in the nineteenth century record the presence of men of two different cavalry regiments and are discussed in detail below (nos. 1 and 2). In addition there is a carved fragment which may come from a third auxiliary cavalryman's tombstone (no. 3). A fourth tombstone and part of a military diploma have also been found. The first probably, and the second conceivably indicate veterans settled at Cirencester but neither should be connected with the first century garrison and are accordingly not dealt with here.[3]

1.   = *RIB* 108, pl. 21. Inscribed tombstone, 0.78 x 1.98 x 0.26 m., with a carving of the deceased, shown as a mounted trooper, riding down a fallen enemy whom he is about to strike with his lance. The tombstone was found in July 1835 in digging house foundations for a Mr Paine at Watermoor, 'about 50 yards outside the old Roman wall' and about 2 feet below the surface[4] and close to the line of Ermin Street: now on display in the Corinium Museum.

Dannicus eq(u)es alae / Indian(ae) tur(ma) Albani / stip(endiorum) XVI cives Raur(icus) / cur(averunt) Fulvius Natalis it / Fl[avi]us Bitucus ex testame(nto) / h(ic) s(itus) e(st)
"Dannicus, trooper of the Cavalry Regiment Indiana, from the troop of Albanus, of 16 years' service, a tribesman of the Raurici, lies buried here. Fulvius Natalis and Flavius Bitucus had this erected under his will"

Discussion

Dannicus, according to the inscription, was tribesman *(civis)* of the Raurici (or Rauraci), who lived in the Roman military district and later province of Germania Superior. The chief town in the territory of this tribe was the Roman colony of Augusta Raurica, the modern Augst, near Basel in Switzerland. The unit in which Dannicus served was a cavalry regiment *(ala)* whose strength was nominally 500 men. In common with many other cavalry regiments the *Ala Indiana* "Indus' Horse", derived its name from that of the commander under whom it had been first raised, but unlike most of these officers, Indus can be identified. According to Tacitus[5] Julius Indus, a tribesman of the Treveri of the Moselle area of east Gaul was put in charge of a band of loyal native cavalry in A.D. 21, to help crush a revolt that had broken out in that year. After the rebels had been defeated, the unit was incorporated into the Roman army. It was subsequently stationed in Upper Germany and it will have been here that Dannicus enlisted in the unit.

According to the older view [6] the *ala* probably came to Britain at the time of the Claudian invasion of A.D. 43. Since Dannicus had served for 16 years at the time of his death, and had been enlisted before the transfer of the regiment to Britain, the tombstone could have been set up at any time between A.D. 43 and A.D. 59. It has recently been argued however[7] that the tombstone is a dozen or more years later in date and was not set up until after A.D. 70

---

3.   For the tombstone see McWhirr, 1973, 191-218, Appendix 1 inscriptions 1969-1973, no. 6, where it is suggested that it may be possible to restore the word *fulminata*, an epithet borne by legion XII. This restoration has not been adopted in the publication of the inscription in Wright and Hassall, 1974, 461, no. 1. For the diploma see the discussion by Margaret Roxan, p. 117.

4.   Information from David Viner quoting from a letter once in the Corinium Museum, now missing. For full bibliography and critical apparatus see *RIB* 108. Note the irregular spelling of *civis* (1.3) and *et* (1.4).

5.   Annals III 42. A daughter of Indus, Julia Pacata subsequently married Julius Classicianus the man sent to replace the unpopular Catus Decianus, the procurator of Britain at the time of the Boudiccan revolt in A.D. 60 or 61 (cf. *RIB* 12). On the history of the unit see Stein, 1932, 141-2; Alföldy, 1968, 19-21.

6.   e.g. cf. Stein, 1932, (n.3).

7.   Alföldy, 1968, (n.3).

21.   Tombstone of the trooper Dannicus, of the *ala Indiana*.

while the unit itself did not come to Britain until after the mid 50s. The reasoning is as follows.

One of Dannicus' heirs was called Flavius Bitucus, if the reading and restoration adopted by R.P. Wright in *RIB* is correct. Now the name Flavius should derive from a grant of Roman citizenship made by the emperor Flavius Vespasianus (or by one of his sons Titus or Domitian). This would mean that the inscription was set up at *earliest* in the year 70 when Vespasian became emperor, so that Dannicus, who had served for 16 years at the time of his death will have enlisted at *earliest* in A.D. 54 and the unit should still have been in Germania Superior at that date. Two conclusions would then follow: there would be epigraphic evidence for the occupation of the fort at Cirencester in the 70s and the *ala Indiana* would seem not to be the original unit in garrison at Cirencester. Unfortunately the stone is damaged at the vital point, and we shall therefore never know whether Bitucus in fact had the *nomen* Flavius, or another similar one such as Florius. The unit may have left Britain for Lower Germany in 83 and was certainly there by 89.[8]

2.   = *RIB* 109, pl. 22. Inscribed tombstone, 0.81 x 2.05 x 0.20 m., with a carving of the deceased shown as a mounted trooper riding down a fallen enemy. In his right hand he brandishes his lance and on his left arm he carries a hexagonal shield and a standard. The tombstone was discovered on 22 January 1836 near to the find spot of no. 1 and purchased by Sir Samuel Rush Meyrick, of Goodrich Court, Ross, and later restored to Cirencester and the Museum by the generosity of Mr G. Moffat, also of Goodrich Court. Now on display in the Corinium Museum.[9]

Sextus Vale/rius Genialis / eq(u)es alae Trhaec(um) / civis Frisiaus tur(ma)/ Genialis an(norum) XXXX st(ipendiorum) XX / h(ic) s(itus) e(st) (h)e(res) f(aciendum) c(uravit)

"Sextus Valerius Genialis, trooper of the Cavalry Regiment of Thracians, a tribesman of the Frisii, from the troop of Genialis, aged 40, of 20 years' service, lies buried here. His heir had this set up"

Discussion

Sextus Valerius Genialis possessed the three names *(tria nomina)* of a Roman citizen, but was also a tribesman *(civis)* of the Frisii, who lived in the Low Countries. He probably enlisted in the *ala Thracum*, a cavalry regiment of 500 men, while it was stationed in the lower Rhineland,[10] although apart from the present inscription, there is as yet no evidence that it was stationed in Germania Inferior in the first century A.D. If this is correct and if, as seems likely, the unit accompanied legion XX from Neuss in Lower Germany to Britain in A.D. 43, then the tombstone would be dated to between A.D. 43 and 63, for Genialis had served for 20 years. The *ala Thracum* in which he served is probably identical to the *ala prima Thracum* known to have been stationed at Colchester at some time between 43 and the Boudiccan revolt in A.D. 60/61.[11] This might suggest that it was the second of the two cavalry *alae* known to have been stationed at Cirencester. However, as shown above, there may be reasons for thinking the other unit, the *ala Indiana*, was still in Upper Germany in the mid 50s (see above), in which case the *ala Thracum* will have been the earlier of the two at Cirencester. Its stay at Colchester may have been very brief for Claudius' first Governor, Aulus Plautius (A.D. 43-47), was probably responsible for building the Fosse Way and its forts at Cirencester and elsewhere both on the line of the road itself and in a screen to the west of it. Alternatively it may have come to Cirencester in A.D. 50 for in that year the

---

8.   Alföldy, 1968, (n.3), p. 20. The unit bears the title *pia fidelis* in an inscription (CIL XI 6123) as do other regiments in Lower Germany which had remained loyal to Domitian during a revolt in Upper Germany in 89.

9.   Information on the discovery and later history of the stone from David Viner. For full bibliography and critical apparatus, see *RIB* 109. Note the irregular spelling of *eques, Thracum, Frisiavus* (an alternative of *Frisius*) and *heres*.

10. For the history of this unit see Stein, 1932, (n. 3 above), 153-4; Alföldy, 1968, n.3 above, 36-7; Jarrett, 1969, 215-224, esp. 218; Bogaers, 1974, 198-220, with English summary 217-219.

11. *RIB* 201. It is not unusual for the first *ala* or *cohors* of a series to lack a numeral on inscriptions.

22.   Tombstone of the trooper Sextus Valerius Genialis, of the *ala Thraecum*.

23.   Stone hand from cavalry tombstone. (Scale 1:1)

colonia at Colchester was founded, and its garrison, legion XX, was moved westward against the Silures. In this case, it may have replaced a third, unknown unit which will have been in garrison at Cirencester for a very brief period (*c.* A.D. 47-50).

3.   Sculptured hand of oolitic limestone (pl. 23), found in 1950 in the garden of no. 157 Watermoor Road. The trench also produced evidence for six burials and it is possible that the fragment comes from a funerary monument although the unweathered state of the stone suggests that it may never have been set up. Around the wrist is a bracelet shown as a broad flat band, the ends of which have been turned back on themselves. The hand itself grasps a rod which could be the shaft of a lance and if so, probably comes from the grave monument of a cavalry trooper[12] similar to nos. 1 and 2. The sculptured hand is the subject of a separate note by N. A. Griffiths, (1978, 396-7).

12.   For parallels from the Rhineland see Gerster, 1938, Type B, "Reitersteine" where an attempt is made to attribute the 36 Rhenish rider monuments to four specific workshops.

THE GEOLOGY OF CIRENCESTER AND DISTRICT
by
H. S. Torrens

INTRODUCTION

Cirencester, being an inland town and one at the far end of the long dip slope of the Cotswold Hills, has never received the amount of attention accorded by geologists to the Costwold Jurassic scarp face, or even better exposed areas of rocks of the same age, such as the Dorset or Yorkshire coasts. Cirencester lies, using S.S. Buckman's (1903) definition of the Cotswold Hills, right on the south-eastern margin of them. The geologically based boundary between the Cotswolds and the Vale of the White Horse farther south-east being effectively the outcrop of the junction between the lithologically quite different Cornbrash limestones and the Kellaways Clay above. This junction runs irregularly just to the south of Cirencester. A further result of the geological position of the town so far down-dip is that natural exposures are rare, being largely confined to those produced first by canals and quarries and then by railway cuttings or more recent road or motorway sections which may be of an unfortunately temporary nature. This lack of permanent exposures means that the adequate recording of temporary sections is a high priority and of course that some parts of the stratigraphic sequence near Cirencester remain badly known to this day.

The notes which follow discuss the development of geology in the Cirencester region and summarize our present knowledge of the stratigraphy within a 5-mile radius of the town. The considerable number of references will, it is hoped, give further information where needed.

HISTORY OF GEOLOGICAL RESEARCH IN THE AREA (TO 1860)

The richly fossiliferous rocks of Middle Jurassic age making up the Cotswolds early on attracted attention. Dr. John Woodward (1665-1728), who is remembered chiefly today for his contributions to geology as author of some important books and founder of the Woodwardian chair of geology at Cambridge University, has recorded how his lifelong interest was first aroused. While botanising on a visit to Sir Ralph Dutton at Sherborne, north-east of Cirencester, he found a fossil brachiopod "in Sir Ralph Dutton's Vineyard at Sherborne, Gloucestershire on Jan 13th, 1689/90. The first fossil shell I ever found." (Eyles, 1973, 7).

An early project to describe these local fossils, which was associated with Cirencester about a century later, was however still-born. Dr. Caleb Hillier Parry (1755-1822) in 1781 issued printed "Proposals for a History of the Fossils of Gloucestershire" which would have been of great interest in view of his Cirencester birth. The promised publication never appeared and the original manuscripts have not been traced. (Torrens, 1978, 221).

The first major impetus to geological investigations near Cirencester came with the excavation of the Thames and Severn Canal and especially the Sapperton tunnel between 1784 and 1789. This canal, running south-west of the town, involved excavation to a massive extent (Household, 1969), especially with the Sapperton Tunnel by far the longest tunnel attempted by then in England. Several important geological visitors to the excavations are recorded including Dr. Charles Blagden (1748-1820) and Henry Cavendish (1731-1810) in July 1785 (Harvey, 1971, 74, 195, 330); and William Smith (1769-1839) – the so-called father of English Geology – in 1788 and again in 1794 (Phillips, 1844, 5, 11). But no details of the sections at Sapperton seem to have been published until the later railway tunnel was constructed nearby in 1843-1845 (Ibbetson, 1847).

Nonetheless the new stratigraphic information and fossils laid bare by the Thames and Severn Canal and other canals connecting with it were certainly used by William Smith in compiling his Geological map of England and Wales of 1815 and his later fine county Geological map of Gloucestershire published in 1819 and reprinted by the British Museum (Natural History) in 1974. A collection of fossils made from the canal near South Cerney enabled him to identify the Kellaways Rock there (Smith, W., 1816-19, 23; 1817) and on his 1819 map the geological formations of the area as then known are shown with remarkable accuracy. He mapped the Inferior and Great Oolite limestones as one in this area; Smith, as others up to the present day, finding it difficult to distinguish the intervening Fullers Earth beds near Cirencester. Above this he mapped Forest Marble limestones and recorded their fossils from Foss Cross, Poulton and Siddington (intervening beds not being recognised here until 1847 – Woodward, 1848). Above he showed Cornbrash and Kellaways Rock separated but mapped as one and capped by Oxford (or for him Clunch) clay.

The next stimulus to the study of geology in the Cotswolds came with the opening of the Literary and Philosophical Institution in Cheltenham in 1833. This brought together those interested in geology in the area and with their encouragement Roderick Murchison published in 1834 his "Outline of the Geology of the Neighbourhood of Cheltenham". Thus aroused, the study of Cotswold geology began to enjoy considerable popularity and a second edition of Murchison's book appeared in 1844 augmented and revised by James Buckman (1814–1884), at this time Honorary Secretary of the Cheltenham Literary and Philosophical Institution, and Hugh Strickland (1811-1853) of Evesham, and later Reader in Geology at Oxford University.

A similar stimulus for the Cirencester area soon followed with the foundation of the Royal Agricultural College there in 1844. Students were accepted from September 1845 and were taught geology by one of the founding professors called Samuel Pickworth Woodward (1821-1865) who was professor of Natural History at the College from 1845-1847 (Woodward, 1884). Woodward had been previously employed as a sub-curator at the Geological Society of London 1839-1845. The same period saw the foundation of the Cotteswold Naturalists Field Club, no doubt encouraged by the newly arrived railway system, which held its first meeting at Birdlip in July 1846. Woodward was one of the founder members, and of the first 25 members nine were from Cirencester, and the publications of the Club soon reflected this Cirencester interest. Volume 1 has a paper by S.P. Woodward "On the Geology of the District Explored by the Cotteswold Club and more particularly the clay subsoil of the College farm" read in 1847 (Lucy, 1888). It was unfortunate that Woodward's tenure of the chair at the College had to cease unexpectedly in 1847 because of financial problems at the College (Woodward, 1884, 289).

The new professor of both Geology and Botany at the College was Cheltenham-born James Buckman who was appointed in 1848. Buckman was a remarkable man with a wide range of interests and the energy to support them. He made fundamental contributions to the geology, palaeontology, botany and archaeology of the Cotswolds. He was also the Honorary Secretary to the Cotteswold Field Club from 1852-1860 and became a regular contributor to its Proceedings. The first volume contains three papers by him, one of archaeological interest, on the Tesserae of a Roman Pavement found at Cirencester in 1849, a subject he expanded in his book published in 1850 with C.H. Newmarch, "Illustrations of the Remains of Roman Art" and two others on the geology of Cirencester and fossil insects.

With the encouragement of the Cotteswold Field Club and the national societies for Geology and Palaeontology based in London, the study of Cotswold geology thereafter greatly prospered and by the time of the publication of James Buckman's paper of 1858 "On the Oolitic Rocks of Gloucestershire and North Wilts.", the major features of the stratigraphy of the Cirencester area had been set down in print and the ground work had been covered. James Buckman resigned from his chair in 1862 having played a vital part in the establishement of Cotswold Geology, and retired to Dorset. The fine collections of Cotswold specimens he had made were left behind at the Royal Agricultural College in Cirencester, where they remained until the first World War. Then "the college was closed . . . but a girls' school in Kent that found it necessary to remove to less nerve-racking quarters occupied it. The Headmistress . . . had no use for this rubbish and turned everything out of the cases helter skelter on the floor of the chemical laboratory and store rooms. By pure accident I (H.H. Swinnerton) heard of this and got permission to secure all the fossils I could. . . . I went systematically through all the heaps picking out everything that I thought would have value, especially when I was informed that what was left would be used for garden paths!! Labels of course were lost . . . Petrological stuff went to Bristol (University) and Cambridge (University)." (Prof. H.H. Swinnerton of

University College, Nottingham *in lit* to S.S. Buckman, April 7th, 1924 – Buckman family archives. See Richardson 1925, 93). This vandalism of the local museum has resulted in the loss of a significant amount of valuable information about the geology of the area and its development.

STRATIGRAPHY OF THE JURASSIC ROCKS WITHIN A 5-MILE RADIUS OF CIRENCESTER

1. *Inferior Oolite*

Of those geological formations found within a five-mile radius the lowest belong to the rocks of the Inferior Oolite Group named by William Smith; because of their inferior position to rocks above called the Great Oolite. The Inferior Oolite outcrops in the floors of the River Churn and Bagendon valleys. Exposures are as a result not often available and our knowledge of the detailed stratigraphy near Cirencester is not good.

The main subdivisions of this group were established by the pioneer work of Cirencester-born S.S. Buckman (1860-1929), the son of James, in papers published in 1895, 1897 and 1901. He showed these rocks could be separated into three major divisions, Upper, Middle and Lower, the base of the Upper division being taken at the base of the lithological unit called the Upper Trigonia Grit and the base of the Middle division at the base of the Lower Trigonia Grit, both of which are deposits laid down unconformably on earlier rocks which had suffered erosion to a greater or lesser degree (see Parsons, 1976). The great majority, if not all, of the Inferior Oolite exposed in our area belongs only to the Upper Inferior Oolite, comprising Upper Trigonia Grit overlain by Clypeus Grit.

At Bull Banks WNW of Duntisbourne Abbots, Richardson recorded (1933, 18-21) 0.6-0.9 m. (2-4 ft.) and 6 m. (20 ft.) of these respectively, and farther east, at Chedworth Wood (1933, 27-28) 1.5 m. (5 ft.) and 6 m. (20 ft.). These thicknesses are considerably increased in the Stowell Park borehole (SP 084118 – Green and Melville, 1956, 13-14) to 2.2 m. (7½ ft.) and 12 m. (38 ft.) respectively. The term Grits applied to these rocks, as with many Cotswold rock terms, betrays their origin in a period when Grit was used for any coarse-grained rock and not only for sandstones. Grit was a term formerly used for what today we would call coarse grain (Arkell and Tomkeieff, 1953, 53). The Clypeus Grit is often but not always a coarse fawn oolitic limestone often with marl partings crowded with the echinoid *Clypeus ploti* (Salter) and common nests of the brachiopod *Stiphrothyris tumida* (Davidson). The Upper Trigonia Grit is a similarly coarse limestone but less oolitic and packed with broken fossils of a large size, often the Trigoniid bivalves, after which the rock is named.

The underlying beds vary greatly in different parts of the Cotswolds depending on the extent of erosion before the deposition of the Upper Trigonia Grit. S.S. Buckman (1897) showed that complications were introduced because these beds had been gently folded before erosion took place, and he produced maps showing the distribution of the rocks immediately underlying the Upper Trigonia Grit (1901, pl. 16) which were modified slightly by Richardson (1904, 143).

At Bull Banks the Upper Trigonia Grit overlay the Upper Freestone as noted by Buckman (see Richardson 1904, 95) but farther east the underlying rocks had been folded by both an anticlinal axis and just east of Cirencester a corresponding synclinal axis. The Notgrove Freestone higher in the sequence was the underlying rock at Chedworth Wood, and when the Stowell Park borehole (1949-51) was drilled Buckman's prediction that this area would show Buckmani Grit beneath the Upper Trigonia Grit was subsequently proven. Other boreholes in the Cirencester area will presumably demonstrate the existence of beds ranging from the Upper Freestone to the Notgrove Freestone as predicted by Buckman. But there is always a very considerable time gap between Middle and Upper Inferior Oolite in the Cotswolds because of erosion.

The beds at the junction of the Inferior Oolite with the overlying Fullers Earth are very badly known throughout the Cotswolds. Near Stroud a unit called the White Oolite forms the topmost part of the Inferior Oolite above the Clypeus Grit, and has yielded critical ammonites of the Zigzag Zone showing it to be Bathonian in age (Richardson, 1904 133; Torrens, 1980, 33).

It was not, however, recognised in sections described farther east at Chalford (SP 900024) west of Cirencester (Channon, 1951) or at Chedworth Wood north-north-east of Cirencester (Richardson, 1933, 27) which exposed the critical junction.

2. *Fullers Earth*

The Fullers Earth near Cirencester is a buff or slaty blue clay about 6.3 m. (21 ft.) thick. It is readily mapped by the clayey soil to which it gives rise and the spring line at its top, but natural exposures are not common and our knowledge of it is limited. At Chalford the normal common occurrence of the small sickle-shaped oyster *Praexogyra acuminata* (J. Sowerby) at or near the top of the Fullers Earth was demonstrated by Channon (1951). The same was found in the Stowell boring where the thickness of the Fullers Earth has increased to over 12 m. (40 ft.). The constant occurrence of this fossil above the Fullers Earth proper suggests that these Acuminata Beds should be separated as a distinct unit, but not one always everywhere of the same age.

Above the Fullers Earth we remain in a part of the geological sequence which is very badly known, because of the large and rapid facies changes over both short distances and small thicknesses, making comparisons between neighbouring sections difficult. Luckily, good sections were described when the railway sections between Cirencester and Chedworth were first made available (Richardson, 1911, 1933; Arkell and Donovan 1952, 246-7). These provide a standard for the development of the higher Great Oolite Group of rocks near Cirencester.

Above the Fullers Earth (with Acuminata Beds at the top about 15 m. (50 ft.) thick) occurred 6 m. (20 ft.) of "Flaggy and shaly coarse shelly limestones" which were assigned by Richardson to the Taynton Stone and the Stonesfield Slates of the area farther north. They have yielded no diagnostic fossils, so their affinities are not clear. Equivalent beds west of Cirencester were recorded by Channon (1951) at Chalford station at the very top of the section he recorded. It is these beds which have been largely quarried for roofing slates in the Cotswolds. Above these beds in the cuttings were a sequence of marls and indurated marls 4 m. (13 ft.) thick. These seem likely to represent the south-westerly attenuation of the Hampen Marly Beds, a series of clays and marls above the Taynton Stone first described at Hampen in Gloucestershire. Farther south at Latton near Cricklade south-east of Cirencester, the Hampen Marly beds are recorded as absent in a borehole (Arkell, 1933).

3. *White Limestone*

Overlying these beds are a series of thick distinctive cream to white micritic limestones named the White Limestone Formation, and comprising one of the most characteristic rock types of the south-east Cotswolds, (Palmer, 1979). The Chedworth to Cirencester railway cuttings again provide a standard sequence for these rocks in this area. Here, the White Limestone can be divided as follows:– (Bed numbers follow those of Richardson, 1911, 1933, but include some *not* assigned by him in the same way).

5– 8	Bladon Member
9–17	Ardley Member
18–32	Shipton Member

Bed characterised by the gastropod *Aphanoptyxis excavata*. (Barker MSS.)

Total 28.5 m. (94 ft.)

The White Limestone of the Cirencester area has yielded an abundance of fossils; of the crucial ammonites, specimens of *Morrisiceras* indicating the Morrisi Zone of the middle Bathonian have been collected from both the railway cuttings (bed 19) and *in situ* from the equivalent bed (2) at Foss Cross Quarry (Torrens (ed.), 1969; Barker, 1976, fig. 1:7). A single ammonite indicating the basal zone of the Upper Bathonian has been collected, also *in situ*, at a higher level at Dagham Downs Quarry (Torrens, 1980, 34-5). The abundant nerineid gastropods which have proved so useful in detailed correlation between sections have been studied recently by Barker (1976). The brachiopods which are very abundant at many levels and which demonstrate all growth stages from juvenile to adult are in serious need of modern research, and are consequently in an unhappy taxonomic state. Corals are locally abundant and those of the celebrated but no longer adequately exposed Fairford Coral bed at the top of the White Limestone at Fairford east of Cirencester have been recently re-described by Negus and Beauvais (1975). One of the most characteristic rock types found within the White Limestone at Cirencester at at least 5 horizons is called "Dagham Stone" (Richardson, 1933, 48) after its occurrence at Dagham Downs. Previously the origin of the irregular ramifying perforations which run characteristically through this stone have been much debated, but Fursich and Palmer (1975) have recently demonstrated their true origin. By making plastic casts of the perforations and then dissolving away the surrounding sediment their fine shape and structure has been demonstrated as the result of burrow systems almost certainly of crustacean origin. These beds have also yielded some unique fossil material, notably the red alga *Solenopora jurassica* Brown which was originally described from Chedworth and where fine material can still be collected of a quality unrivalled in England. A paper defining this taxon on the basis of Chedworth material and discussing its palaeoecology and conditions of deposition is in press (Harland & Torrens, 1981).

Even more remarkable were the fossil reptilian eggs from this horizon collected by a student at the Agricultural College in Cirencester called Dalton and described by James Buckman in 1860. This material, which came from Hare-Bushes Quarry about a mile north-east of Ciren-cester, is now preserved in the British Museum (Natural History), London.

Because of the many sections available, the White Limestone has also been the subject of some interesting work to determine its mode of origin and conditions of deposition. In general, these rocks are thought to have been deposited under normally quiet, shallow and warm seas. Such conditions allowed a considerable variety of animal life to flourish and to be often preserved more or less in the place it originally lived. Both Silva (1976) and Fursich and Palmer (1975) have described the conditions of deposition and both are in general agreement about the White Limestone being the product of sediments deposited on a very shallow current-swept carbonate platform which was subjected to short periods of erosion with consequent non-deposition. Eliott (1975), again basing his work on Dagham Downs Quarry, has used an interesting fauna of new species of fossil algae which grow under particular conditions to demonstrate that they occur here as a transported fauna in broken and rounded pieces of carbonate sediments. This demonstrates that certain beds were subjected to considerable current action during their deposition but again in a warm marine and shallow environment, and a conclusion reached by Harland and Torrens (1981) working at Chedworth.

4. *Forest Marble*

Above the White Limestone at Cirencester are "the Kemble Beds". These were first named by Woodward (1894, 248, 250, 272) and characterised as a series of false-bedded oolites named after the exposures seen at Kemble railway station, where about 9 m. (30 ft.) were visible. The important distinction in lithology and the presence or absence of false bedding was the basis for their separation from the beds below. Separation from the beds above has been, however, a perennial source of difficulty and confusion. Richardson (1933, 49) classified these beds as follows: (in descending order)

Forest Marble	Wychwood Beds ⎫
	Bradford Clay ⎬
Great Oolite	Kemble Beds

but he also acknowledged (1933, 72) that in the general Cirencester area it was "very difficult to determine to which formation rocks belong – whether to the Forest Marble or to the Kemble beds presenting a Forest Marble facies. Locally the lithic structure of the two formations is very similar". Richardson and other workers of his generation also believed in the reality of the Bradford Clay as a distinct geological horizon characterised by a distinct fauna by which it could be recognised. The Bradford Clay was first recognised in the Bath area by William Smith. Recent work by Green and Donovan (1969, 24, 26) has shown that the Bradford Clay fauna is found at more than one horizon even in its type area. Thus its occurrence elsewhere may be correlated with any of these horizons. Palmer and Fursich (1974) have clearly demon-strated that much of the type Bradford Clay fauna is a facies fauna not unique but liable, and now proven, to occur whenever the right conditions for its development were found.

The supposed occurrence of the "Bradford Clay" at Cirencester (Richardson, 1933, 50, 76) is thus not a reliable method of separating the Great Oolite and Forest Marble in this area. The Kemble Beds and the overlying Forest Marble can thus be said to be very difficult to distinguish and it must be asked if they are now worthy of separation. Eliott (1973) has undertaken a recent palaeoecological analysis of a "Bradford Clay" type fauna found at Sunhill east of Cirencester. He concludes that the faunas here were displaced from their original sites and that the bed represents a subtidal accumulation produced by rough coastal seas.

5. *Cornbrash*

The Cornbrash of the Cirencester areas has been famous ever since William Smith recorded fossils from Down Ampney and Latton in his pioneer publications of 1817, 1816-19. Douglas and Arkell (1928) published a major and still unsuperceded study of this Formation, and described the sections then available near Cirencester (pp 134–135), and further details and corrections were supplied by Richardson (1933). Douglas and Arkell demonstrated that, as Smith had pointed out in 1819, the faunas of the Cornbrash allowed it to be separated into Upper and Lower divisions: the Upper Cornbrash because of the affinity of its ammonite faunas now being assigned to the Callovian stage, and the Lower Cornbrash, for the same reason, to the Bathonian stage.

Sections no longer available show that both the Upper and Lower Cornbrash are well developed in the Cirencester area. The Upper Cornbrash is the more notable, and between Fairford and Cirencester forms a notable topographic feature on the surface. It is made up of a sequence of often hard limestones which have been quarried for road metal. The total thickness is only about 2–3 m. (7–10 ft.), (Richardson, 1933, 77–81), of which the Upper makes up about 75%. The Upper Cornbrash can be further divided on the basis of the distribution of brachiopods into a sequence at the top yielding *Microthyridina lagenalis* (Schlotheim), which was particularly abundant at Fairford; and a lower sequence yielding *M. siddingtonesis* (Walker), a species whose type locality is Siddington, south-east of Cirencester, where it was, as at Fairford, extremely common.

The fossiliferous nature of the Lower Cornbrash in the Cirencester region is as celebrated as that of the Upper Cornbrash. It is more condensed in thickness and made up of a more marly softer limestone packed with fossils, of which sections have been described at Ampney Crucis and Sharncote.

6. *Kellaways and Oxford Clay*

Above the Cornbrash come typical Kellaways Beds. These were first described in the area north of Chippenham, Wiltshire, where the hamlet of Kellaways (after which the Callovian stage is named) is situated. In the Cirencester memoir, Richardson almost ignored the Kellaways rock of this area, stating there was "no topographical feature that might indicate the presence of hard Kellaways rock", (1933, 81). It is certainly found, however, and had been described at South Cerney up to 6m. (20 ft.) thick by Harker in 1886. Lithologically it is made up of a sequence of decalcified sands with an inter-bedded series of massive huge doggers which are spheroidal masses of calcareous sandstone up to 1.8 m. (6 ft.) in diameter and yielding an abundant series of ammonites in fine preservation with a great deal of plant material. It was underlain by a few feet of Kellaways Clay, which has been worked for bricks in the past at Siddington as noted by Harker, (1866, 184), and by Richardson and Webb, (1910, 242) wrongly as Oxford Clay. It is worth pointing out that the sequence of these rocks in the Cirencester area has proved highly anomalous on two occasions. At Calcutt, south-east of Cricklade, a well supposedly proved Kellaways Beds to a total thickness of 22 m. (74 ft.) (Richardson 1922); while at Lewis Lane in Cirencester a similar boring is claimed to have proved only a total thickness of 1.8 m. (6 ft.) and even more remarkably to have shown the Kellaways Rock resting direct on the Cornbrash and with no Kellaways clay between, (Richardson, 1925, 93–99), despite evidence published by Harker (1886 and 1891). The answer in this last record surely lies in the fact that the drillers in 1924 recovered no cores at Lewis Lane down to this level, and the sequence must have been misinterpreted. The Kellaways Beds of the type area between

Chippenham and Malmesbury to the south have been recently described by Cave and Cox (1975).

The Oxford Clay of the Vale of the White Horse forms the highest rock type found in the Cirencester area. Details of its stratigraphy are not at all well known for several reasons. In the first place, there are no natural exposures, and man-made exposures in brick yards and clay pits are now almost unheard of; secondly, much of the area immediately to the south and south-east of Cirencester which is floored by Oxford clay is covered by thick gravel river terrace deposits which makes natural or other exposures even harder to find. The Oxford clay of the area nearer Swindon has been described in the old Hills Brickyard near Purton Station north-west of Swindon by Arkell (1941). Here higher zones of the Oxford Clay (Oxfordian) were found with abundant ammonites.

POSTSCRIPT

Cirencester has a remarkable record for the study, marrying geology and archaeology, of the source of the stone used in the construction of the Mosaic pavements in the area, the work of the School of mosaic workers named the Corinium School by D.J. Smith (see summary in Rivet, 1969, chapter 3). This study is especially associated with two men with strong Cirencester associations. The first is Samuel Lysons (1763-1819), son of Samuel Lysons, rector of Rodmarton south-west of Cirencester, where he was born. His interest in the subject was aroused by the study of the Great Pavement associated with the Roman Villa at Woodchester, Gloucestershire, from 1793 to 1796. Lysons had a considerable interest in geology as well as archaeology, and this led him to speculate on the sources of the tesserae of which the pavement was composed, (Smith 1973). He identified the red tesserae as of brick; the bluish-grey as limestone from the Lower Lias of the Vale of Gloucester; a light brown material he suggested came from Lypiatt and thus from somewhere in the Great Oolite group; the dark brown he identified as what is now called Old Red Sandstone, and recognised by him as obtainable from Bristol and the Forest of Dean. Only with the cream-white material did he go seriously astray, wrongly suggesting an Italian marble as the source, (Lysons, 1797, 4). The acuteness of his observations on this subject are remarkable on account of the early date at which they were made.

Lysons' work was continued by James Buckman (1850, 1853) and with C.H. Newmarch (1850), who again combined an active interest in both geology and archaeology. Buckman and Newmarch (1850, 49-54) separated six different natural materials which had been used in the Cirencester pavements as tesserae; as at Woodchester, Old Red Sandstone and Low Lias limestones had supplied Chocolate or Slate coloured materials. In addition, Buckman recognised the occasional use of chalk and more frequently, the often hard, micritic White Limestone of the Cirencester Great Oolite (which Lysons thought was Italian) had supplied white and cream coloured materials. Grey and yellow materials were again both local, the Grey from the same White Limestone which had been heated in a fire, this Buckman was able to prove by experiment; and the yellow from the gravel beds of the area. A modern re-appraisal of Lysons' and Buckman's work would be of great interest, and it is perhaps a fitting reminder of today's specialisation that this has not been attempted.

(This report was revised in August 1981. Editors.)

THE FINDS

Table 2   Correlation of Contexts and Finds

Pottery and finds recovered from individual contexts discussed in this volume are listed below by page reference and/or illustrated figure number.

Pottery: Coarse wares, figs. 50–65
          Mortarium and amphora stamps, fig. 48, prefixes M. and A.
          Stamps on Gallo–Belgic and coarse wares, fig. 49, prefixes G. and C.
          Samian stamps, fig. 41, prefix S.
          Decorated samian, figs. 42–46, prefix D.
          Plain samian, fig. 47
Objects: Figs. 24–40; 66–70

It is hopes that this table will aid all those who wish to reconstitute the finds from specific contexts.

Table 2   CORRELATION of Contexts and Finds

Context	Coarse Wares	Samian	Objects
AE I 10	204	D.7–8; 125	Coin: Vespasian, 87
AE I 12		125	
AE II 10	204	S.12; 125	Coins: Claudius I, Hadrian, 87
AE II P.H. 1	fig. 51, 50; 204		Glass, 106
AE II P.H. 2		D.6; 125	
AE II P.H. 3	fig. 51, 50; 204		
AE III 16	fig. 51, 53–4; 204	D.9; 125	Iron, 101
AE III 17		125	
AE V 19	fig. 51, 52; 204		Coin: Claudius I, 87
AE V 20	204		Coin: Radiate (intrusive), 87
AE V 21	fig. 51, 48–9; 204	125	
AE VII P.H. 1	fig. 51, 51; 204		
AG II 36	figs. 50–51, 28–47; 204	D.4–5; 125	Bronze fig. 28, 41 Iron, fig. 29, 58
AG II 41	fig. 50, 24; 204		Coins: C1st–2nd. illeg., Magnentius, 87
AG II 42	fig. 50, 22–3; 204		
AG II 44			Coin: Claudius I, 87
AG II 48	fig. 50, 21; 204		
AG III 38	figs. 50–51, 28–47; 204		
AG III 39	figs. 50–51, 28–47; 204	125	
AG III 43	fig. 50, 27; 204	D.2–3; 125	Glass, 106
AG III 49	fig. 50, 25–6; 204	S.31; 125	
AH VIII 27	204		Iron fig. 29, 62 Glass fig. 34, 94
AH VIII 28	204		
AH VIII 66			Glass fig. 34, 93
AH VIII 68	fig. 50, 20; 204		
AH VIII 70/74			Coin: Nero, 87 Brooch 91, no. 7 Stone 105, no. 79
AH VIII 75	fig. 50, 6–7; 204	124	
AH VIII 76	204		
AH VIII 78	fig. 50, 17–19; 204	D.1; 124	Stone 105, no. 78
AH VIII 83	fig. 50, 12; 204		
AH VIII 86	204		
AH VIII 91	fig. 50, 8; 204		
AH VIII 93	fig. 50, 5; 204		
AH VIII 96	fig. 50, 13–16; 204	S.49; 124	Coin: Claudius I, 87 Bone fig. 30, 73 Stone 105, no. 80
AH VIII 100	fig. 50, 11; 204		

Context	Coarse Wares	Samian	Objects
AH VIII 103	204	124	
AH VIII 111			Bronze fig. 26, 28; pls. 24, 25; 97, no. 56
AH VIII 116	fig. 50, 2-4; 204	124	
AH VIII P.H.3	204		Brooch fig. 24, 6
AH VIII P.H.4	fig. 50, 9; 204		
AH VIII P.H.7	fig. 50, 10; 204		Graffito fig. 66, 1
AH VIII Pit 1	204		
AK II 22	figs. 60-61, 365-87; 206		
AK II 26	figs. 60-61, 365-87		
AK IV 38	figs. 60-61, 365-87	143	
AK IV 39	figs. 60-61, 365-87; 206		
AK IV 40	figs. 60-61; 365-87; 206		
AK IV 41	figs. 60-61, 365-87; 206		
AL II 39	fig. 60, 335-64; 206	142-3	
AL II 41	fig. 60, 335-64; 206		Glass fig. 34, 93
AL II 42			Brooch fig. 24, 3
AL II 43			Coin: Augustus, 87
AL II 44	fig. 60, 335-64; 206		
AL II 45	fig. 60, 335-64; 206	S.4; D.59; 143	
AL VII 31	fig. 60, 335-64; 206	S.21; D.60; 143	Glass 106
AM I 61	fig. 57, 257-63; 206		
AM I 63	fig. 50, 1		Bronze fig. 26, 22
AM II 58	figs. 57-59, 266-329		
AM II 59	A.1, 149; figs. 57-59, 266-329; 206	S. 1-3, 6, 9, 10-11, 15, 16, 20, 22, 23, 24, 27, 28, 29, 33, 35, 36-37, 42, 44, 45, 47, 48, 52, 53; D. 38-58; 133-142	Coin: H. of Cons., 87 Bronze fig. 26, 19 Glass 107, no. 94; 106
AM II 65			Brooch fig. 25, 15
AM II 66	206		
AM II 67	fig. 57, 264-5; 206		
AM III 35		142	
AM III 43	206		
AM III 44	A.3, p. 149; figs. 59-60, 330-3; 206	142	Coins: Claudius I (x2), 87 Iron fig. 29, 61
AM III 45	fig. 60, 334; 206		
AM IV 41		S.21; 142	
AM IV 44	206	142	
BC I 45	206		
BC I 47			Plant macroremains; insect remains
BC I 48	206		
BC I 52	206		
BC II 34	206	142	
BC II 37	206		
AW I 71	fig. 63, 407-8; 206	D.62; 143	
AW I 72	fig. 63, 403-6; 206	143	
AW I 76		S.5	
AW I 77	fig. 63, 402; 206	D.61	
AW I 79	fig. 63, 409-11; 206	D.63; 144	Brooch fig. 25, 9
AW II 35	fig. 64, 449-52; 208		Iron fig. 29, 57
AX II 36	figs. 63-64, 442-8; 208	144	
AX II 38	figs. 63-64, 442-8; 208	144	
AX II 39		144	
AX II 41	fig. 63, 434-41; 206	S.41; 144	
AX II 42	fig. 63, 425; 206	S.50; 144	

Context	Coarse Wares	Samian	Objects
AX II 43	fig. 63, 415-24; 206	144	Brooch fig. 24, 2 Bronze fig. 28, 53
AX II 44	fig. 63, 427-9; 206	D.64	
AX II 45	fig. 63, 430-3; 206		Iron fig. 29, 68
AX II 47	fig. 63, 426; 206		
AX II 58	fig. 63, 412-4; 206		Plant macroremains
AY I 18	fig. 65, 486-8; 208		Iron 101
AY I 25 & 26	fig. 489-98; 208		Bronze fig. 28, 50 Iron 101 Glass 106, no. 93 Plant macroremains Animal bone
AY V 41			Bronze 97, no. 49
AY V 50	fig. 65, 499-500		
BZ I 12	fig. 64, 453-61; 208	D.65-7; 144	Clay fig. 31, 76
BZ I 15	C.1; 150	D.69-71; 145	Bone fig. 30, 71 Lead fig. 33, 82, 83 Glass 106
BZ I 18	figs. 64-65, 476-83; 208	D.68; 144-5	Bronze fig. 27, 37 Lead fig. 33, 81
BZ I 20	fig 64, 475; 208		
CG III 7		146	
CG III 11		S.26; 146	
CG III 12	fig. 64, 462-9; 208	144	
CG III 14		S.25; 146	
CG III 17	fig. 64, 462-9; 208	144	
CG IV 14	fig. 65, 484-5		
CG IV 16	A.2 & 4; 149	S.55; 145-6	
CG IV 17		145	
CG IV 18		145	
CG IV 19		145	
CG IV 21	fig. 64, 470-4; 208	144	
DA III 166	206	143	
DA III 168	206	143	
DA IV 506	206	143	
DA IV 510	206	143	
DK I 81	figs. 54-57, 156-256	S.30, 32, 43, 46, 54; D.19-27; 128-131	Coins: Claudius I, C1st-2nd, 87 Brooches fig. 25, 12, 14; 92, nos. 16, 18 Bronze fig. 26, 21, 24; fig. 27, 36; fig. 28, 39, 47, 49, 52; 97, no. 49 Iron fig. 29, 64, 66, 67 Bone fig. 30, 72 Stone fig. 32, 77 Glass fig. 34, 92; 106 Animal bone
DK I 90	206	127	Coin: Claudius I, 87 Bronze 97, no. 49 Glass 106 Animal bone Slag
DK I 91	206		Clay fig. 31, 75
DK I 92	206		Animal bone
DK I 94	206		Coin: Claudius I, 87 Brooch fig. 25, 17 Bronze fig. 28, 45 Iron 101 Animal bone
DK I 96			Coin: Claudius I, 87 Animal bone
DK I 97	206	D.12	Animal bone
DK I 99			Animal bone

Context	Coarse Wares	Samian	Objects
DK I 102	fig. 53, 111; 206	D.11; 127	Animal bone
DK I 103	fig. 53, 112; 206	S.38; 127	Animal bone
DK I 104	206		Animal bone
DK I 105	fig. 52, 95; 204	126	Animal bone
DK I 106	M.1, 147; fig. 53, 110; 206	126	Animal bone
DK I 107	fig. 53, 104-9	126	Glass fig. 34, 91 Animal bone
DK I 108	204		Animal bone
DK I 109	fig. 52, 96-103; 204	126	Bronze fig. 27, 29 Animal bone
DK I 110	fig. 53, 115-9; 206	127	Iron 101, no. 69 Graffito fig. 66, 2 Animal bone
DK I 111	204		
DK I 112	206	127	Bronze 97, no. 49 Animal bone
DK I 113	fig. 53, 115-9		Animal bone
DK I 114	fig. 53, 104-9	S.39; 126	Animal bone
DK I 115	fig. 53, 104-9; 204	126	Animal bone
DK I 116	fig. 52, 86-94; 204	S.7; 126	Animal bone
DK I 117	206	127	Animal bone
DK I 119	fig. 51, 58-67; 204	126	Animal bone
DK II 39	figs. 54-57, 156-256	S.51; D.28; 131	Coin: Claudius I, 87 Bronze fig. 27, 38; fig. 28, 55; 97, no. 49 Glass 106 Animal bone Slag
DK II 40	figs. 54-57, 156-256	S.17; D.30; 131	Coins: Claudius I, ?Neronian copy, 87 Bronze fig. 28, 46, 54; 97, no. 49 Glass fig. 34, 87; p. 106; 106, no. 93 Animal bone Slag
DK II 41	figs. 54-57, 156-256	131	Iron fig. 29, 59, 60, 63; 101 Slag
DK II 42	fig. 53, 124-133; 206	S.19, S.56; D.14; 127-8	Brooch 91, no. 5 Bronze fig. 27, 31, 32, 35; fig. 28, 51; 97, no. 49 Iron 99, no. 63 Bone fig. 30, 70 Glass fig. 34, 84; 107, no. 94 Slag
DK II 43	G.2, 150; fig. 53, 114; 206	127	Animal bone
DK II 44	fig. 53, 113; 206	127	Animal bone
DK II 45	fig. 52, 86-94; 204	126	Animal bone
DK II 46	206	D.10; 126-7	Animal bone
DK II 47	204	126	Animal bone
DK II 48	fig. 51, 58-67; 204	126	Animal bone
DK II 94		127	
DM I 19	G.1 & 2; 150; figs. 54-57, 156-256	S.8, 34, 40; D.31-4; 132	Coins: Claudius I (x3), Domitian, Hadrian, 87 Brooch fig. 24, 1 Bronze fig. 26, 20, 25, 27; fig. 27, 33, 34; fig. 28, 40, 43; 93, 97, nos. 36, 42, 49 Iron fig. 29, 66; 101 Shale fig. 30, 74 Clay fig. 31, 75 Glass, fig. 34, 86; 106; 106, nos. 92, 93 Animal bone
DM I 62	figs. 54-57, 156-256	132	
DM I 65	figs. 54-57, 156-256	D.35-6; 132	Animal bone
DM I 120	figs. 54-57, 156-256	132	Iron 101
DM I 130	figs. 54-57, 156-256	D.37; 132	Brooch fig. 25, 13 Glass 106; 107, no. 94

Context	Coarse Wares	Samian	Objects
DM I 131	figs. 54–57, 156–256	132	
DM I 132	204	126	
DM I 133	204	125	Brooch fig. 24, 4 Animal bone
DM I 134	fig. 53, 120–3; 206	127	Coin: Agrippa (Tiberius), 87 Iron fig. 29, 69
DM I 135	figs. 54–57, 156–256	132–3	Coin: Agrippa (Tiberius), 87
DM I 136	M.2, 148; A.5, 149; fig. 53, 120–3; 206	D.13; 127	Bronze fig. 26, 23 Glass 106, no. 93
DM I 137	fig. 54, 140–55; 206	S.14 & 18; D.15–18; 128	Coin: Vespasian, 87 Bronze fig. 26, 26; fig. 27, 30; fig. 28, 44; 97, no 49 Iron 99, no. 68 Glass fig. 34, 85, 88, 89, 90; 106, no. 92 Animal bone
DM I 143	204	126	
DM I 144	fig. 51, 55–7; 204	125–6	
DM I 145	fig. 52, 84–5; 204	S.13; 126	
DM I 150	fig. 54, 137–9; 206		Coin: Claudius I, 87 Bronze fig. 28, 48 Iron 101 Animal bone
DM I 152	figs. 51–52, 68–83; 204	126	
DM I 153			Iron 101
DM I 154	figs. 51–52, 68–83; 204	126	
DM I 158	figs. 53–54, 134–6; 206	128	Bronze fig. 28, 42 Animal bone
Police Station Watching Brief			Coins: Agrippa (Tiberius), Vespasian, C1st–2nd, 87 Brooches fig. 24, 8; fig. 25, 10, 11

AN IRON AGE COIN
by
Prof. S.S. Frere

During excavation of site AH, a bronze coin of Rues (Mack 191) was discovered, unfortunately unstratified, but below the final phase of occupation dated to the fourth century. Coins with the legend RVIIS have some form of association both in style and distribution with the coinage of Tasciovanus issued by the Verulamium mint; one of these coins (Mack 190) may even carry the mint-mark VIR, though this is not certain. It is usually assumed that the word Rues, like Sega-, Dias- and Andoco-, are abbreviated personal names, but they could possibly be mint-names. The coinage of Rues has been discussed by D.F. Allen in his report on the finds from the Harlow Temple (Allen, D.F., 1967, 4) and by Warwick Rodwell who gives a distribution map (Rodwell, 1976, fig. 27). Unlike coins with names Dias, Sego and Andoco, those of Rues do not link his name with that of Tasciovanus, and it is therefore not possible to be sure that his status was similar to that of these others, who appear to be either sons or associates of Tasciovanus. It can be deduced that at the end of his reign Tasciovanus shared his power, whether voluntarily or not, with co-rulers. It is even possible that Rues was his short-lived successor, ruling in Hertfordshire until displaced by Cunobelin. The coins of Rues have a distribution in Catuvellaunian territory centred on Verulamium. The Cirencester example is an outlier, and like other native coins from sites with similar Roman military contexts (e.g. at Wroxeter or Longthorpe) may have arrived there in the purse of a Roman soldier.

THE ROMAN COINS
by
R. Reece

This coin list obviously has an important bearing on the early history of Corinium, but its interpretation poses many problems. It is only fair to future workers to point out the dividing line between fact and supposition and to underline the present short-comings of coin evidence and coin specialists.

The period between the conquest of A.D. 43 and the reign of Domitian is not well served by coins. Gold coins of the period were well struck in reasonable numbers and are usually well dated; they are virtually never found. Silver of Claudius is extremely rare and denarii of Nero struck before 64 are almost equally scarce. From 43 to 64 the only silver coinage in circulation comprised pre-conquest denarii of the Republic, Augustus and Tiberius which can give no more accurate date than "after A.D. 43". After 64 Nero struck more silver, and Flavian denarii are common. The picture in bronze coinage is similar to that in silver except that the conquest troops were supplied with current Claudian asses but very few earlier issues. The one exception is that of the Agrippa memorial coins, and the evidence of British site-finds strongly suggests that these were being struck very shortly before the conquest. Soon after the conquest the supply of newly minted Claudian bronze seems to have ceased, and, it is assumed, local production of copies which ranged from excellent to poor began in response to the shortage. This copying continued through the reign of Claudius and into the next reign, for Nero struck virtually no bronze in the first ten years of his reign. "Claudian copies" may therefore give a date anywhere between 44 and 64 and as yet no one has convincingly demonstrated a chronological sequence from good to bad copying or a link of good or bad copies with civilian or military authorities. From 64 to 68 Nero struck a flood of asses and many sestertii and dupondii, and the good supply continued into the Flavian period. This is the numismatic background.

One subject on which a coin list cannot at present give information is the status of the site – whether military or civilian, Roman or native. This must come from the archaeological record, and the coins can do no more than support the other material evidence.

, Finally we have the assistance of other sites. Colchester is a great help here for it is known from historical sources to go back to the year of conquest, and has another firm date in the sack by Boudicca; Hod Hill and Waddon Hill are Claudian forts abandoned before the introduction of the coinage of Nero, while the Lunt and Exeter have definitely military buildings which must belong in part to late in the reign of Nero. There is therefore a military sequence against which to fit Corinium ranging from the conquest to the Flavian period.

After such preamble the coins from Corinium, at least from the levels described in this volume, must come as a severe disappointment. Only 32 and two halves of coins belong to the military phase. Five coins are presumably intrusive because they date after A.D. 117, four are Flavian, one and two halves are early but illegible, two are Neronian asses, sixteen are Claudian asses of which fourteen are copies, and the total is made up by three Agrippa asses and one late Augustan denarius.

Firstly, by comparison with other sites, the number of coins on which to speculate is small. Then we may note the absence of sestertii and small change, and the virtual absence of silver – it is a very standard series of asses. Finally, the weight of the group falls firmly in the large bracket 44 to 64, with its Claudian copies and only two regular coins.

If these coins result from a military presence on the sites excavated, and the deciding facts here must be the structural results of excavation, that presence seems never to have been large, is probably not as early as Colchester or Hod Hill, and seems to have moved on before the main period of occupation at Exeter or the Lunt. Within the period 44 to 64 the sixteen Claudian asses *cannot* give any more precise information for the reasons outlined above. The coins would fit equally well with a fort occupied for six months in the late forties, or for six months at the time of the Boudiccan rebellion; they could equally result from a small "watchdog" presence over the whole period. Decisions between such alternatives are not the province of numismatists.

Emperer	Reference	Site Reference
Augustus	RIC 350	AL II 43
Agrippa (Tiberius)	RIC (Tib) 32, A.D. 14-54	DM I 134
	RIC (Tib) 32, A.D. 14-54	DM I 135
	RIC (Tib) 32	Police Station 1964
Claudius I	copy as RIC 66	AE II 10
	„ „ „ „	AE V 19
	„ „ „ „	AG II 44
	„ „ „ „	AH VIII 96
	„ „ „ „	AM III 44
	copy as RIC (Claud) 82	AM III 44
	copy as RIC 66, A.D. 41-54	DK I 81
	„ „ „	DK I 90
	RIC 67, A.D. 41-54	DK I 94
	? copy as RIC 66, A.D. 43-64	DK I 96
	RIC 66, A.D. 41-54	DK II 39
	copy as RIC 66, A.D. 43-64	DK II 40
	„ „ „ A.D. 43-64	DM I 19
	? copy as RIC 66, A.D. 43-64	DM I 19
	copy as RIC 66, A.D. 43-64	DM I 19
	„ „ „ A.D. 43-64	DM I 150
Nero	RIC 286	AH VIII 70
? Neronian copy	? A.D. 60-63	DK II 40
Vespasian	Cos. 4	AE I 10
	RIC 740, A.D. 69-79	DM I 137
	Sestertius, rev. illegible	Police Station 1964
Domitian	A.D. 86	DM I 19
Hadrian	RIC 55 (a)	AE II 10
	RIC 795, A.D. 134-8	DM I 19
Clst–2nd	Illegible	AG II 41
	As, halved, illegible	Police Station 1964
Clst–2nd	Sestertius, halved	DK I 81
Radiate	Intrusive, A.D. 270-90	AE V 20
H. of Constantine	A.D. 320 + (intrusive)	AM II 59
Magnentius	copy as CK 8, A.D. 351-64	AG II 41

THE BROOCHES
by
D.F. Mackreth

Although the collections of brooches from Hod Hill and Waddon Hill would seem to be the best with which to compare the present one, there are not enough specimens from Cirencester to make such an exercise useful. The date range of the whole collection, or of the brooches from individual sites, is not narrow enough for any determination of priority of occupation or abandonment to be arrived at; indeed, the small number found stratified beneath sealing layers would have cast grave doubts upon any statements of this kind.

Colchester

1. DM I 19. The pin and half of the six-coil spring is missing. The wings are short and plain. The bow is flat with a slight swell on the front witha buried bead-row. The catch-plate is damaged, but retains part of a rectangular piercing.

The flat sectioned bow is more typical of continental Colchesters than British ones (Ritterling, 1913, Taf.VIII, 81 and 86; Thill, 1969, 32, abb.3, 31-36; van Buchem, 1941, pl.V.2 and 3) and in this country its earliest appearance, perhaps, is in the cemetary at Swarling (Bushe-Fox, 1925, 40, pl.XII, 2; Sieveking, Longworth and Wilson (eds.), 1976, 410, fig. 4.4). Other examples, however, with bead-rows as in the present specimen come from Colchester (Hawkes and Hull, 1947, 310, pl.XCI.35) and Chichester (Hildyard, 1955, 109-112, frontispiece). The first comes from period IV-VI, A.D. 49- *c.* 65, the second has no context. The type is rare in Britain and it is tempting to consider it as being at the end of its life at the moment of Conquest, and specimens like the ones at Chichester and Cirencester as being survivals in use.

Colchester Derivatives

2. AX II 43. The spring is held to the body of the brooch by means of an axis bar which passes through the coils and through the lower hole in a plate which projects from the back of the bow. The chord passes through the upper hole. The wings are curved in section and each has a groove at the end. The bow is humped over the wings, is plain and tapers to a pointed foot. The return of the catch-plate is missing and the catch-plate is filed down behind, but it is not clear if this was part of the original making of the brooch: there is here no trace of the tinned finish which survives in patches on the brooch.

Being plain, there is little to help locate this brooch in any particular group. Very few have come from satisfactorily dated contexts (cf. Wheeler and Wheeler, 1936, 207, fig. 44.26, dated to *c.* A.D. 75-125/150). The method of fixing the spring by means of a piercing with two holes is dated to the first years after the Conquest, but may have evolved at an earlier date: the only Colchester Derivative from the early deposits at Skeleton Green, Puckeridge, Herts., (to be published) has this spring fixing arrangement and another of exactly similar type from Holbrooks, Old Harlow, Herts., (unpublished) has the Colchester's hook and spring arrangement (for decorative type: Wheeler and Wheeler, 1936, 207, fig. 44.22, dated there to the period up to A.D. 50). Another from Verulamium of the same type as the one from Puckeridge has a single rearhook which is recognizable as being a failure in the typological development from the one piece brooch, like the Colchester, and the types which fasten the separate spring to the body by both coils and chord, as in the Cirencester brooch or as in the Polden Hill method (cf. Cunliffe (ed.), 1968, 80, pl.XXVIII.27). On the present specimen the top of the projecting plate behind the head is carefully finished to look like a hook of the Colchester type; this and the absence of a foot-knob may be indicators of an early date, but there is no good evidence other than its context.

3. AL II 42. A complete brooch in which the spring is held as in the last. Each wing is moulded with two wide ridges between narrow ones. From the wings rises a small arched moulded plate which masks the junction of the bow with the wings. The bow is moulded like the wings, only more prominently and with a triangle at the head.

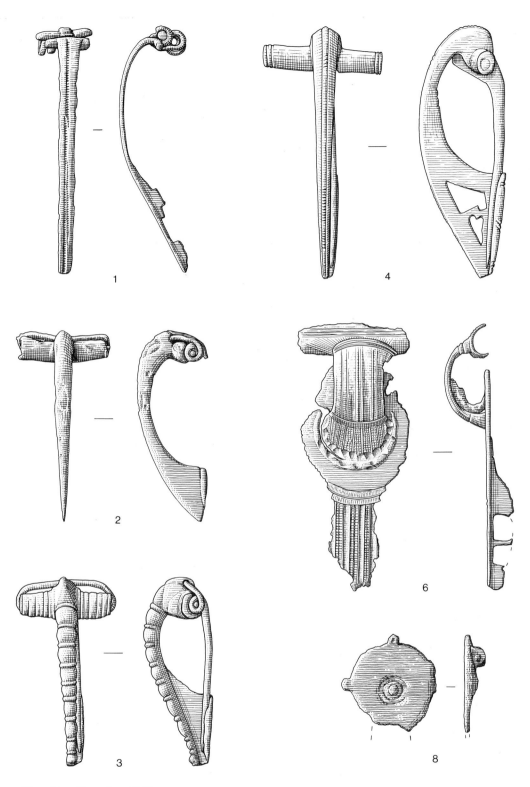

Fig. 24.   Brooches (1:1)

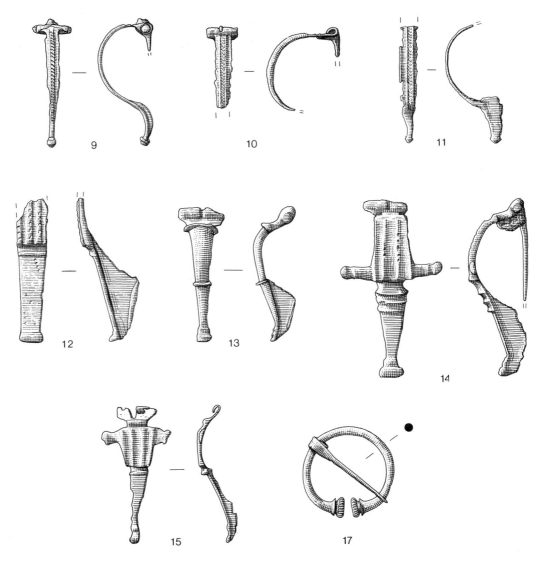

Fig. 25.   Brooches (1:1)

Decoration of this type is very rare and there is no specimen known to the writer which is useful at arriving at a date range for the present example. The comments concerning the spring fixing arrangement under the last brooch are applicable here, but there are no real indicators of a date.

4.   DM I 133.   A complete brooch whose pin is hinged and axis bar is housed in the circular sectioned wings, each of which has a buried ridge at the end. The bow is humped over the wings, has an arris down the centre and down this to the pointed foot run two grooves with a series of cross-cuts between. The catch-plate has two piercings separated by a bar with a dog-leg. The beginning of the catch-plate's return is marked by two grooves and the return itself has two more to top and bottom with another pair set diagonally half-way between.

The hinged pin is present at a very early date after the Conquest on Colchester Derivatives (e.g. Brailsford, 1962, 7; fig. 6, C11-12, C14-15; fig. 7, C.16; fig. 10, C95-96. For date: Richmond, 1968, 117-119), although there is no good evidence to show that its use dates from before that event. Here, the basically simple form and decoration, especially the fretted catch-plate, may suggest a date in the first two decades after the Conquest (cf. Brailsford, 1962, 7, fig. 6, C15).

5.   DK II 42.   Not illustrated. Clearly a brooch, as the lower part of the bow shows, the upper parts are too corroded for the original design to be clear. However, the type was almost certainly a Colchester Derivative whose hinged pin's axis bar was housed as in the last. The

remains of the lower bow show a rectangular section with a ridge on each side in the front, and the stump of the catch-plate behind.

The state of this brooch does not allow any proper comment to be made on its possible date range.

Rosettes

6. AH VIII P.H.3. A corroded brooch heavily stripped during conservation. The spring, now missing, was held in a spring case decorated along the front with grooves forming a panel about the head of the bow from which fine incised lines radiate to fill the panel. The short upper bow is decorated with a series of bead-rows and flutes, set off to top and bottom from the rest of the brooch by grooves and cross-mouldings. Behind this part of the bow are clear signs of a bolt having been present (cf. Hawkes and Hull, 1947, 315, pl. XCIII, 70 and 71). The lower end of the bow proper joins the upper part of a disc which has a series of square punch-marks filling the rest of the area. Around the central disc there is an irregular groove and beyond this a plain surface to the surviving edge which, as can be seen across the top of the foot, was once bordered by two zones of coarse beading. The plain zone was once covered by a repoussé plate probably once cut and decorated (cf. example given above). The foot was once of fantail form as the setting out marks on the back show. The front is ornamented with a repeat of the design on the upper bow. The catch-plate has the remains of two rectangular piercings.

This is a fully developed Rosette replete with virtually all the decorative traits to be found on the type. The Rosette, along with the Langton Down, is characteristic of continental assemblages from Augustan times to the middle of the first century A.D. It has hitherto been difficult to be sure whether or not either of these brooch types was being imported into Britain before the Conquest: Colchester and Bagendon were once the only sites which could be referred to for such information. At Colchester there was next to no material which could be isolated as belonging to period I, although there is a healthy suspicion that a fair proportion of the finds in later periods was residual. The earliest deposits at Bagendon were devoid of brooches and the date of the main deposits has been questioned (Swan, 1975, 59-61). However, the position is alleviated by the occurrence at Skeleton Green, Puckeridge, Herts., of stratified deposits which belong to the earlier part of the first century A.D., and, more importantly in this case, of the presence of a large number of Rosettes in the grave assemblages recovered from the cemetery at King Harry Lane, St. Albans, Herts. (I am grateful to Dr. I.M. Stead for the information in advance of publication), where there are nearly 50 Rosettes out of a total number of over 200 brooches. Thus, on looking at the relatively small numbers of the type which belong to purely Roman contexts, it is possible to suggest that those found are at the end of the type's *floruit* and may be survivals in use only. It is very unlikely that any significant quantities survived as late as A.D. 60, and few of these will belong to the elaborate type to which the present example belongs.

7. AH VIII 74. Not illustrated. Mr. Hull comments: "flat or plate brooch, complete. It is an addition to Hawkes & Hull, 1947, pl.XCVIII, 163 and 164, and Ritterling, 1913, Taf.X.258-260. I have no exact parallels to it. Doubtless mid-first century." For discussion, see after the next brooch.

8. 1964, Police Station Watching Brief. At first sight a circular plate brooch with two axial projections and the remains of a third, but inspection shows that, in place of another such opposite the lugs for the hinged pin, there is evidence for a large projection which was probably in the form of a fantail, (Cotton, 1947, 144, fig. 7, 6). The front of the brooch has traces of tinning and in the centre is the stump of a boss riveted through the bow, surrounded by relieved concentric mouldings.

Nos. 7 and 8 are in effect plate brooches merely shaped to a Rosette silhouette. These should be late in the sequence but the same terminal date should apply to these as that applied to no. 6. Both no. 7 and no. 8 probably had enamelled bosses mounted in the centre of the disc.

Aucissae

9-11. AW I 79, (no. 9); and two more from 1964, Police Station Watching Brief, (nos. 10, 11).   Three precisely similar brooches. All three have bows edged with ridges with swelled fronts, each with a sunken bead-row. Two have surviving foot-knobs sweated on, and two have heads made up of two bead-rows on either side of a flute with a cut-out at each end. In contrast with the Rosette, the Aucissa is not well represented in pre-Conquest collections and the brooch seems to come in with the army of Conquest. It should be pointed out that the writer reserves the name 'Aucissa' for brooches of this form with this particular bow section: there is good evidence that some variants of the general design were being imported before the Conquest. The descendants of the Aucissa arrived in greater numbers: the Hod Hill. It is clear that by A.D. 43 the Aucissa was at the end of its *floruit* and all the specimens coming in with the army and its followers may well be survivors in use. It is unlikely that the Aucissa lasts much beyond the middle 50's of the first century A.D. The three specimens under review here are all unusually small.

Hod Hills

12. DK I 81.   The head is missing. The upper bow has two strong ridges, each with cross-cuts, with a minor ridge on each side. The lower bow is flat with a slight taper and a cross-moulding at top and bottom. The front face has traces of a punched dot design and the whole was once tinned. For discussion, see after no. 16.

13. DM I 130.   A small brooch with a tapering, round-fronted bow which has a cross-moulding at the top, half way down and the usual two-part foot-knob at the bottom. There are traces of tinning. For discussion, see after, no. 16.

14. DK I 81.   The main panel on the bow has three vertical flutes with one cross-moulding above and three more below. On either side of the main panel at the bottom is a wing made up of a knob with a cross-moulding and a flute. The lower bow is flat and tapers to the usual two-part foot-knob. For discussion, see after no. 16.

15. AM II 65.   Very like the last except there is only one cross-moulding below the main panel; the wings are now at the top and each has only a waist and a knob. For discussion, see after the next brooch.

16. DK I 81.   Not illustrated. A heavily corroded brooch on which the details are not fully discernible.

Four of these brooches are developed examples of the type and each differs from the others, the fifth is not preserved well enough to discuss. There is no chronological significance in the differences and the same general date is applicable to each. The type is hardly evidenced before the Conquest and, like the Aucissa, seems to have come in with the army and its followers. Indeed, the contrast in number between the Aucissa and the Hod Hill may suggest that it is more likely to be typical of the early post-Conquest years than any other imported brooch. Like the Rosette and the Aucissa, the Hod Hill is not to be expected beyond *c.* A.D. 60, except that the sheer numbers present in Britain make it inevitable that more would have survived in use beyond that date. However, it is significant that Hod Hills found north of the Humber are rare and the type largely passed out of use by A.D. 70.

Penannular

17. DK I 94.   The ring has a circular section and each terminal is made up of a flat knob with knurling separated from the ring by a thin angular moulding.

This belongs to Fowler's type A4 (Fowler, 1960, 149-177) and is given by her a date range of first to third century. There are not enough specimens to be sure of the main *floruit*, but the presence of a similar one at Waddon Hill (forthcoming), is a sufficient guarantee that it is to be found in the first two decades after the Conquest.

Fragment

18. DK I 81.   Not illustrated. One coil of a spring most probably from a brooch, but the type is not identifiable.

OBJECTS OF COPPER ALLOY
by
Linda Viner

19.   Ligula with probe and cupped oval scoop, decoration on shank consisting of two bands of knotches, one below a band of concentric mouldings.   AM II 59.

20.   Ligula with probe and remains of scoop. Shank decorated with banded mouldings above the scoop. Found twisted but for reasons of clarity illustrated as straight.   DM I 19.

21.   Probe with high patination, knotched shank, and mouldings accentuated with two bands of silver inlay.   DK I 81.

22.   Nail cleaner, circular in section with shank decorated with incised lattice similar to fig. 31, 71.   AM I 63.

23.   Nail cleaner, pierced for suspension, one flat surface only decorated with incised lattice worked prior to forming the hole.   DM I 136.

24.   Ear-scoop, pierced for suspension, impressed dotted flower motif below the hole. DK I 81.

25.   Tweezers.   DM I 19.

26.   Manicure set of three instruments fastened together with a strand of bronze wire. The tweezers alone are recognisable, the other two tools were presumably a nail cleaner and an ear-scoop.   DM I 137.

27.   Length of copper alloy chain, each link formed of a piece of square-sectioned wire formed into a double loop. Two sections of 80 mm. and 100 mm. length are joined by a single loop of thicker wire.   DM I 19.

28.   Seal box lid, with a decorative stud in the form of an eagle held in place by a single copper alloy rivet. The mouldings around the rim, and the feather's of the eagle appear to have once been accentuated with silver inlay of which little now remains.   AH VIII 111.

29.   A duck with green and red enamel inlays in the wings attached to a rectangular grill with open work decoration in the form of a pair of debased Celtic broken back curves. There are four attached tangs at each corner for fastening to a wooden lid, for which the object is the handle. The bird is very similar to those found on brooches (R.C.H.M., Eburacum, 1962, pl. 34, H.31). Information kindly supplied by Dr. Graham Webster.   DK I 109.

30.   Top section of jug handle.   DM I 137.   (cf. Bushe-Fox, 1932, pl. XIV, 49, where the example was found west of Site I, in a deposit mainly first century in date).

31.   Binding, two parallel but now distorted strips held by two rivets.   DK II 42.

32.   Lock-pin with circular domed head.   DK II 42.

33.   Dome-headed terminal with remains of iron pin shank in lower surface.   DM I 19.

34.   Fragment of a baldric or harness fitting.   DM I 19.   (Cf. Webster G., 1960, fig. 6, 153 from the Walbrook, London).

35.   Hollow cast copper alloy object, circular base rising to rectangular slot. Function unknown.   DK II 42.

36.   Cuirass hook from a *lorica segmentata*.   DK I 81.   (Cf. Ulbert, 1969, Taf. 44, no. 13 etc.). The hook end only of a second example was found in DM I 19. Not illustrated.

37.   Sheet of copper alloy, all edges incomplete with two small holes pierced in the centre of the surviving fragment. Possibly from a military armour plate.   BZ I 18.

38.   Rectangular plate of sheet copper alloy, with two punched square holes. A punched circular hole is flanked by two unpunched ones. Possibly part of a belt fitting.   DK II 39.

39.   Rod of circular section with flattened and expanded decorated knob head, the point is missing.   DK I 81.   (Cf. Cunliffe, 1968, pl. XLII, 167, from Inner earth fort ditch at

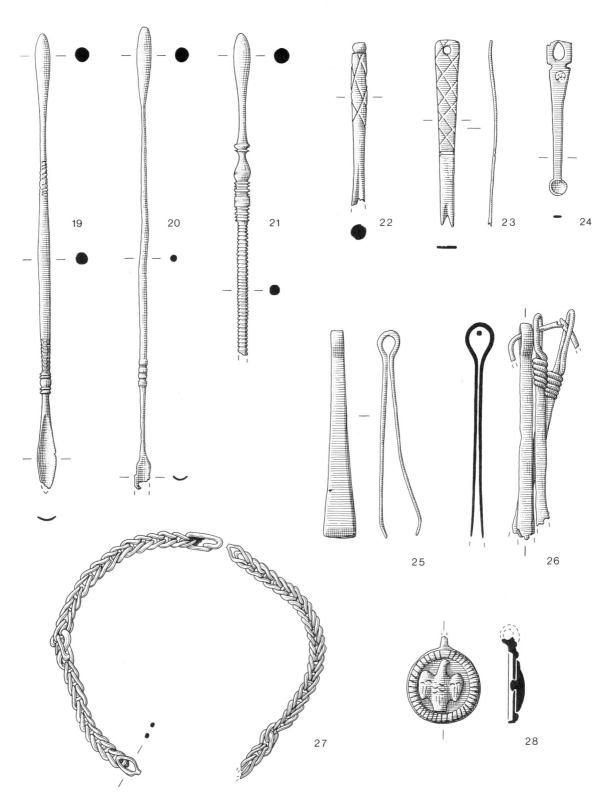

Fig. 26.   Copper alloy objects (1:1)

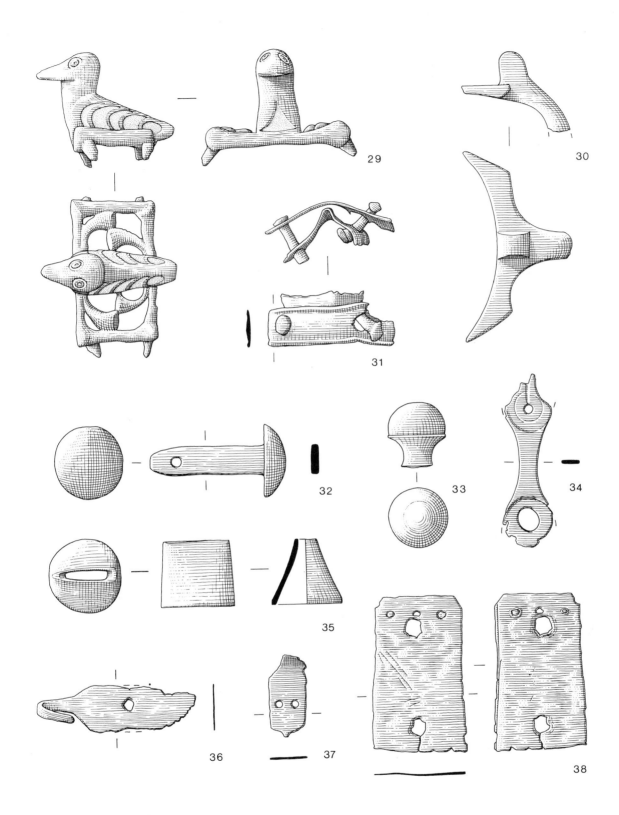

Fig. 27. Copper alloy objects (1:1)

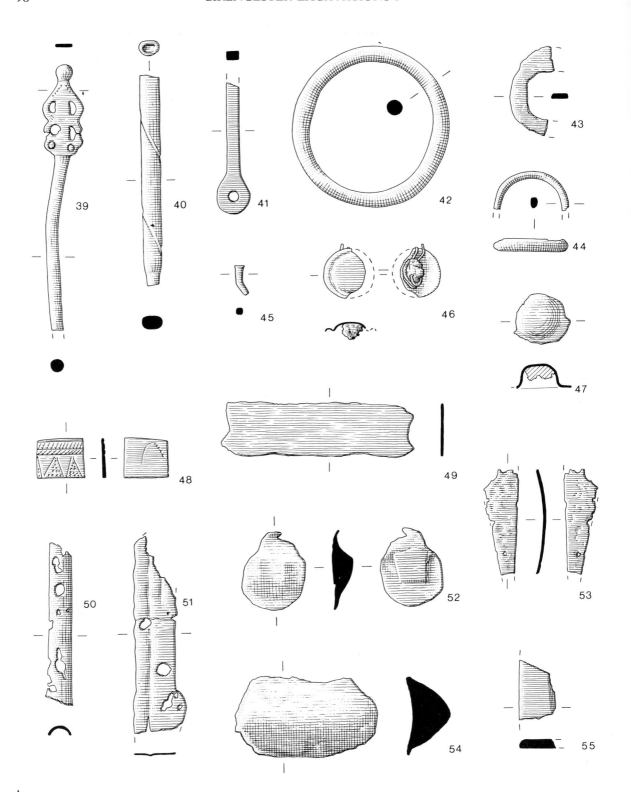

Fig. 28.   Copper alloy objects (1:1)

Richborough, inner side, where it's suggested function is a hairpin). Wheeler (1930, fig. 32, 3) describing an example from Poultry, London, believed it 'somewhat reminiscent of a military standard'. An example from the Walbrook, London (British Museum, 1951, fig. 14, 13) shows spherical pendants attached to two chains which may be indicated on the Cirencester example by the two lower infilled holes.

40. Rod of oval section with scored spiral decoration around the shank. The upper end is hollow, the other constricted to give a circular cross-section. DM I 19.

41. Strip of copper alloy of rectangular section, one end flattened and circular in form with a pierced centre AG II 36.

42. Ring, circular in section with opposing edges unevenly worn thin. DM I 158. A second ring of circular section with a high patination and diameter of 32 mm. was found in DM I 19, not illustrated.

43. Washer, circular flat disc, with a squarish perforation. DM I 19.

44. Finger ring of oval section. DM I 137.

45. Tack with a flat head and square-sectioned shank. DK I 94.

46. Domed stud with a short length of braided chain attached. DK II 40.

47. Stud with domed head, the inner dome filled with lead. DK I 81.

48. Strip of decorated copper alloy sheet, cut down from a vessel. DM I 150.

49. Thin sheet of undecorated copper alloy, function indiscernible. DK I 81. Other similar amorphous fragments were found in AY V 41; DM I 19; DM I 137; DK I 112; DK I 81; DK II 42; DK II 39; DK II 40; DK I 90.

50. Strip of copper alloy of semi–circular section, the surface pitted with corrosion. AY I 26.

51. Strip of copper alloy sheet, both long edges cut in a wavy design; the central circular hole caused by corrosion, the other two sub-rectangular ones punched through the sheet to take small tacks. DK II 42.

52. Working waste soldered together. DK I 81.

53. Triangular sheet heavily pitted with corrosion. AX II 43.

54. Spoon-shaped working waste, heavy in proportion to size, therefore presumably containing some lead. DK II 40.

55. Sheet of cast copper alloy with one finished edge. DK II 39.

56. Shield binding. AH VIII 111 (pl. 24, 25)

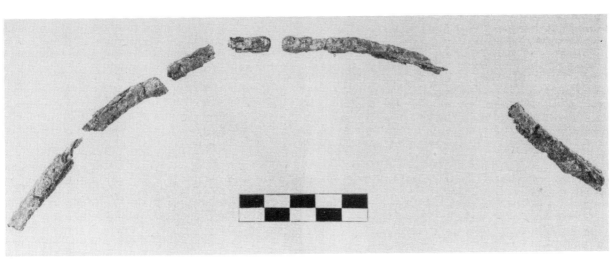

24. Possible copper alloy binding of an auxiliary shield (Copper alloy no. 56).

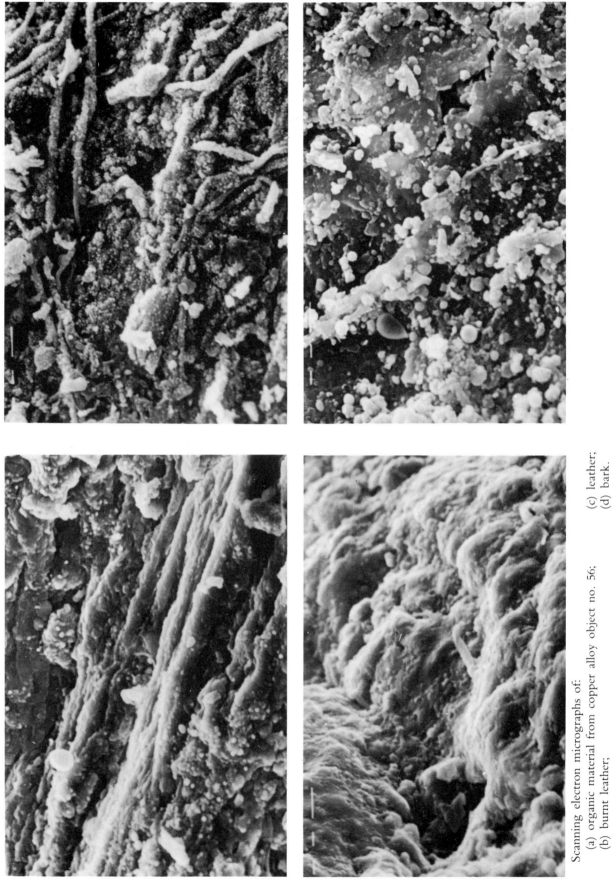

25. Scanning electron micrographs of:
    (a) organic material from copper alloy object no. 56;   (c) leather;
    (b) burnt leather;   (d) bark.
    All x800.

The following note has been contributed by Ann Woods:

The object had been lifted in a block of soil and radiography indicated that it consisted of a fragmentary, slightly curved strip of copper alloy. This was in two main pieces, one *c.* 18.5 cms. in length, the second *c.* 6 cms. in length, and they were separated by a gap of 5 cms. Excavation revealed the presence of thin, copper alloy sheet fragments, nearly all of which were located within the rough arc marked out by the curved pieces. Lying on top of these pieces of sheet, in direct contact with them, were traces of burnt organic matter.

The strip fragments were extensively corroded and very fragile, but visual examination of several fragments indicated that the strip consisted of either a flattened G-section or a flattened, reversed S section. Traces of burnt organic matter were found in the interior of one of the pieces of strip which had split. There were, however, no other signs of contact between the pieces of strip and the pieces of sheet.

In an effort to identify the organic material, some samples were examined with a scanning electron microscope. Samples of leather, burnt leather, and bark were also examined by this method and the results obtained, although not conclusive, indicated that the most similar material was the burnt leather sample (see Plate 25).

It is not impossible that this represents part of a shield-binding. If so, it would have come from an oval, auxiliary, rather than from a rectangular, legionary, shield. (J.S.W.).

OBJECTS OF IRON
by
Linda Viner

57.   Stylus, Type III. Tapering rod flattened to form the eraser, the point at the other end incomplete. AX II 35. Cf. Manning, 1976, 34–36, fig. 10.

58.   Stylus, Type IV. Eraser with decoration below distinctly formed head, the point is missing. AG II 36. Cf. Manning, 1976, 34–36, fig. 10.

59.   Socketed bar, heavily corroded; thickening towards the top may be remains of a blade for a knife or chopper. DK II 41. Cf. Stead, 1976, fig. 118, 174. Wheeler and Wheeler, 1936, 219, pl. lxiv, no. 14.

60.   Set or wedge with a stout rounded stem and battered head. DK II 41. Cf. Manning, 1972, fig. 60, 2–3.

61.   Finger ring with oval bezel, the hoop incomplete. AM III 44.

62.   Tumbler-lock slide key, of simple form, with remains of six teeth at right angles to the bit. The handle was once pierced, but is now filled with corrosion products. AH VIII 27.

63.   Curved strip of rectangular section in two parts, possibly originally a binding for an object. DK II 41. A third strip (not illustrated) 110 mm. in length, of similar section, was found in DK II 42.

64.   Triangular tip of blade. DK I 81.

65.   Remains of socketed tip with tapering, rectangular section. DK I 81.

66.   T-shaped rod, incomplete, with upturned arms. DM I 19.

67.   L-shaped angle bracket, one end originally pierced although the hole is now completely filled by corrosion, and was possibly a hold-fast. DK I 81.

68.   Rectangular-headed pin, probably intended to be driven into woodwork. AX II 45. Cf. Manning, 1972, fig. 69, 97. A ring-headed version, not illustrated, length 105 mm., diameter of head 52 mm., was found in DM I 137.

69.   Chisel with blade tapering into the tang, the top of which is broken. The edge of the blade is formed by even reduction on either side. DM I 134. The head only of one other chisel was

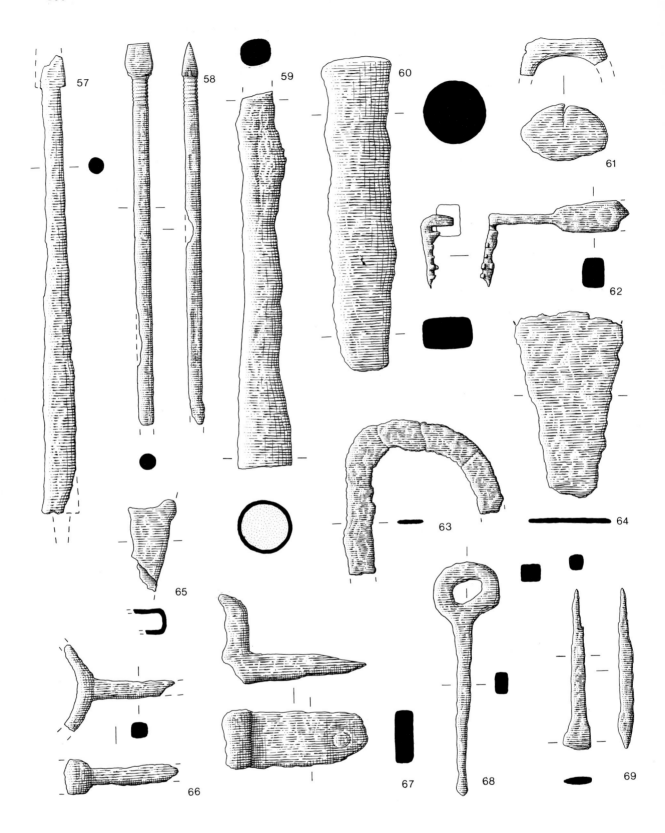

Fig. 29. Iron objects (nos. 57 and 58, 1:1; nos. 59–69, 1:2)

found in DK I 110, length 20 mm, width of blade 15 mm. Not illustrated.

Collection of nails and hobnails, not illustrated: 35 hobnails, dome-headed with average shank length where they survive of 11 mm. Groups of 2, 3, and 4 survive corroded together in lines of former edging to shoes.   DM I 153.

Selection of heads and shanks of nails, round-headed with square-sectioned shanks, lengths 46-50 mm. average.   DM I 150, DK II 41, and AY I 26.

Shapeless and unidentifiable lumps of iron were recovered from AE III 16, DM I 19, DM I 120, DK I 94, and AY I 18.

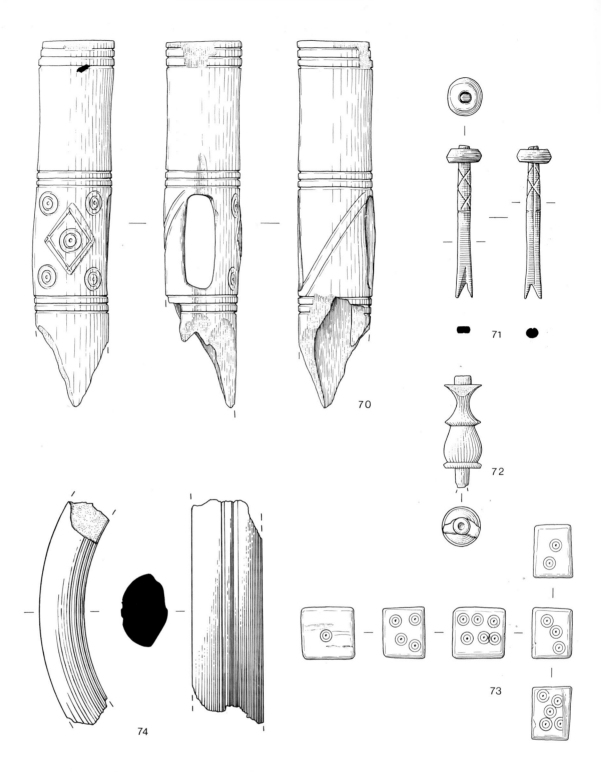

Fig. 30.   Bone and shale objects (1:1)

OBJECTS OF BONE, SHALE, CLAY, STONE AND LEAD
by
Linda Viner

BONE

70.   Cheekpiece, toggle or 'slider', the upper face decorated with incised lines and double-circle-and-dot motifs. The reverse face is marked by a double diagonal. DK II 42. Cf. Fig. 35, 95, Corinium Museum, B 882; fig. 35, 96 in bronze, Corinium Museum, B 302. Macgregor, 1976, 38; 60, no. 4 with parallels and further references.

71.   Nail cleaner, the circular knobbed end of bone held in place by a small bronze stud which has caused heavy green staining on the shank and knob. The shank is decorated with incised diagonal lines similar to fig. 26, 22. BZ I 15.

72.   Lathe-turned and highly polished bone knob. Upper end hollowed, the opposite one broken, presumably detached from the shank of a pin. DK I 81.

73.   Dice, with opposite sides totalling seven. AH VIII 96.

SHALE

74.   Shale bracelet of oval section, the outer circumference decorated with two grooves. Diameter 80 mm. DM I 19.

CLAY

75.   Lamp dish, with pinched spout, in orange clay with grits, the base decorated with two raised concentric circles. The four fragments which survive come from DM I 19 and DK I 91. The spout is blackened with use. Fabric 49, p. 158.

76.   Lamp dish fragment in dark orange gritty ware, with smoothed exterior. Fabric 49, p. 158. Similar to no. 75, with remains on the under surface of a raised circular moulding.   BZ I 12.

STONE

77.   Mortar in oolitic limestone. The rim and interior are smooth-surfaced and well-finished, whilst the outer face below the rim has been left pitted, presumably to ensure a firm grasp of the bowl. DK I 81.

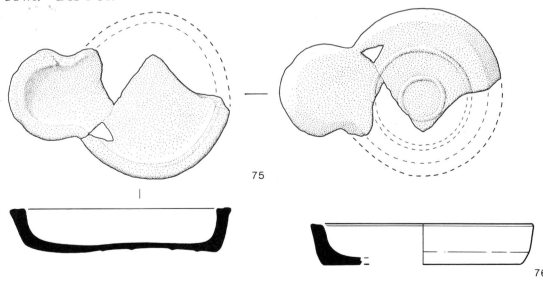

75

76

Fig. 31.   Clay objects (1:2)

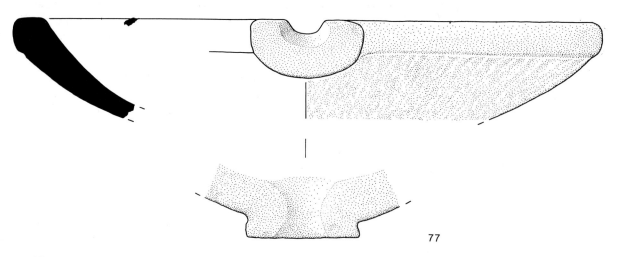

Fig. 32.   Stone mortar (1:2)

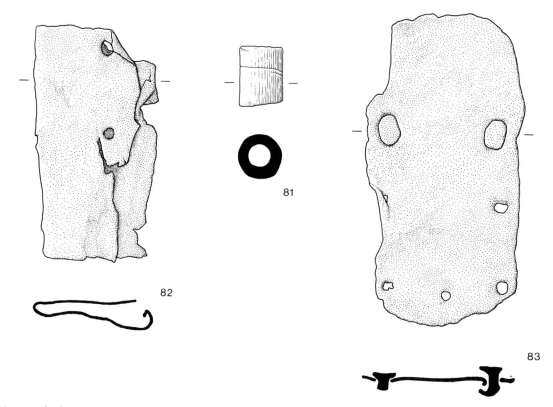

Fig. 33.   Lead objects (1:2)

78. Very fine-grained igneous rock, with crystal lineation parallel to the ground surfaces. Possibly a micro-granite but a thin section is necessary for final proof. The sample is not local to the site and is more likely to be an import, perhaps a glacial erratic. Smooth surfaces are suggestive of its use as a pebble whetstone, discarded after breakage. Fragment 35 mm. long. AH VIII 78. Not illustrated.

79. Fine-grained micaceous siltstone with calcic cement. Possibly of Coal Measures age and a glacial erratic. Fissility is strongly parallel to the bedding. The smooth-surfaced, and rectangular outline, suggests its use as a pebble whetstone, discarded after breakage. Fragment 105 mm. long. AH VIII 74. Not illustrated.

80. Purbeck Marble-Upper Purbeckian, Topmost Jurassic/Lower Cretaceous. Source restricted to the Isle of Purbeck-Swanage area of Dorset. The fragment, *c*. 12 mm. thick, 30 x 35 mm., with two flat and highly polished surfaces, is suggestive of a use as a decorative inlay, wall veneer, or opus sectile?, although the outline is now indiscernible. AH VIII 96. Not illustrated.

Petrological analysis of samples, nos. 78-80, kindly provided by Dr. R.J. King, of the Department of Geology, University of Leicester.

LEAD

81. Cylinder of lead with a lightly incised spiral around the middle. BZ I 18.

82. Rectangular sheet of lead, pierced in six places, folded in antiquity. BZ I 15.

83. Rectangular sheet of lead, similar to no. 82, seven holes pierced around three edges, with two flat-headed lead rivets remaining in two. BZ I 15.

THE GLASS
by
Dorothy Charlesworth

Glass Vessels

The fragments from the military levels represent something like 70 vessels only and there is no window glass. The bulk of the material is unidentifiable fragments of natural green glass used for a variety of bottles, flasks, jars, beakers and bowls in the second half of the first century.

Six fragments of blue glass are featureless (AE II P.H.1; DK I 81, 2 frags.; DK II 40; DM I 130; DM I 137); one is a folded, hollow tubular rim from a small jar or beaker (DM I 19). Five fragments of amber-coloured glass were found – one featureless (AM II 59); one ribbed (DM I 137) possibly from a deep bowl or flagon with a globular body; two with hollow-tubular rims from bowls (DK II 42, fig. 34, 84; DM I 137, fig. 34, 85); and a piece of pillar-moulded bowl (DM I 19, fig. 34, 86). Both colours were popular in the period *c.* 50-100 but less frequently found towards the end of that period when colourless glass generally replaced the coloured metals for the better quality vessels. Only three fragments of colourless glass were found (DK I 90; DM I 137, 2 frags.).

There is a fragment of amber glass with a marvered white trail (DK II 40, fig. 34, 87) possibly from a small ribbed bowl. Isings form 17. (Pfeffer, and Haevernick, 1958, 76-88; Haevernick, 1967, 153-166).

The remaining vessels are all in natural green glass. Few are identified – only two fragments of pillar-moulded bowl (AL VII 31; DM I 137, fig. 34, 88) normally quite a common find on sites of this period; four pieces which can be identified as square bottles (BZ I 15; DK II 39; DM I 19), with one (AG III 43) retaining part of the moulded base markings; and another is certainly from a cylindrical bottle (DM I 137).

Two fragments of a base (DM I 137, fig. 34, 89; and DM I 137) of either a globular-bodied flagon or a deep, globular-bodied bowl, both types are dated *c.* 70-150. A small fragment of a flat, single-ribbed handle is probably from a flagon (DM I 137), and the ribbed convex fragment (DK I 81) could be from either.

84.   Hollow-tubular rim from a bowl, in amber-coloured glass. DK II 42.

85.   Bowl with hollow-tubular rim in amber-coloured glass. DM I 137.

86.   Fragment of pillar-moulded bowl, in amber-coloured glass. DM I 19.

87.   Fragment of amber glass with marvered white trail, possibly from a small ribbed bowl. Isings form 17. DK II 40.

88.   Pillar-moulded bowl, in natural green glass. DM I 137.

89.   Base of globular-bodied flagon or a deep, globular-bodied bowl, in natural green glass. DM I 137.

Glass Objects

90.   Fragment of a 'barley-sugar stick' stirring rod of blue-green glass. DM I 137.

91.   Fragment of a bangle of blue-green glass decorated with a twisted trail of deep blue and opaque white glass. The bangle is Kilbride-Jones' type 2 (Kilbride-Jones, 1937–38, 366-396; Stevenson, 1954–56, 208-221). Examples are most common in the north of England and southern Scotland, but they are widely distributed and not closely dated. DK I 107.

92.   Annular transluscent green glass bead, diameter 18 mm., thickness 6 mm. DK I 81. Two other annular beads, not illustrated, were found: (i) Transluscent green glass, diameter 18 mm., thickness 15 mm. DM I 137; (ii) Blue opaque glass, diameter 13 mm., thickness 6 mm. DM I 19.

93.   Melon bead, complete, diameter 15 mm. AH VIII 66. Five other melon beads, not illustrated, were found in AL II 41, AY I 26, DM I 19, DM I 136 and DK II 40.

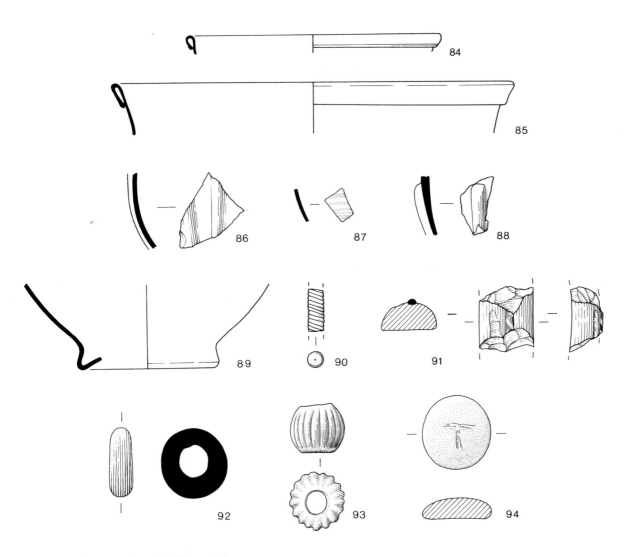

Fig. 34.   Glass vessels and objects (1:1)

94.   White paste gaming counter, with a crude letter T scratched on the top. Diameter 19 mm.   AH VIII 27.

Four other counters, not illustrated, were found:–

Black glass, complete, diameter, 13 mm.   AM II 59.

Blue glass, complete, diameter 15 mm.   DK II 42.

Green–white glass, circumference chipped, diameter 17 mm.   DK II 42.

Black opaque glass, diameter 17 mm.   DM I 130.

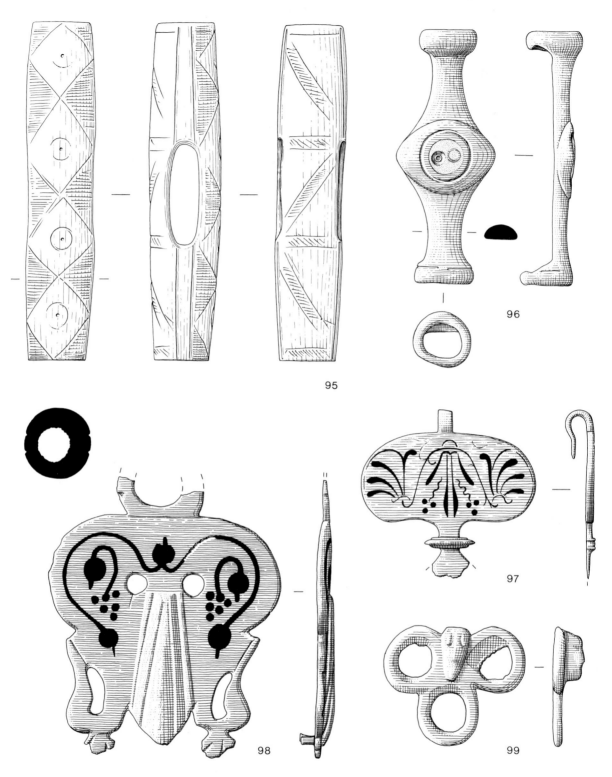

Fig. 35.   Bone and copper alloy objects (1:1)

GAZETTEER OF MILITARY OBJECTS FROM CIRENCESTER
by
Dr. Graham Webster

This section contains a comprehensive inventory of military objects from Cirencester, excluding all ironwork, such as arrowheads and spearheads. Some have been previously described (Webster, G., 1960), but the excavations since 1960 have yielded more. David Viner, curator of the Corinium Museum kindly provided every facility for access to the material in the collections.

The collection is a miscellaneous one but it is evident that the majority are associated with cavalry and that some are of exceptional quality. It is unfortunate that of the 40 items, 28 are unprovenanced or unstratified. The largest group, consisting of 7, comes from the Leaholme excavations, and it could be suggested that the fort in this area was occupied by cavalry.

All objects are of copper alloy, except no. 95 which is of bone.

95. Bone handle or toggle decorated with incised geometric patterns (Bushe-Fox, 1949, pl. LIV, no. 227, where the example is dated before *c.* A.D. 85). Corinium Museum, B 882, unprovenanced.

96. Strap junction with two waisted lengths on each side of a raised central oval feature, which is decorated with two circles inside a larger circle, the whole filled with enamel. There is a loop at each end at right angles to the main bar for admitting the straps. There is evidence that the whole object was originally gilded. An example of similar form has been found at Aldborough (Macgregor, 1976, no. 30). Corinium Museum, B 302, unprovenanced. (Macgregor, 1976, 60, no. 4, under the category of cheek pieces, toggles, or 'sliders').

97. Pendant previously described, but not so accurately drawn (Webster, G., 1960, no. 25, with references). The broken terminal could have been either in trifid form (Ulbert, 1959, Taf. 63, no. 17) or plain (Hobley, 1971-3, fig. 22, no. 20; Bushe-Fox, 1914, fig. 17, no. 22). Corinium Museum, C 109, unprovenanced.

98. (Front cover illustration). Pendant from a horse trapping, the surface would originally have been tinned and the decoration is in the form of scrolls and buds. The lower central area is a much devolved leaf in relief and there are two acorn terminals at the bottom for attachment instead of the usual hook and a circular projecting eyelet at the top. It belongs to a well known series of horse-furniture best exemplified from the Doorwerth hoard (Holwerda, 1913, A and B 2, 3, 4, 5). Other specimens are published from Xanten (in Curle, 1911, fig. 44); Newstead (Curle, 1911, pl. LXXIII); and Aislingen (Ulbert, 1959, Taf. 20, no. 1). The Doorwerth examples are in two sizes, 11 cm. and 8 cm. wide and the larger ones are of finer workmanship, thus the Cirencester·example is of the quality found on the smaller pieces. The Doorwerth hoard has been dated to the time of the Revolt of Civilis (A.D. 69), the Newstead pieces are presumably Agricolan, and Aislingen was occupied up to the time of Vespasian. Thus a date for this type can be suggested as *c.* A.D. 70-80. DM I 56, St. Michael's Field, post-military disturbances.

99. Martingale with three circular loops and a raised, decorated mount, which may represent an animal's head. Examples decorated with a man's head have been found at Richborough, (Bushe-Fox, 1926, pl. XV, no. 29; 1928, pl. XXI, no. 57). Corinium Museum, B 206, unprovenanced.

100. An unusual large pendant with double lobes, presumably designed as a frontlet for a horse, the attached link with two round holes for attachment to the harness was not previously described (Webster, G., 1960, no. 32, pl. XIB, with further references). Corinium Museum, B 315, Nursery Garden, on site of Basilica.

101. Double-lobed pendant with a decorated loop of a rudimentary bird form, and a rivet for fastening to leather. It is a smaller version of no. 100. A similar example has been found at

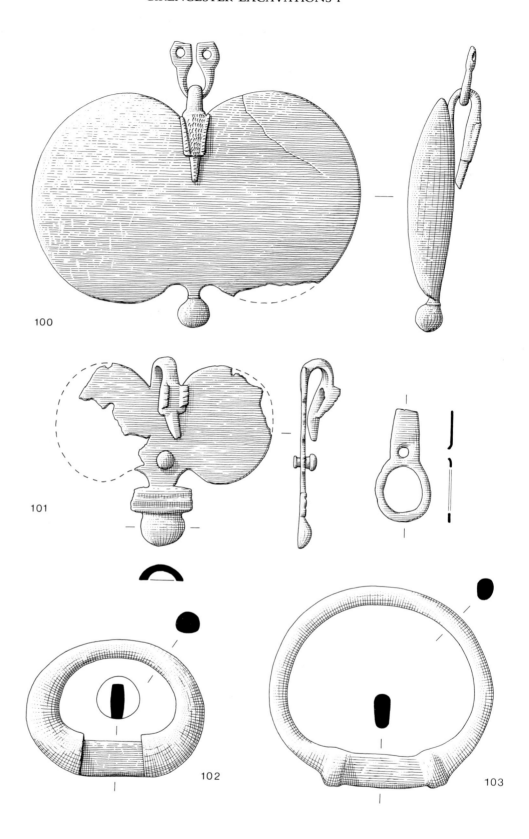

Fig. 36. Copper alloy objects (no. 100, 1:2; nos. 101–103, 1:1)

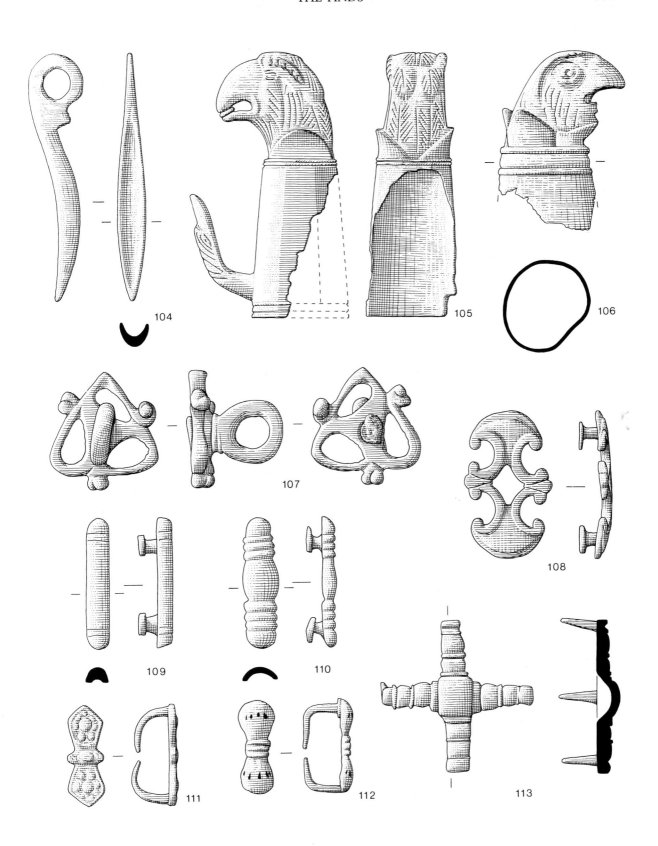

Fig. 37.   Copper alloy objects (1:1)

Valkenberg (Glasbergen and Groenman-van-Waateringe, 1974, pl. 14, no. 52). Leaholme 1961, topsoil.

102.   Plain, but well-shaped terret ring. Corinium Museum, C 1072, unprovenanced. (Macgregor, 1976, 62, no. 9, Simple loop and terret).

103.   Large plain terret ring with swelling-like collars on each side of flat bar of the strap attachment. Similar to no. 102. (Macgregor, 1976, 62, no. 9, Simple loop and terret, with further references and parallels). AM I 42, Leaholme, upper levels of Inner Ditch, pre-building phase.

104.   Barnacle pendant for attaching to horse-harness as an amulet for quietening horses (Cunliffe, 1968, pl. XXXIX, no. 142; Bushe-Fox, 1949, pl. XI, no. 156). DH XII 13, St. Michael's Field, robber trench.

105.   Socket with an eagle's head and projecting hook in the form of a bird's head with long beak. A fitting from a cart, (Webster, G., 1960, no. 37 with references). Corinium Museum, B 291, Querns Lane.

106.   Part of an object similar to no. 105 above. Corinium Museum, B 292, Watermoor Church.

107.   The following note has been kindly provided by Dr. Morna Macgregor:
Triskele-decorated fob. Parallels can be quoted from: Aldborough, Yorks. (Myers, Steer, and Chitty, 1959, 74, fig. 26, 13); Berkshire (Allen, J.R., 1896, 321-36); Haslingfield, Cambs. (Fell, 1951, 65-6); Hunsbury, Northants. (Fell, 1936, 57-100); Kingsholm, Gloucester (Douglas, 1793, pl. XXVII, 1); St. Albans, Herts. (Wheeler and Wheeler, 1936, 217, fig. 48); Seamill, Ayrshire (Munro, 1882, 63, fig. 3); ?South Shields, Co. Durham (Newcastle University Museum 1956.128.69.A); and Tre'r Ceiri, Caer. (Baring-Gould and Burnard, 1904, 8, fig. 5). The dating of these objects is difficult. The Hunsbury examples are of iron 'flashed' in bronze which has been considered to be an early technique (but see Stead, 1965, 41). Tre'r Ceiri and Aldborough have Romano-British associations and the latter is unlikely to be earlier than the Vespasianic foundation; while the St. Albans and Haslingfield examples may be later, the former being ascribed to the fourth century. On stylistic comparisons, the twisted or swirled form at Seamill is paralleled on casket ornament (Gray, 1924, pl. XX, E8); its edge pouncing by the crescent terret from Pentyrch, Glam. (Savory, 1966, 28-33, 29, fig. 1 and pl. II). Both are vague pointers to the mid to late first century A.D. (Macgregor, 1976, 60, no. 10, Triskele-decorated fobs). AL III 15, Leaholme, post-military disturbance.

108.   Mount for attachment to leather in the form of opposed pelta-like features. Corinium Museum, C 301, unprovenanced.

109.   A long cigar-shaped belt mount similar to no. 110. Corinium Museum, B 240, unprovenanced.

110.   Belt mount of common form. (Ulbert, 1969, Taf. 28, nos. 10 and 11, etc.). Corinium Museum, unprovenanced.

111.   A small mount with relief decoration of two rosettes and with two large tangs at the back. Corinium Museum, C 112, unprovenanced.

112.   Dumb-bell button or, perhaps more correctly, a strap slide of a fairly common type, but with unusual inlaid niello dots, (Macgregor, 1976, 134 and 136, fig. 8; Bushe-Fox, 1949, pl. XXXVI, nos 121 and 122). Corinium Museum, C 114, unprovenanced.

113.   Cruciform strap-junction with tangs at the end of each arm for attaching to two or more thicknesses of leather. Corinium Museum, B 370, unprovenanced.

114.   Pendant in the form of a leaf covered with punched decoration and with traces of gilding. The terminal boss is bent to form a hook for attaching a further pendant, and is decorated with an incised cross. This item was published (Webster, G., 1960, no. 33) without the surface decoration. Corinium Museum, C 151, unprovenanced.

115.   Heart-shaped pendant with four lunate openings and a round base terminal. It was attached by means of a small hole in a flat piece of metal projecting inwards at the top.

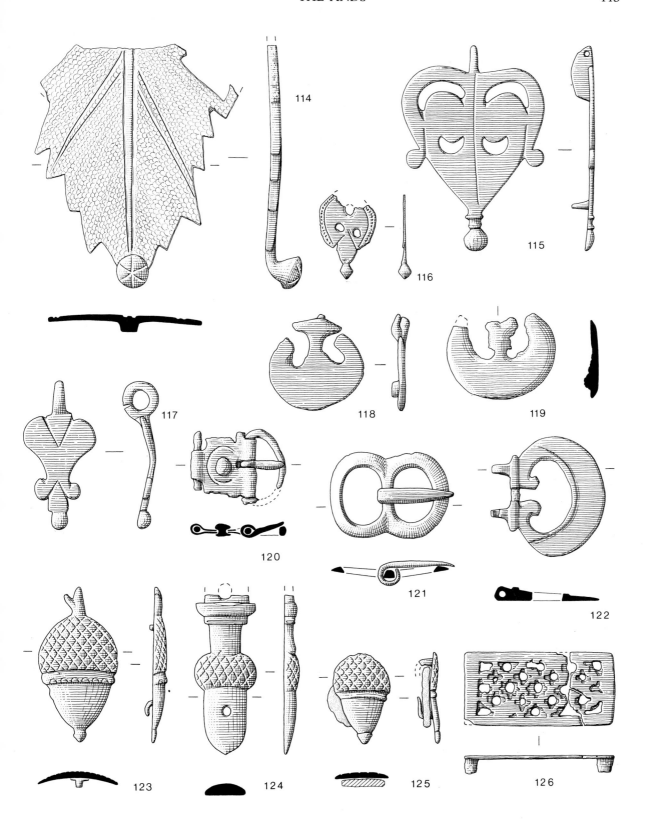

Fig. 38. Copper alloy objects (1:1)

(Webster, G., 1960, no. 35, with references). Corinium Museum, B 403, unprovenanced.

116. The lower part of a small pendant with a conical terminal; it has three asymmetric openings and fine punched decoration round the edge. (Lehner, 1904, Taf. XXXIV for general types). CT XI 121, Extra-mural building and road, adjacent to amphitheatre. Topsoil.

117. Small pendant with a large loop (Webster, G., 1960, no. 31). This is a type normally associated with the second century, but there is a first-century example from Rheingönheim (Ulbert, 1969, Taf. 36, no. 17) which may be an early form. Corinium Museum, C 50, unprovenanced.

118. Pelta-shaped mount, probably a terminal for a strap. Corinium Museum, B 639, unprovenanced.

119. Strap- or belt-terminal of lunate form with a rough unfinished back. There is no indication how it is attached. Similar examples from Rheingönheim are described as 'feet' (Ulbert, 1969, Taf. 37, nos. 5-7) and from Camulodunum as scabbard-fittings (Hawkes and Hull, 1947, pl. 103, nos. 31 and 32) but they are all solid pieces and some could have been sewn into the end of a fabric strip. This could not apply to the decorated pieces unless this was seen through cut-out panels. There is a much heavier example with a hollowed back for filling with lead from Richborough (Cunliffe, 1968, Pl. XLVIII, no. 223). AF I 40, Leaholme.

120. Small D-type buckle of normal military pattern (Ulbert, 1969, Taf. 33, nos. 23-39). AL VIII 29, Leaholme, upper levels.

121. Buckle in the form of a figure of eight. This is not a military type of buckle; a similar example was found on the Telephone Exchange site at Colchester, but could have been from an early *colonia* level (Dunnett, 1971, fig. 11, no. 22). Leaholme 1961, topsoil.

122. Belt-buckle of typical military pattern (Ulbert, 1969, Taf. 26, nos. 1 and 2; Webster, G., 1960, no. 28). Corinium Museum, B 202, unprovenanced.

123. Acorn belt with two tangs at the back for fastening to leather. Decorative mounts of this form are fairly comon on military sites (Hawkes and Hull, 1947, Pl. CII, no. 26; O.R.L., 1901, Taf. xiii, nos. 63 and 64; 'Chesterton Camp' at Water Newton in the British Museum, Acc. No. 82, 6-21, 144). Corinium Museum, unprovenanced.

124. A mount similar to nos. 123 and 125, with a flat back and two rivet holes which could have been a box-mount. (Webster, G., 1960, no. 30). Corinium Museum, B 379, unprovenanced.

125. A mount very similar to no. 123 above, formerly published with a piece of leather still attached, (Webster, G., 1960, no. 29, with references). Corinium Museum, B 327, unprovenanced.

126. Belt plate crudely decorated with what was intended to be a fretted design of the kind in use in the army in the second century (Fox, 1940, fig. 6, no. 19; Nash-Williams, 1932, fig. 33, nos. 32 and 33, pl. ii). The plates of the first century are normally solid with niello decoration. This example could be a poor civil copy. CS I 4, south-western cemetery adjacent to amphitheatre, rubbish scatter, unassociated with a burial.

127. Handle of a strigil decorated with niello inlay. The decoration dates this to the mid-first century, so it probably belonged to one of the military personnel. AH VIII 25, Leaholme, from Flavian shops sealing military levels.

128. Dagger chape, (Webster, G., 1960, no. 27, with references). Corinium Museum, C 145, unprovenanced.

129. Apron-mount with two placements for mounts in the form of domed studs. (Ritterling, 1913, Taf. XII, no. 19; Hawkes and Hull, 1947, Pl. CIII, nos. 24-27; Bushe-Fox, 1932, pl. 14, no. 48). Corinium Museum, C 84, unprovenanced.

130. Scabbard-mount. (Webster, G., 1690, fig. 3, 34, with references). Corinium Museum, C 84, unprovenanced.

131. Strip with silver (?) inlay, probably part of belt- or harness-decoration, very similar to a

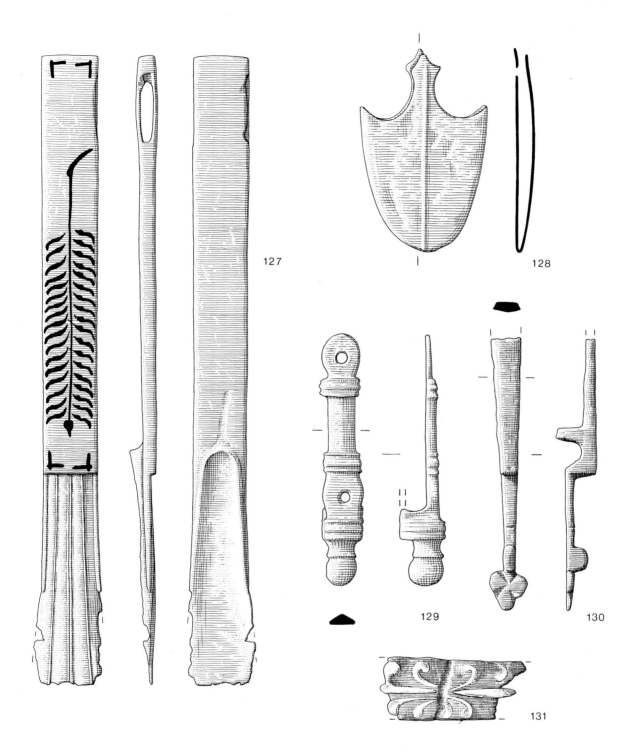

Fig. 39. Copper alloy objects (1:1)

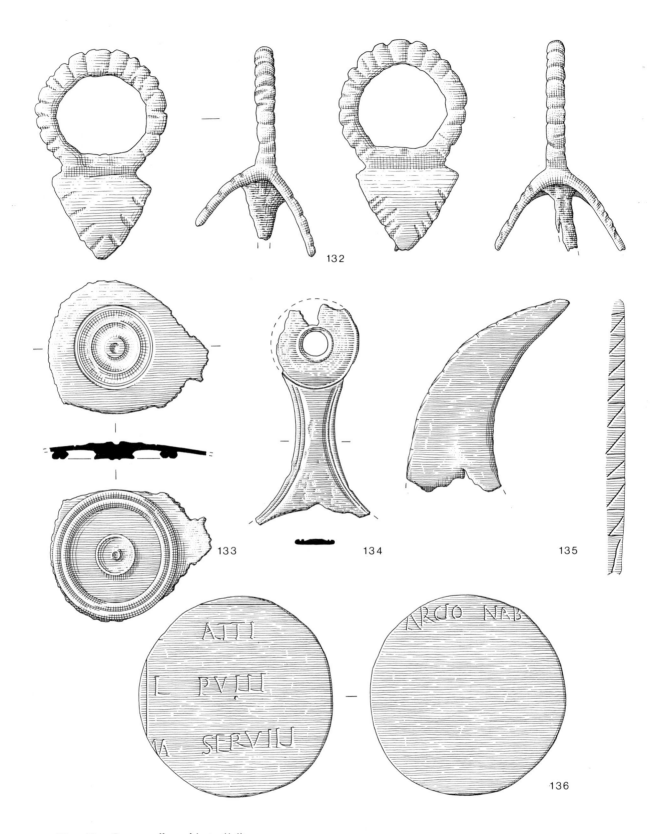

Fig. 40.   Copper alloy objects (1:1)

fragment from Hofheim (Ritterling, 1913, Taf. xi, no. 72). (Webster, G., 1960, fig. 3, 24). Corinium Museum, unprovenanced.

132.   Pair of bronze rings with knobbed decoration and leaf-shaped projections masking an iron nail: probably bucket mounts for the handle. AR IV 9, Police Station excavations, from an upper level producing early material.

133.   Part of base of a skillet with a tinned surface, probably a military type (Boesterd, 1956, nos. 19–34). Similar objects are known from military sites in Britain, e.g. Broxtowe, (Oswald, A., 1939, 441, pl. LXXXVII; Webster, G., 1960, 69, no. 5); Gloucester, (Webster, G., 1960, pl. IX B); and Caves Inn, (Webster, G., 1960, 143–4, fig. 3, pl. 30). AE II 3, Leaholme, upper levels on a site producing early pottery at several levels in the section.

134.   Handle of a skillet similar to no. 133 above. (Webster, G., 1960, no. 36). Corinium Museum, unprovenanced.

135.   Part of heavy bronze mount of horn shape with incised decorations on the outer edge: perhaps from a bucket escutcheon mount (Lehner, 1904, Taf. XXXIII, no. 19) or from a decorated jug handle (Waugh and Goodburn, 1972, fig. 42, no. 137). AF I 3, Leaholme, topsoil.

136.   Circular piece of copper alloy cut from a military diploma.

The following note has kindly been contributed by Dr. Margaret Roxan:
The fragment of a diploma was found on an unrecorded site in Cirencester, and it is at present in the Corinium Museum. It had been reused as a mirror and is a circular disc, measuring 5.3 cm. in diameter. It was first published by Professor Donald Atkinson, (1957, 196). (See also *Ann. ép.* 1958 no. 89, outer face only, 1959 no. 162, both faces). The surviving text reads:

intus: tabella II	extrinsecus: tabella II
ARCIO NAB	ATTI
	L PVLLI
	M SERVILI

A suggested expansion might read:

[*Imp(erator) Caes(ar), divi Hadriani f., divi Traiani Parth(ici) divi Nervae pronep(os), T. Aelius Hadrianus Antoninus Aug(ustus) Pius, pont(ifex) max(imus), trib(unicia) pot(estate) . . . ., co(n)s(ul) . . ., p(ater) p(atriae) (auxilia)[1] . . . . et sunt in Britannia[2] sub . . . . . quorum nomina subscripta sunt . . . . a.d. . . . . alae aut coh(ortis) . . . . ., cui praest . . . . . ., ex . . . . .] arcio Nab [. . . . .f .?[3] . . . . .] [P.] Atii [Severi]; L. Pulli [Daphni]; M. Servili [Getae][4].*

1.   This is most likely to be a fragment of a *diploma* issued to a veteran of the *auxilia* although the same witnesses appear on fleet *diplomata* of this period.
2.   That it was found in Cirencester suggests that the recipient had served in the auxiliary army in Britain.
3.   Atkinson suggested either [M]*arcius* or [L]*arcius* for the *nomen* of the recipient and inferred that he was already a Roman citizen.
4.   The presence of a marginal line above the name ATTI indicates that the names preserved are those of the first three witnesses. From a time late in the reign of Hadrian (134–38) witnesses affixed their names in strict order of seniority and when the first witness ceases to appear the others all move up one place. In December 140 (†36) Ti. Claudius Menander was first witness and the three named above were second, third and fourth respectively. On 19th July 146 the first three witnesses were Severus, Daphnus and Geta (*CIL* XVI 178) but by 9th October 148 Daphnus had replaced Severus in first place (*CIL* XVI 96, 179, and 180).

THE POTTERY

INTRODUCTION

Throughout the processing, the pottery has been dealt with in stratigraphical groups. With the exception of that from the back-filling of the quarried areas and the layers sealing the early occupation, all the pottery found is recorded in the report. As far as the evidence allows, sites have been grouped together into related areas of occupation – the Leaholme fort, the Watermoor Rampart, with the areas which could have been within its circuit; the Sands Rampart, which could have formed part of the same circuit as Watermoor; and the possible *vicus* to the north of Leaholme. Within these groupings, the pottery is arranged stratigraphically, in layers, beginning with the earliest.

The specialist reports on the samian, and the potters' stamps on the mortaria, amphorae, terra nigra and coarse wares, are published separately. Otherwise all the pottery is arranged together in groups, accompanied by a summary of the dating evidence provided by the specialist reports.

The vessel-forms have not been classified; but to aid the recording of small and indeterminate body sherds which could not usefully be drawn, as well as to reduce repetition in the descriptions, the fabrics have been classified. The classification was based on the superficial characteristics of the ware and inclusions – the grain-size and texture of the ware, the presence of visible mica and quartz, the size, colour, type and density of inclusions, and finally the colour which is the combined result of the presence of impurities, particularly iron compounds, and the firing conditions where they are considered relevant, the terms – gritty, sandy, sand-free and smooth have been used only to define the texture of fabrics; they do not denote the actual presence or absence of quartz. When such methods of classification have been used, it is essential to realise that fabrics which are superficially identical need not be from the same source, while dissimilar fabrics need not be from different potteries. Only a long-term and intensive programme of analysis may be able to settle some of the questions raised by the fabric classification, but this is beyond the resources available at present.

Hand-made vessels, a small minority, are specified as such in the report, while in the descriptions of the remaining bulk of the pottery, it is understood that they were wheel-thrown.

The parallels quoted are limited to those which, if not identical, are very similar in both form and fabric and so could be considered to be of the same date and even from the same, or closely related sources, as the Cirencester pottery. All the relevant sherds have been examined. In some cases, although the parallels are from published sites, they could not be identified in the relevant report.

THE SAMIAN
by
B.R. Hartley and Brenda Dickinson

All the sherds are South Gaulish (and almost certainly from La Graufesenque) unless otherwise stated.

ABBREVIATIONS

R forms of dishes: 15/17R etc., with a band of rouletting on the base.

27g: Form 27 with an external groove round the footring, common on South Gaulish cups.

33a: The variant of form 33, common in South Gaul, with external grooves at the base of the wall and below the rim. Internally, these cups generally have an offset at or above the junction of base and wall and a moulding on the base.

D.1.-D.71. refer to sherds illustrated in figs. 42–46.

POTTERS' STAMPS

All the stamps, including those on decorated ware, are listed alphabetically, with the unidentified ones at the end. The numbers for the potters and for individual dies are those which will be used in the forthcoming Index of Potters' Stamps on Samian Ware.

S. 1 - 3 (AM II 59, 1-3)
Amandus ii 4a – twice on form 27, once on form 27g. When complete the stamp reads OFĀMAN. Usually on form 27, more rarely on form 24, this stamp has been recorded from the following contexts significant for date: Camulodunum, Fishbourne Per.IB, Heddernheim, Hofheim I, Rheingönheim (probably) and Wroxeter. Its currency is likely to have been entirely pre-Flavian. *c*. A.D. 50-65.

S. 4 (AL II 45 b)
Bassus i-Coelus 5b – fragment of form 15/17R or 18R, stamped OFB[ASSI·Co]. Stamps from this die occur at La Graufesenque, Risstissen, Ubbergen and Usk, and on form 29. *c*. A.D. 50-70.

S. 5 (AW I 76)
Bassus i 1a – base of a cup of form 24, stamped IC.BAS. The stamp presumably comes from a broken die, giving OFIC·BASSI or OFIC·BASS, rather than recording an association (such as Licinus with Bassus). No other Bassus stamps with OFIC are known. However, there is no difficulty about the date, since the fabric points to the early part of Bassus's career. *c*. A.D. 45-60.

S. 6 (AM II 59, 4)
Cennatus 3a – CENNATI on form 27g. The stamp was used on cups of form 27g and dishes of forms 15/17 or 18 and 18, but there are no records from dated sites. However, other stamps of Cennatus are known from Camulodunum, Hofheim I, one of the pre-Flavian cemeteries at Nijmegen and at Ubbergen. His record of forms includes 16, 17 and 24. *c*. A.D. 45-60.

S. 7 (DK I 116 e)
Cosius Urap(p?)us 1a – form 24, South Gaulish, stamped [COSIV̂S·V̂RÂP The only known stamp of this potter, it occurs at La Graufesenque, Camulodunum, Hüfingen and in a Claudio-Neronian group at Narbonne. *c*. A.D. 45-65.

S. 8 (DM I 19, 1)
Crestio 5a – form 15/17 or 18, stamped OF>CRESTIO.
The stamp occurs at Aislingen, Camulodunum, Chester, the Nijmegen fortress,

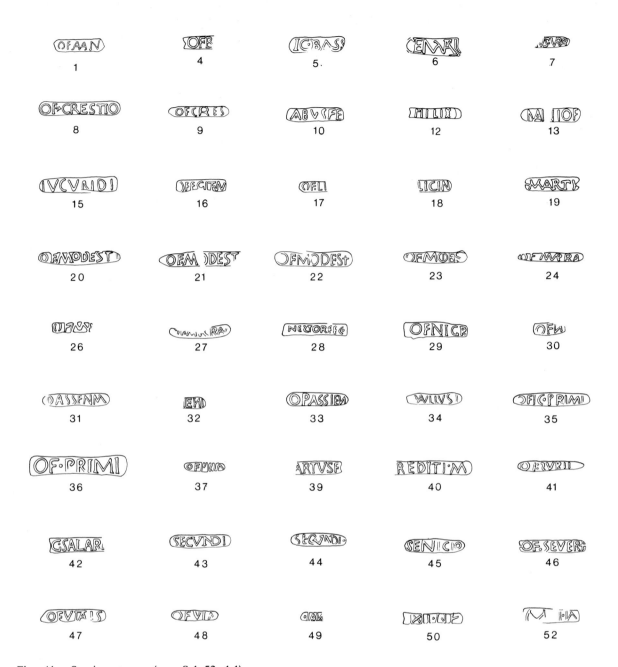

Fig. 41.　Samian stamps (nos. S.1–52, 1:1)

Rheingönheim, York and in the Boudiccan burning at Verulamium. An example from Castle-dykes must be a survival, but the die must in any case have had a long life, and a date *c.* A.D. 50-70 is likely.

S. 9 (AM II 59, 5)
Crestio 9a´ – form Ritterling 8. This stamp is from a broken die, giving OFCRES instead of the original OFCREST(9a). The short version only appears on a dated site at Hofheim I. It was also used on forms 24, 27g and Ritterling 9. *c.* A.D. 50-65.

S. 10-11 (AM II 59, 6-7)
Fabus 5a´ – forms 15/17 and 18. The stamp reads ΛBVSFE instead of the original FΛBVSFE. It was used both on cups (including Ritt. 8 and 9) and on dishes, and appears at Zwammerdam (A.D. 47 onwards) and Valkenburg ZH Woerd (A.D. 50 onwards?). The original version occurs in Period IA at Valkenburg ZH (*c.* A.D. 40 or A.D. 47?). *c.* A.D. 55-65.

S. 12 (AE II 10 a)
Felix i 49g – form 27g, stamped ΗΙΙIX, with an uncommon die of Felix i of La Graufesenque. The potter's activity seems to have been almost entirely pre-Flavian and a likely date for the piece is *c.* A.D. 50-65.

S. 13 (DM I 145 d)
Germanus i 13c´ – three joining fragments giving almost the whole of a cup of form 27g, stamped MΛNIOF, by a broken die of Germanus i (13c) originally reading GERMΛNIOF. Impressions of the original die occur at La Graufesenque and Carlisle, and from the broken version in the Burghöfe Geschirrdepot and at Wilderspool. *c.* A.D. 70-100.

S. 14 (DM I 137 e)
Germanus i 28i – form 15/17 or 18, stamped [GERM]ANI (with MA ligatured) by Germanus i. The stamp, always on dishes, occurs at Heddernheim and the Newton Kyme fort. *c.* A.D. 65-85.

S. 15 (AM II 59, 8 a)
Iucundus ii 12a (see p. 139). *c.* A.D. 65-100.

S. 16 (AM II 59, 9)
Legitumus 1a´ –)FJEGITVM on form 18. The die originally gave a final TVM, and was used on forms 27g, 24 or Ritt. 8, and also dishes. A stamp from one or other version was found in the fort at Great Casterton. *c.* A.D. 45-65.

S. 17 (DK II 40 a)
Licinus 23a – form Ritt. 8, stamped OF·LI[CIN] by Licinus of La Graufesenque, where the stamp has been found. It appears also at Camulodunum and, twice, in Colchester Pottery Shop II. *c.* A.D. 45-65.

S. 18 (DM I 137 d)
Licinus 23b – form 15/17 or 18, stamped [OF]LICIN. One of his less common stamps, it occurs on form Ritt. 1 and at Rheingönheim. Licinus's work is common at Camulodunum and in the Colchester Pottery Shops. *c.* A.D. 50-65.

S. 19 (DK II 42, 1)
Martius ii 2a – form 15/17 or 18, stamped MARTI. The stamp occurs at La Graufesenque and it is on forms 24 and 29 (with pre-Flavian decoration). Another stamp is known on Ritt. form 8. *c.* A.D. 50-65.

S. 20 (AM II 59, 10)
Modestus i 2a – OF·MODESTI on form 18R. This was used only on rouletted dishes and form 29. It is attested from Alphen (possibly in a modified version) and Camulodunum. *c.* A.D. 45-60.

S. 21 (AL VII 31 c & AM IV 41)
Modestus i 2a or 2a´ – two fragments of the same form 15/17R or 18R, stamped OF.M ODEST[I]. Stamps from these dies occur at La Graufesenque and in the Cirencester fort ditch deposit (AM II 59). *c.* A.D. 45-60.

S. 22 (AM II 59, 11)
Modestus i 2g (see p. 139). *c.* A.D. 45–65.

S. 23 (AM II 59, 12)
Modestus i 4e – OFMŌDES on form 18R. This impression was made late in the history of the die, when the two lower bars of the E became joined, as if they belonged to a B. The original stamp occurs at Risstissen and the modified version at Camulodunum. *c.* A.D. 50-65.

S. 24 - 25 (AM II 59, 13; CG III 14 b)
Murranus 10c – OF·MV͡RRA on forms 27g and 15/17 or 18. The stamp was used mostly on dishes, but occasionally on form 27 or 24. It occurs in one of the burnt pottery shops at Colchester (Hull, 1958, fig. 76, 10, 11). *c.* A.D. 50-65.

S. 26 (CG III 11 b)
Murranus (10d) – OFM͡VRR/ on form 15/17 or 18. This stamp is from a broken die. *c.* A.D. 50-65.

S. 27 (AM II 59, 14)
Murranus – OF.[MV?]RRA͡N, not identified, on form 15/17. *c.* A.D. 50-65.

S. 28 (AM II 59, 15)
Nestor 2a – NE2TORFEC on form 18. This stamp has been recorded from Camulodunum and both Colchester pottery shops destroyed in A.D. 60 or 61 (Hull, 1958, 12, and recent discoveries). It was used always on unrouletted dishes, including forms 15/17 or 18 and Ritt. 1. This is the only known stamp of Nestor and only twenty-five examples have been recorded, suggesting that it was probably in use for a short time, *c.* A.D. 55-65.

S. 29 (AM II 59, 16)
Niger ii 4a – OFNIGR on form 18. The stamp is known from Hofheim I, the pre-Flavian cemeteries at Nijmegen, Risstissen, Sels, Valkenburg ZH (Per. 2/3) and Wroxeter. It was used on forms 15/17, 18, 27g, 29 and Ritt. 8. A slightly modified version of the die giving OFNIGV is represented at Rheingönheim, but also at Caerleon and in Period II A at Verulamium. *c.* A.D. 55-65.

S. 30 (DK I 81, 1)
Niger ii 9b – form 27g stamped OFИI[ ].
The stamp was used exclusively on cups, including forms 24 and Ritt. 8 and occurs at Hofheim and Baginton. *c.* A.D. 50-75.

S. 31 (AG III 49 b)
Pass(i)enus 31a – two joining fragments of a cup of form 27g, stamped PASSENM͡A by Pass(i)enus of La Graufesenque, where the stamp (31a) occurs. It has been found also at Baginton, Broxtowe, Usk and the Gloucester Kingsholm site. The cup has a rather flat-topped rim and kiln-grit inside the base. *c.* A.D. 50-65.

S. 32 (DK I 81, 2)
Pass(i)enus 40a – form 15/17 or 18 stamped [OF·PASS]IENI retr. The stamp occurs in Period I at Verulamium, but there is no other evidence of date, though Pass(i)enus's record is mainly pre-Flavian. *c.* A.D. 50-65.

S. 33 (AM II 59, 17)
Pass(i)enus 50a – OPASSIEИ on form 27g. This stamp has been found in both the Colchester pottery shops destroyed in the Boudiccan rebellion, in Period I B at Fishbourne and in Period I at Zwammerdam. It is not known from any Flavian foundations. *c.* A.D. 50-65.

S. 34 (DM I 19, 2)
Paullus i 9c – form 27g stamped PA͡VLLVSF. This stamp occurs at Gloucester, Kingsholm and another of his is in Colchester Pottery Shop I. *c.* A.D. 45-65.

S. 35 (AM II 59, 18)
Primus iii 3d – OFIC.PRIMI on form 18R. The stamp was generally used on form 29, but appears occasionally on dishes, both the rouletted and unrouletted varieties. One example is known from Period I at Valkenburg ZH, but it probably also turns up at Usk. *c.* A.D. 45-60.

S. 36 - 37 (AM II 59, 19 & 20)

Primus iii 12d (see p. 139). *c.* A.D. 45–65.

S. 38 (DK I 103 c)

Primus iii 20b – two joining fragments, with two more in 102, of form 24, stamped OFPRIΛ. The stamp was used exclusively on cups (including form Ritt. 8) and occurs in the Colchester Pottery Shop II. *c.* A.D. 50–65.

S. 39 (DK I 114 a)

Quartus ii 8a – two joining fragments of a dish of form 18, stamped [QV]ARTVSF. The stamp occurs at La Graufesenque and at the pre-Flavian cemeteries at Nijmegen. Quartus's record is Claudio-Neronian and a date *c.* A.D. 45-60 should cover the range.

S. 40 (DM I 19, 3)

Reditus 3b – form 31, stamped REDITI'M by Reditus of Central Gaul (presumably Lezoux). The stamp occurs in the Saalburg Erdkastell and was used on forms 18/31 and 27. *c.* A.D. 130-150.

S. 41 (AX II 41 a)

Sabinus iii 12a – form 27g stamped OI:SABII retr. a poor impression, as often, of a stamp originally giving OI:SΛBIN retr. The stamp is known from La Graufesenque, is common at early Flavian foundations, but reached Camelon (2 examples). It occurs also at Gloucester, Kingsholm, at Hofheim and Risstissen and so should be dated *c.* A.D. 65-85.

S. 42 (AM II 59, 21)

G. Salarius Aptus 3a – G·SALARI·APTI on form 15/17R. Only three examples of this stamp are known, all on rouletted dishes, with one example from Camulodunum. Other stamps of his were used on forms 24 and Ritt. 8 and are recorded from both Periods I and II at Valkenburg ZH. *c.* A.D. 50-65.

S. 43 (DK I 81, 3)

Secundus i 2c – form Ritt. 9, stamped SECVNDI by Secundus i. The stamp is common on forms 24 and Ritt. 8 and 9, and occurs several times at Camulodunum, as well as at Aislingen and Hofheim. *c.* A.D. 45-65.

S. 44 (AM II 59, 22)

Secundus i or ii 1b– SECVNDI on form 27. It is not clear whether this stamp belongs to Secundus i of La Graufesenque, who is a Tiberio-Neronian potter, or to Secundus ii who worked in the Neronian-Domitianic range. However, this stamp is known from the First Colchester Pottery Shop and from Lincoln, so it is clearly Neronian. *c.* A.D. 50-65.

S. 45 (AM II 59, 23)

Senicio 6a – SENICIo on form 27g. The stamp is nearly always on cups, including Ritterling forms 8 and 9. It is recorded in Period I at Fishbourne and in Period IA at Valkenburg ZH and at Camulodunum. Impressions from a worn version of this die just appear in early-Flavian contexts, as at Verulamium (Hartley B.R., 1972, S52), though perhaps always as residual pieces. *c.* A.D. 55-65.

S. 46 (DK I 81, 4)

Severus i-Pud(ens) 3a´ – form 15/17 or 18 stamped OF·SEVERP. The stamp, from a broken version of a die giving OF·SEVERP and far more common than the original, is known from many Flavian foundations, including Caerleon, Corbridge and the Nijmegen fortress. *c.* A.D. 70-95.

S. 47 (AM II 59, 24)

Vitalis i 1d – OFVITALIS on form 18. The only dated site for this stamp is Hofheim I, but impressions from a modified version appear in Valkenburg ZH Period II/III, at Ubbergen and at Gloucester, Kingsholm. *c.* A.D. 55-65.

S. 48 (AM II 59, 25)

Vitalis i 6i – OFVIA probably with TA ligatured, on form 24. The stamp is only otherwise known at Paris, on form 27. The form of the Cirencester cup shows that it cannot belong to the later Vitalis of La Graufesenque. *c.* A.D. 55-65.

ILLITERATE STAMPS

S. 49 (AH VIII 96 b)
Fragment of a cup, probably form 24, stamped ·IFV·[, unidentified and possibly illiterate. Claudio-Neronian.

S. 50 (AX II 42 d)
Form 27g, with an illiterate stamp IX·II·I·ΛIT, only known otherwise from Bonn and Neuss. Late-Neronian or early-Flavian.

UNIDENTIFIED STAMPS

S. 51 (DK II 39 j) (Not illustrated)
..MNII.. – see p. 131.

S. 52 (AM II 59, 26)
M[ ]I·N – on form 27g.

S. 53 (AM II 59, 27) (Not illustrated)
OF⊬ – see p. 139. Possibly Modestus or Murranus.

S. 54 (DK I 81, 5) (Not illustrated)
Form 15/17 or 18 with an unidentified stamp EI[or FI[, South Gaulish, with a double groove on the base and a high, triangular footring. Claudio-Neronian.

S. 55 (CG IV 16 a) (Not illustrated)
Form Ritt. 8 burnt, with an unidentified stamp]INI. Pre-Flavian.

S. 56 (DK II 42, 2) (Not illustrated)
An unidentified, fragmentary stamp on form 15/17 or 18. Pre-Flavian.

THE GROUPS – THE PLAIN AND DECORATED FORMS

THE LEAHOLME FORT

OCCUPATION WITHIN THE FORT AREA

Site AH

Phase I

AH VIII 116
a) Fragments of three dishes of form 15/17, all possibly Claudian.
b) Fragment of form 15/17R. Claudian.
c) Eight fragments, seven joining, of form 27g. The flattened bead lip and pale fabric suggest a Claudio-Neronian date.
d) Fragment of the upper zone of form 29, with scroll decoration. The tie on the scroll, the fabric and glaze, all indicate a pre-Flavian date.

AH VIII 75
Fragment of form 15/17. Pre-Flavian.

Layers sealing-off the military occupation

AH VIII 96
a) Two fragments of the same form 15/17. Claudian.
b) Illiterate stamp – see S. 49.
c) Two joining fragments of the same form 27, with a flattened bead lip. Claudian.

AH VIII 78
a) Two fragments of the same form 15/17, perhaps with rouletting. Neronian.
b) Fragments of two dishes of form 18. Flavian.
c) D.1. Fragment of form 37, with decoration in the style of La Graufesenque, showing a leaf tendril above a wreath composed of small trilobed leaves. These may be the ones occurring on two bowls in the Pompeii Hoard (Atkinson, 1914, pl.vii, 37 and x, 52), where they were used at the ends of scroll tendrils. *c.* A.D. 70-90.
d) Fragment of a panelled form 37. The basal wreath and the broader leaf tips occur on bowls in the Pompeii Hoard. The narrower leaf tips do not seem to occur elsewhere. *c.* A.D. 70-90.

AH VIII 103
Four fragments, two joining, probably all from the same form 27g, with bright Neronian fabric and glaze. *c.* A.D. 50-65.

Site AG

Pit

AG III 49
a) Form Ritt. 1. Claudian or early-Neronian.
b) Pass(i)enus 31a – see S. 31.

Pit

AG III 43 (Above AG III 49)
a) Form 15/17. Early-Flavian.
b) Form 27. Neronian or early-Flavian.
c) D.2. perhaps belonging to d), form 37, with an elongated, heart-shaped leaf on a tendril. The trident-tongued ovolo is on a bowl of form 30 from Kettering made in a mould signed by Vitalis ii. *c*. A.D. 75-90.
d) D.3. Six joining fragments (and possibly one other, with a trident-tongued ovolo), of form 37, with a winding scroll. The basal wreath and ovolo occur on bowls at Newstead and Camelon respectively. The details are: small leaf (Knorr, 1919, Taf.17, 22); leaf with serrated edge (cf. *ibid.*, Taf. 98A on a bowl at Rottweil); hare to right (Hermet, 1934, pl. 26, 53); hare to left (cf. Knorr, 1919, Taf. 53, 2 of Matugenus ii); griffin (Hermet, 1934, pl. 25, 5). *c*. A.D. 75-95.
e) Form 37, with a blurred, trident-tongued ovolo. Flavian.

Layers sealing-off the early occupation

AG II 36
a) Fragments of three or four dishes of form 18. Two Neronian, one, burnt, Neronian or early-Flavian.
b) D.4. Form 29, with a lower zone of saltires flanking a panel with a leafy festoon containing an eagle (Hermet, 1934, pl. 28, 9) in a chevron medallion. The festoon appears on a bowl from Vechten stamped by Labio and, as it is uncommon, there should be a link with him. However, there is no close parallel for the other details. The arrangement of the panels suggests a Neronian date, *c*. A.D. 55-70.
c) Form 18, slightly burnt. Neronian or early-Flavian.
d) A scrap. Probably pre-Flavian.
e) Two joining fragments of form 37 base. Flavian.
f) Fragments of form 37, with a trident-tongued ovolo and zonal decoration with triple-bordered festoons. The decoration can be paralleled at Agricolan sites in Scotland. *c*. A.D. 75-95.
g) D.5. Form 37, with scroll decoration and a lion (Hermet, 1934, pl. 25, 25?) over spirals in the lower concavity. *c*. A.D. 80-100.

AG III 39
Form 27. First century.

Site AE

Occupation on natural

AE I 12
Form Ritt. 9. Claudio-Neronian.

AE V 21
a) Form 18 base, with a high footring and kiln-grit adhering to the inside of the base. Late-Claudian.
b) Four fragments, three joining, of form Ritt. 8 and a tiny scrap from another. Both Claudio-Neronian.

Filling of timber and other features

AE II P.H.2
a) D.6. Form 29, with nautilus gadroons in the lower zone. A bowl from Neuss stamped by Stabilio (Knorr, 1919, Taf. 79A) offers a close parallel, but similar gadroons were used by several potters at La Graufesenque in the Tiberio-Claudian period. Cf. Oswald F., 1951, 149–152 for a discussion of the gadroons. *c*. A.D. 40–55.
b) Form 18, in orange fabric with a patchy orange glaze, typical of Lezoux ware of the Neronian or early-Flavian period.

AE III 17 – filling of timber slot
a) Form 27. Claudian.
b) Form 18. Flavian.
c) Form 37. Trajanic.

Sealing-off Layers

AE I 10
a) Form 18. Neronian.
b) Form 27g. Neronian.
c) Form 27. Neronian.
d) Form 29, with scroll decoration. First-century.
e) D.7. Form 29, with a lower zone of straight gadroons over elliptical festoons, one containing the bird 0.2298, commonly used at La Graufesenque in the Neronian and Flavian periods. The festoons are more typical of the period *c*. A.D. 55-65 than later.
f) D.8. Three fragments, two joining, of form 37, with a winding scroll. The frilled leaf is one of a type used at La Graufesenque in the Neronian and Flavian periods, and cannot be assigned to a particular potter. The other leaf was used by Iucundus ii on a bowl at Vechten. The Nile goose (Hermet, 1934, pl. 28, 68) is a very common type. The seven-beaded rosette and the chevron festoon, rather than medallion, in the lower concavity of the scroll are unusual features. The bowl may just be pre-Flavian, and probably falls within the range *c*. A.D. 65-75.

AE II 10
a) Felix i 49g – see S. 12.
b) Form Ritt. 12, slightly burnt. Pre-Flavian.

AE III 16
a) Form Ritt. 1. Claudian or early-Neronian.
b) D.9. with another fragment in AE III 9, form 29. The upper zone has alternating (?) panels of trilobed leaves and corded medallions. The general size is reminiscent of that of bowls stamped by Bassus i-Coelus (cf. Knorr, 1919, Taf. 13). In any case, the piece falls within the period *c*. A.D. 50-65.

Sites DK and DM

Occupation on natural

DM I 133
a) Form 15/17R (Ritt. 4B). Neronian.
b) Form 24. Neronian.
c) Form 27. Neronian.

Gravel surfaces on natural

DM I 144
a) A fragment from the lower wall of a bowl of form

Ritt. 12 etc. Neronian?
b) Form 15/17. Neronian or early-Flavian.

Silt on natural and Phase I gravel surface

DK I 119
a) Three joining fragments, with two more in DK I 116, of form Ritt. 1 or 18, with a strong external offset. Early-Neronian.
b) Four joining fragments of form 18. Neronian.
c) From 15/17 or 18. Neronian or early-Flavian
d) Form 27. Neronian.

DK II 48
a) Form 15/17 (2). Both Neronian.
b) Form 15/17 or 18. Neronian or early-Flavian.
c) Form 18. Neronian.
d) Form 27. Neronian.

Phase II gravel surface

DM I 132
a) Form Ritt. 12 spout. Neronian.
b) Form 18(R?). Neronian.
c) Inkwell fragment. Neronian(?).
d) Dish fragment. First-century.

Pit Filling

DM I 154 – Bottom Layer
a) Form Ritt. 12 or Curle 11, Neronian or early-Flavian.
b) Form 15/17. Early-Flavian.
c) Form 18 (7, one slightly burnt). All Neronian or early-Flavian.
d) Form 27. Flavian.
e) Form 29. The winding scroll in the upper zone has pointed leaf tips in the lower concavities. Flavian.
f) Form 36 (2). Both Neronian or early-Flavian.
g) Form 36 (?), with an extraordinarily deep groove at the top of the inner wall. Neronian or early-Flavian.
h) Form 37 (?) rim. Flavian.

DM I 154 and 152
a) Form 15/17 (2, one slightly burnt). Both Flavian.
b) Form 18. Neronian or early-Flavian.
c) Form 27g, without a potter's stamp. The inside of the footring is covered with kiln-grit. Neronian or early-Flavian.
d) Form 29 rim. Flavian.
e) Form 30 or 37 rim. Flavian.

DM I 145 – upper levels of pit
a) Form Curle 11 flange. Early-Flavian.
b) Form 15/17. Flavian.
c) Form 15/17 or 18. Neronian or early-Flavian.
d) Germanus i 13c – see S. 13.
e) Form 35/36 with barbotine blobs on the outer wall just below the flange. These appear to be deliberate rather than accidental splashes from the barbotine nozzle. Flavian.

Phase I surface – Silt around stones DM I 148

DM I 143
A scrap. Pre-Flavian.

Second phase of gravel surfaces

DK I 116 (= DK II 45)
a) Two adjoining fragments, with three more in DK I 119 a), of form Ritt. 1 or 18. See DK I 119.
b) Form 15/17. Pre-Flavian.
c) Three fragments of the same dish of form 18. Neronian.
d) Two joining fragments of form 18(R?). Neronian.
e) Cosius Urap(p)us 1a – see S. 7.
f) Form 24. Pre-Flavian.
g) Form 27, with a beaked lip. Early-Neronian.
h) Form 27. Neronian.
i) Form 27. Neronian or early-Flavian.
j) Three fragments. First-century.

DK II 45 (= DK I 116)
a) Form 15/17 or 18. Neronian or early-Flavian.
b) Form 30, with a scroll and webbed leaf used by several potters of La Graufesenque including Scottius i (on a bowl from Urmitz). *c.* A.D. 45-60.
c) Form 18/31 or 31, Central Gaulish. Hadrianic or Antonine.

Silt on Phase II gravel surface

DK II 47
a) Form 15/17 or 18. Pre-Flavian.
b) Form 18. Pre-Flavian.
c) See DK II 42 c).

Gravel layers on DK I 111

DK I 105
Form 24. Neronian.

Occupation on ? Phase II gravel surfaces

DK I 109
Form 18, with an external offset at the junction of the base and wall. Neronian.

Well or Pit Filling

DK I 115 – bottom layer
Form 18. Claudian or early-Neronian.

DK I 114
a) Quartus ii 8a – see S. 39.
b) Two fragments of the same cup of form 27. Neronian.

? Phase III occupation

DK I 107 – top layer
a) Form 18. Claudian or early-Neronian.
b) Five fragments, four joining, of form 24, with a deep band of rouletting above the cordon. Claudio-Neronian.
c) Form 15/17, deep and rather crudely made. Almost certainly Flavian.

DK I 106 – patch over DK I 107
a) Form 18 etc. Neronian.
b) A fragment of form 29 base. Claudian.

DK II 46
a) D.10. Three fragments, two joining, of a bowl of

form 29, with a continuous winding scroll in both upper and lower zones. Identical upper zones are on bowls from Chester and Valkenburg ZH stamped by Crestio and the same scroll, apart from the tie, occurs on an unstamped fragment from Aislingen (Knorr, 1912, Taf. II, 3). The tassel is on form 29s from Heerlen and Leicester stamped by Aquitanus and from Mainz-Weisenau stamped by Celadus. The large, trifid motif in the lower zone was used by several pre-Flavian potters, including Aquitanus (at Vechten) and Crestio (at La Graufesenque). It is also on an unstamped bowl from Per.2 construction at Fishbourne. The five-petalled leaf has no exact parallel, but the cluster of buds is a common type. *c*. A.D. 50–65.

b) See DK II 42 c).

DK I 103
a) Form Ritt. 8. Neronian.
b) Form Ritt. 9. Claudio-Neronian.
c) Primus iii 20b – see S. 38.

DK I 102
a) Form 15/17. Neronian.
b) Form 24. Neronian.
c) Two joining fragments of form 24, from the cup S. 38.
d) Form 27. Neronian.
e) D.11. Form 29, lower zone, with nautilus gadroons and spear heads springing from the trefoil motifs. The gadroons (for which see Oswald, 1951, 149-152), derived from the late-Arretine tradition, were used at La Graufesenque in the Tiberio-Claudian period. The large beads and the rounded profile of this bowl are also typical of the period *c*. A.D. 40-55.

DK II 44
Forms 15/17 or 18 and 18. Both Neronian.

DK II 43
A wall fragment of form 18. Neronian or early-Flavian.

DK I 112
a) Two fragments of a cup of form Ritt. 9. Neronian.
b) Three fragments from a cup of form 27, with a flattened bead-lip typical of Claudian and early-Neronian examples.

DK I 117
Form 24. Claudio-Neronian?

DK II 94
A small scrap. Pre-Flavian.

DK I 90
Forms 15/17 or 18 and 18. Both Neronian or early-Flavian.

DK I 97
D.12. Four fragments of form 37. Mercato(r) i, one of whose ovolos this is, has a similar large scroll on a bowl from London (BM), with the lower concavities divided horizontally with a plant above and an animal below. However, the composition of the plant is unusual, with a fan-shaped motif of spirals, long spindles and poppy heads, none of which seem to be used by him. The dog in one of the lower concavities is Hermet, 1934, pl. 26, 41. The upper concavity of the scroll presumably contained a leaf, though the surviving decoration does not suggest one. Whether by Mercato(r) or not, the bowl

falls witin the range *c*. A.D. 80-110.

Filling of timber slot

DK I 110
Dish fragment. Neronian?

Pit Filling

DM I 136 – bottom layer
a) Form Ritt. 12. Neronian.
b) Form 15/17 or 18. Neronian or early-Flavian.
c) Form 27. Neronian.
d) Form 29, with straight gadroons. Neronian or early-Flavian.
e) D.13. Matches DK I 81 i) and DM I 19. Form 30, with arcades separated by wavy lines topped with tri-lobed motifs. The latter is probably the same as ones appearing on bowls of form 29 stamped by Crispus i, from Vechten (Utrecht) and Primus iii, from Neuss. The draped figure in one arcade is probably a version of Hermet, 1934, pl. 20, 124. The small ovolo was used on form 30s of the pre-Flavian period. *c*. A.D. 50-65.

DM I 134 – upper layer
Form 24. Pre-Flavian.

Pit filling

DK II 42
None of the material here is necessarily later than the Neronian period. The plain ware consists of forms Ritt. 12(3), 15/17(4), 15/17R (burnt), 15/17 or 18 (several, including two stamped pieces), 18 (several, one with a rivet hole, one (burnt) in orange, micaceous fabric typical of first-century Lezoux ware), 24 and 27 (at least 6).

Decorated Ware

a) Form 29 base, burnt.
b) D.14. Three fragments of form 29, with a winding scroll in the upper zone and straight gadroons in the lower. The spirals in the scroll, the small rosette and the five-beaded tie were all used at La Graufesenque by several Neronian potters. The trilobed tassel, supported by a row of beads, is unusual in a scroll, and may have been put in as a space-filler. However, compare a bowl from London (LM) stamped by Gallicanus (Knorr, 1952, Taf. 52, 26A), which has leaf tassels in a scroll which is perhaps freehand. *c*. A.D. 45-60.
c) Two joining fragments of form 30, with a joining flake in DK II 46 and another scrap in 47. The scroll with large and small leaves is similar to those on two form 30s in the Fort Ditch material and the ovolo is the same as on one of these. The latter is also on a signed form 30 of Albinus i from Silchester and on a stamped one of Martialis i from Usk. The larger leaf is on form 29s from Xanten (CVT), stamped by Namus, and Alésia, stamped by Pass(i)enus. The smaller leaf may also be on the Xanten bowl and occurs on a bowl from Neuss stamped by Primus iii. It may be a bad impression of a leaf found on bowls stamped by Crestio (Vichy), Daribitus (Vechten) and Rufinus ii (the London fort). The loosely-curled spirals on the scroll are unusual. *c*. A.D. 50-65.

Potters' Stamps

1) Martius ii 2a – see S. 19.
2) Unidentified fragment – see S. 56.

'Quarry' Filling

DM I 158

a) Form Ritt. 12 or Curle 11. Neronian or early-Flavian.
b) Form 18. Neronian.
c) A fragment of the plain band above the decoration of a bowl of form 30. Neronian or early-Flavian.
d) Five fragments, two joining, from the same bowl as DM I 137 s) *qv.*.
e) Form 30, with an ovolo with traces of a bead row, above it. Neronian or early Flavian.
f) A scrap, slightly burnt. First-century.

DM I 137 – top layer, equivalent to sealing-off layers

a) Form Ritt. 12 flange, slightly burnt. Pre-Flavian.
b) Form 15/17. Neronian.
c) Form 15/17 slightly burnt. Neronian (?).
d) Licinus 23b – see S. 18.
e) Germanus i 28i – see S. 14.
f) Fragments of four dishes of form 15/17 or 18. Flavian.
g) Fragments of dishes of form 18 (3?). All Neronian.
h) Fragments of four dishes of form 18, one slightly burnt. All Flavian.
i) Form 22. Flavian.
j) Form 27 (approximately 14, one slightly burnt). Some Neronian, some Flavian.
k) Form 36. Flavian.
l) D.15. With DM I 19 l) two fragments from the same form 29, with a continuous winding scroll in the lower zone. The serrated leaf was used at La Graufesenque by more than one potter in the Neronian and early-Flavian periods. The spindle and chevron junction-mask are more typical of the Neronian than the Flavian period. *c.* A.D. 55-70.
m) D.16. Form 29, upper zone, with a winding scroll with spindles and spirals. Chevron scrolls of this kind are unusual and tend to occur in the Neronian period at La Graufesenque. The spindles and spirals are on a scroll on a bowl from Mainz stamped by Fabus i. *c.* A.D. 50-65.
n) Form 29, with a basal wreath of chevrons. Neronian or early-Flavian.
o) Form 29 rim. Neronian or early-Flavian.
p) Form 29 rim, Flavian.
q) Form 29, with a winding scroll with spirals in the upper zone and coarse rouletting on the rim. Flavian.
r) Form 29, with a deep upper zone with a panel of pointed leaf tips flanked by diagonal wavy lines. Flavian.
s) D.17. Seven fragments and five more in DM I 158, of form 29, with an upper zone of alternating panels of animals and pointed leaf tips. The chevron wreath below the central moulding can be paralleled on a form 37 from Fishbourne (Dannell, 1971, fig. 135, 93). Below the wreath is a winding scroll with stirrup leaves and spirals. The general characteristics of the bowl are Flavian rather than earlier, with coarse decoration and large beads bordering a clumsy central moulding. The dog (Hermet, 1934, pl. 26, 18) and hare (*ibid.*, 56) and the leaf tips are common on bowls stamped by such potters as Calvus i, Meddillus and Vitalis ii. The scroll can be paralleled (apart from the tiny tulip leaf) on form 29 from Rottweil

(Knorr, 1912, Taf. VII, 8). The potter seems to have had difficulty in joining up the separate elements of the scroll and the tulip leaf is consistently detached from its tendril. *c.* A.D. 70-85.
t) Form 29, with a spiral. First-century.
u) Form 30 rim. Neronian or early-Flavian.
v) D.18. Several fragments, some joining, of form 37, with a trident-tongued ovolo and panels of serrated leaf tips and triple medallions with corner tassels over a chevron wreath. The decoration can be closely paralleled on a bowl from the Pompeii Hoard (Atkinson, 1914, 60). The animals are probably a dog (not identified) and a goat (Hermet, 1934, pl. 27, 36?). *c.* A.D. 75-90.
w) Form 37, with a trident-tongued ovolo and triple festoons containing stirrup leaves. Both were used on bowls from Camelon, but there in double festoons. *c.* A.D. 75-95.
x) Form 37, with an ovolo used at La Graufesenque by Memor (Knorr, 1919, Taf. 70, 16), with a chevron wreath below it. *c.* A.D. 75-95.
y) Form 67 base. Flavian.

Layers sealing the military occupation

DK I 81

Some of the sherds in this group join ones in DM I 19, but the groups have been recorded separately. The plain ware includes forms Ritt. 1, Ritt. 8, Ritt. 9 (two, one stamped), Ritt. 12 (3), 15/17 (several), 15/17R, 15/17 or 18 (several, three with stamps), 15/17R or 18R (several), 18 (many), 18R (several), 24 (several), 27 (many, some with a footstand groove and one with a stamp) and 35. Nearly all the material is pre-Flavian and a few pieces are Claudian or Claudio-Neronian. The proportion of Flavian sherds is low. One sherd of form 18/31 or 31 is Central Gaulish and Antonine.

Decorated Ware

a) D.19. With one sherd in DM I 19, five fragments of form 29, with a rouletted central moulding. The upper zone has a rosette and the lower a winding scroll with a finely-ribbed leaf and a cluster of berries. The leaf occurs on a bowl from Brumath (Knorr, 1952. Taf. 2) stamped by Amandus ii, who made bowls with rouletted central mouldings. This piece is probably to be dated *c.* A.D. 40-50.
b) Form 29, with a straight godroons in the lower zone. Claudian or early-Neronian.
c) D.20. Form 29, with a lower zone of panels of saltires and double medallions probably alternating round the bowl. This arrangement was common at La Graufesenque in the Neronian and occasionally the early-Flavian period and appears on bowls stamped by, for instance, Crestio and Felix i. There are also several examples of the style in the Pompeii Hoard (Atkinson, 1914, pls. II, III). The heart-shaped leaf in the saltire is perhaps the same as one on a bowl from Mainz stamped by Felix i (Knorr, 1952, Taf. 23A). The tassel occurs on a bowl from London (LM) stamped by Rufinus ii. The animal in the medallion is probably a stag. *c.* A.D. 50-65.
d) Form 29, with broad, pointed leaf tips. Neronian.
e) D.21. Two joining fragments of a badly-made bowl of form 29, with a flat scroll in the upper zone. Such scrolls are typical of the Claudian period at La

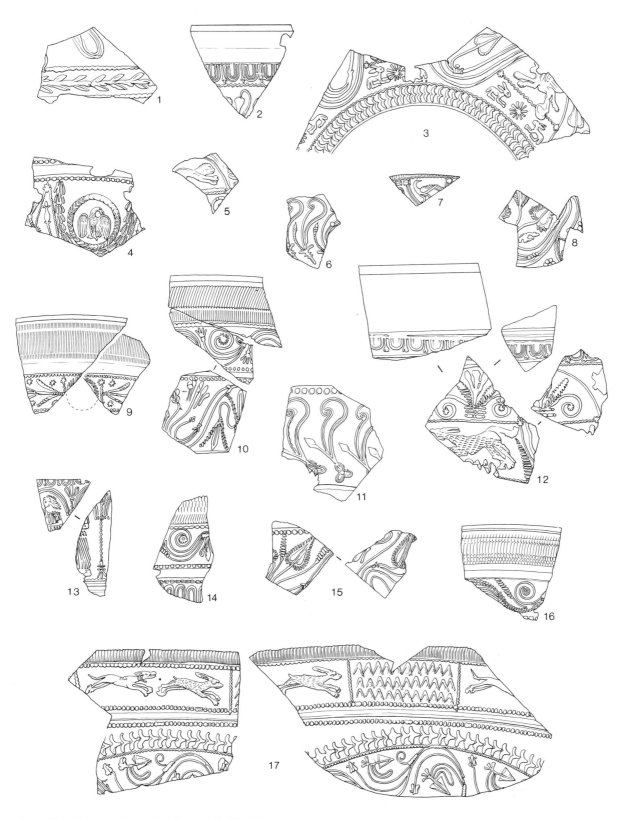

Fig. 42. Decorated samian (nos. D.1–17, 1:2)

Fig. 43.   Decorated samian (nos. D.18–37, 1:2)

Graufesenque, but the lower zone, with panels of saltires and corded medallions is certainly Neronian in style and the fabric and glaze support the later date.

f) D.22. A fragment of the upper zone of form 29, with a head with a wreath (Hermet, 1934, pl. 24, 297), a large thirteen-petalled rosette and a smaller rosette. The rosettes both appear on bowls stamped by Bassus i-Coelus and the head is associated with stamped bowls of Albus i, Rufinus ii and Peregrinus i (identified by G.B. Dannell (1964, 147-152) as Petrecus). These potters have certain motifs in common with Bassus i-Coelus, and it is likely that this piece is by the latter. c. A.D. 55-75.

g) D.23. A small fragment of form 29, with a zone of stubby palisades below the central moulding. An identical zone can be seen on bowls from Fishbourne (Period 2 construction: Dannell, 1971, fig. 128, 31) and Nijmegen, the latter stamped by Pass(i)enus of La Graufesenque. The palisades are also common at Rottweil on form 29 (Knorr, 1912, Taf. VI). c. A.D. 65-80.

h) D.24. Two fragments of form 30, and others in DK II 41, 43. The ovolo, the same as on i), is common on form 30 at La Graufesenque in the pre-Flavian period. The scroll with looped leaf and cluster of berries is of a type current in the Claudio-Neronian period. The basal wreath of trifid motifs is unusual. c. A.D. 45-60.

i) D.13. With DM I 19, two fragments of form 30, with the same ovolo as the last. The draped figure (Hermet, 1934, pl. 20, 124) in an arcade was used by several potters at La Graufesenque in the Claudio-Neronian period (cf. ibid., pl. 73, 13, 14; 74, 12). c. A.D. 45-60.

j) D.25. A small fragment of form 30, with a straight wreath of trifid motifs with broad central blade flanked by diagonally-striated blades. c. A.D. 60-80.

k) D.26. Form 37, with zonal decoration, the upper surviving zone divided into panels. The birds occur on form 29 from London (BM) stamped by Licinus (Knorr, 1952, Taf. 34B). The leaf tips are probably the same as ones on form 29 from London (GH). The lower zone contains a motif used at La Graufesenque on both decorated and plain ware, as a rosette stamp on the latter, and on form 29 from Rheingönheim stamped by Labio (Knorr, 1952, Taf. 32C). This bowl is probably just pre-Flavian, and of the period c. A.D. 60-70.

l) D.27. Form 37, with a stag (D.845) used on form 29 from Vindonissa stamped by Secundus ii (Knorr, 1919, Taf. 74C) and a basal wreath, on form 29 from London stamped by Iucundus ii. c. A.D. 75-90.

m) Form 67. Flavian.

Potters' stamps

1) Niger ii 9b – see S. 30.
2) Pass(i)enus 40a – see S. 32.
3) Secundus i 2c – see S. 43.
4) Severus i Pud(ens) 3a´ – see S. 46.
5) Unidentified stamp – see S. 54.

DK II 39

a) Form 15, slightly burnt. Probably Claudian, to judge by the exceptionally pale fabric and brownish glaze.
b) Form 15/17. Neronian.
c) Form 15/17 or 18. Probably Neronian.
d) Fragments of a least two dishes of form 18. Neronian.

e) Form 18 Neronian or early-Flavian.
f) Form 27g footring. Neronian.
g) Form 27. Neronian.
h) Form 29 rim. Neronian.
i) Form 29, upper zone, with triple festoons containing stirrup leaves, separated by pendants with tulip leaf tassels. An identical zone occurs on two form 37s at Camelon and a similar one at Bainbridge. The standard of workmanship and the fabric and glaze all support a date c. A.D. 70-85.
j) D.28. Three joining fragments of form 29, with an unidentified stamp ..MNII.. (see – S. 51). The upper zone of elliptical festoons containing birds and pendants with heart-shaped tassels can be paralleled in the lower zone of form 29 from Vechten stamped by Censor i (Knorr, 1919, Taf. 22B). The scroll in the lower zone has almond-shaped leaves for which there is no exact parallel. The medallion, composed of concentric striated, plain and large-beaded circles with a rosette at the centre is also unusual. The elliptical festoons suggest a pre-Flavian date, though the poor standard of workmanship is not common in that period. A date c. A.D. 65-80 should cover the range.
k) Form 18R. Neroinan or early-Flavian.

DK II 40

a) Licinus 23a – see S. 17.
b) Form Ritt. 12 flange, with a groove cut after firing on the upper side. Neronian.
c) Form 15/17. Neronian.
d) Fragments of at least seven dishes of form 18. Neronian.
e) Form 27 (2). Neronian or early-Flavian.
f) Form 29 rim. Neronian.
g) Form 29, with an upper zone with a continuous winding scroll, perhaps with a bird on the end of a tendril, as at Castleford, in the Pompeii Hoard and at Verulamium (Hartley, B.R., 1972, D.23) and Wroxeter. Neronian or early-Flavian.
h) Form 29, a fragment of the lower zone with blurred decoration. Perhaps Flavian, to judge by the clumsiness of the workmanship and the thick fabric.
i) D.29. Form 37, partly burnt. The rosette-tongued ovolo and similar chevron wreaths occur on bowls in the Pompeii Hoard (Atkinson, 1914, 45, 48, 49). c. A.D. 70-85.
j) D.30. Form 37, with zonal decoration. The upper zone of festoons containing spirals and pendants with poppy head tassels is a common type at La Graufesenque in the early-Flavian period on both forms 29 and 37 (cf. Knorr, 1919, Taf. 24E for a similar one from Vechten). The lower zone has a scroll with a detached tendril and a fan-shaped leaf. The other leaf is probably a triangular one of the type used by late-Neronian and Flavian potters. c. A.D. 75-95.
k) Form 67, with a small ovolo not recorded on signed bowls. Flavian.

DK II 41

a) Form 29 rim. Neronian or early-Flavian.
b) Form 30, with a small ovolo used at La Graufesenque by potters such as Masc(u)lus i. c. A.D. 55-70.
c) Four fragments of the same bowl as DK I 81 h), qv.

DM I 19

The material is substantially the same as DK I 81 and several sherds of decorated ware join others there. All of it is Neronian, with the exception of forms 15/17R and 35/36, which might be early-Flavian, and form 31, Central Gaulish and Antonine. The plain ware includes forms Ritt. 1, Ritt. 12 (3), 15/17 (4), 15/17 or 18 (several, one stamped), 18 (several), 18R (several), 24, 27 (several with footstand groove and one with a stamp), 31 (with stamp), 35/36 and an inkwell.

Decorated Ware

a) See DK I 81 a).

b) D.31. Form 29, with a basal (?) wreath composed of the same ribbed leaf as in DK I 81 a), *qv.* for comments.

c) D.32. A fragment of the upper zone of form 29, with a scroll containing a shell-shaped leaf and fine-petalled rosette. A bowl with possibly the identical zone occurs at Burghöfe (Ulbert, 1959, Taf. 36, 6). Claudio-Neronian.

d) D.33. Two fragments of the upper zone of form 29. The elliptical festoons suggest a pre-Flavian date. The tassel occurs on bowls stamped by Licinus (*cf.* Knorr, 1919, Taf. 45, 39) and the small rosettes supporting a pendant occur on a bowl from Hofheim stamped by him. *c.* A.D. 45-60.

e) A fragment of the upper zone of form 29. The fine rouletting on the rim suggests a Neronian date, probably early in the period.

f) D.34., with DM I 135 h) two fragments of a bowl of form 29, with the upper zone and the zone below the carination composed of two separate leaves impressed stem to stem. The style, with the minimum of background showing, is reminiscent of bowls stamped by Ardacus, Bassus i-Coelus, Seno and others. A bowl from London (LM) stamped by Seno has the same leaf in the lower zone. The basal wreath is composed of unusual chevrons. *c.* A.D. 50-70.

g) Form 29, with a winding scroll in the lower zone. The leaf was used at La Graufesenque on bowls stamped by Murranus (Knorr, 1919, Taf. 59, 11). Neronian.

h) A small fragment of the lower zone of form 29, with a scroll with an elongated leaf and a boar (Hermet, 1934, pl. 27, 50?) used at La Graufesenque by several potters of the Neronian and early-Flavian periods.

i) see DK I 81 i).

j) Form 37. Flavian.

k) A tiny fragment of form 37, with an ovolo used at La Graufesenque by Paullus iii, but probably by earlier potters too. *c.* A.D. 75-100.

l) see DM I 137 l).

Potters' Stamps

1) Crestio 5a – see S. 8.
2) Paullus i – see S. 34.
3) Reditus 3b – see S. 40.

DM I 62

a) Form 18, two. Pre-Flavian.

b) Form 27. Pre-Flavian.

DM I 65

a) A fragment of the flange and part of the wall of a very small example of form Ritt. 12. Claudio-Neronian.

b) Form 18. Neronian or early-Flavian.

c) Form 18R. Neronian or early-Flavian.

d) Form 18R. Flavian.

e) Form 27. Flavian.

f) Form 29 rim, with coarse rouletting. Early-Flavian.

g) D.35. Form 29, with a deep upper zone of triple medallions, one containing a stirrup leaf, and pendants with five-petalled tassels. Early-Flavian. See DM I 120 for other fragments.

h) Form 35/36. Flavian.

i) A fragment of the plain band above the decoration of a large bowl of form 37. Flavian.

j) D.36. Five fragments, some joining, of a bowl of form 37, with some panels divided horizontally. The saltire has a plant used at La Graufesenque by several potters including M. Crestio, who has it in the basal wreath on a bowl from Nijmegen (Knorr, 1919, Taf. 28B). He also used the cluster of buds (*cf. ibid.*, A on a bowl from Bregenz). The boar below the saltire is Hermet, 1934, pl. 27, 42. The erotic figure in the adjacent panel is D.315. M. Crestio was one of the few potters at La Graufesenque to use an ovolo with a four-pronged tongue. The basal wreath, which also separates some panels, does not seem to have been recorded for him. *c.* A.D. 75-95.

k) Bowl (?) fragment. Neronian or early-Flavian.

DM I 120

a) Form Ritt.12 flange. Neronian.

b) Two fragments of the same form 18. Neronian.

c) Form 24. Neronian.

d) One or two fragments of the same form 29 as DM I 65 g), one with the corresponding stirrup leaf, the other (perhaps from this bowl) with a fragment of the lower zone with a multi-petalled leaf.

e) Form 36 flange. Neronian or early-Flavian.

DM I 130

a) Fragments of two cups of form Ritt. 9. Neronian.

b) Form Ritt. 12 flange, slightly burnt. Neronian.

c) Two fragments of the same dish of form 15/17R (Ritt. 4B). Neronian.

d) Fragments of form 18 (a minimum of four, one with kiln grit on the footring). All Neronian.

e) Form 24. Neronian.

f) D.37. Two joining fragments of a bowl of form 29. The lower zone has a wreath of three-petalled motifs below the central moulding and corded medallions containing three-leaved motifs and separated by columns. A similar, but slightly smaller, medallion occurs on a bowl from Mainz stamped by G.Salarius Aptus (Knorr, 1919, Taf. 85) and a bowl from La Graufesenque with a stamp of his has the leaf. One stamp of this potter occurs on plain ware in the material from the fort ditch. *c.* A.D. 50-65.

g) Footring of a bowl (of form Ritt.12 or, more probably, Curle 11), slightly burnt. Probably Flavian.

h) Footring fragment, probably from a rouletted dish. Neronian.

DM I 131

a) Form 15/17 or 18. Neronian or early-Flavian.

b) Form 18R, with other sherds in DM I 135 e). Flavian.

DM I 135

a) Form Ritt. 12 flange. Neronian.

b) Fragments of three dishes of Form 15/17 or 18. All Flavian.

c) Two fragments of the same form 18, Claudio-Neronian.

d) Fragments of approximately three dishes of form 18. All Neronian.

e) Three fragments, probably all from the same form 18R, with another sherd in DM I 131 b). Flavian.

f) Two fragments of a cup of form 27, with a flattened bead lip. Claudio-Neronian.

g) Fragments of two cups of form 27. Both Neronian.

h) A slightly burnt fragment from the same bowl as DM I 19 f). qv.

i) form 29 rim. Neronian.

j) Form 29, with a chevron scroll used at La Graufesenque by potters of the Neronian period.

k) Three fragments from dishes. All pre-Flavian.

THE MAJOR DEFENSIVE DITCHES

Site AM

Group from Ditch III
AM II 59

It is evident from the nature of the samian found in the ditch that we are dealing with a substantially contemporary group of vessels dumped when complete, and that there is extremely little residual material. The key point is that the footrings of the vessels are unworn, and that they, and the internal bases of the pots, nearly all have particles of fine white grit embedded in them. Such grit was regularly used by samian potters at the points of contact between the footrings of vessels and the bases of the pots stacked on them, in order to diminish the risk of fusion during firing. When the pots were used, and washed, the grit tended to become detached rapidly. It may also be added that the inkwells have no carbon stains of the kind usual with ones which have been in use.

It follows that the group must have been derived from a store in the fort or a shop in the *vicus*, presumably the former.

It will be best to list the samian from the ditch in the categories of (A) decorated ware, (B) potters' stamps and (C) plain forms, before discussing the date of the group as a whole. All of the samian is from South Gaul, and almost certainly all from La Graufesenque.

A. Decorated Ware

i. Form 29

In South Gaul decorated bowls of form 29 were rarely produced from signed or stamped moulds. The internal stamp applied after moulding does not necessarily indicate that the potter stamping had anything to do with making the mould. Indeed it is comparatively rarely (e.g. in the work of Bassus i–Coelus and Germanus i) that a style of decoration can be identified as that of a specific potter or group of workers. Accordingly, we quote parallels for both general styles and details of decoration for the bowls in this group without necessarily firmly indicating connexions with particular workshops.

a) D.38. A more or less complete bowl, diameter 25 cm, stamped IVCV·NDI (Iucundus ii 12a). The tulip-shaped leaf in the scroll of the upper zone occurs on a bowl of uncertain provenance in Roanne museum, stamped OFAQVITĀNI (Aquitanus 2a). Below the carination is an overall zone of pointed leaf tips. Such a scheme is not common, but it occurs, with different leaf tips, on a bowl at London (BM), stamped OFCRESTIO (Crestio 5b). The scroll at the bottom of the lower zone is uncommon, as is the straight line separating it from the zone above.

Iucundus ii worked at La Graufesenque. This stamp seems to have been used exclusively on form 29. It does not occur at any dated sites. Much of his output is Flavian, but he occasionally made forms 24 and Ritt. 9, so must have started work in the pre-Flavian period. This is presumably one of his earliest stamps.

b) D.39. A more or less complete bowl, diameter 24 cm., stamped OFPRIMI (Primus iii 12d). The style of decoration is very common in the Neronian period and similar bowls occur at Silchester, stamped OFMODESTĪ (Modestus i 2d), and, unstamped, at Aislingen (Knorr, 1912, Taf, II, 3) and in the Colchester Second Pottery Shop (Hull, 1958, fig. 102, 14). No

Fig. 44. Decorated samian (nos. D.38–42, 1:2)

identical upper zone has appeared, but there are many similar ones on bowls stamped MANDIO retr. (Amandus ii 9a), from London (Knorr, 1952, Taf. 33F), two from Pompeii, stamped OFBASSI·CO (recorded by D. Atkinson) and GERMANIOF (Germanus i 13a, also with the chevron tie on the scroll), and, unstamped, from the Colchester First Pottery Shop (Hull, 1958, fig 74, 3) and Fishbourne (Period 2 construction; Dannell, 1971, fig. 128, 22).

The Primus stamp occurs at La Graufesenque and was apparently used only on form 29. There is no site-dating for it, but Primus's record and the style of this piece suggest a date *c.* A.D. 45-65.

c) D.40. Approximately three quarters of a bowl of diameter 23.2 cm., stamped OFPRIMI (Primus iii 12d). The upper zone has rather unusual decoration, with a scroll with leaf tips in the lower concavities and roundels instead of rosettes on the ends of the tendrils. Similar roundels were used on a bowl from Mainz, stamped FABVSFE (Fabus i 5a; Knorr, 1919, Taf. 30E, wrongly attributed to Carus i), and in the work of the so-called Canrucatus-Vegetus group (Hermet, 1934, pl. 104, 27-34: the first potter really being Cabucatus). The leaf occurs on bowls stamped ⊖FICBILICAT (Bilicatus 4a), from Leicester and)F·MVR·T[(Mur..-Ter..1a´) from London (LM). The pomegranate seems to be an unusual type. For a similar lower zone ascribed (wrongly) to Melus see a bowl from Rheingönheim (Ulbert, 1969, Taf. 4,21). The chevron scroll was used on a bowl stamped OF·ARDACI· (Ardacus 6a) from Mandeure and on one from Unterkirchberg in the style associated with Daribitus (Knorr, 1919, Taf. 21a). The larger leaf occurs on a bowl from Neuss, stamped DARRA·FE (Darra 2a *ibid.*, Taf. 32). The smaller leaf seems to have no parallel. For the dating of the stamp, see b) above.

d) D.41. Approximately three quarters of a bowl of diameter 15 cm., stamped OFMODESTI (Modestus i 2g). The scroll in the upper zone has a tulip-shaped leaf used on bowls stamped OFAQVITAN (Aquitanus 2a) at Wiesbaden, OFCRESTIO (Crestio 5b) at London (BM), GERMANI (Germanus i 28e) at La Graufesenque (Rodez museum), OFRVFIN (Rufinus ii 4a) at Torre Annunziata (before A.D. 79). The leaf also occurs on bowl p). The whole upper zone is almost identical with one on a bowl from a mould signed before firing Mod (by Modestus i), and stamped after moulding OFFEICIS (Felix i 2d). This bowl has in its lower zone the same leaf as the larger one in the lower zone of the Cirencester piece. The leaf also occurs on bowls from Silchester and Strasbourg stamped OFCRESTIO (Crestio 5b and 5c respectively). The bunch of berries or grapes occurs on bowl m). It was used on bowls stamped OF>CRESTIO (5a) from Camulodunum, OFCRESTIO (5c), without provenance, in the museum at Clermont-Ferrand, and ⌐EDOTVS⌐ retr. (Fedotus 1a) from London (LM). An almost identical lower zone was used on a bowl stamped MELVSFE(CI) (Melus 3a´), from Vindonissa (Knorr, 1919, Taf. 56A). The smaller looped leaf does not appear on stamped bowls, but occurs on a bowl from Aislingen (Knorr, 1912, Taf. IX. 5). This stamp of Modestus i has not been recorded from La Graufesenque, though he certainly worked there. It occurs at Hofheim, Usk and Wroxeter and is likely to be datable to *c.* A.D. 45-65.

e) D.42. Approximately half of a bowl of diameter 24.5 cm., with a scroll in the upper zone and a lower zone consisting of four horizontal wreaths. There is an almost identical upper zone on a bowl stamped GAⱯICANI (Gallicanus 9a) from Mainz-Weisenau (Knorr, 1919, Taf. 33). The fan-shaped leaf was also used on a bowl stamped OFMODESTI (Modestus i 2d) from Silchester and on an unstamped bowl in a Claudian pit at Richborough (Bushe-Fox, 1926, pl. XVII, 2). All the wreaths in the lower zone except for the third one can be paralleled on a bowl from Clermont-Ferrand (Coll. Souchon) where they were also used zonally, stamped MARTI (Martius ii 2a). The third wreath was used on a bowl stamped OFIVCVNDI (Iucundus ii 3a), from Vechten (Knorr, 1919, Taf. 44G). The first three wreaths occur on a bowl from London (CMAE), stamped OⱭMOM (Mommo 9d).

f) D.43. Approximately one third of a bowl of diameter 25 cm., with the lower zone divided horizontally into two bands, the upper one consisting of short, straight godroons. A similar scheme of decoration appears on bowls stamped MANDIO retr. (Amandus ii 9a), from London (Knorr, 1952, Taf. 33F), OF·MODESTI (Modestus i 2a), from Nijmegen, ¶RIMVⱭFE (Primus iii 37a) at York and VⱮDERIo (Vanderio 1a), from Nijmegen. The leaf in the wreaths of the upper zone is a common type and cannot be ascribed to any particular potter. The combination of the dog pursuing a hare to right is a common one, used, amongst others, by Felix i (Knorr, 1919, Taf. 32, 10, 12), Murranus (8a) on a bowl from London (LM), Niger ii (2a) and Niger ii-And.. (1a) at La Graufesenque (Hermet, 1934, pl. 106, 14) and Potitianus i (?) at London (LM). The dog, and possibly the space-fillers, were used on a bowl stamped OFCRESTIO (Crestio 5b) from London (BM). The crouching hare to right occurs on a bowl stamped OF·LABIONIS (Labio 1a), from Cologne (Knorr, 1952, Taf. 32A). Scrolls similar to the one in the lower half of this zone were used on bowls stamped OF·MVRRA (Murranus 10b), from Aachen (ibid., Taf. 44A), OFNIGRI (Niger ii 2a) from London (ibid., Taf. 47D) and one from a mould stamped OF·MVRRAN (Murranus 8a) from Mainz (ibid., Taf. 45D).

g) D.44. Approximately one quarter of a badly-moulded bowl of 27 cm. diameter. A similar upper zone, with elliptical festoons, was used on a bowl from Vechten, stamped OFBASSICO (Bassus i-Coelus 5a). The pendant was used by Melus i (3a), on a bowl from Mainz (Knorr, 1919, Taf. 56B). The larger leaf in the scroll of the lower zone occurs on bowls stamped OFBASSICO (5a) at La Graufesenque (Millau museum) and Trier and OFBASSI·CO (5c) at Hofheim and Strasbourg. In view of the parallels, production by a potter associated with the Bassus i-Coelus workshop seems highly likely.

h) D.45. A small fragment of the upper zone. The horizontal wreath occurs on a bowl stamped OFPRIAMI (Primus iii 12r), from Silchester (May, 1916, pl. VIIA) and on an unstamped vessel from Colchester (May, 1930, pl.XI, 26).

i) D.46 Two joining fragments of the upper zone, with a chevron medallion on the lower concavity of the scroll. This style of decoration is fairly common in the pre-Flavian period, and is used on bowls stamped OFBASSICO (Bassus i-Coelus 5a), at London (GH), OF·LABIONIS (Labio 1a), at Rheingönheim cemetery (Knorr, 1919, Textbild 43), OFMODESTI (Knorr, 1952, Taf. 43L) and on bowls from moulds stamped OF·MVRRAN (Murranus 8a) twice at Mainz (ibid., Taf. 45F, G). It also occurs on a bowl whose stamp has not survived, from the Colchester First Pottery Shop (Hull, 1958, fig. 74, 4, 10). The medallion is perhaps the same as one on a bowl said to be in the style of Masclus i (Knorr, 1919, Taf. 53B), and the motif inside it may have been used by Murranus and Rufinus ii (ibid, Textbild 6, 2).

j) D.47. A small fragment of the bowl. The upper zone has a plain medallion with vertical rows of diagonal beads to one side. The composition of the lower zone is most unusual. The elliptical festoon is the same as one used on a bowl from La Graufesenque (Rodez museum), stamped ME⊕ILLVS (5a). The rosette is probably the same as one used on a bowl at Strasbourg museum, stamped OF·RVFINI (Rufinus ii 2b).

k) D.48. A substantial fragment of the bowl. The larger leaf in the scroll of the upper zone is perhaps one said by Knorr (1952, Taf. 61) to have been used on bowls in the style of Senicio, Seno and Silvius. The smaller leaf is too blurred to be identifiable. The dog looking over its shoulder occurs on two bowls from the same mould stamped, after moulding, ALBIM (Albus i 6a), at La Graufesenque (ibid., Taf. 30A) and GENIALISF (Genialis i 2a) at Vindonissa (ibid.). It is also associated with bowls stamped by Modestus i, at Bayeux, and Primus iii, at Arlesey (BM). The leaping dog seems to be of a type not previously recorded. The arrangement of the lower zone and the elements of the decoration are reminiscent of potters like Amandus ii, Ingenuus ii, Senicio and Seno. The pointed leaf occurs on two bowls from the same mould, stamped OFNIGRI (Niger ii 2a) and OFNIGRI·AND (Niger ii-And.. 1a: Hermet, 1934, pl. 106, 14). This is typologically earlier than most of the material from the ditch and, as it is a single sherd, it is quite likely to be residual.

l) D.49. One fragment of the bowl survives. The leaf, ascribed by Knorr to Daribitus (1919, Textbild 9), appears on a bowl stamped by him at Vechten and on another from La Graufesenque (Rodez museum), stamped ALBVS·FE (Albus i 7a). It was also used on an unstamped bowl at Fishbourne (Period 1a: Dannell, 1971, fig. 126, 3). The leaf on bowls from moulds stamped OF·MVRRAN (Murranus 8a) at Colchester and London (LM) is probably this also. The cluster of buds was used on bowls stamped OFFEICIS (Felix i 2d) at Colchester, GENIALISF (Genialis i 2a) at Vichy, OFLICINI·VA (Licinus-Va.. 1a) at Vindonissa (Knorr, 1919, Taf. 47F) and OFIC·PRIMI (Primus iii 3d) at Vechten (ibid., Taf. 66D).

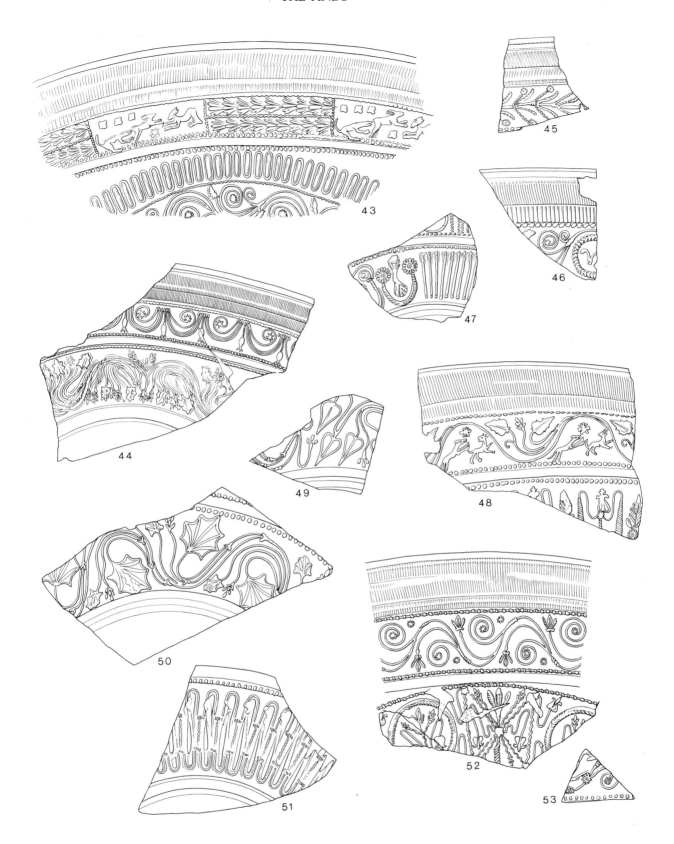

Fig. 45.   Decorated samian (nos. D.43–53, 1:1)

m) D.50. One large fragment of the lower zone. The larger leaf occurs on bowls stamped SEⱮICIO·FE(C) (Senicio 2a), from Aislingen (Knorr, 1912, Taf. 7, 1, 2) and Xanten. The tie on the scroll was used on a bowl with the same stamp from Vechten. For the bunch of berries or grapes, cf. bowl d). For the smaller leaf, cf. an unstamped bowl from Auerberg (Allgaü), with a similar lower zone (Knorr, 1952, Taf. 71D).

n) D.51. A large fragment with a rounded profile, in brown fabric with a dull glaze. The lower zone consists of straight gadroons separated by vertical wavy lines, terminated at either end by four horizontal beads. There are many examples of this general style, though most have bead rows instead of wavy lines, with chevron ends instead of beads. There is no exact parallel for this bowl, but there are similar ones at Neuss, stamped AC·V·T·I·M (Acutus i 24a) and ΘFICBILICAT (Bilicatus 4a), at Vichy (Coll. Morlet), stamped OFIC·FIRMI (Firmo i 1a), at Vechten (Knorr, 1919, Taf. 43C), stamped IVCVNDVS (Iucundus ii 15a) and at Aachen, stamped NÂMVSFE (Namus ii 3a; Knorr 1952, Taf. 46B). A bowl of uncertain provenance stamped SCOTTIVS (Hermet, 1934, pl. 122, 13) has astragalus ends to the wavy lines. In view of the date of most of the potters using this style and the rounded profile of the bowl it is almost certainly a residual sherd of the period c. A.D. 40-50.

o) D.52. Fourteen joining fragments, giving approximately one third of the bowl. The upper zone is rather deeper than usual. An identical scroll was used in the upper zone of a bowl at Rheingönheim (Ulbert, 1969, Taf. 5, 4), with nautilus gadroons in the lower zone. The leaf in the scroll and in the medallion in the lower zone was used on bowls at London (Knorr, 1952, Taf. 42A), stamped OF.MODESTI (Modestus i 2a) and La Graufesenque (Rodez museum), stamped OFNIGRI (Niger ii 2a). Surprisingly, relatively few potters used alternating panels of medallion and saltire in the lower zone, but they are found on bowls stamped by Aquitanus, Darra, Felix i, Macer i, Modestus i, Pass(i)enus and Primus iii. The trilobed leaf in the saltire was used on a bowl stamped OF·AQVITÂNI (Aquitanus 1b), from Vindonissa (Knorr, 1912, Taf. XVII, 4) and on one from a mould signed Ma[, by Masclinus or Masc(u)lus i, at London (BM). For details of the tulip-shaped leaf in the same panel, see bowl d).

p) D.53. A fragment of the upper zone, showing a scroll. Too little survives to indicate the scheme of decoration. The bead tie on the scroll is typical of several potters of the Claudio-Neronian period.

q) A fragment of the base only, with no decoration. The remains of a stamp (S. 53) reading OF[, have not been identified, though Modestus or Murranus are the likely candidates.

r) Rim fragments from several other bowls of form 29.

ii. Form 30

South Gaulish bowls of form 30 are rarely from stamped or signed moulds and almost never carry stamps impressed after moulding. It is accordingly virtually impossible to assign them to individual potters or groups of potters. Even dating is often difficult, since their styles of decoration tended to be very conservative until the mid-Flavian period.

a) D.54. Approximately two-thirds of a scroll bowl of diameter 13.7 cm. There is no ovolo, but its absence is probably intentional, because there is a wavy line at the top of the decoration and that is unusual below the ovolo on form 30 in this style. The two leaves were used on a bowl from Vichy (MAN), stamped OFCRESTIO (Crestio 5b) and, possibly, also by Sabinus iii (Stanfield, 1937, 177, 87, 89). The larger leaf occurs on bowls stamped ΘFICBILICΛT (Bilicatus 4a) at London (BM: Knorr, 1952, Taf. 11A), OFFEICIS (Felix i 2d) in the Colchester Second Pottery Shop (Hull, 1958, fig. 101, 13) and SENOM (Seno 9a) at Vindonissa. It occurs also on a form 30 from a mould signed]us·f, by Masc(u)lus i, at London (de Groot, 1960, Abb. 4, 8). The smaller leaf is perhaps the one used on bowls from the London fort, stamped OFRVFIN (Rufinus ii 2b) and Cologne, stamped SECVNDIO (noted by D. Atkinson).

b) D.55. Two joining fragments, giving approximately one eighth of a scroll bowl. The ovolo with a wavy line above it was used on a bowl at Usk from a mould stamped MÂRTIALIS·F (Martialis i 11c: Boon, 1962, fig. 1). A bowl with decoration almost identical to the Usk one occurs in the Boudiccan burning at Verulamium (Hartley, B.R., 1972, D.4). The larger leaf Hermet, 1934, pl. 9, 43) does not seem to have been recorded on stamped or signed bowls. The smaller one is perhaps the same as one used on bowls from Vindonissa stamped OF·ARDACI· (Ardacus 6a) and Werwik, stamped IVCV.ND (Iucundus ii 12a).

c) D.56. Six fragments, including most of the base, giving about one quarter of the bowl. One pair of gladiators (D.603, 604), was used on bowls of form 29 stamped OFCRESTIO (Crestio 5c) from Mainz (Knorr, 1952, Taf. 17A) and OF·AQVITÃNI (Aquitanus 1b) from Heerlen. The other pair of gladiators is Hermet 172 & 173 (large versions of the types). The leaves in the scroll are not certainly identifiable, but the smaller may be Hermet, 1934, pl. 6, 37.

iii. Form 78

The two vessels of this form in the group have rounded carinations rather than the angular ones of Flavian-Trajanic examples.

a) D.57. One sherd, with rim and scroll decoration.

b) D.58. One fragment, showing a scroll above a band of vertical rows of beads.

B. Potters' Stamps

All the potters with stamps in this group worked at La Graufesenque, though not all the stamps are attested there, and occasionally attribution rests solely on distribution. We list all the stamps in alphabetical order, including those on decorated ware, except for two unidentified ones. The numbers for the potters and for the individual dies are those which will be used in the forthcoming Index of Potters' Stamps on Samian Ware.

1 – 3)	Amandus ii 4a, – see S. 1 – 3.
4)	Cennatus 3a – see S. 6.
5)	Crestio 9a´– see S. 9.
6 – 7)	Fabus 5a´– S. 10 - 11.
8)	Iucundus ii 12a – S. 15.
9)	Legitumus 1a´– S. 16.
10)	Modestus i 2a – S. 20.
11)	Modestus i 2g – S. 22.
12)	Modestus i 4e – S. 23.
13)	Murranus 10 c – S. 24.
14)	Murranus – S. 27.
15)	Nestor 2a – S. 28.
16)	Niger ii 4a – S. 29.
17)	Pass(i)enus 50a – S. 33.
18)	Primus iii 3d – S. 35.
19 – 20)	Primus iii 12d – S. 36 - 37.
21)	G. Salarius Aptus 3a – S. 42.
22)	Secundus i or ii 1b – S. 44.
23)	Senicio 6a – S. 45.
24)	Vitalis i´1d – S. 47.
25)	Vitalis i 6i – S. 48.
26)	Unidentified – S. 52.
27)	Unidentified – S. 53.

The date of the stamps

It is clear from the parallels noted above for the stamps in dated contexts and the frequency with which they appear on forms like 24, Ritt. 8 and 9 and 24, that the group as a whole must be assigned to the Neronian period. There are some parallels from Period I at Valkenburg ZH, but these probably have to be regarded with caution until the stratigraphic evidence (at present being reconsidered by Professor Glasbergen and his team), has been confirmed or otherwise. More precise evidence comes from the links with the Colchester Pottery Shops destroyed in A.D. 60 or 61. The identity of four of the Cirencester group of stamps with one occurring at Colchester is striking in such a small group and may be taken with a high degree of probability to point to the period A.D. 55-65. That a date before A.D. 55 is most unlikely is confirmed by the presence of stamps 16 and 23 (and of 8) in Flavian contexts.

Fig. 46.   Decorated samian (nos. D.54–71 and no. 61, 1:1; for the rest, 1:2)

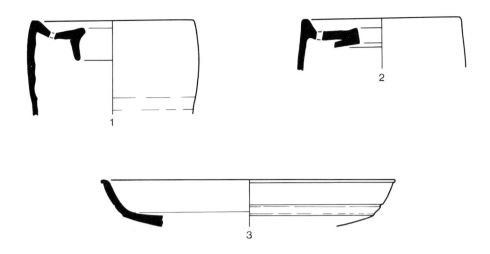

Fig. 47.   Plain samian (1:2)

C. The Plain Samian

Inkwells Two more or less complete inkwells and substantial fragments from three others were in the group. Most of them approximate to Ritterling form 13, but there is considerable variation of the detail of the non-spill collar. The Cirencester examples usually have one air hole in the top as well as the central opening. None has any trace of ink inside. The sizes are almost uniform, with the extreme range of the maximum diameter between 9 cm. and 9.7 cm. (fig. 47, nos. 1 and 2).

Ritterling 8 Only one stamped cup of this form was in the group, by Crestio (Section B5). Sherds from some five or six other examples were included in the group, but some may be residual.

Ritterling 12 There were substantial pieces of four bowls of Ritterling form 12, and fragments suggest that there were at least another five vessels represented. There was nothing particularly distinctive about the Cirencester bowls, which all had diameters of the order 26-27 cm., over the flange.

Form 15/17 There were three dishes of form 15/17, represented by substantial pieces, and five rim fragments, probably all from different vessels. The potters' stamps involved were those of Fabus (B6) and Murranus (B14). The more complete dishes had a diameter of 17.0 cm. and a height of 4.1 cm.   .

Form 15/17R (Ritterling 4B).   One more or less complete dish of this form carried the stamp of G. Salarius Aptus (B21). This dish is a standard example of the form but lacked the rouletting which should have been present between the two concentric circles scribed on the base. The other example of the form consisted of rim fragments only.

Form 18 The five more or less complete examples of form 18 all carried potters' stamps, namely those of Fabus (B7), Legitumus (B9), Nestor (B15), Niger ii (B16) and Vitalis i (B24). Two more dishes were represented by rim fragments only. Slight internal offsets were usual on most of the dishes, but only the dish of Vitalis i had an external offset at the junction of the base and wall. Rim diameters ranged from 14.6 cm. (Vitalis i) to 18.2 cm. (Niger i) but they were mostly around 17.3 cm. The heights ranged from 3.9 cm. to 4.1 cm., except for the Vitalis i dish, which had a height of 3.5 cm.

Form 18R Two more or less complete dishes of form 18R were stamped by Modestus i (B10) and Primus iii (B18). They had diameters and heights of 25.8, 5.5, 26.6 and 6.3 cm. respectively. A third dish, again stamped by Modestus i (B12), had only the base and part of the wall surviving.

Form 24 Only two substantial fragments of cups of form 24 were present, though at least six others were represented by small fragments. The only potter's stamp was one of Vitalis i (B25). There was little variation in the form, though some of the cups had surprisingly coarse rouletting above the external cordon.

Form 27 At least fifteen examples of form 27 were represented in the group, thirteen of them by substantial fragments. The potters' stamps included those of Amandus ii (B1-3), Cennatus (B4), Murranus (B13), Pass(i)enus (B17), Secundus i/ii (B22), Senicio (B23) and one unidentified example (B26). Most of the cups had prominent grooves around the footring, though two of the three by Amandus ii were entirely without grooves. The variation in rims was considerable and included both flat-topped and strongly-rounded ones. Most of the cups belonged to the larger size, with diameters of the order of 11.5 cm. to 13.5 cm., but the three cups of Amandus ii and one or two of the unstamped pieces had diameters in the range 7.4 cm. to 8.0 cm. The corresponding heights for the two sizes were 5.2 cm. to 6.9 cm. and 4.1 cm. to 4.4 cm.

Discussion of date

The parallels quoted above for the styles of decoration involved in the group show that the connections are with potters such as Aquitanus, Ardacus, Bassus i-Coelus, Crestio, Felix i, Gallicanus, Martius ii, Melus, Modestus i, Mommo, Murranus, Niger ii, Primus iii and Rufinus ii, all active in the Neronian period, though some of them still worked under Vespasian. The parallels with the Colchester Pottery Shops, burnt in A.D. 60 or 61, are particularly striking and scarcely less so is the absence of parallels from Flavian foundations. In other words, it seems clear that we are dealing with the relatively early work of the Neronian-Flavian potters. The evidence of the potters' stamps, as already discussed above, points to a similar conclusion and, while the plain ware is not capable of being dated with such precision as either the decorated ware or the stamps, it is quite clearly consistent with a Neronian date, and it would be surprising indeed if the date of deposition of the group did not fall in the decade A.D. 55-65. On the whole, the general impression of the samian ware perhaps favours the second half of the period slightly, but such a judgement is essentially subjective.

Filling of Ditch IV

AM III 44

a) Fragment of a cup in orange micaceous fabric, with a matt orange slip, suggesting origin at Lezoux in the Claudian or early-Neronian period.
b) Fragment of form 18. Neronian.
c) Fragment of form 27. Neronian.

AM III 35

A group of fragments, including forms 15/17(2), 15/17R or 18R, 18 (2), 27 and 27g. The rouletted dish and the form 27 have kiln grit on them. The group is almost certainly Neronian and *c.* A.D. 55-70.

The Inter-ditch areas

AM IV 41

a) Fragment of a bowl, probably of form Ritt. 12. Neronian.
b) Fragment of form 15/17R or 18R, stamped OFMODEST[I], joining AL VII 31, Modestus i 2a of 2a′ – see S. 21.
c) Fragment of the same form 18 as AL VII 12, AL VII 31, AM VII 30. The piece has a flat rim, shallow outward-sloping wall and a step in the profile at the external junction of the base and wall. The fabric shows no mica, but its colour, texture and glaze are typical of Lezoux ware of the Neronian period. (Fig. 47, no. 3).

AM IV 44

Two joining fragments of form 24, with the rouletting carried upwards beyond the groove and downwards onto the top of the cordon. The fabric and glaze are probably Claudian.

Site BC

The Inter-ditch areas

BC II 34

A Claudio-Neronian group, consisting of fragments of form 18, with a flattened bead lip, 24 and a bowl, presumably of form Ritt. 12.

Site AL

Back-filling of the quarried stretches of Ditch III

AL II 39

a) Fragment of the upper zone and rim of form 29, with decoration consisting of overlapping leaf tips. There do not appear to be any parallels for these, but the fabric and glaze of the bowl suggest a Neronian date.
b) Fragment of form 37. The chevron wreath is likely to be the same as one used on a bowl from the Pompeii Hoard (Atkinson, 1914, pl. xv, 75), and the ovolo occurs on two bowls from this group, from moulds signed Memoris before firing below the decoration (*ibid.*, pl. xiv, 73-4). Bowls from moulds signed by Memor occur

also at La Graufesenque and Rottweil. *c.* A.D. 70-90.

c) Fragment of the base of a dish, probably of form 16. The fabric and the double grooving on the base suggest a Claudian date.

d) Fragments of Neronian-Flavian date, including forms 15/17 or 18(2), 18(4), 27 (2 or 3) and 29.

AL II 45

a) Fragment of form 17. Claudian.

b) Bassus i-Coelus 5b, – see S. 4.

c) Fragments of plain ware, including forms 15/17, 15/17 or 18, 18 (2) and 18R. All Neronian.

d) D.59. Fragment of form 29, from the same bowl as AL VII 12, slightly burnt. The general style of decoration is reminiscent of the work of Daribitus. The larger leaf and the mask, which normally has tufts of hair and a detachable beard or bib, occur on a bowl from Vechten (Knorr, 1919, Taf. 31D). The small leaf tips in the upper zone are possibly the same as ones on a bowl from Valkenburg ZH (Glasbergen, 1944, Afb. 55, 1). Both bowls were stamped by Daribitus. The acorn is probably the one used in the upper zone of a bowl from Southwark, stamped by Licinus. The wreath occurs on bowls from Aislingen and London (LM), stamped by Labio, and the same stamp was used on a bowl from Nijmegen which has the small rosette. *c.* A.D. 40-55.

e) Fragment of the upper zone and rim of form 29. Neronian.

f) Fragment of form 29 or 30, with a leafy festoon. Claudio-Neronian. Several of the pieces in this group have kiln grit adhering to their bases and unworn foot-rings, and may be derived from the same source as the fort ditch material.

AL VII 31

a) Two fragments likely to be from the same bowl, probably of form Ritt. 12, with a good Neronian glaze.

b) Fragments of form 15/17 and 15/17R, both probably Claudio-Neronian, to judge by the fabric.

c) Stamp – Modestus i 2a or 2a´ – see S. 21.

d) Fragment of form 18, from the same dish as AM IV 41 c), AL VII 12 and AM VII 30.

e) Fragment of form 18. Neronian or early-Flavian.

f) Fragment of unidentified form, but probably 18R. Pre-Flavian.

g) Fragments of two cups of form 24. Neronian.

h) Several fragments of cups of form 27. All pre-Flavian.

i) D.60 Fragment of form 29 rim, showing part of the scroll in the upper zone. The rosette and tie are very similar to, though perhaps not identical with, ones used on bowls stamped by Senicio, from Aislingen (Knorr, 1912, Taf. VI, 2), Richborough and Xanten. The small leaf may be one recorded for him (Knorr, 1919, Taf. 75, 7). Senicio's work seems to be entirely pre-Flavian and occurs in the Cirencester fort ditch and frequently on forms 24 and Ritt. 8 and 9. *c.* A.D. 45-60.

j) Two fragments of form 29 rims. Both pre-Flavian.

k) Fragment of the lower zone of form 29, so carelessly moulded that the decoration is almost indistinguishable. The fabric and glaze are pre-Flavian.

Site AK

AK IV 38

a) Fragment of form Ritt. 1. Claudian or early-Neronian.

b) Fragment of form 24. Probably Claudian.

Site DA

Pit cut into natural

DA IV 510

a) Form 18. Neronian or early-Flavian.

b) Form 29 rim, in orange, non-micaceous fabric and with a good-quality orange-brown glaze. The fabric, less common than the heavily-micaceous ones, belongs to the range current at Lezoux in the first century. This piece is likely to be either late-Neronian or early-Flavian.

DA IV 506

Form 29, with a lower zone of straight gadroons. The piece is slightly overfired. Late-Neronian or early-Flavian.

DA III 168

Form 15/17 or 18, with the end of the stamp-label just visible. Neronian or early-Flavian.

DA III 166

a) Form 18. Neronian.

b) Form 36 (?). Claudio-Neronian.

THE WATERMOOR RAMPART

Site AW

Base of the Rampart

AW I 77

D.61. A small fragment of form 29, with a rounded carination. The lower zone has most of a bird to right (unidentified). Pre-Flavian, and possibly Claudian.

Intervallum Road

AW I 72

Fragment of the same jar as AW I 55. Form 67, with scored festoons between wavy lines (cf. Hermet, 1934, pl. 91, 35-37). First-century.

AW I 71

a) Fragment of form 18. The piece is badly made, with only a rudimentary bead lip, formed by grooving the wall below the rim. The fabric is rather coarse. Flavian.

b) Fragment of form 27g. Probably Neronian.

c) Fragment of form 27. Neronian or early-Flavian.

d) Fragment of form 29 rim, with a dull, patchy glaze. Neronian-Flavian.

e) D.62. Two joining fragments of form 30, with a possible saltire flanking a narrow panel with a vertical wreath. The scheme of decoration is obscure. The bowl might equally well be Neronian or early-Flavian.

f) Fragment of form 37, with a panel of leaves between horizontal wavy lines. The leaf was used on a bowl from Vechten stamped FIC·PRIM (Primus iii 3a´), which is known from Flavian foundations. *c.* A.D. 75-85.

Gully behind the Rampart

AW I 79

a) Tiny fragment of form 29, with scarcely-impressed leaf tips. Pre-Flavian.

b) D.63. Fragment of a carefully-made bowl of form 30. The ovolo was used on several bowls from moulds signed by Masc(u)lus i of La Graufesenque, including one from Tongres (Knorr, 1952, Taf. 36B). *c.* A.D. 50-70.

c) Fragment of a dish. Pre-Flavian.

Site AX

Occupation of Fort or Vicus

Pit Filling

AX II 43 – layer above 58

a) Form 18. Neronian.

b) Form 24. Pre-Flavian.

c) Form 18 (2). Flavian.

d) Four more fragments, one with a rivet hole, of the form 18R in AX II 41, *q.v.*

e) Form 29, with an upper zone of festoons with beaded tassels and containing spirals. Flavian.

AX II 42 – layer above 13

a) Form 18, burnt. Flavian.

b) A tiny fragment of form 18. Flavian.

c) Four fragments, three joining, of form 18R, with four

more in AX II 43 and one joining piece in AX II 41, *q.v.*

d) Illiterate stamp – see S. 50.

AX II 39

a) Form 18. Late-Neronian or early-Flavian.

b) Form 18R. Late-Neronian or early-Flavian.

c) D.64. Form 37, with a central zone containing a boar (Hermet, 1934, pl. 27, 48). *c.* A.D. 75-100.

Layers sealing-off early occupation

AX II 41

The material is mainly Flavian and consists of forms 18 (without a bead lip), 18R (with a joining sherd in AX II 42) and two cups of form 27g, one pre-Flavian and the other stamped (Sabinus iii 12a – see S. 41). The stamp is known from La Graufesenque, is common at early-Flavian foundations, but reached Camelon (2 examples). It occurs also at Gloucester, Kingsholm, at Hofheim and Risstissen and so should be dated *c.* A.D. 65-85.

AX II 38

Form 42?, slightly burnt, with the edge of the stamp frame. The piece has kiln grit inside the base and on the footring, but was probably in use for a short time. First-century.

AX II 36

Forms 18 (two joining wall sherds), 18R and a dish fragment with a lead rivet. All early-Flavian.

THE SANDS RAMPART

The Rampart

BZ I 12

a) Fragment, slightly burnt, of form 24. Probably Neronian.

b) Fragment of form 18. Neronian or early-Flavian.

c) Fragment of form 18R. Neronian.

d) Fragment of form 18 or 18R. Neronian or early-Flavian.

e) Cf. BZ I 15 i. Fragment of form 29. The zonal arrangement of basal wreath with short gadroons above was a common one in the Neronian-Flavian period. Cf. Iucundus ii (Knorr, 1919, Taf. 43F, from Vechten) and Meddillus (*ibid.* Taf. 55B, from Mainz), both with slightly different wreaths. A wreath, very similar to the one below the gadroons, is on a bowl stamped OFCRESTIO (Crestio 5b), probably from Nijmegen. *c.* A.D. 60-80, or 65-80, if Meddillus.

f) D.65. Fragment of form 37, Central Gaulish, slightly burnt. Most of the decorative details, including the standing figure (D.102), were used by Stanfield & Simpson's X-2, who worked at Les Martres-de-Veyre. The other figure may be the same as one on a bowl from Alchester (Stanfield & Simpson, 1958, pl. 6, 61). *c.* A.D. 100-120.

g) D.66. Fragment of form 37 with an ovolo used both at Les Martres-de-Veyre and (by Sacer i and his associates) at Lezoux. The gladiators (D.1004) were used at Les Martres by Drusus i. This piece is almost certainly from Les Martres and of the period A.D. 110-125.

h) D.67. Small fragment of form 37 with a hare (D.950a), used by many Central Gaulish potters. This

piece is likely to be from Les Martres-de-Veyre *c.* A.D. 100-130.

CG III 12

A chip. First century A.D.

CG III 17 – Rammed gravel base

A flake from form 15/17 or. Flavian.

The Filling of the Ditches

Outer Ditch – bottom layer

CG IV 21 – bottom layer

a) Form Ritt. 12 flange. Pre-Flavian.

b) Form 15/17R, burnt. Pre-Flavian.

c) Form 15/17 or 18, two joining fragments. Pre-Flavian.

d) Form 24. Claudian?

e) Cup fragment. Pre-Flavian.

f) A small scrap in first-century Lezoux fabric. Neronian.

Outer Ditch – middle layers

BZ I 18

a) Fragments of four dishes of form 18, all Flavian.

b) Fragment of form 27. Flavian.

c) Form 29 rim with a fragment of the upper zone with freestyle figures. Probably Neronian.

d) Small fragment of the lower zone of form 29, with festoons at the bottom of the decoration. Probably Neronian.

e) Fragment from the base of a decorated bowl of form

30 or 37. Flavian.

f) D.68. A substantial part of a bowl of form 37 with zonal decoration. All the features of this bowl may be matched from the Pompeii Hoard, where they are common to most of the potters represented (Atkinson, 1914, 26-64) and closely similar bowls appear in Flavian I contexts in Scotland. *c.* A.D. 75-90.

CG IV 19
a) Form 18. Flavian.
b) Form 29. Flavian.
c) Form 29, with pointed leaf tips in the upper zone. Flavian.

Outer Ditch – upper layers

BZ I 15
a) Fragment of form 15/17. Flavian.
b) Fragments of at least five dishes of form 18. Two Neronian-Flavian, the others probably Flavian.
c) Fragment of form 27. Neronian or early-Flavian.
d) Fragment of form 36. Flavian.
e) Fragment of flange from form Ritt. 12 or Curle 11. Neronian or early-Flavian.
g) Two fragments of the same form 30, with an ovolo with single border. Neronian or early-Flavian.
h) Small fragment of form 29, with gadroons in the lower zone. Pre-Flavian.
i) Three joining fragments of form 29, with festoons in the upper zone. The fabric is very similar to that of BZ I 12 e), and may be from the same bowl. There is an almost precise parallel from Mainz stamped by Meddillus (Knorr, 1919, Taf. 55B), and all the elements are on his stamped bowls. *c.* A.D 65-80.
j) Small fragment of form 37, South Gaulish, with an ovolo and wreath which both occur in the Pompeii Hoard. *c.* A.D. 75-90.
k) D.69. Fragment of a panelled bowl of form 37 with a ramshorn wreath (not known on stamped bowls?) and a gladiator (Hermet, 1934, pl. 21. 152). Although not assignable to a particular potter or group of potters, this bowl is unlikely to have been made before about A.D. 85.
l) Two joining fragments of form 18/31, Central Gaulish, probably from Les Martres-de-Veyre. Trajanic or early-Hadrianic.
m) Rim fragment from a similar dish to the last.
n) D.70. Fragment of form 37 with the common ovolo of Igocatus of Les Martres-de-Veyre. The surviving decoration is characteristic of him. *c.* A.D. 100-120.
o) D.71. Fragment of a panelled form 37 with sea-horse (O.34) and Victory (D.484), both used by one of the mould-makers who worked for Ranto and his associates at Les Martres-de-Veyre. The general style is that of Stanfield's Medetus-Ranto group. *c.* A.D. 100-125.
p) Burnt fragment of form 37 with a closing zone of beaded circles of the kind used by several potters at Les Martres-de-Veyre. *c.* A.D. 100-125.

CG IV 18
Two joining fragments of form 37, Central Gaulish, with a basal zone of beaded circles (Rogers, 1974, C 292) and panther (D.795) used at Les Martres-de-Veyre by mould makers for Donnaucus and Ioenalis i. *Cf.* two bowls from London (Stanfield and Simpson, 1958, pl. 40, 462, 471). *c.* A.D. 100-125.

CG IV 17
a) Form Ritt. 12. Neronian.
b) Forms 15/17 or 18(2), and a fragment of form 29 base, all Neronian or early-Flavian.
c) Form 18. Flavian.
d) Form 37, with unusual basal wreath and a vertical band of leaves. Early-Flavian.
e) Two scraps, one burnt. Undatable.

CG IV 16
a) Form Ritt. 8 burnt, with an unidentified stamp]INI. Pre-Flavian. see S. 55.
b) Plain ware of Neronian or early-Flavian date, includes 15/17(2?), many examples of forms 15/17 or 18, and 18, 27(2?), 35 and 36(4?).
c) Form 27g bases(2). Neronian or early-Flavian.
d) Form 29, with a badly moulded scroll. Medallions in the upper concavities of the scroll, as here, are not common, but appear on bowls stamped by such potters as Modestus i, Mommo and Primus iii. A bowl from Mainz stamped by Primus has a similar layout in the upper zone (Knorr, 1919, Taf. 66B). The tulip leaf and the bird (Hermet, 1934, pl. 28, 39) are too common to be diagnostic. *c.* A.D. 60-80.
e) Forms 30 or 37 rim, and 37 rims(3). Flavian or Flavian-Trajanic.
f) Form 37, a tiny fragment of a trident-tongued ovolo. Flavian or Flavian-Trajanic.
g) Form 37 with upper zone of alternating plants and animals, and a lower with a winding scroll. Zones of this type appear on form 29s stamped by such potters as Calvus i and Vitalis ii. Cf. Knorr, 1919, Taf. 84 for similar animal zones. The stag (Hermet, 1934, pl. 27, 15), was used by several potters. *c.* A.D. 75-90.
h) A small fragment of form 37 with a straight wreath of bifid motifs over a panel with a large four-petalled corner tassel. The wreath is of a general type found on many of the bowls in the Pompeii Hoard (Atkinson, 1914), although it does not exactly match any of them. This bowl is likely to be Flavian rather than later. *c.* A.D. 70-90.
i) Five fragments, four joining, from a bowl of form 37, with straight wreaths above and below a zone of chevron festoons containing spirals. The details were all used by Mercato(r) i, and the trident-tongued ovolo is particularly characteristic of his work. The ovolo, festoons with the same spirals and tassels, and the basal wreath are all on a stamped bowl of his from Nijmegen, and the upper wreath of bifid motifs is on one from Epinal. *c.* A.D. 80-110.
j) Form 37, with a trident-tongued ovolo. The tree made up of separate impressions of tendrils with striated spindles, is a common feature of bowls by Germanus i and potters working in the same tradition. This particular piece is likely to belong to the period *c.* A.D. 80-110.
k) Form 37, with a zone of opposed spirals below a zone with a plant composed of overlapping impressions of conventional grass tufts. Flavian-Trajanic.
l) A small fragment of form 37, without significant decoration. Flavian or Flavian-Trajanic.
m) Form 37, with a scroll with a triangular leaf. Flavian-Trajanic.
n) Plain ware from Les Martres-de-Veyre, consisting of forms 27 (seven fragments, most joining), 33a and 36.

All Trajanic or Hadrianic.

o) Form 37, with an ivy leaf (Rogers, 1974, J89) and a seven-beaded rosette (*ibid.*, C280?) used at Les Martres by potters supplying moulds to Donnaucus. Both are on a bowl from London ((BM) Stanfield and Simpson, 1958, pl. 45, 518). *c.* A.D. 100-125.

p) Form 37 in the fabric of Les Martres. Only the wavy line below the decoration survives. Trajanic or Hadrianic.

q) Form 37 with a small rosette-tongued ovolo (Rogers, 1974, B14) used at Lezoux by Sacer i and Criciro v. The surviving decoration, probably a zone of festoons, suggests the work of the former. *c.* A.D. 125-145.

Inner Ditch – middle layers

CG III 14

a) Five fragments, most joining, from form 15/17R (Ritt. 4B). Neronian. Two sherds in CG III 11 a).

b) Form 15/17 or 18 stamped OFMVRRA by Murranus (10c). For dating see S. 25.

c) Plain ware of Neronian date, comprising forms 15/17 or 18, 18R and 27.

d) A fragment from the upper zone of form 29, with a scroll similar to, or possibly identical with the one in the upper zone on the bowl in DK II 46 a), *q.v.* The sherds do not join.

CG III 11

a) Two fragments joining the dish in CG III 14 a), *q.v.* Neronian.

b) Form 15/17 or 18, stamped OFMVRR/ by Murranus, with a broken die (10d). See S. 26.

c) Cup fragment. Pre-Flavian.

d) Form 37, with leaf tips flanked by diagonal wavy lines, as in CG III 7 a) below, but probably from a different bowl. *c.* A.D. 80-110.

CG III 7

a) A fragment of a bowl of form 37, with a panel of pointed leaf tips flanked by diagonal wavy lines over a basal wreath. All the details can be paralleled in the work of Mercato(r) i of La Graufesenque (cf. Knorr, 1919, Taf. 57, B, J, on bowls from Nijmegen and Baden-Baden). *c.* A.D. 80-110.

b) Six joining fragments of a bowl of form 37, with zonal decoration. The basal zone of flattened S-shaped godroons, kneeling stag (D.862) and tree were used on form 29s from Vindonissa stamped by Secundus ii (Knorr, 1919, Taf. 74 B, C), and by contemporaries. The dog is Hermet, 1934, pl. 26, 41. *c.* A.D. 75-90.

c) Nine fragments, eight joining, of a bowl of form 37, with a panel containing a saltire. Six additional fragments in CG III 6, an upper level layer over the Rear Ditch. *c.* A.D. 75-95.

d) An undatable scrap from a cup (form 27 etc.).

MORTARIUM STAMPS
by
Katharine F. Hartley

M.1 (DK I 106) fig. 53, 110

The spout and adjacent parts of a mortarium in softish, fine slightly yellowish cream fabric, with flint and quartz-like trituration grit, combined with internal scoring. Fabric 67. The stamp is one from at least ten dies used by Q. Valerius Veranius. Veranius is one of the few mortarium potters to have had Roman citizenship, and also one of the few whose work is both common in Britain and well represented on the Continent. Indeed, he has more stamps there than any other potter whose products are well represented in Britain. Eighty-five of his stamps are known from sites throughout Britain, and 18 from the Continent and the question of where his workshops were situated cannot be resolved. It is reasonably certain that early in his career he had worked at Bavai (Nord), where eight of the nine mortaria stamped by him are in the local brown fabric, with rim-forms similar to those made by other local potters like Privatus; these are stamped by two dies which are otherwise unknown. There is no reasonable doubt that the remainder of his known mortaria were made elsewhere, in north-east France, with perhaps a subsidiary pottery in Kent. The concentration of his mortaria in areas accessible to the coast implies distribution by coastal or sea-going traffic. (Hartley, K.F., 1973, fig. 4, 47; 1977, Group II).

Apart from the eight mortaria in brown fabric at Bavai, his mortaria are all of Gillam type 238 (Gillam, 1957, 204). There were several other less important potters, including Q. Valerius Esunertus, Q. Valerius Suriacus, Gracilis and Litugenus II, whose products are identical save that many of them are not represented at all on the Continent. The work of all, including Veranius, is to be dated within the range *c.* A.D. 70-100. There is ample site-dating evidence for Veranius' alone, from Agricolan sites in Scotland, such as Camelon and Cardean, in England from Richborough and Exeter, and in Wales, Caerleon (Bushe-Fox, 1949, 92, Pit 125; Fox, 1951, fig. 2, 6; and 1940, 139, no. 2; Hartley, K.F., 1977, Group II).

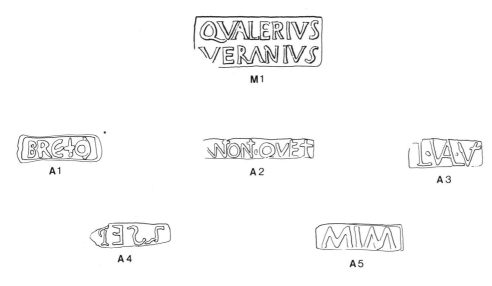

Fig. 48. Mortarium and amphora stamps (M.1, 1:1; for A.1–5, 1:2)

M.2 (DM I 136) fig. 52, 120, stamp not illustrated
A very worn mortarium in slightly abrasive, brownish pink ware, fired to cream at the surfaces, with quartz-like and probably also flint trituration grit, both on the interior and on top of the rim. Fabric 68. A small potter's stamp is impressed along the flange, but damage to the surface and the presence of grits have made it virtually illegible. It is, however, almost certainly from one of the six dies of Q. Valerius Se.. which reads QI·VA·S *c.* A.D. 55–85. Valerius is one of a number of potters making mortaria of similar form and fabric who worked either in Gallia Belgica or in Kent, (Hartley, K.F., 1977, Group I).

POTTERS' STAMPS ON AMPHORAE, GALLO-BELGIC, AND COARSE WARES
by
Valery Rigby

Amphora Stamps

The identification and dating is based on M.H. Callender, (1965). See fig. 48.

A. 1 (AM II 59) (see p. 182)
BROC·OD – Callender 205, Broc ( ) Oduciense. The nearest die is fig. 4, 22, from Windisch. No dates given for his working life, but the presence of this amphora in the filling of Ditch III of the Leaholme fort suggests that he was working by the Neronian period at the latest. One stamp on the handle of a Dressel type 20. Fabric 40 – South Spanish.

A. 2 (CG IV 16)
[G A]NTONI QVIETI – Callender 243, G. Antonius Quietus. Probably from the same die as Callender, 1965, fig. 5, 2, from Richborough. South Spanish. *c.* A.D. 70-120. Callender considers that the products of this potter are the most numerous and widely spread of all. One stamp on the handle of a Dressel type 20. Fabric 40.

A. 3 (AM III 44) (see p. 187)
L.·VAL·VI – Callender 973, L. Valeri Vituli. The nearest die is fig. 10, 16, from Silchester. South Spanish. Mid-first century A.D. One stamp on the handle of a Dressel type 20. Fabric 40.

A. 4 (CG IV 16)
L̂S SEP retrograde – possibly Callender 944, L.S ( ) Sept ( ). No dies illustrated resemble this one. One stamp on the handle of a Dressel type 20. Fabric 40 – South Spanish.

A. 5 (DM I 136) (see fig. 53, 121)
MIM – Callender 1114, M. Iulius Mopsi. The nearest die is fig. 11, 18, from Windisch. The potter worked in Baetica. *c.* A.D. 30-80/90. One stamp on one handle of a Dressel type 20. Fabric 40. There is a stamp, possibly from the same die, from Chichester, in a Period I, first century context (Down and Rule, 1971, fig. 3.10, 105).

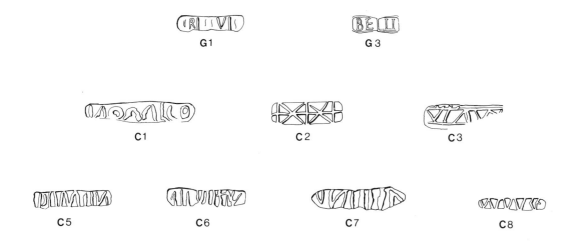

Fig. 49.   Stamps on Gallo-Belgic and coarse wares (G.1 and 3; and C.1–3, 5–8, 1:1)

Stamps on Gallo-Belgic Wares

G. 1 (DM I 19) (see p. 173, 159b)
CRISSVIS – central stamp on the base of a bowl with a moulded footring. In terra nigra (TN) – pale grey dense paste; dark blue-grey surfaces, with a smoothly polished interior finish. There is a stamp from the same die on an identical cup base from Southampton, Bitterne (Southampton Museum). No other examples are known, and the kilns have not been located. An import. *c.* A.D. 45-80.

G. 2 (DK II 43) (see p. 172) (not illustrated)
A small fragment showing only the border of the stamp, the die and therefore the potter cannot be identified. The stamp is on the base of a platter, Camulodunum form 16, in TN – pale blue-grey dense paste, darker blue-grey surfaces, with a polished finish on the inside. Almost certainly an import. *c.* A.D. 45-85.

G. 3 (DK II 5) (U.S. upper levels, Site DK, Admirals Walk).
BELLI – on the underside of a small jar with a moulded footring, possibly a carinated jar similar to Camulodunum 120 or to no. 336. Fine-grained sand free ware; grey core, rust cortex and dark grey-black surfaces, with traces of a highly polished external finish. There is an identical jar base, with a stamp from the same die, from Gloucester (Gloucester City Museum). Stamps from different dies, but probably the work of the same potter have been found at Margidunum (Oswald, 1948, pl. III, 11), Fishbourne (Cunliffe, 1971, fig. 80, 6), Aachen, Trier (Koethe, 1938, Abb. 2, 18) and Bavai, a possible source (Hénault, 1934-6, 196-7; 267-8). An import. *c.* A.D. 40-75.

Stamps on Coarse Wares

C. 1 (BZ I 15)
A probable name stamp placed centrally on the base of a bowl or platter with a plain functional footring. Fabric 17 – brown core; patchy blue-grey surfaces; worn, with traces of a burnished finish inside and out.

The stamp is made up of a combination of O, Λ and I motifs, and appears to have been an attempt to reproduce a name for it can be read as NOMITO – Nomitos; this reading may however be strictly fortuitous. There are no other stamps from this particular die. The fabric suggests that the potter was working locally at the potteries to the south of Cirencester, near Swindon. The few examples of coarse ware platters or dishes stamped with recognisable names are in no way closely related – e.g. Sace(r), Cen(tus) and Reditas, a group of potters working in the north Midlands, possibly near Doncaster, whose products have been found at Old Winteringham, Doncaster, Templeborough, Ilkley, Manchester and Burrow in Lonsdale.

Locally, the few name stamps on coarse ware products fall into two groups, the first represented by one stamp from Gloucester, and the second by stamps from Eastington, Bourton on the Water, and Wanborough (Excavations by Mr B. Rawes; Stroud Museum; the private collection of Mr C. Renfrew; Greene, 1974, fig. 2, 4). The stamp from Gloucester, on a small cup in red ware, is from the same die as one on a bowl from a burial found at Winchester (Nuns Walk – Winchester Museum), and since a similar stamped bowl occurred in a burial at Neatham, Hants, the source would appear to be in Hampshire rather than Gloucestershire.

The second group of stamps occur centrally on the bases of flanged bowls decorated with arcs in white slip on the flange, and should eventually be decipherable as name stamps, although at present the known examples are too fragmentary to be recovered. Examples of the form have been found at Cirencester and Alchester, however the source is not known, and there need be no connection with the Cirencester bowl stamp. The Wanborough bowl is from a group dated *c.* A.D. 90-120, while a date in this period is indicated by the context and fabric of the Cirencester stamp.

C. 2 (DM I 19) (fig. 55, 193)
A potter's mark centrally placed on the base of a platter copying the imported Gallo-Belgic form Camulodunum 14. Fabric 13 – brown core; mottled buff and blue-grey surfaces; burnished upper surface and rim.

No other stamps from this particular die have been identified, but there are close parallels, with the same arrangement of the motifs, on platters also in coarse wares, in Cemeteries KL and WW, at Nijmegen (Holwerda, 1941, nos. 1152-4, 1164). The cemeteries apparently belonged to the Colonia Ulpia Noviomagus, which was founded by Trajan, and were in use until the early third century.

The fabric suggests that the platter was made fairly locally, since there are a number of jars in the same fabric and with the same finish. The source may have been in the area of Savernake where platters of a similar form, in Fabric 6, were found in the filling of the first century well at Mildenhall, and from a kiln at Savernake (Annable, 1966, fig. 2, 12; fig. 4, 56; *ibid*, 1962, fig. 5, 2). A very similar platter, but with a footring, in Fabric 6, was found at Little Bedwyn, Wilts (Ashmolean Museum). The edge of a central stamp survives, but it is illegible, but along with this piece, it suggests that the practice of stamping platters occurred at the Savernake potteries.

The platter could date to any period between A.D. 50 and 160, however the fabric and form indicate a date in the Flavian-Trajanic period.

C. 3 (AG II 10)

An illiterate Mark placed centrally on the base of a platter with a functional footring. Fabric 16 – light blue-grey ware; burnished surfaces.

Probably a local product from the potteries south of Cirencester, no other stamps from this die have been identified, nor are there any close parallels. The fabric and form suggest a date in the Flavian-Trajanic period.

C. 4 (AH VIII 25) (not illustrated)

A name stamp or Mark, illegible, but with an unusually large die-face, placed centrally on a platter copying the Gallo-Belgic import form Camulodunum 16. The fabric is a good quality copy of TN, with a rust fine-grained sandy core; grey cortex; dark blue-grey surfaces, with a very convincing smoothly polished TN finish.

There are sherds from an identical platter, no stamp surviving, DH XL 91.

Although officially a copy, the platter could still be an import from Gaul or the Rhineland, and is probably to be dated to almost the same period as its "prototype", *c*. A.D. 50-85.

In addition to those from the excavations, there are three stamps apparently found in Cirencester in the Bathurst Collection of the Corinium Museum, C. 5-7, and one in the Ashmolean Museum, C. 8. They are included because they provide more information about the local potteries.

C. 5 (B.1613)

An illiterate Mark placed centrally on the base of a cup with a functional footring.

The simple Mark is made up of a combination of I and V motifs. There are no other stamps from this die although it is very similar to C. 6 below, a stamp on a bowl found at Wanborough, and one on a cup from Bourton-on-the-Water (in the private collection of Mr C. Renfrew). They are sufficiently similar to have been used by the same potter who probably worked locally. The form and fabric suggest a date *c*. A.D. 50-85.

The combination of motifs is probably the most common one found on platters and bowls made in Britain, so that examples occur widely, if sparsely, suggesting a number of different sources. Very similar stamps have been found at Alchester, Verulamium, Leicester, and Southwark (Ashmolean Museum. Excavations of 1960, by Prof. S.S. Frere. Kenyon, 1948, 221, No. 4. Excavations by Mr H. Sheldon publication forthcoming). Excluding bowls in Oxford red colour-coated wares, the practice of stamping platters and cups appears to have been most common in the first and second century, *c*. A.D. 50-120, presumably inspired by the imports which provided so many of the prototypes for the forms.

C. 6 (B.2868)

An illiterate Mark placed centrally on the base of a platter with a functional footring.

Almost certainly from the same source as C. 5, see above for the dating and discussion.

C. 7 (B.1614)

An illiterate Mark placed centrally on the base of a cup with a functional footring.

The mark comprises a combination of the motifs, V, Λ, И and I, it is therefore more complex than C. 5 and 6, as well as being larger and cruder, but it is sufficiently similar to suggest the same source and date.

C. 8

An illiterate Mark placed centrally on the base of a platter with a footring. Although not from the same die, there is a very similar stamp on a bowl from Wanborough, and it seems likely that they are from the same local source. Other stamps comprising repeated V motifs have been found at Wanborough and Braintree, Essex. The fabric and form suggest a date in the Flavian-Trajanic period.

To date, a dozen stamps, all from different dies, but all closely related in their motifs, and also in form and fabric, have been found at Cirencester and Wanborough, sites which are less than 20 miles apart. It suggests that the practice of stamping cups and platters was employed at a pottery local to both sites, possibly on a fairly large scale, in the Flavian-Trajanic period. Given the absence of any evidence for kilns in the immediate area of Cirencester, the obvious candidate for the source is the area of the known potteries, south of Cirencester, part of which are in the area of Wanborough, (information from Mrs V.G. Swan and A.S. Anderson). Some stamping appears to have taken place at one, or more, sources of Savernake wares, while there is evidence for a third pottery, with a regional market rather than a local one, which stamped decorated flanged bowls at least, and which was probably at work at the same time.

THE COARSE POTTERY
by
Valery Rigby

Fabric Classification

Fabric 1 – fine-grained sand-free ware. Heavily tempered with fine angular dull cream non-calcareous grit, occasional white flints and also straw-like voids – probably shell grit, although possibly 'grass-tempering'.

Normally fired with a blue-grey core and yellow ochre surfaces, with an even smooth finish, but not glossy. Examples occur first in the occupation layers on natural, on site AH VIII and so could be derived from the occupation which preceded the Leaholme fort, Period II A. The fabric has not been identified in the material from Bagendon and Rodborough Common discovered to date.

Fabric 2 – fine-grained sand-free micaceous ware. Heavily tempered with fine grit, dull angular cream non-calcareous grits and also angular voids, probably from calcareous grit, chalk or limestone.
Normally fired with a blue-grey core and orange-brown surfaces, with a smoothly burnished glossy finish. As in the case of Fabric 1, possibly from occupation preceding Period II A.

Fabric 3 – fine-grained sand-free smooth ware. See p. 201, Fabric C. Almost certainly from the same source as Fabric 24, but whereas all the jars in Fabric 24 are hand-made, those in Fabric 3 are wheel-thrown. Normally fired with a grey core and red-brown surfaces, with a smooth soapy burnished finish. Iron Age technique.
As in the cases of Fabric 1 and 2, possibly derived from occupation preceding Period II A. The fabric has been identified amongst the material from Bagendon, the forms being non-Roman standard local Iron Age types.

Fabric 4 – fine-grained sand-free micaceous ware. Mixed tempering which varies in quantity but is usually fine, fine brown clay grains, fine dull cream non-calcareous, and red ferrous and grog grits, with occasional flake-like black carbonaceous inclusions.
Normally fired with orange-brown or yellow ochre surfaces, often with a blue-grey core, and given a rather uneven faceted burnished finish which wore readily to produce a powdery surface through which the grits protrude. Some at least of the less-tempered versions fall within the definition of Severn Valley wares, while the more heavily tempered examples could be classified as oxidised versions of Savernake wares (Webster, P.V., 1976, 18. Swan, 1975, 42). Examples occur at Bagendon, where fairly common, and Rodborough Common, and in both cases where the forms could be classified, they fall within the range of common Severn Valley ware types. (Clifford, 1961, fig. 52, 6 & 16; fig. 53, 1 & 4; fig. 62, type 36; fig. 64, 91B; fig. 5, 4 & 6; fig. 6, 12). The quantities suggest that there was at least one source local to Cirencester and Bagendon.

Fabric 5 – even textured fine-grained sandy ware, with mica and quartz. Normally fired with a dark grey or brown core, darker grey or black surfaces and given a highly burnished finish. When worn the surface has the texture of fine sand-paper.
Present in the earliest occupation on site AH, at least one example has been identified at Bagendon (Clifford, 1961, fig. 65, 116D). From the Neronian period the range of products was much wider, but there was still specialisation in shallow platters and bowls and wide-mouthed necked bowls. Variations in the fabrics and forms suggest that more than one source was involved, but wherever the source it was a consistently important one for Cirencester until the mid-second century, and its early products also reached Kingsholm, Gloucester (Darling, 1977, fig. 6, 9).

Fabric 6 – fine-grained generally sand-free ware. Heavily tempered with a mixture of different types of tempering between 0.5 and 4.0 mm. in length: –
A. dark grey grog and ferrous grits. The core is normally pale grey of off-white, with darker

blue-grey surfaces; a slurry finish masks the grits at the surface which can be left matt, rilled or smoothed to a more or less glossy finish. When worn the grits are visible and produce a speckled effect.

B. heavily tempered with blue-grey grog grits, the same colour as the core, the surfaces are rather darker, and have a rilled or matt lumpy finish.

C. heavily tempered with dull white angular grog. Normally fired and finished like A.

D. heavily tempered with brown and white flint, and grey grog and ferrous grits. Finished as A.

E. heavily tempered with dull white grits, as in variant C, but with a high proportion of dull light and dark grey grog and iron grits as in variant A. Normally fired and finished as A.

F. heavily tempered with white siltstone grit, dark grey grog and ferrous grits. Fired as A.

All the variations closely resemble Savernake ware, the products of potteries established in the immediately post-Conquest period near Mildenhall, in Savernake forest, where two kilns have been excavated, and possibly also Pewsey and Oare (Annable, 1962, 142-55. For the definition and distribution of Savernake ware – Hodder, 1974, 67-84; Swan, 1975, 36-47). Without further detailed research it is not possible to determine the significance, if any, of the different tempering mixtures. Possibly the basic clay may prove more helpful, for in certain varieties it is almost free of impurities, in particular iron. The similarities in the forms suggest that the varieties are closely related, and they appear to be contemporary, although variant 6A occurs in the earliest contexts and therefore may have been the earliest to be introduced, before *c.* A.D. 55. Examples also occur at Bagendon and Rodborough Common, in the same forms as Cirencester, large necked storage jars and jars with bead rims, which supports an early date for their introduction; the same forms occur also at Sea Mills (Bristol Museum). The early groups from Cirencester are too small to provide conclusive evidence, but together, the varieties of Fabric 6 occupied an important and increasing sector of the market for kitchen-wares throughout the second half of the first century, and continued to be important in the second century even after the apparent reintroduction of products of the Black Burnished Ware workshops *c.* A.D. 120. The quantities and different versions of Fabric 6 found at Cirencester and Bagendon suggest that there could be at least one local source, and that not all supplies were from the Savernake area.

Fabric 7– even-textured coarse-grained sandy ware. Usually fired with a pale grey or brown core and dark blue-grey surfaces with an even burnished finish. A comparatively rare fabric at Cirencester, but examples have been identified from Bagendon and Rodborough Common, so that its source may have been fairly important in the immediate area. Examples occur first in the Period II A of gravel surface on site AH VIII which means that the earliest pieces could be derived from the occupation which preceded the Leaholme fort. Supplies appear to have ceased by the time the Leaholme fort was abandoned.

Fabric 8 – fine-grained sand-free soapy smooth ware. No tempering.

Normally fired with a grey core and orange-brown surfaces which even when worn are soapy smooth in texture. Comparatively rare and apparently used for good quality table wares. Not found in the early layers on site AH VIII. Examples occur first in the earliest gravel surface on sites DM and DK, which post-date *c.* A.D. 55. However, the earliest examples could be derived from earlier occupation.

Fabric 9 – fine-grained ware, more of less micaceous. Probably not tempered although there are frequently occasional grits present – red-brown iron, white calcareous and some mixed colour very coarse waterworn gravel. Used for flagons and honey-pots, it was normally fired to orange-red sometimes with a blue or grey core, and with or without a matt cream slip.

Not found in the earliest layers on site AH VIII, the first examples occur in the lowest gravel surface on sites DK and DM, which post-date *c.* A.D. 55. After *c.* A.D. 70/5, the source, or sources, became the most important supplier(s) of flagons to Cirencester which suggests that the site was close by. This, the similarity in texture and the date range of the major groups of finds suggests that Fabrics 16 and 17 were closely related.

Fabric 10 – fine-grained smooth sand-free highly micaceous ware. Heavily tempered with fine grit, bright red ferrous and sparse white calcareous inclusions. Normally fired to a bright orange or orange-red ware which even when very worn has a soapy smooth texture, often with a grey core at the rim and base. It appears to fall within the definition of Severn Valley wares. Absent from the earliest gravel surfaces on sites AH VIII, DM and DK. Examples occur first in the silt which seals the earliest surface on the latter sites, post-dating *c.* A.D. 55.

Fabric 11 – fine-grained sand-free smooth micaceous ware. Probably not tempered but there are occasional inclusions, bright red ferrous, dull cream non-calcareous and white calcareous grits. Used for flagons and honey-pots, it was usually fired to a pale pink, buff or cream colour with a self-slip, or less frequently with a cream slip. Absent from the earliest gravel surfaces on sites AH VIII, DK and DM. Examples occur in the lowest silt layer on site DK. However, the largest group was found in the filling of Ditch III which tends to confirm the Neronian dating. Supplies appear to have been for the army, so ceased in the early Flavian period.

Fabric 12 – fine-grained ware, heavily tempered with coarse sand comprising mainly white, brown and translucent quartz grits with some black grains. Normally fired to grey, but occasionally oxidised. The grits protrude to produce a rough pimply surface with a matt finish. Absent from the earliest gravel surfaces on site AH VIII, examples have been found in the gravel surface on sites DM and DK which post-dates *c.* A.D. 55, as well as in the fillings of timber features attributed to the military occupation of the Leaholme fort.

Fabric 13 – differs from Fabric 6 in that all varieties include a fairly high proportion of white calcareous grit in the tempering. The forms, finish and firing conditions appear almost identical to Fabric 6 with the exception that the surfaces are rather vesicular. It may be an accidental or regional variant of Fabric 6.
A.   generally fine angular white calcareous grits, some large, 3 to 5 mm., dark grey iron and grog, with occasional flake-like voids – probably shell grit, but possibly carbonaceous;
B.   white calcareous, grey grog and ferrous, white and brown flint grits.
It is less common than Fabric 6, but still forms a significant proportion of the jars and storage jars of the early period at Cirencester. Absent from the earliest layers on site AH VIII, examples occur in the occupation layer on the second phase gravel surface on site AG and the lowest gravel surface on sites DM and DK, the latter post-date *c.* A.D. 55. Fabric 13, therefore, appears to have been introduced rather later than Fabric 6, but since the groups concerned are so small they may not be representative.

Fabric 14 – fine-grained highly micaceous ware, with no obvious tempering. Used for small thin-walled vessels, fired to a fairly dark grey, with a smoothly burnished finish which is highly micaceous. Extremely rare. Pre-Flavian.

Fabric 15 – even-textured sandy ware with much glittering quartz and mica, like Fabric 5 but coarser in texture. Normally fired to dark grey or black with a highly burnished finish. Less common than Fabric 5, it appears to be introduced rather later in date although it was used for a very similar range of forms and may be from the same source. On the site of the Leaholme fort, it occurs in the main filling of Ditches II and IV so that its use may post-date *c.* A.D. 60. It has also been identified in the area of the Watermoor fort or Vicus, which tends to support a Neronian or early Flavian date.

Fabric 16 – fine-grained even-textured ware, with no tempering. It was both oxidised and reduced, with a burnished finish which is usually very worn. No examples occur in the earliest deposits. Examples occur first in the lowest gravel surfaces on sites DK and DM which post-date *c.* A.D. 55. Pottery in this fabric appears to be from a local source and to have continued in production into the second century. Possibly related to Fabrics 9 and 17.

Fabric 17 – fine-grained even-textured, slightly abrasive to the touch. Normally fired to blue-grey with a burnished finish which is usually very worn. Not found in the earliest groups from site AH. Examples do occur in the trample on natural on sites AE and DM which suggests that it was not introduced until after A.D. 55. The range of forms for which it was used, particularly the rustic jars, support a Nero-Flavian rather than a Claudian date for its introduction. Presumably from a local source (or sources). Examples are very common until the late second century.

Fabric 18 – fine-grained sand-free highly micaceous ware. Tempered with fine white calcareous grit, with some other accidental inclusions. Used for hand-made jars whose form is late Iron Age in tradition, but this fabric is Romanised. In texture and appearance it closely resembles Fabric 10, but lacks the red iron grit. Examples have been identified only in the area of the Watermoor fort or Vicus, and it appears to represent the introduction of a new Iron Age tradition in pottery in the Neronian or early Flavian period.

Fabric 19 – fine-grained sand-free smooth ware, micaceous, with no tempering although there are sometimes occasional grits. Like Fabric 11, but with a high iron content since it fires to a bright orange or red. Some examples have a thick cream slip. Used for flagons and honey-pots. Absent from the earliest gravel surfaces on sites AH VIII, DK and DM. Examples occur first in the layers which post-date c. A.D. 55.

Fabric 20 – even-textured close-bodied sandy ware, with no obvious tempering although some occasional grey iron and white calcareous grits. Usually fired to grey, but there are some orange-brown and brown examples, with a burnished finish which is now extremely worn. Probably a local product. Absent from the earliest gravel surfaces on site AH VIII and the main filling of Ditch III, AM II 59, examples occur first in the lowest gravel surface on sites DK and DM which post-date c. A.D. 55. Sherds also were found in the core of the Sands Rampart.

Fabric 21 – fine-grained iron-free ware, some incidental red iron grits. Fired to a creamy white colour, with a self-coloured slip on the outside and a brown slip confined to the interior. Used only for flagons and honey-pots, it is an import, possibly from Lezoux (a suggestion put forward by Mr G.B. Dannell). Examples have been identified at Winchester, Hants; Oare, Wanborough and Mildenhall, Wilts; Sea Mills, Avon; Chichester and Fishbourne, Sussex. The most complete example is from the main filling of Ditch III, AM II 59, which suggests a military connection and a date after c. A.D. 60.

Fabric 22 – fine-grained sand-free smooth ware with no tempering. Usually has a brown core and black or dark grey surfaces, or a sandwich effect of grey core, brown cortex and dark grey surfaces, with a soapy smooth finish. Absent from the earliest gravel surfaces on site AH VIII, it occurs in the lowest gravel surface on sites DK and DM, which post-date c. A.D. 55.

Fabric 23 – fairly fine-grained ware, heavily tempered with coarse sand grit. Usually fired to grey with a matt rough finish. Used for necked jars and carinated bowls. The fabric also occurs at Kingsholm, Gloucester, and appears to be from the same source. The earliest context for examples of the fabric is the lowest silt layer on site DK, so that it was probably supplied to the army after c. A.D. 55. The existing examples are all from the area of the Leaholme fort, within Cirencester itself, and none have been identified from Bagendon or Rodborough Common.

Fabric 24 – fine-grained ware, heavily tempered. See p. 201, Fabric C. Usually fired to brown or with a grey core and brown surfaces, the fabric is reserved for hand-made jars of Iron Age forms. Almost certainly from the same source as Fabric 3, but all vessels in the latter are wheel-thrown. See below nos. 396-8.

Fabric 25 – fine-grained ware; heavily tempered.
A.   see p. 201; Fabric A.
B.   see p. 201; Fabric B.
Usually fired to dark grey with a soapy smooth burnished finish. It is essentially Iron Age in tradition. Absent from the earliest gravel surfaces on site AH VIII, it occurs in the filling of Ditch II, AM I 61, where it appears to be part of a residual, Tiberio-Claudian group, possibly from the initial silting. See below nos. 396-8.

Fabric 26 – fine-grained smooth micaceous ware. Heavily tempered with fairly coarse sand which results in a rather rough and sandy surface finish. Normally fired to a light orange-brown. The fabric was used for a limited range of flagons. Absent from the earliest gravel surfaces on sites AH VIII, AG, DK and DM, examples occur in the main filling of Ditch III, AM II 59.

Fabric 27 – fine-grained ware, heavily tempered with fine white calcareous and red-brown ferrous grit. Not a common ware, it was used for some flagons and was fired with a blue-grey core and red-brown surfaces. Possibly intrusive, examples of this fabric are absent from all layers but those sealing-off the early occupation which include second century material.

Fabric 28 – fine-grained sand-free smooth micaceous ware. Orange-brown ware, with traces of a thick coral red slip inside and out, so that it resembles Pompeian Red ware. Rare. Possibly pre-Flavian or Flavian.

Fabric 29 – fine-grained ware, with varying amounts of tempering – dull white calcareous grits which vary considerably in size, up to 0.7 cm. in length and sparse brown ferrous grits. Fired to buff or yellow-buff in colour, it was used almost exclusively for flagons the majority of which were found in the filling of Ditch III (see fig. 58). Identical flagons have been found at Kingsholm, Gloucester (unpublished, Gloucester museum). Examples are absent from the earliest gravel surfaces, so the use of flagons in this fabric appear to post-date *c.* A.D. 55, and they ceased to be supplied after the military withdrew from Cirencester. The flagons may have been supplied under contract to the military at Gloucester and Cirencester (see p. 179).

Fabric 30 – even-textured, open-bodied sandy ware. Fired to grey. Examples occur only in the layers sealing-off the early occupation which include second century material.

Fabric 31 – hard fine-grained sand-free white ware, with varying amounts of red grog tempering. Used for flagons and associated liquid-carrying vessels, examples are scarce compared to Fabrics 11, 29 and 9, and are absent from the earliest gravel surfaces, the first examples being in layers which post-date *c.* A.D. 55.

Fabric 32 – coarse-grained gritty ware, extremely abrasive. Cream ware, with matt rough and gritty surfaces. Probably from the potteries of the Verulamium region, or possibly the Oxford region. Examples are absent from all layers which pre-date the sealing-off layers which suggests that its introduction to Cirencester did not occur before *c.* A.D. 70. It may be significant that no mortaria from the Verulamium region occur in contexts earlier than the sealing-off layers also.

Fabric 33 – fine-grained slightly micaceous sand-free ware, tempered with red grog. Fired to orange-red, the burnished finish is streaked by the grog tempering. Rare. Pre-Flavian or Flavian.

Fabric 34 – fairly fine-grained slightly abrasive micaceous ware, with no obvious tempering, although there are occasional intrusive grits. Creamy buff or pink, with a cream exterior slip. Used for amphorae of Camulodunum form 186. Imported from Cadiz.

Fabric 35 – fine-grained smooth micaceous ware, with some fine sand. Pinky brown ware, with paler surfaces. Used for amphorae of Dressel type 30.

Fabric 36 – fairly fine-grained dense ware with no tempering. Cream ware, with a self-coloured slip. Origin unknown, possibly South Gaul.

Fabric 37 – hard sandy micaceous ware with fine white calcareous grits. Brick red ware with a cream slip. Origin unknown. Not illustrated.

Fabric 38 – dense fine-grained micaceous ware, with white calcareous grits. Pinkish-brown ware with a cream slip.
A. Imported from Rhodes.
B. Similar fabric, in the same form as 38A, but probably a copy.
Possibly imported from the Mediterranean area.

Fabric 39 – orange-brown fine-grained sandy ware, with much coarse black volcanic 'bombs'. Orange-brown ware. Used for amphorae of Dressel type 2/4. Imported from Italy. Not illustrated.

Fabric 40 – fine-grained ware with much coarse mixed sand. The typical fabric of amphorae of Dressel type 20 and imported from Southern Spain. By far the most common amphorae type found in the early occupation.

Fabric 41 – fine-grained sandy ware similar to Fabric 17. Sparsely tempered with dark grey ferrous and coarse white grog inclusions. Possibly the reduced version of Fabric 4, but it was not apparently used for typical Severn Valley forms. Fired to blue-grey. Absent from the earliest gravel surfaces, examples occur in the main filling of Ditch III and in the layers sealing-off the early occupation. Its introduction appears to post-date *c.* A.D. 60.

Fabric 42 – fine-grained sand-free smooth ware. Heavily tempered with fine red iron grits. Fired to orange-red with a burnished finish. Absent from the earliest gravel surfaces, examples occur in the main filling of Ditch III, AM II 59.

Fabric 43 – fine-grained micaceous sandy ware, similar to Fabric 17. Some tempering with coarse brown sand and fine white calcareous inclusions. Fired to a blue-grey colour with a dirty white slip. The only example is from the ditch behind the Watermoor rampart. Although the technique is different, it is possibly from the same source as Fabric 17.

Fabric 44 – fine-grained ware, slightly abrasive in texture. Tempered with fine white calcareous, dull cream non-calcareous, red-brown ferrous inclusions.
Used for flagons, it was fired with a blue-grey core and orange-red surfaces. Rare compared to Fabrics 11 and 29, examples occur in the third gravel surface on site AH VIII, which post-dated *c.* A.D. 55.

Fabric 45 – even-textured sandy ware, coarser in texture than Fabric 30. Fired to blue-grey, with a burnished finish. Scarce, found only in the area of Watermoor fort or *vicus.*

Fabric 46 – fine-grained slightly abrasive in texture, probably not tempered although occasional grits occur. Fired with a brown core and dark grey-black surfaces. Used in particular for small jars with rouletted decoration. Absent from the earliest gravel surfaces, examples were found in the main filling of Ditch III, so that its introduction probably post-dated A.D. 55.

Fabric 47 – coarse-grained gritty orange-brown ware. Used for small carrot-shaped amphorae with horizontal rilling on the body.

Fabric 48A – fine-grained ware, slightly abrasive in texture, with some sparse and possibly accidental grog grits. Represented here only by butt beakers of Camulodunum form 113, which although they resemble the products of the Camulodunum region are clearly not from that source. Examples are rare, the most complete being in the main filling of Ditch III, so that it is probable that beakers were still being supplied after *c.* A.D. 60. There are at least two beakers from Bagendon, type 57 (Clifford, 1961, fig. 62).

Fabric 48B – fine-grained slightly sandy texture, with occasional red grog grits. Usually white or cream, but under some firing conditions the exterior can be covered with a grey, pink or mauve 'haze'. The typical fabric of butt beakers of form 113, manufactured at Camulodunum, and probably elsewhere also, and found commonly south and east of a line from Flamborough Head to Southampton Water, with outliers beyond which include Bagendon, type 57 (Clifford, 1961, fig. 62, 57). Much more common at Bagendon than at Cirencester, where represented by five sherds.

Fabric 49 – coarse-grained gritty ware, with much quartz. Similar in texture to B.B.1, but fired to a light grey colour, and not in the forms typical of the Black Burnished workshops. Probably not local since the basic clays of the "local" products are markedly fine-grained.

Fabric 50 – fine-grained dense powdery ware, with no tempering; orange core with duller orange-buff or smoky orange surfaces.

Fabric 51 – Pompeian Red ware. Fine-grained dense ware, with few obvious inclusions; the colour varies from pale buff to darker pink.
A.   Thick pink slip over the whole vessel usually. In some examples the slip is very highly micaceous, but it apparently wore quickly so that only traces of a thin slightly micaceous wash survive.
B.   Comprises slip A, confined to the exterior and lower surfaces, while a thick coral red slip, with a highly polished finish, is on the interior (upper) surface, over-riding the edge of the lip and the exterior slip.
One of the finer-grained varieties of Pompeian Red ware recently studied by Dr. Peacock, it is presumably Peacock Fabric 3, although he does not include the variant with the highly micaceous slip, for which he suggests a source in Central Gaul, possibly even Lezoux itself.

(Peacock, 1977, 154). The similarity of the paste to that of some Lezoux samian noted by Boon, is particularly noticeable in the case of one of the chance finds from Cirencester, while the similarity of the micaceous slip on the lids, nos. 266 and 268, to that on the early first century Lezoux wares from Bagendon is marked (Boon, 1967, fig. 3, 13). Examples with the less micaceous external slip are identical to finds from Chichester and Winchester (Down, 1978, 201, no. 4. Cunliffe, 1964, fig. 22, 2). The most complete examples are from the filling of Ditch III (AM II 59; nos. 266-9), so it appears that sets of platters and lids were still being supplied to Cirencester after *c*. A.D. 60. For more detailed discussion see Peacock, 1977, 147-162.

Fabric 52 – fine-grained ware; orange ware with a thin mica-coating all over. Possibly from Gloucester, where mica-coated wares were made in the late first and early second century (Rawes, 1972, 27).

Fabric 53 – fine-grained sand-free smooth ware. Orange-brown sometimes with a grey core, and mica-coating on the exterior, visible surfaces. Probably imported from the Rhineland.

Fabric 54 – fine-grained sand-free red ware, with a thin matt maroon slip. Possibly not an import, certainly not from the usual sources of imported colour-coated wares. Sherds from nine different vessels have been found in Cirencester, two from the layers sealing-off the early occupation, and the rest in post-military levels.

Fabric 55 – even-textured sandy orange-brown ware, with a mica-coating on the exterior and visible surfaces. Possibly an import.

Fabric 56 – fine-grained sand-free powdery ware; cream, entirely covered with a slip which varies in thickness and quality of colour from dark metallic brown to patchy orange-brown. Some examples have a fine sand rough-casting on the inside, below the slip. Most examples were imported from Lyons, Central Gaul, but some may be from Camulodunum. The earliest context for a beaker in this fabric is in the group trampled into natural on Site AH VIII, the bowls appear first in later layers (see p. 179–185).

Fabric 57 – fine-grained sand-free smooth very pale cream ware, thick metallic orange and brown slip. Probably an import from Lezoux, Central Gaul.

Fabric 58 – fine-grained sand-free smooth micaceous ware, with no tempering. Pale pinkish buff ware with a red slip overall. An import, probably Central Gaul.

Fabric 59 – dense sand-free smooth ware. Egg-shell ware. Imported, probably from Italy.

Fabric 60 – fine-grained sand-free cream ware, with a green lead glaze. Imported from Central Gaul.

Fabric 61 – fine-grained sandy ware, with some fine red iron grits; dark cream ware with a self-coloured under-slip and a thin mica-coating on the visible surfaces only. Possibly from the Rhineland.

Fabric 62 – typical Italian amphora ware.

Fabric 63 – fine-grained sand-free ware, with occasional black grits. Dark grey or brown core, with black highly polished exterior. Possibly imported. Rare, identified examples are confined to the back-filling of the quarried stretches of the defences and the layers sealing-off the early occupation. For discussion see p. 150, G. 3.

Fabric 64 – fine-grained sand-free white ware, with a thin mica-coating overall. Possibly an import.

Fabric 65 – fine-grained slightly abrasive ware, cream with highly polished smoky pink surfaces. Not typical TR 3 *(terra rubra)*, but possibly still an import.

Fabric 66 – fine-grained oragne-brown ware; mixed coloured sand, and a high proportion of large mica flakes used as tempering. Amphora, origin unknown.

Fabric 67 – fine-grained ware, with no obvious tempering. The fabric is often yellowish-cream, sometimes white and occasionally brownish-pink with a pink core; grey and white flint, and transparent quartz-like trituration grit. Used for mortaria in the Claudian and Flavian periods. The Flavian form, Gillam 238, usually has concentric scoring combined with the trituration grit both inside and on top of the flange. Manufactured in north-east Gaul or less probably in Kent. Examples are absent from the earliest gravel surfaces which might pre-date *c.* A.D. 55, but common in the layers sealing-off the early occupation.

Fabric 68 – dense fine-grained sand-free ware, heavily tempered with white flint, transparent quartz-like grits, mica flakes and occasional brown grains. The trituration grit is like the tempering and is combined with horizontal scoring on the inside. Manufactured in north-east Gaul or less probably in Kent. Absent from the earliest gravel surfaces, an example occurs in the main filling of Ditch III, so that the type does not appear in contexts pre-dating *c.* A.D. 55, and is most common in the sealing-off layers.

Fabric 69 – fine-grained sand-free smooth micaceous ware, with no tempering. Sparse white flint trituration grit survives. An import from Aoste (Isère), France.

Fabric 70 – fine-grained ware, with varying amounts of sand tempering. Grey core; pinkish brown surfaces, with a self-slip. Probably of local origin, with Gloucester as a possible contender. Absent from the earliest gravel surfaces, examples were found in the filling of timber features attributed to the Leaholme fort and the main filling of Ditch III, AM II 59. Apparently in use *c.* A.D. 50-75.

Fabric 71A – Hard fine-grained sandy ware. Brick red with grey core; cream slip. Probably a Gloucester product.

Fabric 71B – fine-grained sandy ware, tempered with sparse large white chalk grits. Grey core; orange surfaces, with a cream slip. Sparse grey flint trituration grits. Probably from sources south and east of Cirencester. Absent from the earliest gravel surfaces.

Fabric 72 – coarse-grained sandy ware. Cream or orange-brown with lighter surfaces, with grey, white or brown flint trituration grit. Manufactured in the Verulamium region. Only two examples occur and they are confined to the layers sealing-off the early occupation and are typologically Flavian.

Fabric 73 – sandy ware, heavily tempered with fine white calcareous grits. Bright red ware. No evidence of the type of trituration grit used, if any. Possibly of local origin. Examples are confined to the back-filling of the quarried stretches of Ditch III.

Fabric 74 – B.B.1

All examples appear to be from Dorset, Williams Group I. The fabrics and forms have been described in detail by Gillam, Gillam and Mann, and Farrar, and analysed by Peacock and Williams, so that no further descriptions are needed here (Gillam, 1960, 113-129; 1968. Gillam & Mann, 1970, 1-44. Farrar, 1973, 73-6. Peacock, 1967, 97-100. Williams, 1977, 177-199). None of the examples are securely stratified in layers which definitely can be attributed to the military occupation or to occupation contemporary with that occupation. They are all typologically early, with the exception of no. 254, they are all from Dorset – Williams Group I, and they are in contexts which pre-date the mainstream trade in B.B.1 by a considerable depth of stratigraphy, which hopefully reflects accurately the length of time involved. Early B.B.1 has been identified at Gloucester, Kingsholm, a military site receiving much of its pottery supplies from the same sources as Cirencester, Leaholme, Usk, and Sea Mills, so that the discovery of equally early B.B.1 at Cirencester was predictable (Darling, 1977, fig. 6, 9, 26; Greene, 1973, 33; Bristol City Museum). Yet no. 254 remains an embarrassment, since elsewhere the most optimistic dating for its use is A.D. 120, a date more than justified by finds from Cirencester, which tend to favour a date nearer A.D. 140. There is other intrusive late material from the sealing-off layers of sites DK and DM, including an Antonine coin, but work to date appears to prove that the Antonine pieces are intrusive, either during excavation or processing.

Fabric 75 – fine-grained sand-free highly micaceous ware, with no tempering. Cream ware with a green glaze. An import from Central Gaul, possibly the Lezoux area.

Fabric 76 – off-white fine-grained ware, tempered with white calcareous grit, fairly coarse sand, including transluscent brown quartz. Probably from the Oxford region.

Fabric 77 – highly micaceous fine-grained sandy ware. Orange-brown, with a thin cream slip.

Amphora of unknown form. Origin unknown. Not illustrated.

Fabric 78 – the ware resembles that of Fabric 40 in texture and composition. Light pinkish-brown, with a thick cream slip. There is only one example from the site, a base, with an unusually shaped knob. Origin unknown, probably Spain. Not illustrated.

Fabric 79 – fine-grained sand-free ware heavily tempered with fairly coarse calcareous grit. Cream ware. Used for amphorae of Camulodunum type 185A. Imported from southern Spain. Not illustrated.

Fabric 112 – Blue-grey fine-grained sandy ware; thin orange-brown cortex. Lead glaze on interior and/or exterior with colours ranging from light green to dark green-brown.

Fabric 153 – Pompeian Red ware. Coarse-grained gritty orange-brown ware. External red polished slip. This is Peacock's Fabric 1 (Peacock, 1977, 149) considered to have been imported from southern Italy before A.D. 43 and used for platters and matching lids of Camulodunum form 17. The examples from Bagendon, type 6, are in this ware.

The Groups

THE LEAHOLME FORT

CONSTRUCTION LEVELS OF THE RAMPART

AM I 63

1. The base from a jar with a foot-ring. Hand-made. Fabric 3. Grey core; light red-brown surfaces; vertically burnished exterior. Burnt and discoloured.

Similar bases, also with vertical burnishing occur on a range of hand-made necked jars and bowls from Bagendon, types 96, 116 and 126, and Rodborough Common (unpublished, Stroud Museum), so this base appears to be part of the local pre-Roman pottery tradition. Only one other has been identified to date,

which probably belonged to no. 92. It is more probably pre-Conquest in date although the production of such hand-made finer wares may have continued well into the Claudian period and may have been supplied to the Roman Army.

The base from a jar or necked bowl. Fabric 3. The piece can be paralleled at Bagendon so that it too could be pre-Conquest in date, but is more probably early Claudian, made locally and supplied to the army. Tiberio-Claudian.

OCCUPATION WITHIN THE LEAHOLME FORT

Site AH VIII

The quantity and quality of the groups are comparatively poor, the sherds are small and rather worn, therefore the information available on the forms and fabrics is limited. There are few matches between different layers, and where they occur, they all involve the filling of features and the sealing-off layers. Only a limited range of forms and fabrics are represented, with imported vessels restricted to a few samian vessels, and bowls and beakers in colour-coated ware.

Vessels in the local hand-made Iron Age tradition are absent, the basic wares being Roman in technique and traceable at least until the end of the second century. They are fine-grained, more or less micaceous, and tempered with varying quantities of white, red-brown or grey grog, white calcareous, red or grey ferrous grits, i.e. Fabrics 1, 2, 4, 6 and 13. Those tempered with fine grit tend to have been oxidised rather than reduced, to have a glossy burnished finish and to be table rather than kitchen forms. The fabrics tempered with coarser grit were normally reduced, were less well finished and were for use in the kitchen, although some attempt had been made usually to mask the grits with a wet-hands or slurry finish, to smooth the rim, also sometimes the shoulder, and even decorate a few vessels. Chiefly on the type and quantity of the tempering, Fabrics 6 and 13, could be considered to fall within the definition of Savernake wares, while Fabrics 1, 2 and 4, could be defined as Severn Valley wares (Swan, 1975, 42; Hodder, 1974, 67-84; Webster, P.V., 1976, 18). In the context of the Leaholme Fort, it seems unlikely that the vessels which fall within the range of Severn Valley wares actually came from a source in the Severn Valley itself, unless it was located at or near Gloucester. Considering the possible sources for the related fabrics, Fabrics 6 and 13, and their association with the Savernake area, a source for the so-called Severn Valley wares from Leaholme may lie near Cirencester, or to the south-east. The quantities in which Fabric 4 and 6 occur elsewhere in Cirencester and at Bagendon suggest that the source, or sources, should be considered as local (see p. 153). There is a marked scarcity of coarse-grained sandy or gritty wares, made with naturally abrasive clay or tempered with coarse sand. This is true at Bagendon and Rodborough Common and is probably due to the geology of the area. The range of forms is confined to tankards, necked jars, jars with bead-rims and necked storage jars, but it is almost certainly artificially restricted by the shortage of diagnostic sherds as well as the size of the sample. Few pieces are decorated, and where decoration exists it is restricted in area and simple in execution – a band of burnished or incised lattice on the shoulder, single grooves, or pairs forming low-relief cordons, or a combination of all three. No examples of rustic decoration occur below the sealing-off layers and even here there is just one sherd. It is noteworthy that despite the small size of the groups, there is one definite and one possible tankard, the first in the earliest group from the site, the second in the filling of a post-hole belonging to Period II B (p. 204) & no. 9). The form appears to have been in common use in the Claudian period and in both cases, the fabrics, although different in detail, fall within the definition of Severn Valley ware (Webster, P.V., 1976, 18). Tankards apparently of equally early date have been identified at Bagendon, type 109, and Rodborough Common, although they were apparently not recognised as such in the reports, and they too are in so-called Severn Valley wares (Clifford, 1961, fig. 65, 109. Unpublished Stroud Museum). Generally, the assemblage is different to those from equivalent layers elsewhere within the Leaholme fort, but this could be due to the small and consequently unrepresentative size of the sample. All the samian is post-Conquest but pre-Flavian in date, and at present there is no reason to date the coarse wares any later. The groups from the sealing-off layers include three sherds of Flavian date suggesting that nothing amongst the coarse wares need be later than *c.* A.D. 85.

Phase I – occupation on the natural gravel

AH VIII 116

2. Fabric 1 – originally heavily tempered; vesicular; smoothed but matt finish.
3. Fabric 2 – highly micaceous; vesicular. Burnt and discoloured. Burnished exterior. The rim from a necked bowl.
4. Fabric 3 – worn orange-brown surfaces, slightly vesicular; burnished finish. The rim from a necked jar. Possibly pre-Conquest in date. See p. 201, Fabric C.
The miscellaneous sherds are from four different vessels.

Phase II – Gravel surface on natural

AH VIII 93

5. (Match in AH VIII 78). Fabric 6A – hard; matt lightly rilled slurry finish. A storage jar; the form and fabric are paralleled at Bagendon, type 173.

Occupation on Phase II surface

AH VIII 75

6. Fabric 7 – burnished exterior. Rare compared to versions in Fabrics 6 & 13, but examples have been found at Bagendon (Clifford, 1961, fig. 54, 21) and Rodborough Common (Rennie, 1959, fig. 6, 17).
7. Fabric 4 – smooth ware. Sparse tempering. Blue-grey core; soapy smooth burnished finish. The rim from a necked bowl.
The miscellaneous sherds are from one vessel.
Samian – pre-Flavian.

Occupation on the Phase III gravel surfaces

AH VIII 91

8. Fabric 6A – surfaces shade from light grey to dark blue-grey; smoothed exterior. Identical jars from Bagendon, type 147 (Clifford, 1961, fig. 54); Mildenhall, the Well deposits (Annable, 1966, fig. 2, 6); Oare (Swan, 1975, fig. 3, 29); Savernake kilns (Annable, 1962, fig. 5, 13).

The filling of Phase III Timber features

AH VIII P.H.4

9. a. Fabric 4 – blue-grey core; brownish-orange surfaces. Worn, with traces of a highly burnished finish.
b. The base is almost certainly from the same tankard. Other examples – AH VIII 116 – Fabric 4. Similar tankards in orange-brown fabrics occur at Bagendon, type 109 (Clifford, 1961, fig. 65), Rodborough Common (Unpulished, Stroud Museum), Mildenhall well (Annable, 1966, fig. 3, 49), Sea Mills (Bristol Museum). Tankards appear to have been made in orange-brown fabrics from the earliest stages of the Roman occupation of the area.
The miscellaneous sherds are from one vessel.

AH VIII P.H.7 (Matches in AH VIII 111)

10. Fabric 70 – blue-grey; pinky-brown surfaces. Considerably worn, the few surviving trituration grits are grey and dark brown. Heavily burnt and discoloured on the inside along the line of the bead. The inscription on the outside was cut when the vessel was leather-hard, before firing (see fig. 66, 1). The Fabric can be attributed

to Gloucester where at least one example occurs at Kingsholm (Darling, 1977, fig. 6, 9, 18). Pre Flavian. Samian – Neronian or early Flavian.

Phase IV gravel surfaces

AH VIII 100

11. Fabric 44 – cream slip on the exterior and over the rim. The rim from a honey-pot (see nos. 312-314). The miscellaneous sherds are from three vessels, one possibly matches no. 20 (AH VIII 68).

The filling of a timber-slot

AH VIII 83

12. Fabric 6A – light blue-grey ware; smoothed exterior.
Also a body sherd from a large beaker. Fabric 56.

Layers sealing the military occupation

AH VIII 96

13. Fabric 56 – metallic brown slip. Fine sand rough-casting, outside only. Probably an import. Pre-Flavian or Flavian. Two examples from Bagendon, type 45 (Clifford, 1961, fig. 63).
14. Fabric 5 – burnt and discoloured. Worn, crudely smoothed finish. (Matching sherds in layers 97 & 57). Other examples – AM III 14.
15. Fabric 5 – worn surfaces. (Matching sherd in AH VIII 58). There is an identical jar from the construction levels of the Watermoor Rampart, no. 402. At least one example from Bagendon, type 116D (Clifford, 1961, fig. 65).
16. Fabric 6A – rilled matt surfaces.
There are miscellaneous sherds from two flagons, one as no. 308.
Samian – pre-Flavian (S. 47).

AH VIII 78

17. Fabric 10 – sparse tempering; grey core at the rim. (Matching sherds in layer 4).
18. Fabric 8 – burnt in patches; highly burnished exterior. Probably a butt beaker.
19. Fabric 4 – orange core; streaky orange and grey surfaces; burnished exterior.
In addition – sherds from two vessels.
Samian – Flavian (D.1).

AH VIII 68

20. Fabric 5 – burnished shoulder, burnished bands on the neck.

Site AG II & III

With the exception of the complete jar from the pit AG III 49, the pottery is little better than that from site AH VIII. The assemblages are rather different for there is an increase in the proportion of reduced wares apparently at the expense of the oxidised finer-tempered wares although the coarse-tempered kitchen wares (reduced) maintain their position. The difference could be chronological since the general trend in the second half of the first century A.D. appears to be away from oxidised wares, it is probably due to the small size of the samples.

There is no samian from the actual occupation layers and unfortunately the coarse ware vessels are of types which survived in production beyond the mid-second century A.D.. Pit AG III 49 was more productive, with two sherds of pre-Flavian samian in the lower filling and a decorated sherd dated c. A.D. 75-95 (D. 3), in the upper layer which means that the sealing-off silty layers cannot have been deposited before A.D. 75 at the very earliest. The sealing-off layers produced larger and more helpful groups than AH VIII, for besides the usual group of pre-Flavian residual material, there are three sherds of Flavian samian, including a decorated piece dated A.D. 80-100 (D. 4-5). Amongst the coarse wares, nothing need date to later than c. A.D. 95, although a number of indeterminate rims might be later, as could the rustic jars in Fabrics 17 and 20 (nos 41-42). However, the absence of other forms and fabrics characteristic of second century groups at Cirencester, supports the samian dating.

Occupation on natural

AG II 48

21. Fabric 5 – highly burnished finish. Rim sherd from a typical necked bowl.

Occupation on the second phase of gravel surfaces

AG II 42

22. Fabric 13A – dark grey, burnt and sooty exterior; matt slurry finish.
23. Fabric 6B – hard; mottled grey surfaces; rough and lumpy finish due to the grits protruding. Sooty lip.

Occupation on the third phase of gravel surfaces

AG II 41

24. Fabric 6A – heavily tempered; lightly rilled neck and shoulder.
There are miscellaneous sherds from two vessels.

Filling of Timber and other Features

AG III 49

25. Fabric 14 – dark grey surfaces; highly burnished exterior, with an incised spiral on the neck.
26. Fabric 6A – over-fired. Unusually fine tempering;

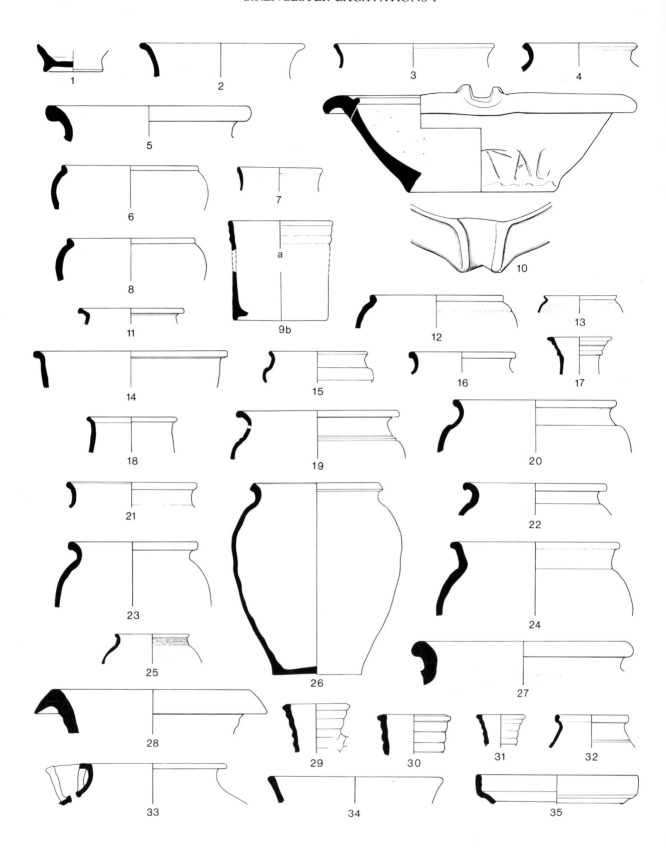

Fig. 50.   Coarse pottery (1:4)

surfaces shade from dark grey to grey buff; matt slurry finish.
Also sherds from a flagon.
Samian – Claudio-Neronian (S. 29).

AG III 43
27. Fabric 13 – hard. Heavily tempered. Smoothed slurry finish; slightly vesicular.
Samian – *c.* A.D. 75-95 (D. 2-3).

Layers sealing-off the early occupation

AG II 36; III 38 & 39
28. Fabric 34 – amphora, Camulodunum form 186B. AG II 36.
29. Fabric 9 – buff core at the rim. AG III 39.
30. Fabric 19 – orange-brown, cream slip. Also a rim and neck and handle sherds from two others similar in Fabrics 19 and 9. AG II 36.
31. Fabric 11 – pale orange; cream slip. AG III 38.
32. Fabric 9 – bright orange; thin cream slip. AG III 38. Other examples – AS II 75, in Fabric 9, orange with a cream slip.
33. Fabric 19 – cream slip. There is no evidence for the precise number of spouts, and whether or not there was a handle. AG II 36. There is an identical jug from BC I 58, and several similar jugs from the area of the Leaholme fort but since all are in the sealing-off layers, it seems probably that they were not in use until after A.D. 65. The basic type is present amongst the early pottery from Usk (Darling, 1977, fig. 6.4, 18).
34. Fabric 5 – highly burnished faceted finish. AG III 39. Other examples – CG IV 19; layers sealing the Sands rampart.
35. Fabric 5 – burnished finish. AG II 36.
36. Fabric 4 – sparse tempering; burnished rim and interior, smoothed exterior. Discoloured by smoke and soot. AG III 39.
37. Fabric 16 – blue core; pale orange surfaces dis-coloured with smoky grey patches. Faceted burnishing on the rim and shoulder. Decoration – uneven burnished lattice on a matt ground. AG II 36 and 30.
38. Fabric 16 – orange-buff. Worn. In addition a small rim sherd from another. Fabric 16 – orange ware, buff surfaces. AG II 36.
39. Fabric 4 – light grey; smoothly burnished finish. AG II 36.
40. Fabric 17 – burnished exterior. In addition there are rim sherds from two necked jars – Fabric 16 – mottled grey ware; Fabric 17 – grey ware. AG II 36.
41. Fabric 17 – grey core; mottled grey and brown surfaces. Highly burnished rim top, smoothed shoulder. Decoration – low relief nodular rustication. AG III 39.
42. Fabric 20 – some fine sand; mottled brownish grey surfaces. Decoration – low relief nodular rustication. AG III 39. Rim and body sherds from another. Fabric 17. Decoration – low relief nodular rustication. AG III 39. Rim and body sherd from a third example. Fabric 8 – grey core; brown cortex; black surfaces. Decoration – low relief nodular rustication. AG II 36.
43. Fabric 6A – slurry finish, lightly rilled. Rim sherd from another similar jar. Fabric 6A. AG II 36.
44. Fabric 6E – brown core; sooty black surfaces. AG III 39.
45. Fabric 13 – hard. Grey ware; lumpy, matt finish. AG II 36.
46. Fabric 6C – thin grey core; rust cortex; blue-grey surfaces, lightly rilled exterior finish. AG II 36.
47. Fabric 6C – brown core; grey surfaces; burnished rim and shoulder. Decoration – burnished lattice on a matt ground. AG III 39. Rim sherd and body from two other storage jars. Fabric 6A. AG II 36. Storage jars with similar burnished decoration occur at Bagendon, type 174 (Clifford, 1961, fig. 68, 174), Sea Mills (Bristol Museum), Mildenhall Well (Annable, 1966, fig. 3, 41). There are miscellaneous sherds from five other vessels. The group includes much residual material.
Samian – *c.* A.D. 80-100 (D. 4-5).

Site AE

The quality and quantity of the groups continued to be poor but the assemblages are rather different to those from both site AH and AG. Oxidised wares are scarcer than on site AH while the dark grey or black ware, Fabric 5, is proportionally much more important than on sites AH or AG, and Fabric 17 is better represented. The range of forms is wider, with the presence of platters imitating Gallo-Belgic forms and imitation butt beakers, both in Fabric 5, and narrow-necked jars or flasks in Fabric 17. The samian trampled into natural is Claudio-Neronian which matches that on site AH for date, but the coarse wares may be somewhat later, after A.D. 55, due to the presence of sherds from two jars in Fabric 17, coupled with the greater importance of reduced at the expense of oxidised wares.

Occupation on natural

AE V 21
48. Fabric 26 – sparse fine sand. Pinky buff. The rim from a honey-pot (see nos. 312-315).
49. Fabric 6A – very worn.
There are sherds from four other vessels, including Fabric 21 (see below no. 300) and two examples in Fabric 17.
Samian – Claudio-Neronian. After *c.* A.D. 50.

The presence of sherds of Fabric 17 suggests that this layer is later in date than the equivalent layer on site AH VIII.

Filling of timber and other features

AE II P.H.3 + P.H.1
50. Fabric 5 – burnished finish. Other examples – Ashcroft Road, 1961 – A VIII 11, in Fabric 5; AL I 27; Dyer Court, 1957 (Webster, G., 1959, fig. 14, 15).

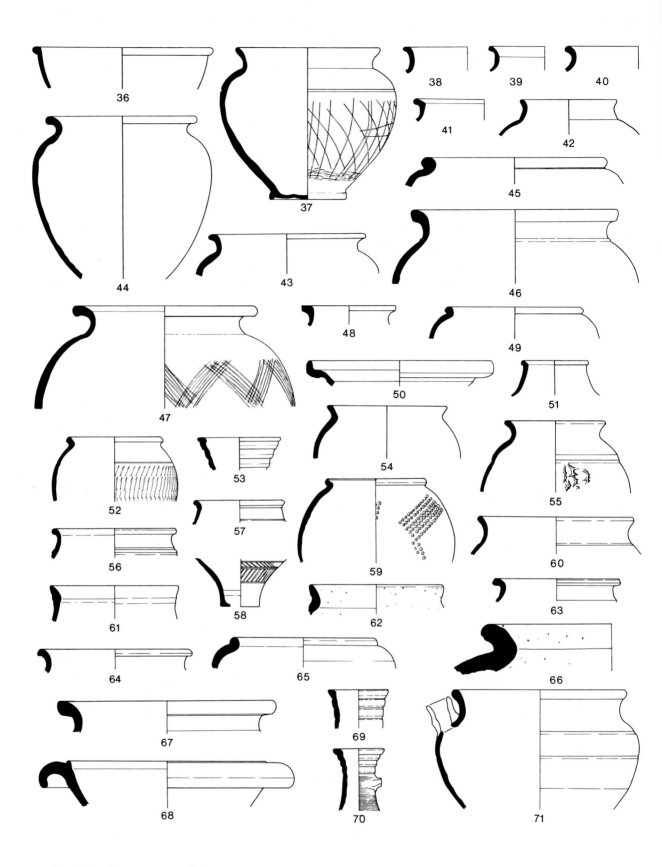

Fig. 51.   Coarse pottery (1:4)

There are miscellaneous sherds from three vessels, including one like no. 52.

AE II P.H.2
Samian – Claudian (D. 6).

AE VII P.H.1
51. Fabric 5 – burnished exterior. Miscellaneous sherds from another jar in Fabric 5.

AE V 19 – timber-slot
52. Fabric 17 – powdery ware; some sparse dark grey grog grits. Worn, but traces of a burnished finish on the rim and shoulder. Decoration – rouletted. Other examples – AL II 33; AD IV 31; AD III 27; DK I 72. The miscellaneous sherds are from two vessels.

Sealing layers

AE III 16
53. Fabric 11 – buff dirty cream slip.
54. Fabric not classified.
Samian – Claudio-Neronian. After *c.* A.D. 50.

Sites DK and DM

The groups from sites DK and DM are in marked contrast to those from equivalent layers on sites AH, AG and AE. The areas excavated are markedly larger, and the features included rubbish deposits, so that the quantity is much greater whilst the quality of the sherds is better, with larger sherds, relatively unworn, and with numerous matches between features and layers. Since the difference in size of the samples is so great, the differences between the various assemblages have certainly been magnified and may have been distorted.

The range of forms and fabrics from the occupation layers are much wider than those from equivalent layers on the sites previously discussed, and resemble more closely the material from the sealing-off layers of the latter. There is a real difference but it may have been exaggerated by the presence of more diagnostic sherds in the larger groups. More fine and imported wares are represented, terra nigra, glazed and mica-coated wares, amphorae and mortaria being added to samian and colour-coated wares. Amongst the coarse wares the additional forms include platters, nos. 89, 99, 106 and 107, bowls, no. 74, beakers, no. 59, and jars, no. 94, while there is a marked increase in the number of rustic jars and necked bowls in Fabric 5. Partly as a result of the increase in the number of rustic jars, there is a marked increase in the importance of untempered blue-grey wares, particularly Fabrics 16, 17 and 20, along with the probably related flagon ware, Fabric 9. In the context of the Leaholme fort, the dating of the new material is made difficult because little of it appears in the filling of the ditches assigned to the final period of occupation, particularly the large group from Ditch III. With the exception of two pieces which could be later, all the samian from the lowest layers on sites DK and DM, including the material trampled into the natural clay, is Neronian in date so giving a later *terminus post quem* than equivalent groups from site AH and so appears to support a later date for the coarse wares, after *c.* A.D. 55. A comparison with groups from site AE shows that although the samian could be earlier, the coarse ware assemblages, despite their small size resemble those from sites DK and DM more closely than sites AH or AG.

The material from the second and third phase of occupation shows no marked difference to that from the lowest layers, the latest samian continues to be Neronian, with just one piece which could be early Flavian, and an apparently intrusive Hadrianic or Antonine sherd.

The groups from pit DM I 145/154 and from the pit DK I 106/115 are crucial for dating the deposition of the silty sealing-off layers. The rubbish accumulation in pit DM I 145/154 includes a group of material contemporary with that in the filling of Ditch III, but the majority is later, Flavian or Flavian-Trajanic. Ten sherds of samian are of Flavian date, while the mortarium no. 68, has been dated A.D. 80-120. Amongst the coarse wares there are many types which are paralleled only in the sealing-off layers on sites DK and DM, and otherwise occur in Flavian or Flavian-Trajanic contexts elsewhere in Cirencester, e.g. nos. 71, 73, 74, 79 and 82. The accumulation of the rubbish in this deposit could have begun as early as A.D. 60/65, but its final deposition cannot have taken place until after A.D. 80. The group from the pit DK I 106/115 is less diagnostic, but in the upper layers includes Flavian samian and a mortarium dated A.D. 80-120, no. 68. The silty sealing-off layers not only include the most extensive group of pre-Flavian samian from the sites, they also include the earliest mortaria and a considerable number of early coarse wares. Although much of the group parallels the assemblages from pit DM I 145/154, it does include additional forms. Severn Valley ware could be said to be already represented by the early tankards and by the necked jars or bowls, nos. 9, 3 and 7, and here the range of forms is widened by the platters nos. 72 and 197 and possibly by the carinated bowls nos. 125 & 191. The range of forms in Savernake-type wares is extended from just necked jars and jars with bead rims, of various sizes, to include platters, carinated bowls and lids, nos. 193 and 82-3, while there are two additional bowl types in Fabric 5, nos. 74 and 199. However, probably the most notable introduction is a small group of dishes and jar(s) in B.B.1, nos 254-256.

Given the presence of two sherds of Antonine samian and a coin dated A.D. 134/8, there is some doubt as to whether the group of B.B.1 products should be dated to the late first or second century. Elsewhere in Cirencester, jars in B.B.1 occur in Flavian contexts (see below no. 428), so it appears that a trickle of those products was reaching the area in the later decades of the first century. However, supplies seem to have been intermittent until the mid-second century, after which they were continuous and rapidly expanding. Typologically, the dish, no. 255, and the jar, no. 256, could be Flavian, but recent research cannot date the platter or dog-dish, no. 254, to earlier than A.D. 120 (Farrar, 1977, fig. 14.3, 52). It is possible that the vessels B.B.1 from the sealing layers could be part of two different trading patterns in the first and second century.

Notably absent from the large group of samian are products of the potters working at Les Martres-de-Veyre A.D. 100-135, while the latest of the South Gaulish products are dated A.D. 70-95. Also absent are any mortaria, and, with the exception of the platter in B.B.1, coarse wares which were not produced before the early years of the second century. It is, therefore, unlikely that the rubbish in the silty layers was accumulating continuously until the Antonine period. The bulk of the pottery dates from the Claudian to the Flavian-Trajanic period, while the Antonine material, either marks the final deposition of the uppermost layers, or was intruded during the re-development of the site in the late second century.

Gravel surfaces on natural

DM I 144 (= DK I 111)

55. Fabric 17 – worn. Decoration – low relief linear rustication. (Matching sherd from the lower layers of the pit DM I 145/154). There are base sherds probably from this pot. This jar is unlikely to date to before *c.* A.D. 80 at the earliest, since there are matching sherds in the Pit DM I 145/154, it was probably intruded at the time that the pit was being filled.
56. Fabric 16 – dark grey-brown core; lighter surfaces. Burnished exterior and rim.
57. Fabric 22 – dark grey-black surfaces.
There are sherds from 10 different vessels including a hand-made jar in the local Iron Age tradition.
Samian – Neronian or early Flavian.

Silt on natural and Phase I gravel surfaces

DK I 119 & DK II 48

58. The base from a butt beaker. Fabric 4 – worn. Decoration – bands of lightly burnished chevrons.
59. Fabric 17 – metallic blue-grey slip on the rim and exterior, with a burnished finish. Decoration – matt pale grey barbotine spots.
60. Fabric 4 – hard. Sparse tempering; smoothed finish. Smoky grey patches at the rim.
61. Fabric 6D – overfired. Blue core; thin and smeared orange surfaces. Matt finish.
62. Hand-made. Fabric 24 – soft. Brown core; black surfaces with a soapy burnished finish. Local Iron Age tradition. See p. 201, Fabric C.
63. Fabric 23 – light orange; rough and gritty matt finish. Also body sherds from two jars in Fabric 23 –

grey ware. Other examples – nos. 228, 324-327.
64. Fabric 6A – matt slurry finish. Also body sherds from two other jars in Fabric 6C – grey ware.
65. Fabric 6A – smoothed rim and shoulder.
66. Hand-made. Fabric 24 – soft. Grey core; light red-brown surfaces; soapy burnished finish. Local Iron Age tradition, examples occur at Bagendon. Possibly pre-Claudian. (Match in DK II 43). See p. 201, Fabric C.
67. Fabric 13A – hard; smoothed finish; slightly vesicular. Also body sherds from two other storage jars in Fabrics 6A and 6C, both grey.
The miscellaneous sherds are from eight different vessels, some join a vessel in DK I 116 & DK I 81.

Pit Filling – DM I 154, 155, 152, 151, 140, 146, 145. Apparently below the second phase of gravel surfaces, DM I 132.

DM I 154 – Bottom Layer (Joining sherds from three different vessels in layers 144, Phase I gravel surface; and DM I 145, upper level of the pit filling).
68. Fabric 72 – pinkish orange; cream surfaces. Sparse flint trituration grits. Verulamium region. *c.* A.D. 80-120. Base sherd Fabric 67 – cream ware, typical. Very worn. Kent or north-east Gaul. First century.
69. Fabric 9 – orange, cream slip.
70. Fabric 9 – cream tempering. Blue core; light orange surfaces with rilling on the neck. Also sherds from 10 different flagons. Neck sherds: Fabric 9 – orange-red ware. Neck and handle sherds: Fabric 23 – orange ware. Base sherds: Fabric 9 – orange ware, cream slip. Body sherds: Fabric 11 – pinky buff (2). Fabric 4 – orange ware (2). Fabric 9 – orange (2).

71. Fabric 10 – orange; burnished exterior. There is evidence for only one spout although there could have been more. Other examples – AR IV 7. Ashcroft 1951, IV 8. The form occurred at Wroxeter in red ware with a white slip (Bushe-Fox, 1913, fig. 18, 39).
72. Fabric 16 – some intrusive white grits. Grey core; orange surfaces. Highly burnished finish, with a metallic sheen.
73. Fabric 5 – burnished interior, smoothed exterior. See below, no. 434 (AX II 41). Other examples – AD III 22.
74. Fabric 5 – highly burnished rim and exterior, matt interior. Burnt and sooty inside and out. Dyer Court, 1957 (Webster, G., 1959, fig. 16, 59).
75. Fabric 5 – burnished exterior. (Matching sherds in layer 152).
76. Fabric 153 – Traces of a red polished slip on the exterior and rim. (Matching sherds from DK I 41; 54; 78).
77. Fabric 17 – burnished rim and shoulder. Decoration – low relief, nodular rustication. (Matching sherds in layer 152).
78. Fabric 17 – reddish-brown core; patchy grey and buff surfaces; smoothed rim and shoulder. Decoration – low relief rustication. In addition there are body sherds from three other jars with rustication; Fabric 17 – (1); Fabric 20 – (2). There is also another jar with a band of rouletting below the low relief rustication. Fabric 17.
79. Fabric 4 – grey tempering. Dark grey core; brown cortex; dark sooty grey surfaces; smoothed matt finish. Sooty patches. Also a rim sherd from another similar vessel.
80. Fabric 17 – burnished rim and shoulder. Also a complete base, probably from the same pot.
81. Fabric 17 – over-fired; traces of a burnished finish on the shoulder.
82. Fabric 6C – brown core; exterior soot encrusted. (Matching sherds in layer 152). Other examples – DK I 46; DK I 41; DK I 35; AM III 17.
83. Fabric 6C – dark brown core; patchy dark brown and grey surfaces. (Matching sherds in layer 152).
There are miscellaneous sherds from over ten vessels including a necked jar decorated with deeply incised evenly spaced strips, in Fabric 17.
Samian – Neronian–Flavian

DM I 145 – Upper levels of the pit
84. Fabric 5 – burnished rim and exterior; rilled interior. Sooty patches on the outside.
85. Fabric 17 – rusty core; worn grey surfaces so that the core colour shines through in patches. No finish survives.
The miscellaneous sherds from five vessels include a heavily burnt jar in Fabric 12.
Samian – Flavian (S. 13).
After c. A.D. 70.

Second phase of gravel surfaces

DK I 116 & DK II 45
86. Fabric 28 – traces of a coral slip on both surfaces. The rim from either a shallow platter or the deep flange from a bowl; probably the former.
87. Fabric 22 – dark grey surfaces. Traces of a highly burnished finish on the rim, facetted burnishing on the inside.
88. Fabric 19 – blue core; orange surfaces; matt finish. Also the base from a flagon in Fabric 9 – light orange ware.
89. Fabric 28 – sparse red grits; soapy smooth burnished finish.
90. Fabric 5 – worn with traces of a burnished finish on the exterior.
91. Fabric 5 – highly burnished finish. Sooty patches inside and out. Also rim sherds from three other jars in Fabric 5.
92. Fabric 25 – facetted burnished finish. (Matching base sherds in DK I 119). An unusual fabric here, more closely related to late Iron Age fabrics than to Romano-British. The base has a fairly tall foot-ring, like no. 1. Tiberio-Claudian.
93. Fabric 5 – matt finish. Sooty exterior.
94. Fabric 23 – rough and gritty matt finish.
There are miscellaneous sherds from 15 different vessels, including three amphorae, Dressel type 30 and a thin-walled butt beaker copying Camulodunum 113 in fine grained orange ware, possibly a local product.
Samian – Neronian to early Flavian group, with Hadrianic-Antonine. (S. 7).

Gravel layers on ?Phase II gravel surface (DK I 111)

DK I 105
95. Fabric 23 – overfired. Orange core; blue-grey shading to brown surfaces. Smooth finish on the rim and between the cordons on the shoulder; remainder has a matt rough finish. (Matching sherds in layers DK I 109, 103 and 102). Also rim sherd possibly from another similar jar in typical Fabric 23.

Occupation on ? Phase II gravel surfaces

DK I 109 – Dump of intensely burnt material
96. Fabric 34 – amphora, Camulodunum form 186A.
97. Fabric 57 – metallic brown slip. Fine grog rough-casting on the exterior. Pre-Flavian or Flavian.
98. Fabric 53 – mica gilt coating on the exterior and rim.
99. Fabric 17 – Brown core; worn dark grey surfaces; burnished interior. A very accurate copy of an imported G-B platter type. It is probably a local product judging from the fabric which makes it particularly interesting since the imported Tiberio-Claudian prototypes themselves did not reach Cirencester, although they did reach Bagendon, type 2 (Clifford, 1961, fig. 47, 4–6).
Other examples – AL II 29, Fabric 17 – grey ware.
100. Fabric 5 – blue-grey core; very worn grey surfaces, no finish survives.
101. Fabric 5 – burnished exterior. Also base and body sherds from at least two others in Fabric 5.
102. Fabric 6E – light brown core; dark grey-brown surfaces; burnished rim and shoulder, rilled lower body.
103. Fabric 6A – burnished rim and shoulder, matt below the decoration. Decoration – burnished stripes on a matt ground. Also a sherd from a handmade version in Fabric 6A – oxidised; orange-buff ware and red grog grits.
There are miscellaneous sherds from nine different vessels.
Samian – Neronian.

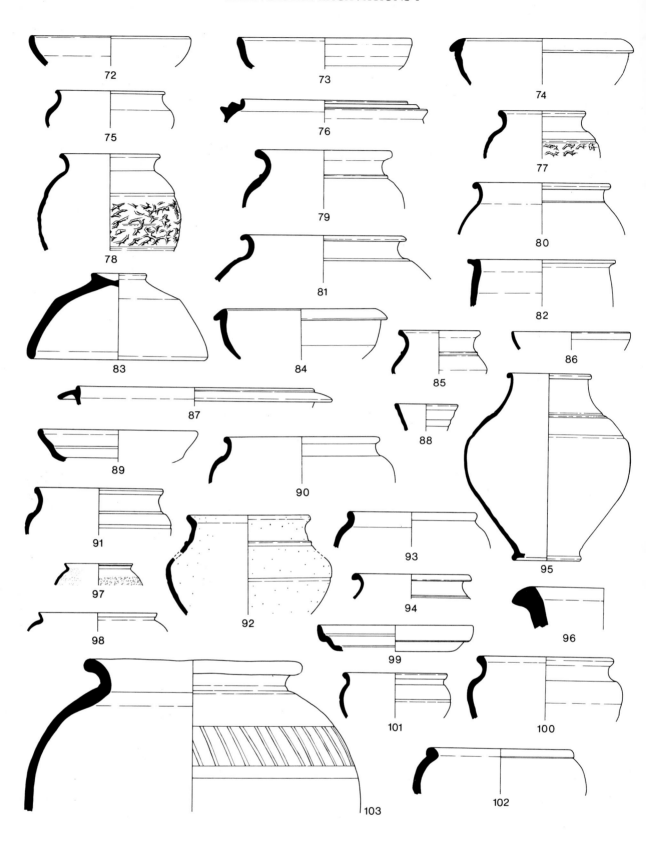

Fig. 52.   Coarse pottery (1:4)

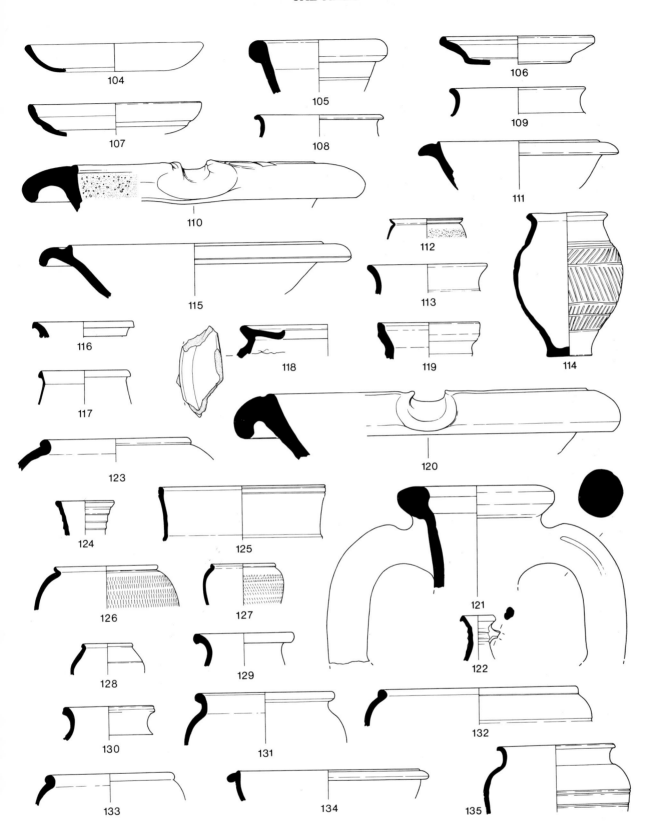

Fig. 53. Coarse pottery (1:4)

Well or Pit filling

DK I 115, 114, 107, 106.

104. T.N. – pale blue ware with sparse grey grits; blue-grey surfaces; polished finish. An import. *c.* A.D. 45-80. About one-third of the rim circuit. There are sherds from 29 similar platters from Cirencester.

105. Fabric 35 – amphora, Dressel type 30.

106. Fabric 23 – streaked and patchy grey and orange surfaces; smoothed finish. Also bases from three platters, two in Fabric 5, one in Fabric 23.
Other examples – Ashcroft 1961, A VII 38.

107. Fabric 5 – burnished interior, smoothed exterior.

108. Fabric 17 – paler surfaces; burnished rim top and in bands on the neck.

109. Fabric 23 – light grey core; dark blue-grey surfaces, smoothed matt finish.
There are small miscellaneous sherds from eleven vessels, including an Italian amphora, Dressel 2-4, Fabric 39.
Samian – pre-Flavian–Flavian (S. 37).
The group appears to be related to the earliest silt layers on sites DM and DK.

? Phase III occupation

DK I 106

110. Fabric 67 – softish fine slightly yellowish-cream fabric with flint and quartz-like trituration grit combined with internal concentric scoring. The stamp belongs to Q. Valerius Veranius (see M.1). *c.* A.D. 70-100.
There are miscellaneous sherds from nine vessels, including a flagon like no. 180.
Samian – Claudio-Neronian.

? Phase III occupation

DK I 102

111. Fabric 71B smoky grey and orange patchy surfaces, with traces of a smoky cream slip. Sparse flint trituration grits. Possibly local. Probably pre-Flavian.
In addition, a rim fragment from a mortarium, of either Group I or Group II, (Hartley, K.F., 1977) Gillam type 238. Fabric 67, very worn, A.D. 50-100, (Matches in DK I 81, see no. 168).
There are miscellaneous sherds from nine vessels. They include a bead-rimmed jar in a fabric heavily tempered with shell grit and a carinated beaker similar to Camulodunum 120, in Fabric 22.
Samian – Tiberio-Claudian and Neronian. (D. 11).

? Phase III occupation

DK I 103

112. Rim sherd from a beaker, Camulodunum form 94B, in Fabric 57; pink slip; sand rough-casting, which includes mica flakes. Possibly made at Colchester, but could be imported from Lezoux, Central Gaul. Pre-Flavian or Flavian.
The small group of remaining sherds include joining sherds from no. 95.
Samian – Claudio-Neronian. (S. 33).

DK II 44

113. Fabric 10 – traces of a highly burnished finish.

DK II 43

114. Fabric 10 – very worn powdery surfaces, no finish survives. Decoration – three zones of burnished stripes, with two superimposed grooves on the lower body. There are miscellaneous sherds from two vessels, one heavily burnt.
Samian – Neronian or early Flavian.

Fillings of Timber and other Features

DK I 110 & DK I 113 Timber-Slot

115. Fabric 70 – fine-grained smooth ware. Dark blue-grey core; pinky-orange surfaces. Very worn. A local product, probably from the Gloucester area. Pre-Flavian.

116. Fabric 19 – blue core; orange surfaces, with traces of a cream slip. There is a base sherd and a handle which are probably from the same flagon. Also sherds from five other flagons; one in Fabric 21; two in Fabric 29; one in Fabric 4; two in Fabric 9 – orange ware, cream slip; one in Fabric 11.

117. Fabric 9 – burnished rim and neck. Smoky patches on the outside. A butt beaker.

118. Fabric 10 – hard. Very sparse tempering. Smoothed surfaces. There is an inscription incised on the shoulder (fig. 66, 2). The actual form and function of the vessel is unknown, it has been drawn out as if to form a spout.

119. Fabric 6A – burnished exterior, rilled interior.
In addition:– a. Body sherds from a small globular jar decorated with undefined bosses, Fabric 55.
b. Body sherd from a beaker. Fabric 56 – rough-cast.
There are small miscellaneous sherds from at least fifteen different vessels, all jars, in oxidised versions of Fabrics 4, 5, 8, and 27; in reduced versions of Fabrics 5 (3), 6A (3), 12, 16 (2), 25.
Samian – Neronian?

Pit cut into DM I 132

DM I 136 & 134

120. Fabric 68 – extremely worn. Pink core, cream surfaces. The tempering and trituration grit include white calcareous and red-brown ironstone grit. (See M. 2, p. 148).

121. Fabric 40 – amphora, Dressel type 20. The stamp on the handle reads – MIM (See A. 5, p. 149).

122. Fabric unclassified. Hard sandy ware, overfired. Grey core; orange cortex; dirty grey-white, thin and patchy slip. Intrusive, third and fourth century.

123. Fabric 6A – burnished band on the rim and upper shoulder, matt lower body.
There are miscellaneous sherds from five other vessels, including two amphorae, Camulodunum 186 in Fabric 34.
Samian – Neronian or early Flavian. (D. 13).

Pit cut into DK II 45 (= DK I 116)

DK II 42

124. Fabric 9 – orange; cream slip. See also Dyer Court, 1957 (Webster, G., 1959, fig. 17, 76).

125. Fabric 9 – hard. Matt surfaces.

126. Fabric 17 – burnished rim; decoration – rouletted. Also bases from three and body sherds from two similar

jars, with rouletted decoration.

127. Fabric 4 – blue core; brown cortex; black surfaces; highly burnished rim and shoulder. Decoration – rouletted.

128. Fabric 9 – hard. Blue core; orange surfaces; facetted burnished exterior. Smoky patches.

129. Fabric 20 –highly burnished rim and exterior.

130. Fabric 17 – burnished lip, smoothed matt neck.

131. Fabric 4 – fine tempering. Blue-grey core; orange cortex; dark grey surfaces; matt finish. Sooty patches.

132. Fabric 6E – burnished rim and shoulder.

133. Fabric 13 – rilled finish.

There is a large group of miscellaneous sherds from over 50 vessels, including 17 flagons, a spouted jug, a jar with a pierced strainer base and a jar with rustic decoration.

Samian – c. A.D. 50-65 (S. 19 & 53) (D. 14).

The group appears to be part of the lowest silt layer on sites DM and DK.

'Quarry' filling

DM I 158

134. Fabric 5 – burnished rim and exterior; matt interior with a burnished band.

135. Fabric 5 – variegated light and dark brown surfaces; burnished rim and shoulder, matt neck and a band below the top pair of grooves.

136. Fabric 6E.

There are miscellaneous sherds from four vessels.

Samian – Neronian–early Flavian (D. 17, match in DM I 137).

DM I 150

137. Fabric 40 – amphora, Dressel type 20.

138. Fabric 5 – burnished from the rim to the groove, lower body smoothed.

139. Fabric 4 – blue core; orange cortex; greyish buff surfaces; smoothed matt finish.

The group appears to be related to those above the lowest silt, including the thick upper silts.

DM I 137 – Upper Layer

140. Fabric 32 – smoky grey patches along the rim. Not local, probably from potteries in the Verulamium region. (Wilson, 1972, nos. 102, 103, 107 etc).

141. Fabric 19 – brown core; apricot coloured surfaces. Decoration – rouletted.

142. Fabric 32 – pink core. Probably from the Verulamium region.

143. Fabric 17 – burnt and discoloured surfaces. Worn.

144. Fabric 23 – very worn, no finish survives. Other examples – DM I 47, Fabric 5. Ashcroft 1951, I 8.

145. Fabric 5 – burnished exterior, and interior to the groove, lower body matt.

146. Fabric 17 – grey core; rust cortex; blue-black surfaces. Worn, traces of a burnished finish.

147. Fabric 12 – matt rough finish.

148. Fabric 20 – grey core; very worn brown surfaces.

149. Fabric 5 – burnished exterior and rim; interior matt, with narrow burnished bands or a spiral. Sooty interior.

150. Fabric 74 – B.B.1. Highly burnished surfaces. Possibly a lid or shallow platter.

151. Fabric 32 – smoky grey edge to the rim. Probably from potteries in the Verulamium or the Oxford region.

152. Fabric 6E – blue-grey core; brown cortex; dark grey surfaces. Matt finish. Heavily encrusted with soot.

153. Fabric 6C – rust core; khaki surfaces, exterior heavily burnt and sooty. Matt finish.

154. Fabric 13 – brown core; patchy grey and brown surfaces; matt slurry finish. Similar jar, with cordon, from Mildenhall, the Well deposit, said to be a product of the Savernake kilns (Annable, 1966, fig. 2, 30).

155. Fabric 6C – matt slurry finish.

Samian – Flavian (S. 14 & 18) (D. 15-18).

Layers sealing the military occupation – contexts as listed

Fine Wares

156. Fabric 60 – moulded decoration, cf. gadroons with a row of separate beads above. The wall sherd from a flagon, Déchlette form 62; see also Greene, 1972, 35, fig. 10, no. 3. Imported from Central Gaul. Pre-Flavian. In addition, an abraded sherd, probably from the lower wall of a similar moulded flagon, imported from Central Gaul. DK I 81.

157. Fabric 54 – very thin and patchy maroon slip. Decoration – low relief linear rustication. DK I 81. Other examples – AM I 61, identical.

158. Fabric 57 – variegated brown and orange slip which has flaked on the shoulder where the rough-casting should be. Possibly imported from the Rhineland, or Lezoux, Central Gaul. DM I 131. Also sherds from a bowl and four beakers; all in Fabric 56. A bowl, with scaled decoration, like no. 330, and beakers, with rough-casting in sand, like no. 334 (DK I 81 (5) & DM I 19).

Gallo-Belgic Imports

159a. T.N. – hard pale blue-grey fine-grained dense core; dark blue-grey surfaces; highly polished rim top, paler and less glossy finish elsewhere. The rim from a hemispherical bowl, Camulodunum form 46. An import. DK II 39.

159b. The base from a cup, with a plain functional foot-ring, probably Camulodunum form 58. T.N. A central stamp reading CRISSVIS (see G. 1, p. 150) DM I 19.

Amphorae

160-161. Fabric 40 – Dressel type 20. DM I 19 + DM I 135. Also 10 handles, four necks and a large number of body sherds from a minimum of 14 amphorae of Dressel type 20 in typical Spanish ware.

162. Fabric 34 – Camulodunum form 186A. DM I 19. Also four handles, a base and body sherds from a maximum eight different vessels.

163. Fabric 36 – cream ware. DK I 81.

There is an unusually large group of body sherds from other types otherwise scarcely represented – (not illustrated). Handles from two amphorae, Dressel type 30, in Fabric 35; a handle, Camulodunum form 185A, in Fabric 79; handle, Camulodunum form 185B, Fabric 34; a two-column handle, Dressel type 2/4, Fabric 62; body sherds from an amphora like no. 290 (AM II 59), Fabric 38; a neck sherd from an amphora, possibly Camulod-

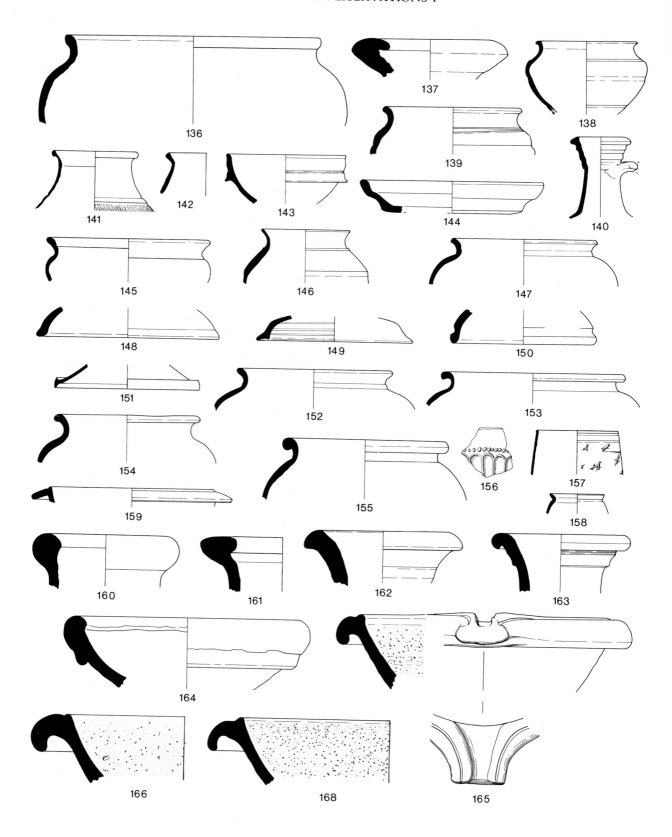

Fig. 54.   Coarse pottery (1:4, except no. 156, 1:2)

unum form 186, Fabric 34; body sherds from an amphora of unknown form, Fabric 77; a base from a small amphora with a bulbous knob, Fabric 78.

Mortaria

164. Fabric 67 – cream fine-grained ware. No trituration grits but faint scoring on the inside. Either an import (?Germany) or made in south-east England. Claudian, although the type survived in use into the Neronian period. DK I 81 + DK II 41.

165. Fabric 68 – soft cream ware; no obvious wear so that the trituration grit is masked; concentric scoring on the inside. (Hartley, 1977, Group I). *c.* A.D. 50-85. DM I 19. Rim sherds from two others identical.

166. Fabric 68 – cream fine-grained ware; fine brown, grey and translucent quartz-like trituration grit. Moderate wear and superficially burnt. As no. 165. *c.* A.D. 50-85. DK I 81.

167. Fabric 67 – cream fine-grained ware; grey and white flint, and quartz-like trituration grit. Superficially burnt. As no. 165. DK I 81 + DK I 102.

168. Fabric 68 – hard cream ware; typical trituration grits, none on the rim. Very worn, but traces of scoring survive below the bead on the inside. As no. 165. DM I 19.

169. Fabric 67 – cream. The grit extends onto the rim. Scored inside. As no. 165. DM I 65. Rim sherds from two others identical (DM I 135), also base sherds from six others in the same fabric. Also rim fragments from two in Fabric 72. Verulamium region. Flavian. DK I 81: DM I 19.

Coarse Wares

170. Fabric 53 – pink, thick mica-coating on the exterior. DK II 40.

171. Fabric 29 – heavily tempered with white calcite and brown grits. Blue-grey core; thin light orange-brown surfaces. DM I 19 + DM I 130.

172. Fabric 19 – orange; creamy buff slip on the outside. DK I 81.

173. Fabric 9. DM I 131. There is an identical flagon from the filling of Ditch III, layer AM II 59, no. 301.

174. Fabric 29 – grey core; buff surfaces. DK II 40. There are identical flagons from the filling of Ditch III, layer AM II 59, nos. 302-304.

175. Fabric 21. There is an identical flagon from the filling of Ditch III, layer AM II 59, no. 300. Also the rim sherd from another example. DM I 19.

176. Fabric 31 – yellowish-cream slip. DM I 135. Rim sherd from another. DK II 40.

177. Fabric 17 – orange, with a thin grey core at the rim; thin cream slip. DM I 65.

178. Fabric 19 – hard. Sparse white tempering. Orange core; pink surfaces. DM I 19.

179. Fabric 19 – Also rim sherd from two others. DK I 81.

180. Fabric 19 – dark orange ware, cream slip. DM I 131.
Also rim sherds from five others identical and three others in Fabric 9 – orange ware, cream slip. DK II 40; DK I 81; DM I 19; DK II 39.

181. Fabric 9 – overfired. Red core; blue surfaces, cream slip. DK I 81.

182. Fabric 19 – no trace of a slip. DM I 131. Also the rim from another identical flagon. DK I 81.

183. Fabric 4 – brown ware; buff surfaces. Also a rim sherd from another similar. Fabric 9. DM I 19. Other examples – DK I 106.

184. Fabric 29 – overfired. Sparse tempering. Blue core; patchy buff and blue-grey surfaces. DM I 130.

185. Fabric 19 – badly flaked surfaces. DK II 39. Also the rim from another similar. DK II 42. Other examples – AL I 21, Fabric 26; DM I 94, Fabric 26.

186. Fabric 4 – pinky buff; very worn and flaked surfaces. DK I 81.

187. Fabric 9 – orange, patchy cream slip. DM I 19. There is a similar honey-pot from layer DM I 139.

188. Fabric 5 – highly burnished rim and neck. DK I 81.

189. Fabric 9 – hard. Buff core; orange-buff surfaces streaked with grey. Matt finish. Possibly a tankard. DM I 19.

190. Fabric 1 – slightly vesicular; burnished exterior. The rim from a tankard. DM I 19.

191. Fabric 1 – slightly vesicular; matt finish. DM I 120.

192. Fabric 5 – highly burnished finish. DM I 135. A close copy of the imported T.N. platter form, Camulodunum 14. Probably pre- or early Flavian. Other examples – DM I 104.

193. Fabric 13 – smooth, burnished interior, matt and lumpy exterior finish. DM I 19, (C. 2. – p. 150). Other examples – Parsonage Field, 1958. CW/58/20; Fabric 6A.

194. Fabric 5 – sandy ware. Dark grey-black; highly burnished interior; smoothed exterior. DK II 40 + DK I 81. Other examples – AX V 12; CJ I 17; CG III 16. Ashcroft 1951, II 4. Parsonage Field 1958, CW/58/240.

195. Fabric 5 – burnished finish. Sooty patches on exterior and rim. DM I 130. Other examples – DK I 28; Fabric 5, AD V 92 + 99.

196. Fabric 5 – burnished finish. Sooty patches. DM I 19.

197. Fabric 23 – coarse sand and white grits. Grey core; orange-brown surfaces; burnished interior; matt exterior finish. DK I 81 + DK I 97. Other examples – DQ I 92; DQ I 169.

198. Fabric 5 – burnished surfaces. DK I 81.

199. Fabric 5 – grey-black surfaces; burnished rim, matt exterior with burnished bands. DK I 81.

200. Fabric 5 – burnished rim and interior, matt exterior. DM I 137. Dyer Court 1957 (Webster, G., 1959, fig. 16, 61).

201. Fabric 5 – burnished rim and exterior, matt interior with burnished bands. DM I 19 (2). Other examples – AG II 22; AS III 47; DQ I 177.

202. Fabric 5 – burnished rim, worn interior, burnished exterior. DM I 19.

203. Fabric 5 – burnished exterior; smoothed interior, with burnished bands. Decoration – burnished arcs. DM I 19.

204. Fabric 5 – very worn brown surfaces. DM I 19. A rim from a second identical jar. DK I 81.

205. Fabric 6B – unusually fine tempering. Dark grey, smoothed surfaces. Sooty patches. DK I 81.

206. Fabric 10 – pale orange; smoothed exterior. DM I 19.

207. Fabric 5 – rilled exterior finish. DM I 135.

208. Fabric 20 – very worn. Sooty patches. Also rims

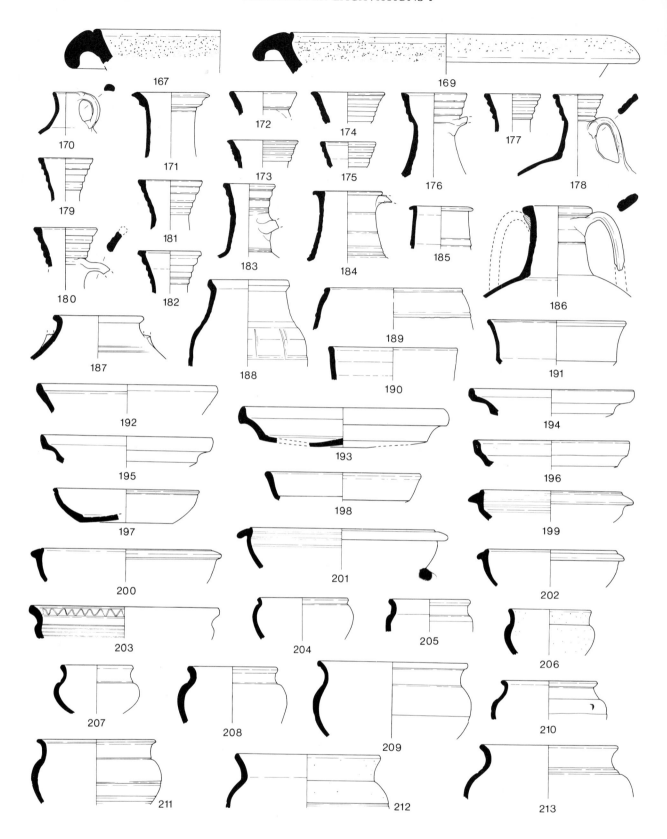

Fig. 55.   Coarse pottery (1:4)

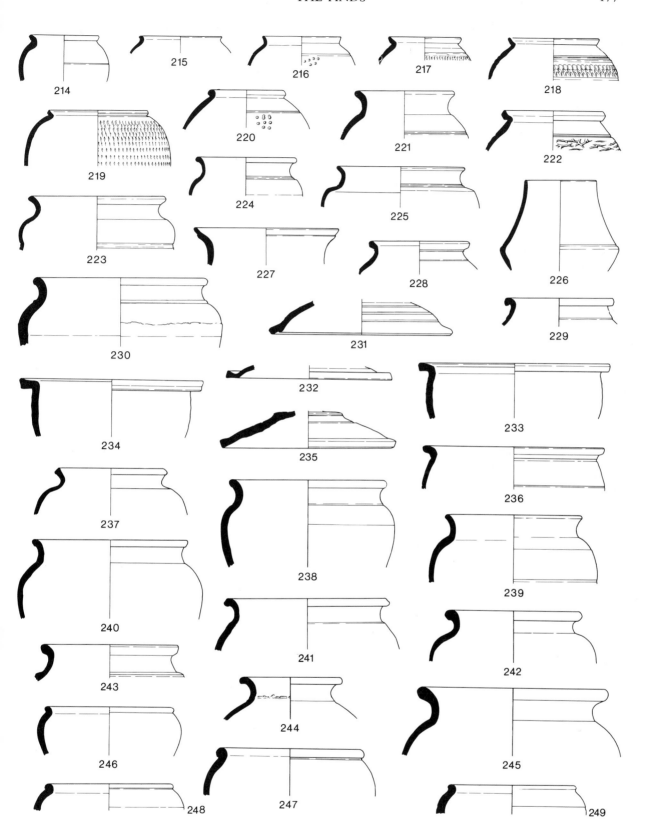

Fig. 56.   Coarse pottery (1:4)

from two other similar in Fabric 5 – dark grey. DK I 81.

209.   Fabric 7 – light blue-grey surfaces; burnished finish. DM I 131.

210.   Fabric 15 – brownish-grey surfaces. Matt rough finish. DK I 81.

211.   Fabric 7 – dark blue-grey surfaces; burnished from the rim to the top groove; matt lower body, with narrow burnished bands. DM I 19. Similar jars from Mildenhall, the Well Deposit. (Annable, 1966, fig. 3, 43).

212.   Fabric 10 – yellow-orange; worn, with only traces of a burnished finish. Smoky grey patches. Cordon defined by two grooves on the maximum girth. DK I 81. Severn Valley ware form, paralleled at Gloucester (Hassall & Rhodes, 1974, fig. 10, 32).

213.   Fabric 17 – worn, traces of a burnished finish. DK I 81.

214.   Fabric 31 – sparse red grits; smoothed surfaces. DM I 19.

215.   Fabric 10 – grey core; orange-brown surfaces. Burnt and discoloured. DM I 19 + DM I 62.

216.   Fabric 22 – blue-grey core; grey surfaces; worn smooth exterior. Decoration – low relief barbotine spots in grey slip. DM I 130.

217.   Fabric 22 – grey-black surfaces; highly burnished rim and shoulder. Decoration – rouletted. DK II 40.

218.   Fabric 17 – worn, traces of a highly burnished finish on the rim and shoulder. Decoration – rouletted bands separated by grooves. DK II 40.

219.   Fabric 16 – heavily burnt and discoloured. No finish survives. Decoration rouletted. Also rims from two and body sherds from at least four others similar in Fabric 17 – grey ware. DK I 81.

220.   Fabric 5 – highly burnished smooth exterior. Decoration – low relief barbotine spots. DK I 81. Other examples – AM III 14.

221.   Fabric 16 – burnished rim top and shoulder. Probably decorated with rustication, see no. 55. DK II 40.

222.   Fabric 17 – orange core; blue-grey surfaces; burnished rim and shoulder. Decoration – low relief rustication. DM I 131. Other examples – Ashcroft 1951, I 9. Parsonage Field 1959, CW 2 A18. Similar jar from Mildenhall, the Well Deposit (Annable, 1966, fig. 2, 26).

223.   Fabric 16 – burnished from the rim to the groove. Probably decorated with rustication. Also two rims from others similar, Fabric 16 – dark grey; in Fabric 17 – grey ware. DK I 81.

224.   Fabric 17 – burnished. Probably decorated with rustication. DK I 81.

225.   Fabric 4 – overfired. Dark grey core; pale grey-buff surfaces; matt finish. DM I 19.

226.   Fabric 5 – highly burnished exterior. DK II 41.

227.   Fabric 1 – slightly vesicular, matt finish. DM I 135.

228.   Fabric 23 – DK I 81. Similar jars occur in the filling of Ditch III, layer AM II 59, no. 324.

229.   Fabric 12 – matt rough finish. (See above, no. 228). DK I 81.

230.   Fabric 17 – some sparse grey and calcite grits; lightly rilled rim and shoulder; roughly smoothed lower body – smudge lines where the finish changes. DK I 81.

231.   Fabric 5 – smoothed exterior, with narrow burnished bands; matt interior. DK II 40.

232.   Fabric 25 – matt surfaces. DM I 19. See p. 201 Fabric B.

233.   Fabric 6C – matt slurry finish. Sooty patches below the rim. DK II 40.

234.   Fabric 6E – rilled slurry finish. Rim sherds from two others in Fabric 6C – grey ware. DK II 40.

235.   Fabric 6C – overfired. Blue-grey; poorly finished with deeply scored and pitted surfaces. DK II 40.

236.   Fabric 6E – matt finish. DK II 40.

237.   Fabric 6E – matt slurry finish. Sooty patches on the exterior. DK I 81.

238.   Fabric 13 – lightly rilled matt slurry finish on the rim and shoulder; vertically smoothed lower body. DK I 81.

239.   Fabric 13 – matt slurry finish with a band of rilling on the shoulder. DK I 81.

240.   Fabric 6E – Orange core; grey cortex; blue-grey surfaces; rilled slurry finish. DM I 65. Rim sherd from two other similar in Fabric 6E – grey ware. DK I 90.

241.   Fabric 6B – matt slurry finish. DM I 19.

242.   Fabric 13 – sooty patches. DK I 81.

243.   Fabric 6E – burnished slurry finish so that the grits are masked. DM I 65.

244.   Fabric 6E – smoothed slurry finish so that the grit is masked. DK I 81.

245.   Fabric 6C – grey core; orange cortex; light blue-grey surfaces. Matt slurry finish. DM I 19.

246.   Fabric 6E – Orange core; dark blue-grey surfaces. Matt slurry finish. Rim sherds from two others similar. DK I 81. Other examples – DM I 134.

247.   Fabric 6A – burnished exterior. DM I 19. Rim sherds from two other identical. DK I 81.

248.   Fabric 20 – some fine grits leached out. Brown core; grey and brown patchy surfaces; burnished rim and shoulder. DK I 81.

249.   Fabric 6E – slurry finish, highly burnished rim and shoulder, matt lower body. DK I 81.

250.   Fabric 6D – sandy texture. Orange core; pale blue-grey surfaces. Burnished rim and shoulder. Decoration – burnished lattice on a matt ground. DM I 131.

251.   Fabric 6E – matt slurry finish. Burnt and dis-coloured. DM I 19.

252.   Fabric 6E – burnished slurry finish on the rim and shoulder. DK II 40.

253.   Fabric 25B – hand-made. Black core; brownish-grey surfaces; smoothed exterior. Other examples – Ashcroft 1961, I 40 (2); Parsonage Field 1958, CW/58/196. (See below no. 507). See p. 201, Fabric B.

254.   Fabric 74 – B.B.1. hand-made – facetted burnished interior; smoothed exterior. Rim sherd from a second example. DK I 81. Not before A.D. 120 at the earliest. Almost certainly intrusive.

255.   Fabric 74 – B.B.1. hand-made – highly burnished surfaces. A carinated bowl. Probably Flavian. DM I 19.

256.   Fabric 74 – B.B.1. hand-made – highly burnished rim. Probably Flavian. DK I 81.

Amongst the large quantity of miscellaneous sherds three vessels are of particular interest.

a.   Rim sherd from a butt beaker, Camulodunum form 113 – Fabric 48B in typical ware. A late variant, with no cordon below the rim on the outside, and a slight angle at the base of the rim on the inside. The form and fabric are identical to examples from Camulodunum, Verulamium and Chichester, and it could be from the same source, possibly Camulodunum. Pre-Flavian. It is

rare at Cirencester, only small sherds from five vessels have been identified – three on the line of the Leaholme defences – AL II 41; AD V 31; AD V 87.
b. – c. Rim sherds from two carinated bowls in typical Fabric 23 – matt rough finish. The fabrics match those used for necked jars like nos. 228-9, 325-7. Examples of both the jars and the bowls are common at Kingsholm, Gloucester, and it appears that both were from the same source as these from Cirencester.
Samian, S. 8, 28, 30, 32, 38, 41, 44, 49, 52. D. 19-37.

THE MAJOR DEFENSIVE DITCHES

Filling of Ditch II

The group is small, the sherds too are small but they are in fairly good condition. The assemblage appears to divide into two groups, the first is comprised of forms and fabrics common in the filling of Ditch III, AM II 59, including nos. 2, 3 and 6, the other is comprised of those which are of late Iron Age tradition, nos. 1, 4 and 7. There appears to be an actual difference in the date of the two groups, the latter group being in use in the pre-Claudian or early Claudian period and occurring here merely as survivals, otherwise the main filling of Ditch II appears to have taken place at the same time as Ditch III, after c. A.D. 60.

AM I 61
257. Fabric 25 – dark blue-grey surfaces; burnished exterior. Rim sherd from a second example. Iron Age tradition – but the form is not paralleled exactly at Bagendon or Rodborough.
258. Fabric 25B – hand-made. Burnished exterior. Iron Age tradition, a typical bead-rimmed jar of the region. See p. 201, Fabric B.
259. Fabric 24 – hand-made. Burnished exterior. Iron Age tradition. See p. 201, Fabric C.
260. Fabric 4 – sparse tempering; very worn, but traces of a highly burnished finish on the rim and shoulder at least.
261. Fabric 41 – grey-brown core; paler cortex; dark grey-black surfaces; worn, traces of a burnished finish on the rim and shoulder.
262. Fabric 15 – burnished exterior.
263. Fabric 6F – rather soapy matt finish.
The miscellaneous sherds from nine vessels include the base from a large flagon in Fabric 29, and two handles, probably from the same very worn amphora, Dressel 20, Fabric 40.

Filling of Ditch III

In quality, this is the best group in every respect from the early areas of occupation. At least 30 vessels must have been complete and many others virtually complete at the time of deposition in the ditch, including a large group of imported colour-coated vessels and samian, and this has given rise to the hypothesis that the group was comprised of discards from a quarter-master's store. In marked contrast, the number of miscellaneous and possibly residual sherds is small and appears to form a separated group since few parallel the more complete vessels.

The forms, fabrics and functions are not representative of the groups from the early occupation layers. Fine wares, samian, colour-coated, glazed and Pompeian Red wares, comprise over half the number of vessels, while flagons and honey-pots too are more than usually well represented, while ordinary kitchen wares are comparatively scarce. Colour-coated wares imported from Lyons appear to be next in importance to samian amongst the finer table wares.

The bulk of the samian is pre-Flavian in date, much being Neronian, with the emphasis on the period A.D. 60-5, rather than earlier (see p. 133), but there is one bow of Iucundus (D. 38), which is Neronian-Flavian and which probably helps to date the deposition of the groups, rather than its accumulation. On the evidence from Cirencester, the flagons, nos. 302-4 & 308-9, the honey-pots, nos. 310-314, and the jars, nos. 324-7, along with bowls in the same fabric, also date to the Neronian or Neronian-early Flavian period, while nothing amongst the more fragmentary sherds is any later, and at least nos. 296-7, 300, 318 & 329 could be Claudian.

Probably the most important aspect of the group is that certain common forms and fabrics can be paralleled exactly in the material from Kingsholm, Gloucester, in particular, flagons, nos. 302-4 and 308-9, in Fabric 29, jars, nos. 324-7, in Fabric 23, with their associated carinated bowls, an assemblage which on form can be paralleled also at Usk. It appears that the Leaholme and Kingsholm forts were contemporary and received at least some of their pottery supplies from the same sources, in which case the lack of parallels with the Flavian fortress below the Colonia at Gloucester may be significant. It suggests that the arrival of a new unit at Gloucester resulted in new arrangements for the supply of pottery in which the Leaholme fort was not included, implying that it had been abandoned.

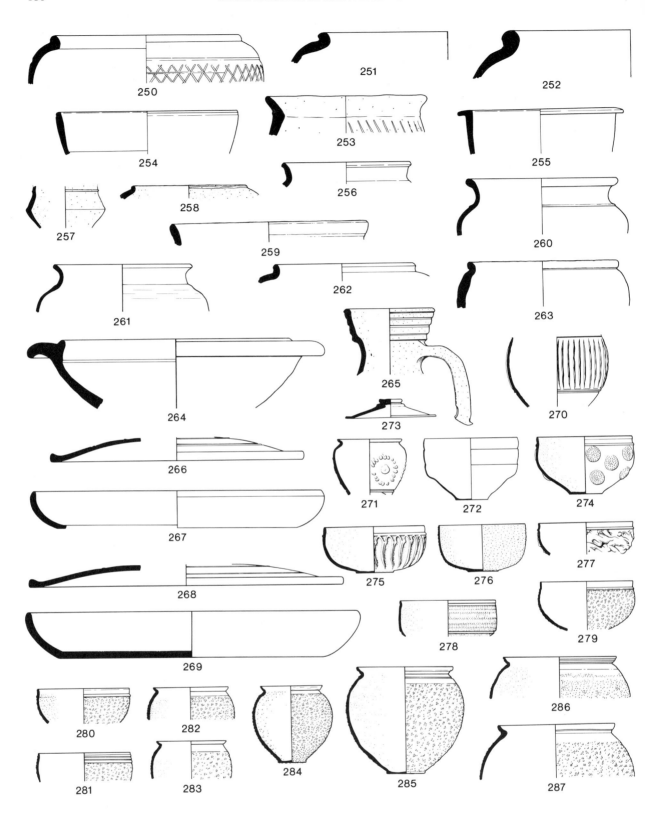

Fig. 57.   Coarse pottery (1:4)

Parallels with material from Bagendon and to a lesser extent, Rodborough Common, are confined to the group of small sherds and in particular, those forms found in the earliest occupation layers. No examples of the complete vessels nor of the Fabrics 11, 23, 29 have been identified. That there was contemporary occupation is attested since the sites share certain forms and fabrics which are Roman in technique and Claudio-Neronian in date, including post-Conquest imported colour-coated wares. The differences may be due to the inadequate size of the samples, socio-economic or chronological reasons, or probably a combination of all three.

The samian from Bagendon is generally earlier than that from the Leaholme fort, with a notable absence of the Neronian material which dominates the group from Ditch III. There is a comparatively large group of Gallo-Belgic imports, covering a much wider range of forms and fabrics than that from Cirencester as a whole, and as a group it is dated A.D. 25/30–60/5. In addition there are two sherds which could be earlier, since they are essentially late Augustan, and five which could date to the Flavian period but are probably more at home in this context in the pre-Flavian period. The platters in Pompeian Red ware, form 6, are more likely to be post-Conquest, while the imported colour-coated ware beakers are definitely post-Conquest, being identical to those in the filling of Ditch III. The mortaria are of types found at Leaholme, they have been examined by Mrs K.F. Hartley, and she dates type 80, Claudian, type 81, *c.* A.D. 50-85, and type 82, in typical Oxford cream ware, third century. Probably the most common fabric at Bagendon, certainly amongst the classifiable rims is the Cirencester Fabric 6, which may or may not be from kilns in the Savernake Forest, but is certainly closely related, while the earliest forms in which it occurs at Cirencester, jars with bead rims, type 148, and necked storage jars, types 171–5, are very common. Proto-Severn Valley wares and forms, if not the real thing, are present at Bagendon and in the earliest layers of the Leaholme fort, with Claudio-Neronian and Neronian samian on the latter site. Flagons are comparatively poorly represented at Bagendon, and where they occur they are from quite different sources to those from the Leaholme fort, some of the difference is almost certainly the result of chronology, but it is possible that the flagons supplied to the forts of Leaholme and Kingsholm were not available to the local native population, and the same could be true of the necked jars and carinated bowls in Fabric 23. As the collections stand at present it appears that occupation of the area sampled by excavation at Bagendon ceased before the complete vessels dumped into ditch III came into general use. The samian suggests that this could have been as early as the early Claudian period while the other fine and imported wares suggest that it was during the Neronian period.

Bottom filling

AM II 67

264. Fabric 70 – fine-grained smooth ware heavily tempered with sand, some calcareous and red ferrous grits. Blue-grey core; pinkish-brown surfaces. No trituration grit. Little wear. From a local source, probably the Gloucester area. Pre-Flavian. (Matching sherds in AM II 48).
265. Fabric 44 heavily tempered; smooth matt finish.

Main Filling

AM II 58 and 59

Pompeian Red ware

266. Fabric 51A – traces of a thick highly micaceous slip survive over all surfaces although the lid is worn and superficially burnt. Claudian-early-Flavian.
267. Fabric 51B – identical paste to no. 266. The micaceous slip is confined to the exterior; the coral red slip on the inside has a highly polished finish. There are small rim sherds from two other platters.
268. Fabric 51A – identical to no. 266. Worn and burnt.

267. Fabric 51B – identical to no. 267. Complete. The upper base is decorated with groups of incised concentric circles.

Only five other platters and one lid have been identified elsewhere in Cirencester, the lid and three platters are chance finds, the others being no. 414; AM IV 34, probably disturbed from the filling of the Leaholme ditches; Ashcroft 1961, A IV 1, unstratified.

Glazed wares

270. Fabric 60 – very worn thin and patchy green glaze, inside and out. Decoration – vertical ribs in white slip; fairly high relief. Pre-Flavian.
271. Fabric 60 – ware as no. 270. Very thin and patchy glaze. Decoration – rosettes made up of high relief barbotine spots in white slip. Pre-Flavian. There is a body sherd from a second example.
271A. Fabric 75 – fig. 62, a sherd from the body of a flagon, Déch. 62. Thick green glaze, with a brownish tinge. Decoration – moulded, in low relief, showing a plain wreath and part of an olive branch with small pointed leaves and one round berry. Arranged within the decorative zone is a signature, similar to those found on decorated samian bowls, and originally cut into the

mould. It reads]OTISA.S and is presumably incomplete. The signature appears to be unparalleled. In addition there is a body sherd from the same flagon, showing olive leaves (AM II 60).

Eggshell ware

272. Fabric 59 – overfired. Dark red core; patchy black, brown and blue-grey matt surfaces. A 'second' – the bowl is rather distorted. Identical bowls have been found at Camulodunum, form 64, and Exeter (May, 1930, pl. XXXIII, 13; Hawkes and Hull, 1947, pl. LIII, 64; Exeter Arhcaeological Field Unit, forthcoming.) For further discussion see Greene, 1973, 30.

Colour-coated wares – imports from Central Gaul

273. Fabric 58. – pale orange; very worn surfaces but there are traces of a red slip. (Matching sherds in AM II 61).
274. Fabric 56 – patchy brown slip; fine sand rough-casting inside. Decoration – applied roundels with barbotine spots, below the slip. Almost complete. Also, a sherd from a second example (AM II 58). Other examples – AM II 47; AM III 33. Both probably disturbed from early levels.
275. Fabric 56 – patchy brown slip shading from red-brown; fine sand rough-casting inside. Decoration – gadroons in barbotine below the slip. Complete bowl.
276. Fabric 56 – fine rough-casting inside, coarser sand on the outside; dark brown slip overall.
277. Fabric 56 – fine rough-casting inside; thick metallic brown slip. Decoration – rustication.
278. Fabric 56 – fine rough-casting on the inside; dark brown slip. Decoration – all-over rouletting.
279. Fabric 56 – no grits on the inside; fairly coarse sand rough-casting on the outside. Patchy bronze and light brown slip. Complete base from another bowl, but with fine rough-casting on the inside also.
280. Fabric 56 – fine rough-casting inside; coarser sand outside; bronze slip. Rim sherd from a second indentical example.
281. Fabric 56 – sparse fine rough-casting on the inside, dense coarse sand on the outside. Very worn on the inside. Rim and body sherd from another identical example.
282. Fabric 56 – very fine rough-casting on the inside, coarser sand on the outside; dark brown metallic slip.
283. Fabric 56 – identical ware and slip to no. 282. Rim sherd from another identical example.
284. Fabric 56 – identical ware and slip to no. 282. Complete beaker. There are also rim sherds from five other similar beakers in Fabric 56.
285. Fabric 56 – identical ware and slip to no. 282. Complete beaker.
286. Fabric 56 – identical ware and slip to no. 282. Very worn inside. Rim sherd from another example, very worn.
287. Fabric 56 – identical ware and slip to no. 282.
288. Fabric 58 – thin red-brown slip. Decoration – a broad band of coarse rouletting. In addition:– a small base sherd from a tripod bowl, Camulodunum 63. Fabric 56 – thin worn red-brown slip.
A sherd from a lamp with moulded decoration. Fabric 56 – very worn, pale brown slip.

Mica-coated wares

289. Fabric 61 – self-coloured underslip; mica-coating on the rim and exterior only; very worn and patchy. Decoration – rows of undefined bosses, raised from the inside using a tool of this diameter. Possibly from the Rhineland. Other examples decorated with bobbles of the same type, all in mica-coated wares – AF I 43; AH VIII 50 + 58; AH VIII 43; AS I 80; AS I 37.

Amphorae

290. Fabric 38A. There is also a second handle and body sherds from possibly the same vessel.
Amphora, Dressel type 20. (Not illustrated). Fabric 40. The stamp reads – BROC.OD (see fig. 48, A. 1).
291. Fabric 47 – Camulodunum form 189. Badly finished rilled exterior. There is also a handle and body sherds from a second example.
292. Fabric 34 – an amphora stopper. There are rim sherds from two others. The miscellaneous body sherds include: a two-rib handle, Camulodunum form 185; body sherds, Camulodunum form 186; body sherds, Dressel type 30.
293. White dense smooth ware, with a highly burnished exterior finish. Part of a small unguent flask or a model egg. Imported. (Rouvier-Jeanlin, 1972, no. 1261).

Mortaria

294. Fabric 68 – cream powdery smooth ware; grey and white flint and coarse mica flakes in the tempering and used also as trituration grit. The existing sherd is from an unused vessel. The form and fabric are typical of Q. Va. Se... (Hartley, K.F., 1977, Group I). A large number of similar vessels were found in the Boudiccan burning levels at Camulodunum and Verulamium. c. A.D. 55-85.
295. Fabric 68 – cream ware; self slip, with a rilled finish. No trituration grit, but the fabric is tempered. Unworn. Pre-Flavian.

Coarse wares

296. Fabric 48A – smooth finish on rim, neck and base. Decoration – a broad band of rouletting.
297. Fabric 48A – identical ware and finish to no. 296. Other examples from the same source – AL II 45; AD V 31; AD VI 40; AD XI 11 – all on the line of the Leaholme defences, in disturbed stretches. The butt beakers sherds from the Mildenhall Well deposit are from the same source.
298. Fabric 29 – heavily tempered, some grits more than 10 mm. in length.
299. Fabric 11 – sparse temper. A complete rim circuit. Others from the same source – AM II 29; AM II 34; AM II 48; AM II 53; AM III 33. All found along the line of the Leaholme defences, and probably disturbed from the main filling of the ditches.
300. Fabric 21. There is also a base sherd which may be from the same vessel. The form and fabric are scarce on the site, but there is another identical example and body sherds from the layers sealing the military occupation (DM I 19).
301. Fabric 9 – hard. There are identical examples from layers AM III 21 and DM I 137, the latter seals the

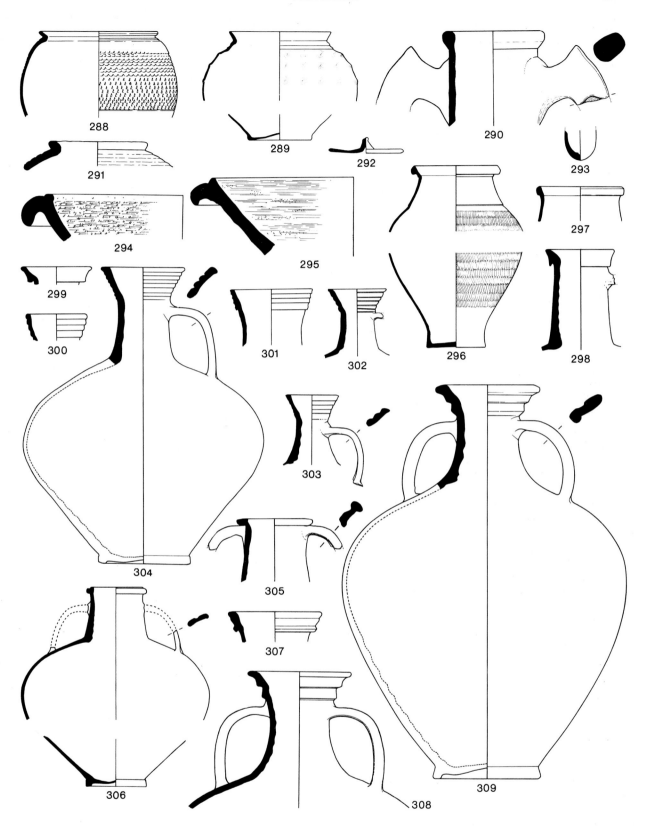

Fig. 58.   Coarse pottery (1:4)

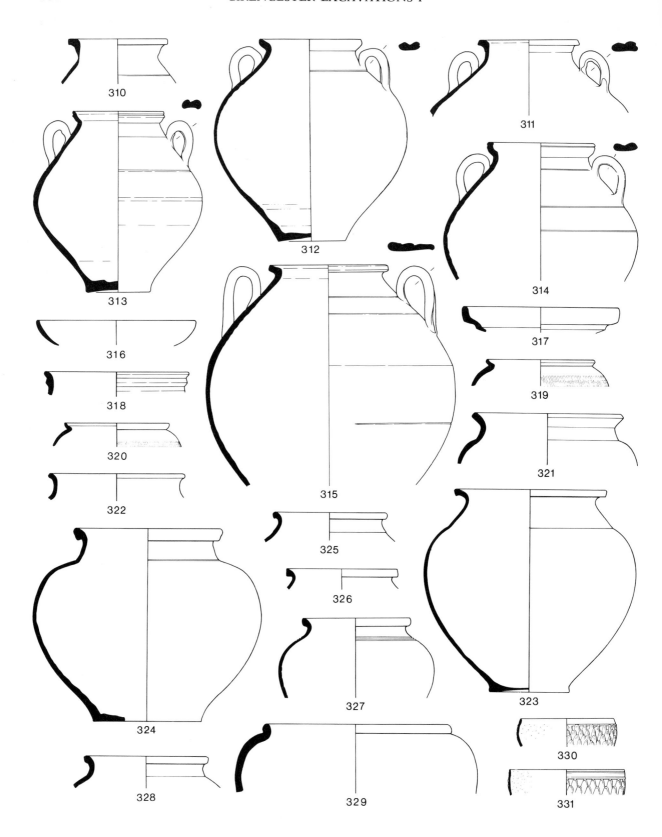

Fig. 59. Coarse pottery (1:4)

military occupation.

302. Fabric 29 – pinky buff surfaces. It is a genuine screw-neck, with a single spiral groove forming the narrow rings. There are examples of five others from the site, in layers AM II 66; AM VI 8; AD VI 54; DK I 96; DK II 40; the latter two examples are from the levels sealing the military occupation.

303. Fabric 11 – some sparse incidental fine white and coarse brown grits. Also rim and neck of a second, complete neck and handle of a third, and three bases. There is an identical example from one of the layers sealing the military occupation – DM I 135.

304. Fabric 29 – complete. Also two identical examples in Fabric 29 and four in Fabric 11 – identical in colour and finish to no. 304. There are three others identical from the site, in layers AL VII 12; DK II 37; AM II 49 – all on the line of the Leaholme defences and probably disturbed from the ditches. Despite the differences in the degree of tempering, it seems likely that all the screw-neck flagons in both Fabrics 11 and 29 were from the same source. At least one flagon, identical to no. 304, has been found at Kingsholm, Gloucester, (unpublished, Gloucester museum).

305. Fabric 26 – the basic ware is like that of Fabrics 11 and 29, but the tempering includes a large amount of sand, which resulted in a rather rough and gritty surface finish. It is probably from the same source as no. 298 etc., and also the mortaria like nos. 10 and 264.

306. Fabric 31 – badly fired and discoloured. Tempered with fine grit, fired to grey on one side and red on the other side of the pot. Presumably meant to be pale cream, but has a pale blue core; cream inner surface; patchy blue-grey, buff and cream exterior; smoothed exterior streaked by the grit.

307. Fabric 44 – hard. Heavily tempered. Brown core; red-brown surfaces, very worn and smooth. (Matching sherd in AM III 33). Probably from a two-handled flagon like no. 308.

308. Fabric 29 – heavily tempered, much of it coarse, including some shell; pinky buff. The broad flat two-rib handle has a deep thumb-print at the centre, top and bottom. Probably complete when deposited. There are necks from three others and bases from four.

309. Fabric 29 – identical to no. 308. Complete. The two-handled flagons, like nos. 308 and 309 are probably from the same source as the screw-neck flagons.

310. Fabric 11 – some sparse white calcareous grits.

311. Fabric 11 – identical ware to no. 310. Also rim sherds from four others in Fabric 11, identical in colour and texture; one other in Fabric 44 – pinky buff also. There is one other from the site, DM I 99, from a second century context.

312. Fabric 11 – sparse and probably incidental fine white calcareous grit. Discoloured by iron stains.

313. Fabric 11 – identical ware to no. 310. There are rim sherds from three others with the same type of rim.

314. Fabric 11 – identical ware to no. 310. Also a second almost complete example and the rim from a third. In addition, three examples from the rest of the site, layers AM II 48; AM III 18; AM IV 16; – the first two may have been disturbed from the main filling of Ditch III and ?Ditch IV.

There are bases from seven examples, the exact rim variant cannot be determined, and handles from two

others. The honey-pots appear to be from the same source as the one- and two-handled flagons, like nos. 304 and 309.

315. Fabric 21 – sparse red grits. This particular honey-pot is unique on the site, although it must be from the same source as the ring-necked flagon, no. 300. Complete base, probably from a honey-pot, in Fabric 31 – heavily tempered with fairly coarse red grogs.

316. Fabric 22 – well-finished matt surfaces. (Possibly from the same platter as sherds from AM III 44).

317. Fabric 5 – burnished interior, smoothed exterior.

318. Fabric 5 – burnished exterior. The rim from a carinated bowl.

319. Fabric 46 – very worn, no finish survives. Decoration – rouletted. Dyer Court 1957 (Webster, G., 1959, fig. 16, 68).

320. Fabric 46 – identical to no. 319. Very worn. There are four examples from the rest of the site; layers AD III 24; AL VII 24; AM II 48; DM I 124.

321. Fabric 41 – grey core; pale cortex; very dark grey surfaces; well finished matt surfaces.

322. Fabric 5 – burnished exterior. There are small rim and body sherds from four similar necked jars, a sherd from one with a deep shoulder groove and bases from two examples.

323. Fabric 41 – like no. 321. Worn, so it is possible that the rim was burnished originally. There is a base from another jar in Fabric 55. Similar jars from Kingsholm, Gloucester (Darling, 1977, fig. 6.9, 19).

324. Fabric 23 – patchy grey and buff surfaces.

325. Fabric 23 – like no. 324, blue-grey in colour. There is a rim from a similar jar, in fabric 23, from layer DK II 45.

326. Fabric 23 – like no. 324. Grey ware.
Also a rim sherd from another identical jar. Other examples – DK I 81; DK I 119; AD V 111.

327. Fabric 23 – like no. 324; blue-grey core; pale grey-buff surfaces. Grooves at the neck base form low cordons. There are examples of necked jars similar to nos. 324-327 in gritty fabrics similar to Fabrics 12 and 23, from Kingsholm, Gloucester. (Darling, 1977, fig. 6.9, 20-23). It seems probable that they were from the same source as the Cirencester examples, and procured for the military detachments garrisoned in the area. Cremation burials from Barnwood include a range of similar jars. (Cheltenham Museum).

328. Fabric 6E – darker blue-grey surfaces.

329. Fabric 6E – sooty patches. The bases and body sherds in Fabric 6 all belong to large storage jars, two of which were hand-made; at least 11 vessels. There are few small miscellaneous sherds.

a. Small rim fragment and body sherds from a carinated jar like Camulodunum form 120 – probably an import. Fabric 59.

b. Body sherds from a necked jar with a shoulder groove. Fabric 30.

Samian – Neronian (S. 1-3, 6, 9, 10-11, 15-6, 20-1, 23-7, 31, 34-6, 40, 42-3, 45-6, 50-1) (D. 38-58).

Filling of the ? Middle Ditch

AM III 44

330-1. Fabric 56 – identical ware and finish to no. 282. Very worn brown slip. Joining sherd in AM III 45 below. Imported from Central Gaul. Pre-Flavian. Other

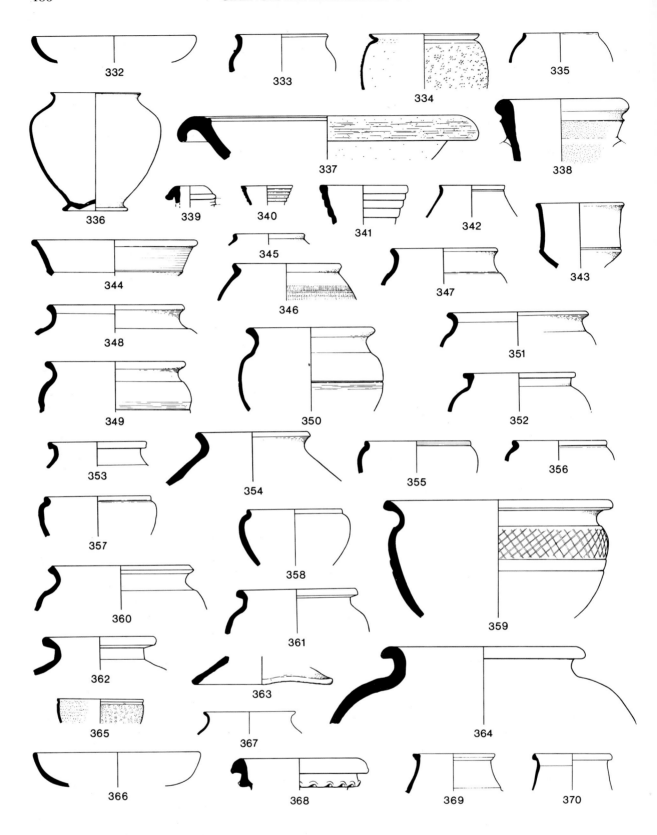

Fig. 60.   Coarse pottery (1:4)

examples – AH VIII 77; AH VIII 78; AL VII 29; DK I 81.

332. Fabric 22 – identical to no. 316, and possibly from the same platter.

333. Fabric 15 – very worn grey ware, no finish survives. Also a body sherd from a beaker like no. 334; amphora, Dressel type 20 (not illustrated). Fabric 40. The stamp reads – L.VA.L (see fig. 48, A.3). There are miscellaneous sherds from six vessels, including one or two platters like no. 194. Samian – Neronian.

Inter-ditch area

AM III 45

334. Fabric 56 – identical fabric and finish to no. 282. There are miscellaneous sherds from three vessels, including a mortarium identical to no. 264 and a necked jar in Fabric 29.

Layers back-filling the quarried stretches of Ditch III (Sites AK and AL)

The quality of the pottery is good, the sherds are fairly large and the fractures not particularly worn, so that the material had not lain around for a long period before deposition.

One samian sherd is dated c. A.D. 70-90, the remainder being pre-Flavian, with several sherds from unused Neronian bowls like those in the undisturbed stretches of Ditch III. Many of the forms and fabrics parallel those found in the undisturbed stretch of Ditch III, the layers sealing-off the early occupation on sites DK and DM, and the core of the Sands rampart. However, it is noticeable that like the former, but unlike the two latter contexts, there is a marked shortage of rustic jars, jars with carinated shoulders and so-called Severn Valley ware forms, and no sherds in B.B.1. New forms include the flagons, nos. 339 & 368, the bowls, nos. 344, 372-3, the necked jars, nos. 352 & 354, and the jar with the lid-seated rim, no. 382. Examples of these types occur in Flavian contexts elsewhere in Cirencester so none need be later. The back-filling of the quarried stretches of Ditch III probably took place in the Flavian period, between A.D. 70 and 85.

AL VII 31

335. Fabric 22 – highly polished facetted exterior finish. Probably also an import like no. 336.

336. Fabric 63 – highly polished finish. The form of the base suggests that the piece is an import and that it may have been stamped. c. A.D. 50-85 (see G. 3, p. 150). Other examples (rims only) – AM IV 23; AM III 17. Kingsholm, Gloucester (Darling, 1977, Fig. 6.8, 7).

337. Fabric 73 – orange-red sandy ware, with fine white calcareous tempering. Very worn inside so that no trituration grits survive, if they ever existed; scored on the rim. Origin unknown, possibly a local product; the form and fabric are consistent with a first century date. Other examples – AD II 34. Also rim sherds from a wall-sided mortarium, like no. 164. Fabric 67 – cream ware; superficially burnt; no trituration grit. Claudian; not made after c. A.D. 50/5, but still in use in the Neronian–early Flavian period. Sherds from a mortarium similar to no. 165.

338. Fabric 66 – dense ware, with some tempering which was also used as rough-casting on the neck, outside, between the handles. The rough-casting includes a high proportion of mica flakes and white calcareous grits, as well as coarse sand, of mixed colour. Orange-brown with cream exterior surface. The fabric resembles that of the mortarium Fabric 69. Origin unknown, but possibly Kent or north-east France judging by the fabric.

339. Fabric 11 – pale mauve core; dark pink; creamy pink slip on the exterior rim.

340. Fabric 19 – lighter yellow-orange surfaces.

341. Fabric 21 – a larger version of the type found in the filling of Ditch III, AM II 59, no. 300 etc. Also a base sherd possibly from the same flagon.

342. Fabric 48A – smoothly burnished exterior finish.

343. Fabric 4 – smoothed finish. There is an identical bowl from the core of the rampart at the Sands, CG III 12, no. 462. There are also three others from layers DK I 58; AW 1 67; DQ I 128. A typical Severn Valley form.

344. Fabric 15 – burnished interior; facetted burnished exterior.

345. Fabric 10 – sparse tempering; burnished.

346. Fabric 17 – very worn, with traces of a greyish-white slip. Decoration – rouletted.

347. Fabric 5 – burnished exterior.

348. Fabric 5 – highly burnished exterior. Rim sherds from two others. Fabric 5.

349. Fabric 7 – crudely burnished exterior.

350. Fabric 17 – very worn, no finish survives.

351. Fabric 41 – burnished exterior.

352. Fabric 32 – pink; matt and rough finish.

353. Fabric 23 – blue-grey surfaces; gritty rough matt finish. Identical examples from the filling of Ditch III, no. 324-7 etc.

354. Fabric 15 – worn darker grey surfaces; rough and gritty to touch. Badly shaped, apparently hand-made.

355. Fabric 7 – pale brown core; blue-grey surfaces; burnished exterior. Other examples – no. 6.

356. Fabric 17 – burnished rim and shoulder.

357. Fabric 5 – burnished rim and exterior. There is a rim sherd from a similar jar in the layers sealing the military occupation, (Unpublished DM I 19).

358. Fabric 6A – burnished rim and exterior, the tempering shows as dark grey flecks.

359. Fabric 13A – grey core; red-brown cortex; dark blue-grey surfaces; matt soapy-textured slurry finish. Decoration – burnished lattice.

360. Fabric 6E – grey core; rust cortex; grey-black surfaces, matt finish.

361. Fabric 6E – lightly rilled matt finish.

362. Fabric 13 – grey core; orange cortex; streaky buff and orange surfaces; burnished slurry finish.

363. Hand-made. Fabric 24 – dark grey with roughly

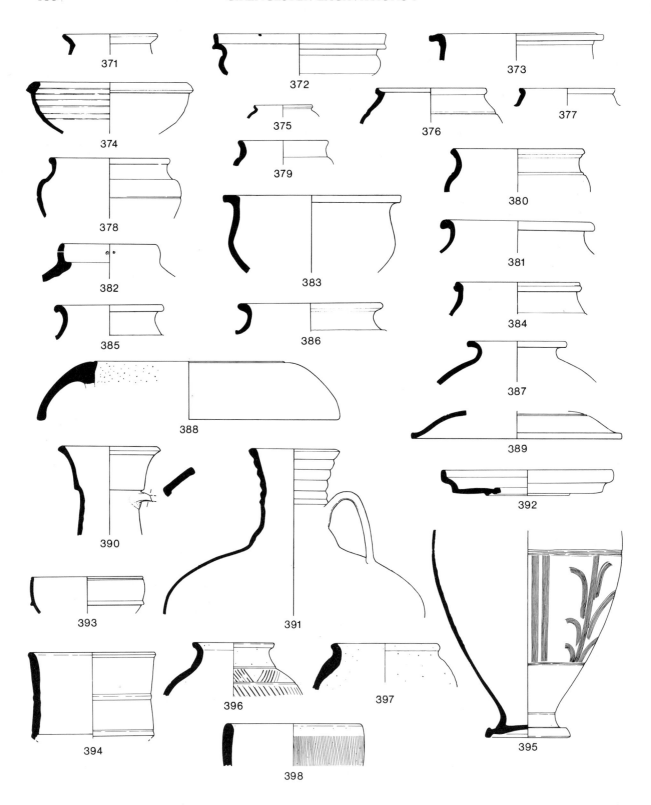

Fig. 61.　Coarse pottery (1:4)

tooled surfaces.

364. Fabric 6E – well smoothed slurry finish.
There are miscellaneous sherds from a large number of different vessels, including a body sherd from a typical butt beaker, Camulodunum form 113 – Fabric 48B. Pre-Flavian.
Samian – A.D. 70-90 (D. 59-60).

AK II 22 + AK IV 39-42

365. Fabric 56 – thick metallic orange-brown slip. Fine rough-casting inside. Also:– a base sherd from a beaker. Fabric 56 – coarse rough-casting outside, none inside; a sherd from a lamp with moulded decoration. Fabric 56 – patchy light brown slip.
366. T.N. – pale blue-grey fine-grained paste; mottled blue-grey surfaces; highly polished interior, facetted polished exterior. An import. c. A.D. 50-80.
367. Fabric 63 – identical to no. 336 possibly from the same jar.
368. Fabric 19 – overfired. Hard. Blue-grey core; orange-red cortex; cream slip. The lower edge of the rim is frilled.
369. Fabric 9 – bright orange; traces of a thick cream slip. Probably a honey-pot, with two small applied handles, like no. 312 etc.
370. Fabric 33 – burnished rim and neck. A locally-made butt beaker.
371. Fabric 65 – highly burnished rim and exterior. Similar to the imported TR 3 wares, but not from the usual source.
372. Fabric 5 – highly burnished surfaces. Other examples – AD IV 40 – an identical bowl, and also no. 470.
373. Fabric 45 – matt surfaces. A carinated bowl.
374. Fabric 5 – burnished bands on a matt ground inside; burnished rim; matt exterior. Other examples – nos. 74 and 84; AG I 3.
375. Fabric 5 – burnished exterior.
376. Fabric 16 – burnished rim and shoulder, matt finish below the groove. Possibly decorated with rustication.
377. Fabric 20 – orange core; pale grey surfaces; burnished rim and exterior.
378. Fabric 5 – traces of a dark grey-black burnished finish outside.
379. Fabric 4.
380. Fabric 4 – facetted burnished finish. Sooty lines along the lip, and a patch on the shoulder.
381. Fabric 45. Lightly rilled matt finish.
382. Fabric 15 – grey surfaces; crudely finished. A single hole at the rim, pierced after firing. Other examples – no. 344; also AK I 16; AL II 32: DK II 13; AH VIII 4; AW I 54; AE III 6. Flavian-Trajanic. The type was represented in Savernake, Kiln 2, (Annable, 1962, fig. 5, 35), and there are rims of at least 12 vessels from Sea Mills, including pierced examples, as well as distorted 'seconds', some of which appear to be from the same source as the Cirencester examples.
383. Fabric 6E – brick red core; grey surfaces; matt finish. Soot encrusted exterior. Other examples – AM II 47.
384. Fabric 6A – rilled exterior.
385. Fabric 6A – burnished slurry finish.
386. Fabric 6E – overfired.

387. Fabric 6A – red-brown core; dark grey surfaces; burnished slurry finish. Other examples – AL VIII 13; AM III 22 + AM VI 8.
Amongst the miscellaneous sherds is a rim fragment from a mortarium cf. no. 264 in Fabric 70, possibly from the same source as no. 264. Pre-Flavian.
Samian – Claudio-Neronian.

EARLY POTTERY DISTURBED FROM EARLY LAYERS

388. Fabric 69 – pink cortex; darker cream surfaces. Very worn, but some white trituration grits survive. Gillam 236. Manufactured in Gallia Narbonensis, at the vicus of Aoste (Isère). (Hartley, K.F., 1977, 8; and 1973, 40) c. A.D. 55-85. AM I 44.
389. Fabric 64 – pale orange mica-gilt slip. Two grooves define a low cordon on the outside. The lid appears to be of the same form as no. 266 (AM II 59), Camulodunum form 17B, but the fabric is completely different, being like that of the white ware flagons, Fabric 21. The use of mica on a white fabric is rare, and appears to be confined to jars with barbotine decoration, Camulodunum form 114, absent from Cirencester, but identified at Bagendon, type 46, (Clifford, 1961, fig. 62, 46) and several other sites with pre-Roman occupation in southern England. AM II 60 & 49.
390. Fabric 29 – this is the only identifiable example of the form but the fabric is identical to the screw-neck and two-handled flagons etc., like nos. 298, 303 & 308. AM III 18,
391. Fabric 31 – hard. Blue-grey core; white surfaces. Judging from the number of body sherds from the early layers, flagons in white sand-free ware were not common. AM III 16, 17, 18, 20.
392. Fabric 24 – fine tempering burnished surfaces. The foot-ring is moulded and there is a raised cordon on the upper surface, with a rouletted wreath on the outside. The fabric belongs to the Iron Age tradition, although many variants of the form occur in Fabric 5, this is the only identified example in a late Iron Age ware and with a raised cordon. Platters with such cordons are not common, but have been identified at Silchester, Baldock, Herts, Brafield and Duston, Northants (AL I 32).
393. Fabric 22 – dark brown core; dark grey black surfaces, rilled interior, burnished exterior. Probably from the same source as the platters nos. 316 and 332. The form copies the imported G-B cup, form 58 or the samian form 24/5. Pre-Flavian–early Flavian. It appears that close copies of imported forms have a very similar range to the prototypes. Possibly an import. AM II 49.
394. Fabric 1 – vesicular; yellow-buff surfaces; worn, but traces of a burnished finish survive on the outside. Severn Valley ware, source unknown. No close parallels have been identified although cordoned and carinated cups and bowls are widely found in the region. AD XI 11.
395. Fabric 22 – evenly burnished exterior. Decoration – deeply incised combed stripes with swags in a band below the maximum girth. There is no evidence of stamps or concentric arcs but it is probable that the upper body was more elaborately decorated, in zones delimited by cordons. The vessel, which was probably a

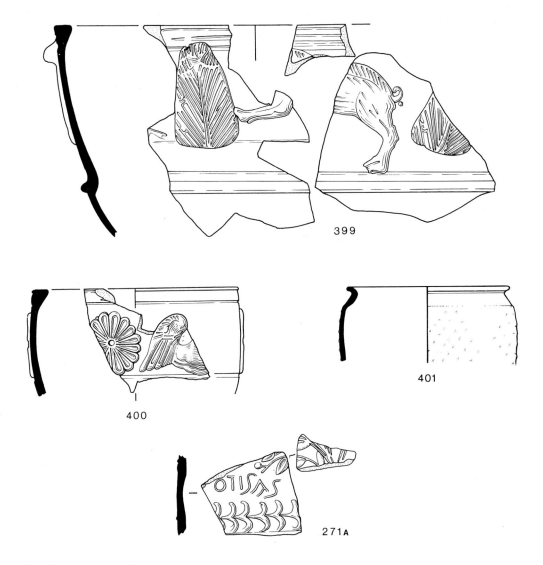

Fig. 62.   Coarse pottery (1:4)

narrow-necked jar or flask, had had the upper body, above the maximum girth, trimmed off in antiquity, presumably so that it could continue to be used but as a wide-mouthed drinking cup, rather than as a flask. Although in many pieces, the complete lower body could be restored so that it was obvious that the base was complete when it was discarded.

The vessel is unique in Cirencester, but it paralleled quite closely a tall flask from Silchester (May, 1916, pl. lxxi, 113). The pedestal is almost identical to a series of bases found in London, and wrongly identified as pedestals from Belgic urns, which may have been made in the Walbrook Valley (Hawkes & Dunning, 1930, fig. 23. Marsh & Tyers, 1976, 239). Bowls imitating Drag. 37, with decorated comparable stripes combined with concentric arcs, in smooth dark grey or black ware are sufficiently rare in Cirencester to suggest that they were not from a near-by source (there appears from the fabrics to be more than one) but were brought in from a distance. None are securely stratified, although three do occur in Antonine contexts. The small group of other sherds with which it was found are pre-Flavian in date, suggesting that the group could have been disturbed

from an earlier position. AM III 33.

396.   Fabric 24 – patchy dark grey and brown surfaces; soapy burnished finish. Decoration – at least two bands on the shoulder, lightly incised lines on a burnished ground. Iron Age tradition; see p. 201, Fabric C. The fabric closely resembles a common type at Bagendon which was used for both hand-made and wheel-made vessels, platters, necked bowls and jars, but neither the form nor the decoration can be paralleled there. On analogies with similar jars in south-eastern England, it could be Tiberian and should not be later than Neronian, so it is residual in its context here. DM I 129.

397.   Fabric 24 – hand-made, dark grey and brown patchy surfaces; unevenly smoothed shoulder. A variant of the basic local Iron Age type paralleled at Rodborough, Bagendon, Frocester, Gloucester, Wycomb and Salmonsbury, as well as the Malvern area and Camerton, Somerset; see p. 201, Fabric C.

398.   Fabric 25A – hand-made. Black ware, the exterior is finished with vertical burnishing. The form has a long Bronze and Iron Age tradition, while locally it can be paralleled at Rodborough, Cleeve Hill, Oxenton Hill, Salmonsbury, Sutton Walls and Camerton, in very

similar Malvernian wares, and presumably many other contemporary settlements. None have been identified in the material from Bagendon, but this is unlikely to be of importance either culturally or chronologically. The example from Cirencester may indicate that the form continued in use into the Roman period, but it is almost certainly residual and redeposited in its context, which is early second century. DM I 122; see p. 201, Fabric A.

399. Fabric 60 – Patchy yellowish-green glaze inside and out. Decoration – applied motifs below the glaze:–
a. the front and rear quarters of a boar. The sherds do not join so that at least two animals could be represented. Representations of boars in metal and stone occur frequently in pre-Roman, Celtic, and Roman contexts:
b. two identical leaves, with incised veins, placed on either side of the boar figure.

The vessel is a large *Skyphos*, and was made in Central Gaul. Pre-Flavian. (For detailed discussion of the glazed wares from Cirencester see Greene, 1972). AM III 17, 18, 22, 27.

400. Fabric 60 – incidental red grog grits; the green glaze is rather thin and patchy on the outside, but is thicker and more even on the inside. Decoration – applied before the glaze:–
a. a complete stylised rosette, identical to one found at Vindonissa (Ettlinger & Simonett, 1952, taf. 30, 7);
b. the outstretched wing of a bird, possibly an eagle, rather than Victory. Central Gaul. Pre-Flavian. AM III 14 & 22.

401. Fabric 60 – lime-green glaze, thick and glossy. Decoration – barbotine spots arranged in a diamond-shape; below the glaze. Central Gaul. Pre-Flavian. AH VIII 25.

THE WATERMOOR RAMPART

There is insufficient pottery for conclusive dating of the construction of the rampart. There is a small group of Roman pottery in the surviving base itself, so that any fort here cannot have been the earliest Roman establishment in the immediate area. The samian is Claudio-Neronian, while the necked jars can be paralleled exactly in the sealing–off layers of site AH within the Leaholme fort. Sherds from the Leaholme rampart itself are of Iron Age tradition and although the vessels could have been in use in the Claudian period, it suggests that this is the earlier of the two ramparts. The surfaces of the intervallum road produced Neronian or early Flavian samian with accompanying coarse wares which need not be later than the early Flavian period. The filling of the gully behind the rampart probably marks the end of the useful life of the rampart, the latest samian sherd has been dated A.D. 50-70, while none of the coarse wares need be later than Flavian.

Site AW

Surviving levels of the Rampart

AW I 77
402. Fabric 5 – worn surfaces, no finish survives. Identical necked bowl, no. 15.
Also a body sherd from a necked jar, with a raised cordon at the neck base. Fabric 1 – slightly vesicular surfaces.
Samian – pre-Flavian, possibly Claudian (D. 61).

Surface of the Intervallum Road

AW I 72
403. Fabric 19 – sparse white grit. Grey core; light orange-buff surfaces. Two rib handle. Also neck sherd from a flagon with a three-rib handle. Fabric 19. Body sherds from a jar or flagon. Fabric 26.
404. Fabric 4 – worn matt surfaces. The rim from a dish or a carinated bowl.
405. Fabric 7 – burnished finish. Probably a pedestal base rather than a rim.
406. Fabric 17 – worn, no finish survives. Miscellaneous sherds from two vessels.
Samian – first century. Matches a sherd in the layer above, AM I 55.

Upper levels of the Intervallum Road

AW I 71
407. Fabric 6 – heavily burnt and discoloured. Matt lumpy finish; soot encrusted. Other examples – AX I 43 (not illustrated); AS III 25.
408. Fabric 6E – smoothed slurry finish.
Miscellaneous sherds from two vessels.

Filling of the Gully behind the Rampart

AW I 79
409. Fabric 5 – very worn; only traces of the burnished finish survive. The form was apparently also made in B.B.1. in the first century A.D. (Farrar, 1977, fig. 14, 3, 47).
410. Fabric 43 – overfired. Whitish-grey slip on the exterior only; burnished finish on the rim and upper shoulder. Decoration – low relief rustication. Complete rim circuit.
411. Fabric 41 – matt surfaces.
There are miscellaneous sherds from at least 13 different vessels.
Samian (D. 63).

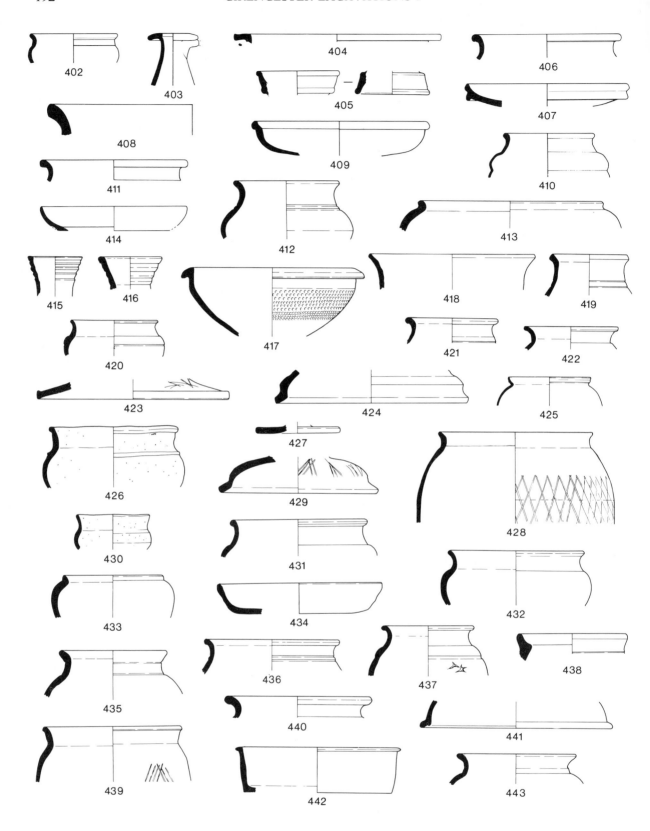

Fig. 63.   Coarse pottery (1:4)

Site AX

The pottery suggests that the area was markedly disturbed in the Roman period for matching sherds were found in virtually all the lower layers, in particular AX II 35, 36, 38, 39, 41-45. Alternatively, the matches may have resulted from the fact that all these layers represented different stages in the same levelling-up of the ground surface for a major building phase.

In Layers AX II 47, 44 and 45, there are hand-made vessels in fabrics which belong to the Iron Age rather than the Roman tradition in both form and fabric (nos. 426, 430 and p. 201). Pottery belonging to the local native Iron Age tradition is scarce in the earliest occupation layers in Cirencester, although more sherds occur presumably residually in higher levels, and here all three vessels occur in contexts which post-date the Claudian period, at the earliest. Their occurrence is noteworthy because, in detail they represent vessel-types not paralleled in the material from Bagendon or Rodborough, although no. 426 is paralleled closely at Salmonsbury. The groups also include two hand-made jars and a lid in B.B.1, typologically of first century date and almost certainly from a source in Dorset, nos. 429, 439 & 447. The stratigraphically earliest groups appear to be later than equivalent groups from sites AH and AG, being closer to those from sites DK and DM. There is no samian from the lowest layers while that in the upper levels is essentially Neronian and Flavian. The material from the adjacent sites in Parsonage Field, excavated by Misses M. Rennie and K.M. Richardson in 1958 and 1959 respectively, include no samian earlier than Neronian, while none of the mortaria are earlier than Flavian.

The pottery from all the sites excavated to date implies that occupation in the area of Parsonage Field did not begin before the Neronian period and so is definitely later than the earliest occupation within the Leaholme fort. It has not provided any evidence to support or refute the theory that Parsonage Field was within the circuit of the Watermoor rampart. The presence of B.B.1 products from Dorset, may indicate the arrival from the area where B.B.1 was the native indigenous pre-Conquest pottery, of military units.

Occupation of Fort or Vicus

AX II 58 – pit filling
412. Fabric 15 – burnished exterior. (Matching sherds in AX II 45).
413. Fabric 6A – matt slurry finish.
414. Fabric 28 – highly micaceous; very worn but traces of a coral red slip survive inside and out. Possibly an import.
There are miscellaneous sherds from five other vessels.

AX II 43
415. Fabric 11 – some sparse grits. Also a neck sherd from a flagon. Fabric 31 – very pale buff.
416. Fabric 10 – smooth surfaces. Handle and body sherd from two others in Fabrics 19 and 29.
417. Fabric 5 – burnished rim and interior; very worn exterior. Decoration – rouletted. Sooty patches inside. Also a flange fragment from a similar bowl. Fabric 5. Other rouletted examples – AT I 19; AW III 37. Plain examples – nos. 74 and 84; AS I 80; AS I 84; AS I 93; AS I 86; AS III 36; AS III 37; AL III 14; AH VIII 44; AH VIII 44 + 33. Dyer Court 1957 (Webster, G., 1959, fig. 16, 59).
418. Fabric 46 – matt finish. Rim from carinated bowl.
419. Fabric 5 – very worn but traces of a burnished finish. Grooves define a cordon at the base of the neck, and possibly on the shoulder.
420. Fabric 5 – very worn brownish-grey surfaces.
421. Fabric 17 – worn burnished exterior finish.
422. Fabric 45 – burnished rim and shoulder. Possibly decorated with rustication.
Also a rim sherd from a similar jar. Fabric 45. Shoulder sherds from two jars. Fabric 17 – orange-brown core; grey surfaces; low relief and high relief rustication respectively. Body sherd from a jar. Fabric 20 – high relief rustication.
423. Fabric 8 – very worn. Traces of a possible inscription cut when the lid was leather hard survive towards the knob.
There are miscellaneous sherds from 11 vessels, including a bowl like no. 407 an Italian amphora, Dressel 2-4, and a Spanish amphora, Camulodunum 186.
424. Fabric 5 – highly burnished exterior; matt interior. Samian – Flavian.

AX II 42
425. Fabric 52 – mica slip on the rim and shoulder. The miscellaneous sherds include a body sherd from a jar or beaker decorated with cordons in Fabric 10. Decorated with burnished lattice between the cordons which joins sherds in AX II 36 and 39.
Samian – Flavian.

AX II 47 – Second layer above natural?
426. Hand-made. Fabric 18 – the exterior is discoloured to a smoky grey. Freehand smoothed finish. (Matching sherds in AX II 44). Iron Age tradition, but not closely paralleled locally, although there is a similar unpublished example from Salmonsbury (Cheltenham Museum). See p. 201, Fabric B.
Also the base from an amphora, Dressel type 30. Fabric 35 – off-white ware, heavily burnt and discoloured.

AX II 44
427. Fabric 38 – typical amphora stopper.
428. Fabric 74 – B.B.1 hand-made – burnished rim and shoulder. Burnished lattice on a matt ground. Typical

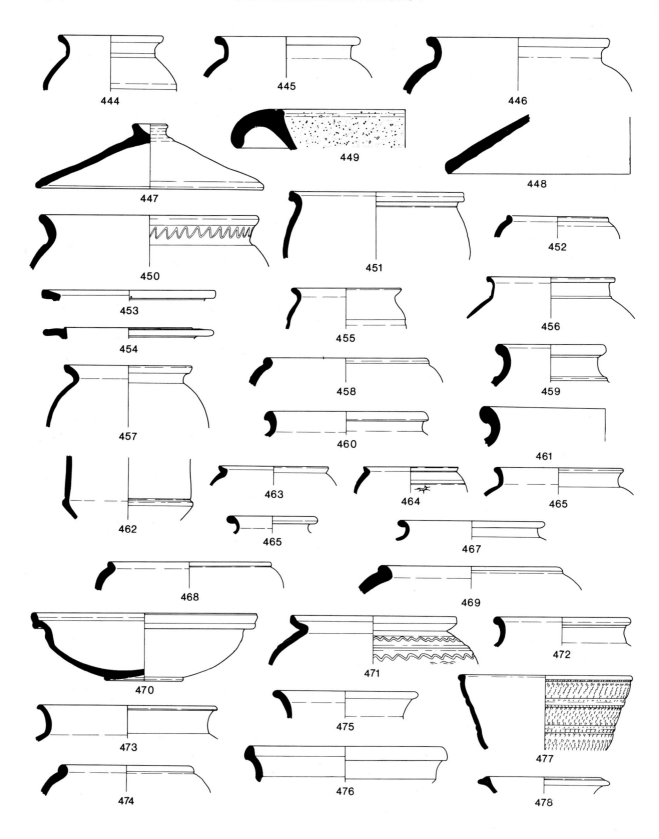

Fig. 64. Coarse pottery (1:4)

fabric of the Dorset B.B.1 potteries.

429. Fabric 15 – decoration – burnished lattice. Very worn, no finish survives.

Miscellaneous sherds from three vessels include a body sherd from a shallow necked bowl (as no. 402), in Fabric 5.

AX II 45

430. Fabric 18 – hand-made. Sparse tempering; burnished finish. Iron Age tradition, although not paralleled closely locally.
431. Fabric 5 – highly burnished finish.
432. Fabric 5 – highly burnished exterior.
433. Fabric 6A – smoothed exterior.

There are miscellaneous sherds from eight vessels, including the base from a flagon in Fabric 31 with joins in AX II 35 and a body sherd from a spouted jar, like no. 71, in Fabric 10. Decorated with burnished lattice on a rilled matt ground.

Samian – Flavian. (D. 64).

Layers sealing-off the early occupation

AX II 41

434. Fabric 5 – facetted burnished surfaces. Other examples – no. 73.
435. Fabric 16 – smoothed matt exterior finish.
436. Fabric 45 – burnished exterior. Rim sherd from another similar. Fabric 17.
437. Fabric 17 – burnished rim and shoulder. Decoration – low relief nodular rustication. Rim sherd from another jar similar. Fabric 17 – blue-grey.
438. Fabric 46 – smoothed matt finish. Other examples – see no. 382.
439. Fabric 74 – B.B.1 hand-made – burnished rim and shoulder. Decoration – burnished lattice on a matt ground. Probably from Dorset.
440. Fabric 17 – burnished exterior.

441. Fabric 5 – highly burnished exterior; matt interior. Knob from another, in fabric 44 – burnished exterior. A relatively large group of sherds, includes a base from an amphora, Dressel type 30 in Fabric 35, and a rim sherd from a spouted jar, like no. 33 in Fabric 19, red ware with cream slip, a rim sherd from a bowl, like no. 74 and a rim sherd from a necked bowl, like no. 15 in Fabric 5, and a rim sherd from a jar, like no. 52. Fabric 17, with rouletted decoration.

Samian – c. A.D. 65-85.

AX II 36 & 38

442. Fabric 52 – sparse accidental grits; worn mica-coating all over. A "second", it is blistered.
443. Fabric 16 – burnished finish.
444. Fabric 45 – highly burnished rim and shoulder. Decoration – low relief nodular rustication.
445. Fabric 6E – rilled exterior finish.
446. Fabric 6E – matt surface.
447. Fabric 74 – B.B.1 hand-made – uneven freehand burnished exterior; matt interior.
448. Fabric 17 – orange-brown; facetted burnished exterior; rilled interior.

Samian – c. A.D. 75-100.

AX II 35

449. Fabric 67 – hard. Deep pink core; pinky-cream surfaces. Mixed grey and white flint trituration grit which does not extend onto the flange; internal scoring. Moderate wear, related to Gilliam 238. c. A.D. 65-90.
450. Fabric 74 – B.B.1 hand-made – burnished finish. Decoration – burnished scroll on the outside of the rim. Possibly second rather than first century.
451. Fabric 6A – matt rilled lumpy exterior finish.
452. Fabric 6C – burnt. Matt rough exterior.

Samian – Neronian and probably Flavian.

THE SANDS RAMPART

Generally the pottery from the construction layers of the rampart is fairly fragmentary, while some is very weathered, as if it had been exposed for sometime before its deposition with the rampart material.

The samian covers the pre-Flavian to early Hadrianic period. There is a small sherd of Flavian samian from the rammed gravel base of the rampart, CG III 17, and a group of small Neronian and early Flavian sherds from the core, CG III 12, which indicate a date of after c. A.D. 70 for its construction. The first section through the rampart also resulted in a fairly large group of samian from the core, BZ II 12, but it included three vessels form Les Martres-de-Veyre, dated A.D. 100-25. Comparison with the large group of samian from the lower layers over the collapsed rampart, in particular BZ I 12, shows that the latest samian here is also from Les Martres and dated A.D. 100-25. It appears therefore that the core BZ II 12 had been contaminated, but whether the later material was intruded from the layers above during excavation or got in during the disturbance of the core when the rampart was in the process of collapse, is not clear. When the Les Martres material is removed, the resulting group from BZ II 12 supports a date between A.D. 70 and 85 for the rampart's construction. The complete absence of samian from Lezoux and of Hadrianic-Antonine pottery from the lower and middle layers filling the ditches, could indicate that in this section at least, the rampart had collapsed by c. A.D. 125.

Both sections through the rampart produced fairly large groups of coarse wares a proportion of which are paralleled in the occupation and sealing-off layers of the Leaholme forts, nos. 453-4, 456, 458, 462-3, suggesting that it was derived from there. The remaining sherds are rather indeterminate, but two jars at least, nos. 455 and 457, are early-second century in date, so should be part of the intrusive group. The absence of B.B.1 and local products common in the Flavian-Trajanic period, in particular bowls like no. 74, and jars like nos. 78 and 79, suggest that the rampart was constructed before A.D. 85.

The coarse wares from the lower layers of the ditches, CG IV 21, BZ I 20 and BZ I 18, include a range of Flavian-Trajanic forms and fabrics. In addition, some pieces are contemporary with the groups from the core of the rampart, and some may actually have fallen into the ditch when the collapse took place; in particular there are matching sherds from the core CG III 12, the middle of the ditch, CG III 11, and the upper levels CG III 6. There are sherds from at least two jars in B.B.1, one in the bottom of a ditch (CG IV 21), the other, a jar like no. 429, from the higher levels, BZ I 15. The coarse wares appear to support the date of *c.* A.D. 125 for the collapse of the rampart.

The Rampart

BZ I 12

453. Fabric 16 – burnished rim top. The rim from a shallow dish or a carinated bowl. Similar bowls were found in the layers sealing-off the early occupation in the Leaholme fort, the sherds are small and were not illustrated (see p. 204).

454. Fabric 22 – powdery ware; very worn surfaces, originally dark grey-black surfaces, burnished rim. Other examples – no. 87.

455. Fabric 77 – worn rough surfaces. Probably decorated with rustication. Possibly early second rather than first century in date.

456. Fabric 17 – hard; smoothed exterior finish. Other examples – see no. 80.

457. Fabric 50 – powdery ware; worn surfaces, with smoky grey patches; no finish survives. Probably second century.

458. Fabric 6E – burnished slurry finish.

459. Fabric 13 – smoothed finish.

460. Fabric 13 – orange core; smoky grey and buff worn surfaces; no finish survives.

461. Fabric 6E – smoothed finish.

There is a fairly large group of very worn, small body and base sherds, from at least 14 vessels including body sherds from two jars with low relief nodular rustic decoration, in Fabrics 20 and 45.

Samian – a fairly large group, from the pre-Flavian to the Hadrianic period in date. (D. 65-67).

CG III 12 & 17

462. Fabric 10 – worn, no finish survives. A carinated bowl. Other examples – see no. 343. The form occurs commonly in the area with identical versions from Bagendon, type 36, and similar bowls from Rodborough.

463. Fabric 46 – very worn, no finish survives. Probably originally decorated with rouletting. Identical jars in the filling of the Ditch III, nos. 319-20.

464. Fabric 17 – smoothed rim and shoulder. Decoration – relatively high relief nodular rustication for the size of the pot.

465. Fabric 6A – unusually fine tempering; very worn grey patchy surfaces; traces of a burnished finish.

466. Fabric 17 – burnished rim top, matt neck.

467. Fabric 13 – very worn surfaces.

468. Fabric 6A – very worn surfaces so that the tempering visible as dark grey flecks. Body sherds from four jars in blue-grey Fabric 6 and one in orange-buff.

Body sherds from four storage jars. Fabric 6 – blue-grey.

469. Fabric 6E – smoothed slurry finish. (CG III 17). There is a fairly large group of miscellaneous sherds from at least 12 vessels including base and body sherds from a small necked bowl in Fabric 10. The base has a shallow groove on the inside forming an imitation footring, similar to bases found at Bagendon, types 101 & 116; also the base from a mortarium, Fabric 67. First century.

Samian – a group of small Neronian sherds, with two Nero-Flavian pieces.

The filling of the Outer Ditches

CG IV 21 – Bottom layers

470. Fabric 5 – very worn surfaces, only small patches of the highly burnished finish survive. Almost complete. Other examples – AD VIII 40; similar to no. 372. The form also occurs at Kingsholm, Gloucester (Darling, 1977, fig. 6.9, 32).

471. Fabric 49 – mottled rough surfaces. Decoration – incised scrolls (Matching sherds in CG IV 19).

472. Fabric 17 – hard; highly burnished finish on the lip and in bands on the neck. Rim sherd from another similar.

473. Fabric 17 – burnished lip, matt neck. Rim sherd from another similar.

474. Fabric 6E – smoothed finish. Also the rim from another. Fabric 6E – heavily burnt and discoloured with soot. There are miscellaneous sherds from over eight vessels including a base from a bowl or a jar in Fabric 11 which is possibly from the same pot as no. 484, and a sherd from a hand-made jar, in Fabric 74 – B.B.1 with burnished stripes on a matt ground. Probably Flavian rather than later.

Samian – pre-Flavian.

BZ I 20 – bottom layer

475. Fabric 10 – smoothed surface.

BZ I 18 – middle layer

476. Fabric 5 – with some large water-worn grits. Badly burnt and discoloured so that no original colour and finish survive.

477. Fabric 4 – ochre core; bright orange surfaces; exterior smoothed before being decorated. Decoration – three bands of rouletting. Other examples – Parsonage Field 1958, CW/58/241. Layer 6, Bldg 2; 1973 Site D, Sewer-pipe trench.

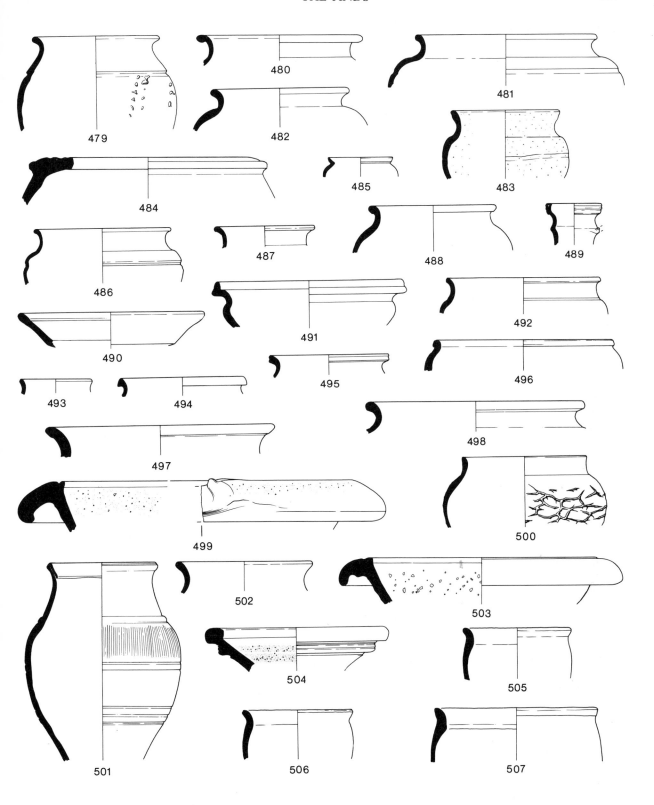

Fig. 65.   Coarse pottery (1:4)

478. Fabric 45 – traces of burnished finish on the rim. Lid or bowl.

479. Fabric 30 – burnished rim and shoulder. Decoration – crudely executed light grey barbotine spots. (Matching sherds in BZ II 14).

480. Fabric 16 – blue-grey surfaces; burnished rim-top, remainder matt.

481. Fabric 49 – badly-fired grey ware; worn, but trace of a burnished finish. Sooty patches of exterior.

482. Fabric 15 – matt lumpy finish.

483. Fabric 24 – hand-made; facetted burnished finish. Iron Age tradition (see p. 201 Fabric C).

The miscellaneous sherds include over 20 vessels including body sherds from an amphora, Camulodunum. 185 in Fabric 35 and body sherd from a jar in Fabric 16. Decorated with high relief rustication. Samian – Nero-Flavian. (D. 18).

Selected pottery from layers over the Rampart

484. Fabric 11 – thin cream slip on the exterior. The base may be in CG IV 21. Probably pre-Flavian.

485. Fabric 112 – patchy dark green glaze, inside and out. Not an import from Central Gaul, possibly from the pottery at Savernake, Wilts. (Information from Mrs V G Swan). (BZ II 4).

THE VICUS

The pottery from site AY is in poor condition, the sherds are small, worn and weathered suggesting exposure to the elements for some time. It includes pieces which post-date *c.* A.D. 70, as well as sherds which could have been derived from the earliest occupation. The lowest layers seem to be make-up and levelling layers rather than actual occupation. Datewise the groups support occupation in the area contemporary with the Leaholme fort.

Layers on natural

AY I 18

486. Fabric 17 – orange core; light blue-grey surfaces; worn but smooth surfaces. Many small sherds.

487. Fabric 17 – very worn, no finish survives. Decoration – probably low relief nodular rustication. Many small sherds but restoration of a profile was not possible.

488. Fabric 41 – very worn, no finish survives. Many small worn sherds. There are small miscellaneous sherds from five vessels.

Second levels above natural

AY I 25 + 26

489. Fabric 31 – hard. Off-white; burnished exterior. Body sherd from a flagon. Fabric 21. Rim sherds from two ring-necked flagons. Fabric 19. Neck sherd from a flagon. Fabric 29.

490. Fabric 5 – worn, with traces of a burnished finish on the inside only. Base sherd with a shallow foot-ring, probably from the same platter.

491. Fabric 5 – traces of a burnished finish. Base sherd probably from the same bowl. Rim sherd from a second example.

492. Fabric 5 – worn surfaces. Rim and body sherd from two others. Body sherd from a version with a deep groove on the shoulder. Fabric 5.

493. Fabric 10 – worn, smooth surfaces.

494. Fabric 41 – very worn but smooth surfaces.

495. Fabric 23 – black slurry surfaces. Body sherd from a similar jar. Fabric 23 – light grey ware.

496. Fabric 6C – over-fired. Matt finish.

497. Fabric 10 – sparse tempering; worn, no finish survives. Falls within the definition of so-called Severn Valley wares.

498. Fabric 6E – matt lumpy finish. There are body sherds from three jars. Fabric 6. There are miscellaneous sherds from 14 different vessels, including a rim sherd from a typical jar like no. 319 in Fabric 46 and a base sherd from a butt beaker in Fabric 48A, from the same source as no. 296.

Filling of features cut into natural

AY V 50

499. Fabric 67 – hard cream ware. Very worn, little trituration grit and internal scoring survive. The flange was not gritted. *c.* A.D. 60-90.

500. Fabric 17 – burnished rim and upper shoulder. Decoration – low relief rustication. Identical jars from AL VII 13; Ashcroft 1951, I 9.

RESIDUAL EARLY POTTERY

501. Fabric 2 – vesicular; burnished exterior. Decoration – a continuous band of light vertical combing. The rim was formed by folding over the top edge. The fabric falls within the definition of Severn Valley ware. AS III Pit 5 – a pit cut into natural in the areas of the possible vicus for the Leaholme fort.

502. Fabric 4 – sparse grits; highly burnished finish. The fabric falls within the definition of Severn Valley ware, and the glossy finish suggests a source at Gloucester (see no. 72). (AS III Pit 5).

503. Fabric 71A – Brick red, with a grey core at the rim; thin cream slip. Probably made at Gloucester whee A. Terentius Ripanus made generally similar mortarium *c.* A.D. 60-90. (AS I 90).

504. Fabric 67 – fine yellowish-cream ware. Translucent crystalline trituration grit. Well worn. Pre-Flavian, but the used grit in this mortarium may indicate a date after *c.* A.D. 55. (1964 Observation, Site AS).

HAND-MADE POTTERY OF LOCAL IRON AGE TRADITION FROM OTHER SITES IN CIRENCESTER

505. Fabric 25B – glossy vertically burnished exterior finish which masks the grits; burnt and sooty. Parsonage

Field, 1958, CW/58/186. See p. 201, Fabric B.
506. Fabric 24 – glossy vertically burnished finish
which masks the grits; burnt and sooty patches inside
and out. Ashcroft 1961, A I 40. Found with 507 in a

context post-dating A.D. 140. See p. 201, Fabric C.
507. Fabric 25B – glossy burnished finish on the
exterior, horizontal on the rim and vertical on the body.
See p. 201, Fabric B.

Under superficial examination, the jars in Fabrics 24 and 25, in particular nos. 505-7 appear identical in form, fabric and finish, only further investigation proves that the tempering is totally different and that widely separated sources could be involved. The obvious source for the limestone tempering is the local Cotswold stone, however the tempering proved to be Paleozoic limestone and the Malvern area is the obvious source, given the distribution of the particular vessel-forms involved, characterised by nos. 398 and 505. Jars of the same type as no. 505 etc. have been identified over an extensive area on both sides of the Severn, impinging on the area of the Upper Thames, with finds at Sutton Walls, Beckford, Bredon, Salmonsbury, Lechlade, Bagendon, Rodborough and Camerton. The distribution of the plain vertically burnished Malvern-type jars corresponds closely to the distribution of Dobunnic coins.

Despite their obvious Iron Age affinities, no example of either Fabric 24 or 25 occur in the earliest deposits at Cirencester. A typical jar form, in Fabric 24, no. 62, was found in the lowest silt layer of the Leaholme fort with Neronian samian. A bead-rimmed jar, in Fabric 25B, no. 258, occurred in the filling of Ditch II, with a group of possibly residual Tibero-Claudian sherds, but in the absence of other evidence, it could be contemporary with the Neronian-early Flavian remainder of the group. Typical Malvernian products occur first in the thick silts sealing-off the Leaholme fort from deposits from the later town (no. 253), otherwise they occur in areas which could have been within the defensive circuits of the Watermoor and Sands ramparts, which are thought to post-date after A.D. 70 for the introduction of vertically burnished Malvernian jars like nos. 398 and 505. The evidence from other sites suggests that those types were in use in the area before the Roman occupation, in which case the Cirencester examples could indicate survival well into the Roman period.

The presence of plain, vertically burnished Malvernian wares at Cirencester and Bagendon is unexpected given the absence of examples of the decorated products. The number from Cirencester is small, so that it constitutes far less than 1% of the total, and all the relevant sherds were submitted for analysis, but the importance of Malvernian wares at Bagendon is much greater. The sample from Bagendon was chosen from the illustrated material and this comprises only part of the total amount excavated. Examination of the types 161-164 with the aid of hydrochloric acid, shows that 23 have limestone tempering, probably Malvernian (Clifford 1961: fig. 55, 1-16; 59, 13; 60, 24 and 35; 68, 161-164). There appears from these figures to have been considerable trade with the Malvern area, however the sample could be distorted.

Although no groups comprised exclusively of hand-made pottery in the local Iron Age tradition have been found on sites within the town, a number of vessels have been identified, of which 14 are published in this volume – nos. 1, 62, 66, 253, 258-9, 397-8, 426, 430, 483, and 505-7. It is presumably significant that there are rims from only five wheel-made vessels which on the combination of form and fabric, could also be considered as part of that tradition, nos. 3, 92, 257, 392 and 396. Wheel-thrown pottery was obviously a late introduction which may not even have preceded the arrival of the Roman Army. The basic local forms can be extrapolated from the collections from Bagendon, Cirencester, Salmonsbury, Rodborough and Lechlade. The finer hand-made jars frequently have a foot-ring base, or else a recessed base which forms a shallow foot-ring, and they are confined to wide-mouthed necked bowls of varying size and proportions, and tripartite carinated bowls, Bagendon type 126-7, whose typological affinities appear to belong to the Upper Thames area, although chronologically this is difficult to substantiate. Those wheel-made vessels which may just be pre-Conquest in date are almost all finer wares, and are mainly limited to copies of Gallo-Belgic imports – butt and girth beakers, and platters – and cordoned and carinated vessels of so-called 'Belgic' derivation, and are present at Salmonsbury and Bagendon. Some may be of local manufacture, but some were probably traded into the area with actual imported fine wares from Gallia Belgica, South and

Central Gaul, which came in via the Fishbourne-Chichester area. Neither the vessels themselves, nor their typological traits can be attributed to the region north of the Thames valley, but they are closely paralleled at Silchester and the Fishbourne-Chichester areas. Before the trade in wheel-made pottery could greatly affect local techniques, the advance of the Roman Army lead to their widespread adoption, with the consequent introduction of forms and fabrics of obvious Roman character, but still derived form the tribal region of the Atrebates and hence bearing marked resemblances in form and decoration to the original traded wares.

IRON AGE AND ROMAN POTTERY FROM CIRENCESTER AND BAGENDON
by
D.F. Williams

A representative selection of Iron Age sherds from Bagendon and Cirencester were submitted for examination. All the sherds were studied macroscopically with the aid of a binocular microscope, and the majority were thin sectioned and examined under the petrological microscope. In addition, a number of Roman sherds from both sites were examined for comparison with those Iron Age sherds which make up Fabric D.

Fabric A fig. 61, 398.
Hard fabric, dark grey throughout. Inclusions of feldspar and quartz are visible in fresh fracture. Large angular grains of altered plagioclase feldspar can be seen in thin section, together with epidote, hornblende and quartz, and a large fragment of quartz diorite. This sample falls into Peacock's Group 'A' (1968), with a likely origin in the Malvern Hills. Burnished vertical lines occur on the outside surface of the sherd, similar to one from Sutton Walls (ibid., fig. 3, no. 3).

Fabric B fig. 56, 232; fig. 57, 253, 258; fig. 63, 426; fig. 65, 505 and 507; Clifford, 1961, figs. 55.5, 55.9, 60.24, 68.161, 68.163 and 68.164.
Soft, slightly soapy fabric, darkish grey throughout. Numerous angular fragments of white limestone can be seen throughout the fabric. Fig. 63, 426 and fig. 65, 507, and Clifford, 1961, fig. 55.9 were thin sectioned showing the limestone to be shelly limestone or 'biosparite', containing fossil fragments set in a matrix of recrystallized calcite. These samples fall into Peacock's Group B1, (1968), 'Palaeozoic limestone', with a suggested origin in the Malvern Hills area.

Fabric C fig. 50, 4; fig. 51, 62, 66; fig. 57, 259; fig. 61, 396, 397; fig. 65, 483 and 506; and Clifford, 1961, figs. 55.15, 65.116c, 67.148 and 70.179.
The fabric varies from soft to hard and is usually reddish-brown through to dark grey or black. Numerous argillaceous material occurs throughout the fabric. The majority of sherds were thin sectioned, confirming that the most distinctive feature of the fabric is the presence of frequent argillaceous inclusions. It is difficult to say whether this material is grog (crushed up pottery) or not. In some examples, often in the same sherd, the inclusions are large and fine-grained suggesting that the material occurs naturally in the clay or else represents the addition of a secondary clay; while in others the inclusions are smaller, more angular and contain a great deal of quartz, suggesting grog. Possibly both elements are a characteristic feature of this type of fabric. In addition to the argillaceous matter, many of the sherds contain quartz sandstone, a few have fragments of limestone and all have discrete quartz grains present.

Samples of Roman pottery from both sites were examined by thin section, and the characteristic argillaceous inclusions were recognized in fig. 50, 8, 22 and fig. 51, 47, and Clifford, 1961, figs. 52.26, 54.11 and 56.24. A similar range of inclusions have also been noted in pottery from Iron Age contexts at Lechlade, 15 miles east of Cirencester, and in second century A.D. levels at Gloucester (= Type-Fabric 2). This would seem to suggest a continuation of Iron-Age pottery-making traditions into the Roman period in the form of either the deliberate addition of grog or the use of similar raw materials. The source (or sources) for this type of fabric is difficult to predict at this stage of recognition, given the ordinary nature of the inclusions. A great deal of work obviously needs to be done if we are to tie down the source area, and assess the distribution and scale of production of this distinctive ware.

Fabric D Clifford, 1961, fig. 60.3

Moderately hard fabric, reddish-brown throughout, and heavily charged with ooliths. Thin sectioning reveals the ooliths more clearly, and it is possible to see their concentric structure within the limestone body. Bagendon is situated on Great Oolite Beds and so a local origin is quite possible, though oolitic grains were noted in a sherd from Cleeve Hill in Peacock's B2 Group, which may suggest a source further afield.

GRAFFITI
by
Mark Hassall

1. AH VIII + P.H. 7, (see also fig. 50, 10)
Sherds from the body and rim of a mortarium in orange fabric with grey core found in a post hole attributed to the first century military occupation. A graffito cut before firing reads

...] AIVP N FAC

The last three letters might stand for n(umero) fac(ta) or similar. (Hassall and Tomlin, 1977, 440, no. 76)

2. DK I 110, (see also fig. 53, 118)
Sherd of vessel with spout in orange fabric found in 1974 in the filling of a slot for a timber sleeper beam attributed to the military phase. A graffito, probably complete at the beginning, traced before firing on the flat horizontal shoulder of the vessel reads

]LIVII LIVII

(Hassall and Tomlin, 1977, 440, no. 75)

Fig. 66.   Graffiti (1:2)

TABLE 3 POTTERY UNILLUSTRATED

During the editorial stage the main text of the pottery report was reduced by the removal of all unillustrated groups as well as some of the unillustrated material from the published groups. This material appears in the following tables where contexts are listed in the same sequence as the pottery report.

	COARSE WARES						
	1–5	6–10	11–15	16–20	23–27	28–33	41–6; 49; 74;76
AH VIII 116	1(2):2(1): 3(1):4(1): 5(1)						
AH VIII 93		6(1)					
(AH VIII 76)	4(1)						
AH VIII 75	4(2)	7(1)					
(AH VIII P.H.3)	5(1)						
(AH VIII Pit 1)			12(1)				
(AH VIII 86)		7(1)					
AH VIII 91		6(1)					
AH VIII P.H.4	4(1)	10(1)					
AH VIII P.H.7							
AH VIII 100	4(1):5(1)						44(1)
AH VIII 83		6(1)					
AH VIII 96	5(2)	6(1):9(1)	11(1)				
AH VIII 78	3(1):4(1)	8(1):10(1)					
AH VIII 68	5(1)						
(AH VIII 103)				17(1)			
(AH VIII 28)	4(1)	9(1)					41(1)
(AH VIII 27)					22(1)		
AG II 48	5(1)						
AG II 42		6(1)	13(1)				
AG II 41		6(2)	14(1)				
AG III 49		6(1)	14(1):19(1)				
AG III 43			13(1)				
AG II 36:46; & III 38 + 39 }	4(3):5(4)	6(7):8(1) 9(3)	11(1):13(1)	16(4):17(3) 19(3):20(1)	23(1)		
AE V 21	3(1)	6(1)		17(2)	26(1)		
AE II P.H.3 + 1	5(1)			17(1):20(1)		31(1)	
(AE V 20)		6(2)		17(2)	25(1)	28(1)	
(AE VII P.H.1)	5(2)						
AE V 19		8(1)		17(1)	25(1)		
AE III 16			11(1)				
AE II 10 + III 16 }				17(½)			
AE I 10	5(1)	6(1)		17(2)			
(DM I 133)	4(3)	6(3)	13(1)	17(5)			
DM I 144	1(1):4(1) 5(2)	6(2):8(1) 9(1)		16(1):17(2)	24(1)		
DK I 111					25(1)		
DK I 119 ≡ DK II 48 }	4(2):5(1)	6(7):8(1) 9(2):10(1)	13(1)	17(3)	23(3):24(2)	31(1)	
(DM I 132)	4(2)		13(2)				
Pit Filling DM I 154 etc. }	4(5):5(4)	6(3):9(6): 10(1)	11(2)	16(2):17(9): 20(4):	23(1)		
U.L. DM I 145 }	5(1):	6(2):9(1)	12(1)	17(1):20(1)			
(DM I 143)		6(1)	13(1)	17(2)			
DK I 116 DK II 45 }	4(1):5(7)	6(4):9(4)		17(1):19(1)	23(1):25(1)	28(2):31(1)	
(DK II 47)		6(1)		17(1)		31(1)	49(1)
DK I 105		10(1)			23(2)		
DK I 109	4(1):5(5)	6(3):8(2) 9(2)		16(2):17(1) 20(1)		31(1)	
(DK I 108)					23(1)		
Pit DK I 115 etc }	4(1):5(5)	6(4):9(1)		17(2)	23(3):27(1)		

Contexts in parentheses indicate those groups containing no illustrated material. The numbers appearing in the columns are fabric numbers followed by the minimum number of vessels in parentheses. The presence of samian and Gallo–Belgic (TN) wares in a context are indicated by 'X' in the two final columns; dating is given in the relevant specialist reports.

COLOUR-COATED+ GLAZED 54–8: 61: 64: 75: 112	MICA-COATED WARES 52–3: 55: 61: 64:	FINE-WARES 21: 22: 48: 51: 59: 63: 65: 113:	MORTARIA 67–73	AMPHORAE 34–40: 47: 62: 66: 77–9	T-N	SAMIAN	
56(1)						X	AH VIII 116
				47(1)			AH VIII 93
							(AH VIII 76)
						X	AH VIII 75
							(AH VIII P.H.3)
56(2)							(AH VIII Pit 1)
							(AH VIII 86)
							AH VIII 91
		70(1)					AH VIII P.H.4
						X	AH VIII P.H.7
56(1)							AH VIII 100
56(1)							AH VIII 83
56(1)						X	AH VIII 96
56(1)						X	AH VIII 78
							AH VIII 68
						X	(AH VIII 103)
							(AH VIII 28)
							(AH VIII 27)
							AG II 48
							AG II 42
							AG II 41
						X	AG III 49
						X	AG III 43
				34(1)		X	AG II 36:46 & III 38 + 39
		21(1):48(1)				X	AE V 21
							AE II P.H.3 + 1
							(AE V 20)
							(AE VII P.H.1)
							AE V 19
						X	AE III 16
						X	AE II 10 & III 16
56(1)				40(1)		X	AE I 10
						X	(DM I 133)
		22(1)				X	DM I 144
							DK I 111
						X	DK I 119 = DK II 48
		22(1)				X	(DM I 132)
			67(1):72(1)	35(1)		X	Pit Filling DM I 154 etc.
						X	U.L. DM I 145
						X	(DM I 143)
		22(1)		40(3)		X	DK I 116 DK II 45
						X	(DK II 47) DK I 105
57(1)	53(1)			35(1)		X	DK I 109
						X	(DK I 108)
				35(2):39(1) 40(1)	X	X	Pit DK I 115 etc

	1-5	6-10	11-15	COARSE WARES 16-20	23-27	28-33	41-6; 49; 74;76
DK I 106	4(3):5(1)	6(3)				29(1)	
DK II 46		6(1):9(1)					
DK I 102	4(1):5(1)	6(1):9(1): 10(1)	13(1)				
DK I 103	4(1)				23(1)	31(1)	
DK II 44		10(1)					
DK II 43	4(1)	10(1):6(1)					
(DK I 112)	4(1):5(1)				25(1)		
(DK I 117)	4(2)			20(1)			
(DK I 94)	5(1)	6(1):9(1)					
(DK I 90)	5(1)	6(1):9(2)	11(1)	17(1)			
DK I 97	4(1)	6(3)		16(1):17(4)		31(1)	
DK I 110	4(1):5(1)	6(4):9(3) 8(1)	10(1):11(1) 12(1)	16(2):19(1)	25(1):27(1)	29(1)	
Tank Feature							
DK I 104 etc	5(2)	6(1)					
DM I 136 + 134		6(1):9(1)	11(1)	17(1)	23(1)		
DK II 42	4(3):5(2)	6(3):9(5)	13(1)	17(10):19(1) 20(3)		29(1):32(1)	
DM I 158	5(2)	6(4)		17(1):20(1)			
DM I 150	4(1):5(1)						
DM I 137	5(2)	6(3)	12(1):13(1)	17(2):19(1) 20(1)	23(1)	32(1)	74(1)
(DK I 91)	5(1)						
(DK I 92)	4(2):5(1)			17(1)			
(AM I 63)	3(2)						
AM I 61	1(1):4(1): 5(3)	6(2):10(1)	15(1)		24(1):25(2)	29(1)	41(1)
AM II 67							44(1)
AM II 59	5(7):	6(13):9(1)	11(22)		23(5):26(1)	29(10):30(1)	41(2):44(1) 46(2)
AM III 44	5(1)		11(2):15(1)	17(1)		29(1)	
AM III 45			11(1)			29(1)	
(AM III 43)	5(1)						
(AM IV 44)							
(AM II 66)			11(1)			29(1)	
AL II 39-45 ⎫	4(1):5(5)	6(4):7(2)	10(1):11(1): 13(2):15(2)	17(3):19(1)	23(1):24(1)	32(1)	41(1)
AL VII 31 ⎭							
AK II 22 ⎫	4(2):5(4)	6(5):9(1)	15(1)	16(1):19(1): 20(1):		33(1)	45(2)
AK IV 39-42 ⎭							
(BC I 48)	5(1):	9(1)					
(BC I 52)				20(1)			
(BC I 45)	4(1)						
(BC II 37)		6(2):10(2)		19(1)			
(BC II 34)		6(1)	13(1)			30(1)	
(DA IV 510)	4(1)	6(1):9(1): 10(1)					
(DA IV 506)							
(DA III 168)	5(1) Contaminated with late 3rd- early 4th- century A.D. sherds						74(2)
(DA III 166)		6(1)	15(1)	17(2)			
AW I 77	1(1):5(1)						
AW I 72	4(2)	7(2)		17(1):19(2)	26(1)		
AW I 71		6(2):9(1)				29(1)	
AW I 79	5(2)	6(7):9(1)	12(1)				41(1):42(2) 43(1)
AX II 58		6(2):9(2)	15(1):17(1)			28(1)	
AX II 43	5(6)	6(2):8(1): 10(1)	11(1):15(1)	16(1):17(6) 20(1)		31(1)	45(2):46(1)
AX II 42	5(1)	6(1):10(1)		17(1):20(1)			
AX II 47				18(1)			
AX II 44	5(1)	6(2)	15(1)				74(1)
AX II 45	5(2)	6(1):10(2)	13(1):15(5)	17(2):18(1)		31(1)	
AX II 41	5(4):	6(3):		16(1):17(5) 19(1).			44(1):45(1) 46(1):74(1)

COLOUR-COATED+ GLAZED 54-8: 61: 64: 75: 112	MICA-COATED WARES 52-3: 55: 61: 64:	FINE-WARES 21: 22: 48: 51: 59: 63: 65: 113:	MORTARIA 67-73	AMPHORAE 34-40: 47: 62: 66: 77-9	T-N	SAMIAN	
			67(1):72(1)			X	DK I 106
						X	DK II 46
		22(1)	67(1):71(1)	40(1)		X	DK I 102
						X	
57(1)						X	DK I 103
							DK II 44
						X	DK II 43
						X	(DK I 112)
						X	(DK I 117)
				39(1):62(1)		X	(DK I 94)
			70(1)			X	(DK I 90)
	52(1)					X	DK I 97
56(1)	55(1)	21(1)	70(1)			X	DK I 110
							Tank Feature
		48(1)					DK I 104 etc
			68(1)	40(1):34(1)		X	DM I 136 + 134
						X	DK II 42
		22(1)				X	DM I 158
				40(1)			DM I 150
						X	DM I 137
							(DK I 91)
							(DK I 92)
							(AM I 63)
				40(1)			AM I 61
			70(1)				AM II 67
56(26): 58(2):60(3) 75(1)	61(1)	21(2):22(1): 48(2):51(4) 59(1)	68(2)	34(3):38(1) 40(1):47(2)		X	AM II 59
56(2)		22(1)		40(1)		X	AM III 44
56(2)			70(1)				AM III 45
							(AM III 43)
				38(1)			(AM IV 44)
							(AM II 66)
		21(1):22(1): 48(1):63(1)	67(1):68(1): 73(1)	66(1)		X	AL II 39-45
							AL VII 31
56(3)		63(1):65(1)	70(1)		X	X	AK II 22
							AK IV 39-42
							(BC I 48)
							(BC I 52)
							(BC I 45)
				35(1)			(BC II 37)
					X	X	(BC II 34)
						X	(DA IV 510)
			68(1)			X	(DA IV 506)
						X	(DA III 168)
							(DAIII 166)
						X	AW I 77
						X	AW I 72
							AW I 71
						X	AW I 79
		21(1)					AX II 58
				34(1):77(1)		X	AX II 43
	52(1)					X	AX II 42
				35(1)			AX II 47
				38(1)			AX II 44
						X	AX II 45
		22(1)		35(1)		X	AX II 41

				COARSE WARES			
	1–5	6–10	11–15	16–20	23–27	28–33	41–6; 49; 74;76
AX II 36 + 38		6(2):17(1)		16(1)			45(1):74(1)
AX II 35		6(2)					74(1)
BZ I 12	1(1):4(1)	6(3):9(1)	13(1):13(2) 15(1)	16(1):17(3) 20(1)	24(1)		45(1):50(1)
CG III 17 + 12	4(1):5(2)	6(11):10(2)	13(1)	17(2):20(1)			46(1)
CG IV 21	5(1)	6(5):9(1)	11(1)	17(3)			42(3):49(1) 74(1)
BZ I 20		10(1)					
BZ I 18	4(1):5(2)	9(3):6(15)	15(1)	16(3):17(6)	24(1)	29(3):30(1)	49(6)
AY I 18	5(2)	6(1)		17(2)	25(1)		41(1)
AY I 25 + 26	4(2):5(7)	6(4):7(1): 9(1):10(2)	17(5):19(1)		23(2)	29(1):31(1)	41(1):42(1) 46(1)

COLOUR-COATED+ GLAZED 54–8: 61: 64: 75: 112	MICA-COATED WARES 52-3: 55: 61: 64:	FINE-WARES 21: 22: 48: 51: 59: 63: 65: 113:	MORTARIA 67-73	AMPHORAE 34–40: 47: 62: 66: 77-9	T-N	SAMIAN	
	52(1)					X	AX II 36 + 38
			67(1)			X	AX II 35
		22(1)				X	BZ I 12
			67(1)			X	CG III 17 + 12
						X	CG IV 21
							BZ I 20
57(1)				35(1)		X	BZ I 18
							AY I 18
		21(1):48(1)					AY I 25 + 26

SLAG SAMPLES
by
G. C. Morgan

Several samples of iron slag were found and subsequently examined by G.C. Morgan and L. Biek. They appear to have come from a smelting furnace. Mr. Morgan reports:

i.   Tap slag – smelting furnace and corroded piece of iron. Apparently a round bar with a taper. Traces of random wood fibre. DK II 41.

ii.   Earthy slag with some fayalite. Very mixed smelting furnace residues. DK II 42.

Three further samples await analysis by L. Biek. They are DK II 39; DK II 40; and DK I 90.

THE ANIMAL REMAINS
by
Clare R. Thawley

The total number of fragments associated with the military occupation of Roman Cirencester was 823, that could be identified accurately. These have been divided for the purposes of this report into three groups:

   I   Military layers DK I 112, 113, 114, 115, 116, 117, 119
                              DK II 43, 44, 45, 46, 47, 48
   II   Layers sealing the military occupation
                      DM I 19, 65, 133, 137, 150, 158
                      DK I 81, 90, 92, 94, 96, 97, 99, 102, 103, 104, 105, 106, 107, 108, 109, 110
                      DK II 39, 40
   III Vicus   AY I 26.

The pottery found in these areas suggests that much of the material consisted of redeposited rubbish, in which case the animal bones have to be approached with caution since they cannot be classified according to historical age in the same way that pottery can. The aim of this report is, therefore, to extract as much information as can be considered valid, and no attempt has been made to speculate on topics such as agricultural management, autumn killing, meat yield, method of procuring meat, or husbandry techniques, etc. The small size of the sample prevents statistical tests being carried out (minimum numbers of animals and metrical analysis of bones to determine sex), and so this report will deal with basic data, and butchery marks only.

   The animals represented in the three groups were:

TABLE 4 ANIMAL BONE FRAGMENTS FOUND IN EACH GROUP

Species	I	II	III	Totals
Ox	48 (12)	258 (31)	85 (7)	391 (50)
Sheep/Goat	10 (7)	190 (36)	59 (5)	259 (48)
Pig	22 (9)	84 (17)	36 (3)	142 (29)
Horse	2 (2)	1 (1)	9 (1)	12 (4)
Goat		1 (1)		1 (1)
Dog		2 (2)		2 (2)
Roe Deer		1 (1)		1 (1)
Fowl	1 (1)	14 (7)		15 (8)
Totals	83	551	189	823

The figures in brackets represent the minimum number of individuals per species per group, assuming that all layers within each group are discrete. This is only a small number of species compared with the range so far found on other sites within Cirencester, which include cat, red deer, hare, goose, vole, mouse, shrew, badger and fish (King, 1975; Thawley – unpublished) and is probably the consequence of the sample size rather than the result of any cultural factors. Considering the evidence presented in table 4, the three most commonly occurring species are Ox, Sheep and Pig respectively, followed after a large gap by Fowl and Horse. Of all the animal remains only two species showed no signs of butchery, namely Horse and Dog; this also applies to remains of these animals from the whole area of Roman Cirencester examined so far, suggesting that they were kept as working beasts or pets and did not constitute part of the diet. Dead dogs and horses seem to have been buried elsewhere or were not common animals. No sieving was carried out on the site, so the bones found can be expected to be heavily biased towards the large animals as shown by Payne (1972).

Tables 5-7 show the bones recovered from each species of large mammal. For the three main food animals (Ox, Sheep and Pig) bones are shown to occur from most parts of the body, more so in group II where the sample is larger and more varied and where there is a greater probability that small or unfragmented bones may be found.

TABLE 5:   BONES FROM ANIMALS IN GROUP I (FRAGMENTS)

Bone	Ox	Sheep	Pig	Horse
Skull	2		3	
Mandible	4		3	
Teeth			1	
Vertebra	2	1	1	
Ribs	18	3	6	
Scapula	4	2	2	
Humerus	1	1	1	
Radius		1		1
Ulna			1	
Metarcarpals	4			
Phalanges	5			
Pelvis	4			1
Femur	2			
Tibia	1	2	1	
Fibula			1	
Tarsals	1			
Metatarsals			2	
Totals	48	10	22	2

TABLE 6:   BONES FROM ANIMALS IN GROUP II (FRAGMENTS)

Bone	Ox	Sheep	Pig	Horse
Skull	13	11	11	
Mandible	20	22	14	
Teeth	6	4	1	
Vertebra	20	15	9	
Ribs	100	42	17	
Scapula	19	7	4	
Humerus	8	7	3	
Radius	7	11	3	
Ulna	1	2	3	1
Metacarpals	11	4	2	
Phalanges	14	2		
Pelvis	7	5	10	
Femur	2	9	5	
Tibia	9	26	6	
Tarsals	1	1	3	
Metatarsals	12	8	2	
Totals	258	190	84	1

TABLE 7: BONES FROM ANIMALS IN GROUP III (FRAGMENTS)

Bone	Ox	Sheep	Pig	Horse
Skull	5	5	2	
Mandible	7	2	1	
Teeth	4		3	2
Vertebra	19	4	1	
Ribs	10	19	13	4
Scapula	9	2	3	
Humerus	4	3		
Radius	6	4		
Ulna	1	1	1	
Metacarpals	1	2		1
Phalanges	4			
Pelvis	2	5	4	1
Femur	2	6	3	
Tibia	8	5	1	
Tarsals	3	1	3	
Metatarsals			2	1
Sesamoid				1
Totals	85	59	36	9

The apparent abundance of certain bones on the site can be attributed to differential preservation and fragmentation as much as it could be to local habits in butchery and cooking. Bones from the region of the head and longbone shafts are usually more compact and survive better than spongy bone from the epiphyses. Bones from the spine and ribs should be commoner than bones from the limbs, simply because there are many more of them. The larger bones will become more fragmented during butchery in order to produce small enough cuts of meat of a size that is easy to cook and eat.

These factors alone could easily account for the variation in the abundance of the different bones. There is one point of interest though, in that fragments from the feet of cattle and sheep occur, which could indicate that the carcasses were not dressed before being brought into the area, and thus that they may have been slaughtered and butchered within the area being dealt with in this report.

The variation in occurrence of the different bones seems to be fairly consistent over the three groups, varying in proportion to sample size.

The number of fragments of the three main food animals shows the Pig to be the least frequent. If butchering an Ox, many more fragments must be generated to produce enough small enough pieces of meat than would be necessary if butchering a Sheep. A Pig being intermediate between these two would again need to be cut up more than a Sheep to produce the same sized pieces of meat. On this basis Ox would appear the most abundant, then Pig, then Sheep. This only appears to be the case in group I, which is such a small sample that no conclusions may safely be drawn from it. In groups II and III the picture seems to be somewhat altered with Sheep occupying second place, by quite large margins. In terms of fragments, Ox and Sheep were probably equally popular and Pig constituted a much smaller part of the diet. This could in part be due to the functions of these animals before being killed. Cattle provide milk, breeding stock and traction, sheep provide wool and breeding stock but pigs are less easy to keep, but are quite useful foragers on the land. Pigs may have been kept as urban scavengers, fulfilling a very useful task, but in large numbers could be a serious menace. If this was the kind of existence that Pigs led then the numbers would need to be controlled, and they would be far less abundant than Cattle or Sheep.

Table 8 shows the age at death of those bones which could be recognised to be of a certain age, which comprises 43.4% of all fragments.

TABLE 8: AGE AT DEATH

Group I	Juvenile	Prime	Old age
Cattle		8	
Sheep		2	1
Pig		7	
Group II			
Cattle		42	6
Sheep	2	31	1
Pig	2	20	
Group III			
Cattle	1	85	8
Sheep	6	87	1
Pig	2	43	1
Overall totals			
Cattle	1	136	15
Sheep	8	120	3
Pig	4	71	1

The small amount of historical information on the subject of epiphyseal fusion indicates that bones fused later in life than they do today, because modern stock has been selectively bred over the centuries to mature as early as is economically possible. By modern standards, taken from Silver (1963), the age ranges shown in the above table are: "juvenile" 0-1 years, "prime" 1-3½ years (sheep), 1-4 (pig) and 1-5 (ox), and "old age" lies above all the upper age limits for "prime" meat. The above figures will be biased to some extent, through being determined from modern aging data, but far less than they would be if divided neatly into the "exact" year in which death occurred.

The figures in table 8 show at least that the minority of fragments were from animals that had lived for more than one year at a bare minimum. This could point to an organised agricultural community which was capable of keeping stock over a few years, and so solving the problems of over-wintering. The beasts would then be culled before the meat became too tough. The occurrence of young animals amongst the bones is probably an indication of the killing of weak or sickly individuals, and probably before the winter months. To make most use of the animals before they were killed, Roman farmers in Italy would put their stock out to work in the fields, so as to provide some active service to the community. White (1970) reports that these farmers preferred a heifer to work 2 years before being put to calf, thus putting less of a strain on the animals. Animals killed while still young (less than a year old) generally provide little meat compared with older and more developed beasts, but if death was unavoidable for economical or health reasons, then their meat was apparently regarded as something of a delicacy. One reaons for the apparent shortage of young animal bones is their fragility, rendering them more susceptible to decay and crushing post burial, giving a poorer chance of survival than those of an adult.

There could have been land around the fort that was farmed in peacetime, and, according to Davies (1971), this was a common practice.

The presence of dogs on the site is testified by the number of fragments found to have been gnawed by them. 10.2% of all the fragments recovered were gnawed, and no doubt many more were at the dogs' disposal and were completely demolished or taken elsewhere and buried. Table 9 shows the number of gnawed fragments that survived:

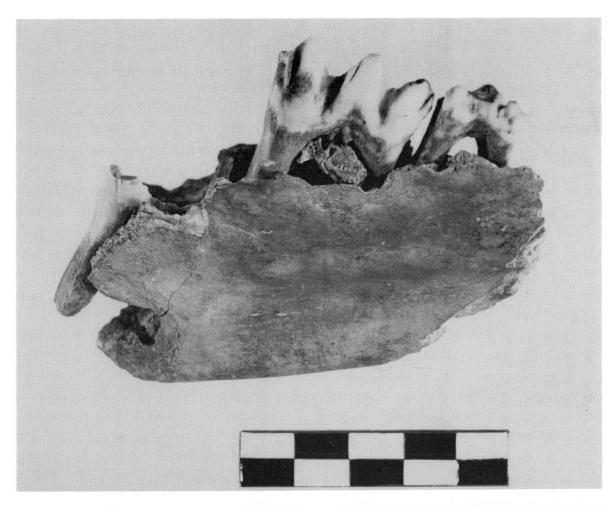

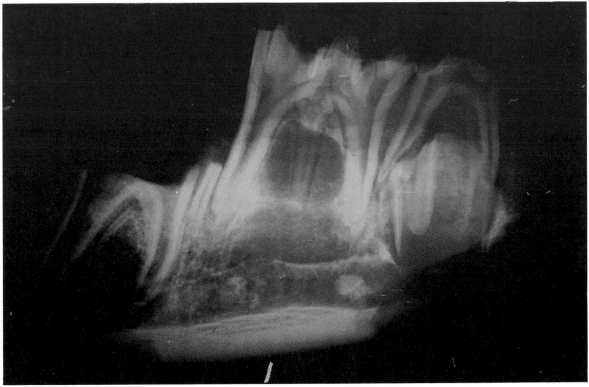

26.   Photograph (a) and X-radiograph (b) of the complete absence of adult premolar 4 in the socket below milk premolar 3, from DM I 137.

TABLE 9: BONE FRAGMENTS GNAWED BY DOGS

	Ox	Sheep	Pig	Horse
Group I	7	2	5	1
Group II	25	27	9	
Group III	5	2	1	
Totals	37	31	15	1

In addition to bones gnawed by dogs, there was a small amount of evidence of other activities. Five bones, from groups II and III, were charred. There were no calcined bones, however, so these charred bones may be the remains from cooking or more widespread fire at some stage, rather than incineration or cremation. Another five bones, again from groups II and III, had green stains like those from decayed copper alloy objects, and were probably juxtaposed to such objects after burial.

There were some bones which showed signs of disease. These will be briefly described but not diagnosed, since this is a highly specialised subject rather beyond the scope of this report. The bones are:

1. part of an Ox mandible with milk premolars 2 and 3 and a broken part of molar 1 (group II). A radiograph shows that the adult premolar 3 (P3) is developed and ready to erupt below milk P2, but that there is an empty socket below milk P3 (plate 26). The mandible is complete at this point so that there is no way that the adult tooth could have dropped out. It would thus seem that this tooth was absent through a developmental abnormality, probably of congenital origin. There are similar cases found in the jaws of ancient cattle and sheep, as shown by Andrews and Noddle (1975), but the tooth absent in these cases is always P2 (adult) and not P4 as in the jaw described above;

27.   Proximal end of a diseased ox metatarsus.

2. an Ox metatarsus with a diseased proximal end (plate 27), possibly arthritis or infection of the joint (group II);
3. an Ox rib (group II) with extra bony growth on the shaft, probably a healed break;
4. a Sheep mandible (group II) with a decayed stump of a tooth in the place of molar 1, and a porous and swollen socket, probably a peridontal abcess (plate 28);
5. a Sheep mandible (group II) with a small porous growth on the ventral of the jaw below milk P3.

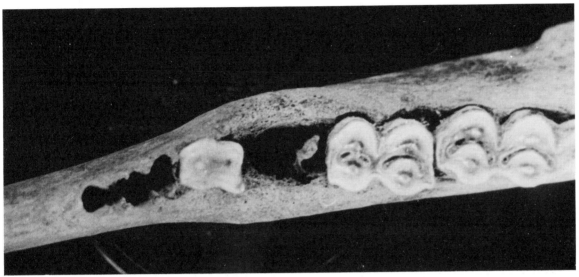

28.   Peridontal abscess of sheep mandible, showing decayed tooth stump in swollen socket, from DK I 81.

Butchery Techniques

The butchery methods employed in Roman Cirencester will be dealt with in rather more detail than most of the previous topics, since the bones of the whole "military" sample give more information on this subject than they can on anything else, albeit of a qualitative rather than quantitative nature. Also the techniques are markedly different from those used later in history e.g. on Mediaeval sites, and may show regional variation within the Roman period. On preliminary investigation, the butchery within the three groups did not show itself to be significantly different, so the following discussion of butchery will cover the combined material.

OX

For convenience the bones will be dealt with in three sections, namely "head", "forequarters" and "hindquarters".

Head

The bones from the "head" region are: skull, horn cores, mandible, hyoids and atlas vertebra; the last is included since it can give an indication of how the head was removed from the neck.

Most of the bones from the head region have cuts showing that the head was deliberately butchered once it had been removed. There were no fragments showing signs of pole-axing, as there have been from other parts of Roman Cirencester, or other means of slaughtering. The horns had all been deliberately cut from underneath by a lateral blow and torn off, and would probably have been sent to the local horner. The head seems to have been severed from the body either by cutting into the occipital condyle from the side or underneath, splitting it off and leaving it attached to the neck, or by cutting into the atlas vertebra from above and splitting it to leave the front part attached to the skull.

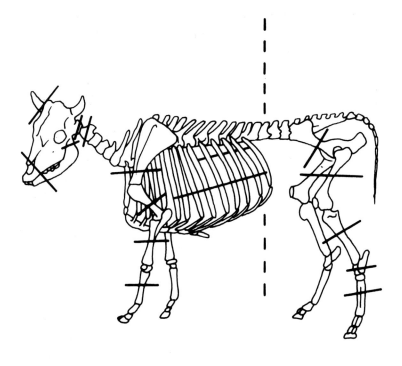

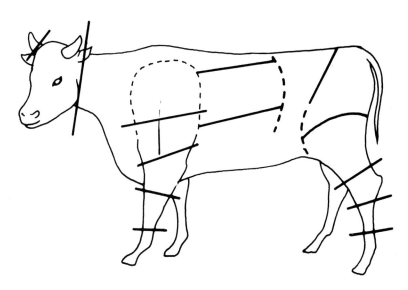

Fig. 67.   The butchery of an ox

The bones around the "cheek" region (temporal, zygomatic) show cuts from the posterior, which could have been associated with removal of the mandible. Other parts of skulls show odd cuts probably associated with fleshing activities, and a number of fragments around the cranial region have been torn along sutures, possibly to extract the brain.

There are cuts of a rather blunt nature, as if made with the blunt side of an axe, in the snout region, which coincide with the diastema of the mandible. The mandible fragments can be divided into "cheek" and "hinge" fragments of which there are 23 and 8 respectively. The mandibles have cuts from the lateral mainly, with some from the medial, which could only have been made once the jaws had been separated, and then split. The reason for cutting up the mandibles is uncertain, but it has been found in a number of sites that the writer has examined. The hyoid fragments show some cuts, probably associated with the removal of the tongue.

Forequarters

The bones included in this category are: cervical and thoracic vertebrae, ribs, scapula, humerus, radius, ulna, carpals, matacarpals and phalanges (sternebrae would be included here, but none were found).

The modern method of butchery is to separate the fore- and hindquarters after the carcass has been split longitudinally, by an electrical saw, and then cutting roughly between the thoracic and lumbar vertebrae. The position of severing of the Roman carcass into fore- and hindquarters is very difficult to determine, and reference to these two areas in this report will be made using a hypothetical line between the thoracic and lumbar vertebrae.

The cervical vertebrae are few in number here with only 3 fragments as against 25 thoracic showing any signs of butchery, and give no clue to the method of dealing with the neck. There is one axis vertebra which shows a ventral cut on its odontoid process, probably another means of separation of the head and neck.

The thoracic vertebra tend to have become very fragmented due to the removal of the long neural spine, and the centra of the vertebrae were usually avoided by cutting down each side of the vertebra to remove the rib articulations, mainly from the ventral. The ribs show varied butchery, depending from which part of the rib the fragments were originally cut. The ribs are the most abundant of all bones for two reasons: 1) there are more of them than any other bone on the body to start with, and 2) because they have become highly fragmented during the process of butchery, since whole ribs are more difficult to cook as they are so long. The usual cut was that of an axe stroke made to one side of the rib, the rib then being broken through manually. The blade fragments were usually cut from the lateral side, cutting through the meat, with only about half this number cut from the medial. The shaft fragments (where the rib narrows nearer the proximal end) were predominatly cut from the ventral leaving the proximal ends attached to the thoracic vertebra, or as separate cuts of meat. The evidence from the ribs and thoracic vertebra all point to the carcass being laid on its back to remove the ribs and split the backbone, and to do this the organs within the thoracic cavity must first have been removed and the sterebrae cut through. The scapula fragments show four fairly common practices:

1. the severing of the shaft region from the blade by cutting into this area from the medial, the carcass lying on its back. This was probably done to leave the blade attached to the chest while the lower leg was torn away with shaft and proximal scapula attached. The blade could then be easily removed as a separate "joint" of meat;
2. the puncturing of the blade portion for hanging by a meathook or a similarly pointed tool. The holes made by these tools are always in the thinnest part of the blade; they were made by a pointed object being forced through the bone, and are not at all similar to a bone gnawed by a dog;
3. the cutting of the spine of the blade, usually from the ventral, possibly part of fleshing actvitities, the spine then being torn off;
4. the cutting or slicing of the proximal end, probably severing it from the humerus.

Many of the humerus fragments have shafts split by spiral fracture, probably to extract the marrow and to break the bones down into smaller fragments to facilitate cooking. The distal ends were usually cut to avoid hitting the olecranon process of the ulna, and broken at the humerus-radius/ulna joint. Some superficial cuts occur on the shafts, often in the form of small "scoops", probably from carving the meat.

The ulna and radius fragments again show spiral fracturing to the shaft, usually from cuts nearer the end of the bones. The proximal end of the radius was cut again to avoid the olecranon process, and split through, probably removing the olecranon process and the distal humerus, to form a whole "elbow" joint. No carpal bones were found, and many of the metacarpals were split from blunt blows to the shaft. There were 23 phalanges which could have come from front or back legs, and they will all be dealt with here. Most of them showed little or no signs of butchery except for small surface slices on their posterior sides, about half way down the bone. In view of the small amount of edible meat on the lower leg, it seems likely that the foot would have been taken off at the mid-metacarpus whilst dressing the carcass, and that any cuts on the phalanges could be associated with activities outside the butchery trade.

Hindquarters

The bones from this category are: lumbar, sacral and caudal vertebrae, pelvis, femur, patella, tibia, (fibula absent in cattle), tarsals, metatarsals and phalanges (the latter already dealt with in the forequarters discussion). The lumbar vertebrae, like most of the thoracic vertebrae, have cuts to the centrum from the ventral or from the posterior, from which the centrum would be split in half if the axe-stroke hit it, while, if it missed, the transverse processes would be cut off, as is often the case in the lumbar vertebrae. All this tends to suggest that the carcass was either hung up by its hind legs and axed in successive strokes through the backbone so as to produce posterior cuts to the centra, or else it was laid on its back and axed into the spine to produce ventral cuts to the centra. There is only one sacral vertebra, cut centrally, which offers little information on the method of severing the pelvic girdle from the backbone.

The pelvis fragments show cuts to the shafts of the ilium, pubis and ischium, with occasional cuts to the acetabulum. Modern butchery separates the pelvis by a cut to the ilium shaft, leaving the blade as one part and the "aitchbone", including the acetabulum, pubis and ischium, as the other. Whether the Romans did this is hard to tell, since the sample here is rather small. The cuts to the acetabulum could indicate that the hind leg was removed by lying the carcass on its back and cutting down into this joint with successive axe-strokes. There is no evidence in the femur fragments to support this, though. Most of the femur fragments show shafts split by spiral fracture, in the same manner as the long bones from the forequarters.

There were no patella fragments, and the tibia fragments are again all split mid-shaft, from cuts aimed from all directions, sometimes multiple cuts showing where the butchers had some difficulty in penetrating this bone.

The tarsal fragments all bore cuts to their posterior or medial sides, some cuts being deeper than others, particularly on the calcaneus and astragalus. The metatarsal fragments frequently show spiral fracturing to the shaft, often from lateral blows of a rather blunt nature. This was probably when the hind foot was removed during the process of dressing. The phalanges have already been dealt with in the section on the forequarters.

The butchery of cattle described above is shown in fig. 67, with the position of the cuts marked against both a skeleton and a solid animal. The diagram is not, however, complete, as, for instance, the longitudinal splitting of the backbone cannot be shown, and can therefore only be used in conjunction with the text.

There is an interesting comparison with the butchered material from the Saxon Shore fort of Portchester (Grant, 1975) where the cattle longbones appeared not to have been split for marrow, the pelvis was cut through the acetabulum and the thoracic vertebra showed more lateral cuts. There are, nevertheless, some similarities in the general butchery, e.g. horns, ribs, and longbone joints. These differences and similarities could be due to regional variation in butchery techniques.

Fig. 68.   The butchery of a sheep

SHEEP

Like the Ox, the Sheep butchered fragments will be subdivided into head, fore- and hind-quarters, to include the same bones.

Head

The removal of the head from the neck seems to have occurred between either the axis–atlas, or the atlas–occipital condyle interfaces. One occipital fragment has been deliberately torn off, possibly to extract the brain. All fragments in the horn region show that the horns were deliberately torn off, and like the Ox bones, may have been used as a source of keratin for other trades. There is one frontal fragment which shows possible signs of slaughter: stunning, before bleeding. A parietal fragment shows a similar mark. Most of the mandible fragments came from the "cheek" region, being cut or torn in the diastema and/or across the angle. The diastema is the thinnest part through which to cut the mandibles and would also avoid having to cut into the teeth. Cuts around this part of the jaw are something of a mystery, since there is little edible meat. Perhaps these cuts were associated with removal of the tongue, or for other use such as production of "stock" for cooking. The teeth bore no signs of being used as a raw material, but a number had a build up of calculus, which could yield information on their diet (Armitage, 1975). Samples have been saved for this purpose, in case this kind of analysis is ever developed.

Forequarters

The cervical vertebrae bear cuts to the neural arch rather than to the centrum, so removing the arches. The thoracic vertebrae are cut either from the posterior or ventral, and split in half along the centrum, suggesting that the carcass was either hung up and axed down the backbone or laid on its back and cut into the spine, in a similar way to that already observed in the Ox. The rib fragments were usually cut on the medial side near the proximal ends, probably leaving these ends attached to the thoracic vertebrae, as in modern "lamb chops", while the rib blades were usually broken at both ends.

The scapula fragments consisted mainly of proximal ends with part of the shaft attached, which was cut on its medial side at a slight ventral oblique, with the carcass probably laid on its back to facilitate this. This would not be the most sensible way to detach the foreleg, as it is simpler to slice through the meat between the scapula and ribs to remove the entire scapula and then proceed to cut up the limb.

The humerus fragments came mainly from the distal end, with part of the shaft attached, cut from all directions. One distal end bore an antero-medial cut which severed the condyle, articulated with the ulna and radius, and so avoided the olecranon process. The shortage of proximal ends may be in part due to the stage in the animal's life at which this region fuses. If most of the animals were killed in their prime and before all the epiphyses fused, the proximal humerus epiphysis, which is one of the last to fuse, would be susceptible to decay.

Cuts to the radius are all in the shaft region, usually from the medial and split by spiral fracture, which avoided cutting near the proximal end. One ulna fragment was cut on the posterior side, and the olecranon process split off. There were no carpals, and the feet seem to have been severed at the metacarpus, by splitting the shaft. There were no butchered phalanges.

Hindquarters

Of the hindquarter vertebrae only the lumbars were found, which have very few centra split in half. Instead, these were avoided and the transverse processes broken. The pelvis fragments appear to have been cut so as to leave the hindleg and acetabulum attached, by cutting into the shafts on either side of the acetabulum, mainly from the ventral, with the carcass laid on its back. The femur was severed mid-shaft with cuts from the medial or lateral, and split. Most of the femur fragments were of small pieces of split shaft. One distal end showed ventral cuts to the articulation.

Distal ends predominated among the tibia fragments, and the shafts bear cuts from the medial, lateral and posterior, quite often the cuts being of a blunt type, made possibly with the back of an axe. Surface scores on the bones are probably signs of fleshing activities, using a knife. There were two tarsals, but neither was cut. The metatarsals were generally split mid-shaft with no signs of cuts, and this could be the site of removal of the foot. There were no phalanges.

The butchery is shown in fig. 68, in a similar fashion to that of the Ox. It is perhaps worth mentioning that two Sheep bones (from different layers) showed unusual "holes" or cuts. These were a metacarpus and a metatarsus, each with a nearly hexagonal hole made in the proximal end.

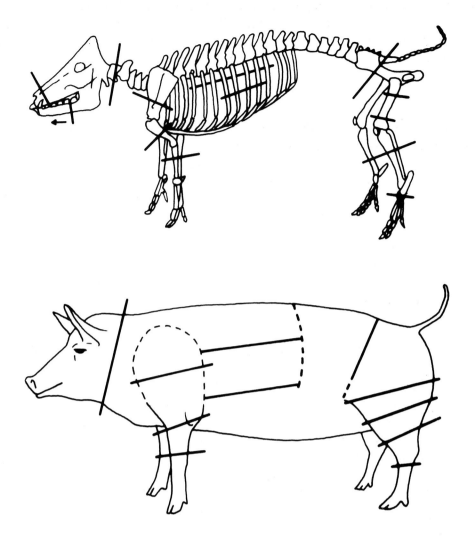

Fig. 69.   The butchery of a pig

PIG

Head

Head fragments were quite common amongst the Pig remains, which could be a more accurate indicator of the economic importance of the Pig than the overall number of fragments. Taking differential preservation of bones into consideration (see p. 213), the head is more durable than many of the more porous bones from the rest of the body, especialy from the area around the teeth.

Most of the skull fragments show deliberate butchery or breakage. There are two fragments with cuts made to the temporal arch, probably to remove the mandibles. Another has had the occipital condyle sliced off from the posterior; a frontal fragment was deliberately split down the mid-frontal suture and had slice marks within the cranial cavity, presumably to remove the brain. Another fragment was severed from a blunt blow from the dorsal into the premaxilla, similar to the cuts, already described, that were found in the cattle.

Unlike sheep and cattle, the symphysis of the mandible fuses in pigs, and prevents the two jaws from being pulled apart. Frequently this region was cut through, by the Romans, from either the posterior or ventral and then split through. The "cheek" fragments usually show medial cuts, which must have been made once the two jaws had been split. Cuts at the posterior end of the jaw were usually from the lateral, corresponding to cuts on the temporal arch, and this could show how the jaws were detached from the skull.

There were two atlas vertebrae, both cut into the neural arch from the dorsal then broken through, which would probably have been left attached to the skull.

Forequarters

There are very few vertebrae, but a possible trend does emerge for the thoracics. The centra seem to have been consistently avoided and the rib articulations cut instead. One cervical vertebra has been cut from the posterior into the centrum, which was then split in half. The ribs show cuts varying with the position of the fragment within the whole rib: cuts near the proximal end are from the dorsal/lateral, but a little further down the shaft they are from the medial, as with modern pork chops, and on the blade cuts occur with equal frequency from either side (lateral or medial). Many fragments bore surface slices, probably from fleshing. The scapula fragments consisted largely of broken pieces of blade, an area susceptible to post-burial decay and fragmentation. The more durable proximal ends show surface slices, and the shafts show cuts to the spine and blade from the medial or lateral.

Of the butchered humerus fragments, all had split shafts, so the proximal humerus may have been left attached to the scapula as part of a shoulder "joint". The humerus shafts bore cuts from the lateral, medial and anterior. None of the humerus epiphyses were cut. The radius fragments consisted only of distal ends whose shafts had been split from cuts to the lateral or medial. The ulna fragments consisted of shafts, cut laterally either side of the incisura semilunaris, probably leaving this attached to the distal humerus and proximal radius as one joint. There were no butchered carpals, metacarpals or phalanges, which may be due to the small sample size or because the foot was cut off and eaten as the "hock and trotter" are today.

Hindquarters

There were two butchered lumbar vertebrae fragments: one with cuts removing the transverse processes from the posterior, and the other cut across the centrum leaving a front and back half, unlike cuts described in the cattle which showed longitudinal splitting. The vertebra cut in half laterally could have been at the point of separation of the hind- and forequarters.

There were no sacral vertebrae. The pelvis fragments consisted predominantly of the acetabulum with parts of the three shafts, cut from all directions. Some of the ilium fragments have cuts which suggest that the ilium and sacrum were left attached and the rest of the pelvis left with the hind leg. No proximal femur fragments were found, and the shaft fragments were usually cut at both ends from the same direction (medial or lateral). There were also surface scores from fleshing. Many of the fragments were of diaphyses and therefore from young animals. Tibiae were cut only in the shafts, generally from the lateral, but towards their distal ends cuts were heavier and deeper (anterior or medial) probably associated with severing the tarsal area. The tarsals show anterior and surface cuts, the latter from severing of the tendons or fleshing. There were no butchered metatarsals or phalanges, so the hind foot was possibly eaten, like the fore foot may have been.

This butchery is shown in fig. 69, as for the cattle and sheep previously described.

There is in addition to the above information on butchery, a small amount of evidence about tools used. There are signs of the use of axes, knives and meathooks or fleshhooks, all from the bones themselves. This information, in the general absence of small finds from the area, can give an indication that such tools were in use. Some bones bear possible signs of sawing, but are rare and rather dubious. It would appear that axes and knives were then primarily used for butchery, not, as today, saws, which could nevertheless have been used in boneworking; any bone small finds might show this.

Breeds

This is a subject which cannot possibly be taken to any depth, since all that survives of the various breeds that might have occurred are the bones. There is no means, other than from historical records, of determining the colour of the skins, hides, fleeces, or the conformation of the beasts. Yields of milk, meat, wool, fat and other by-products cannot be accurately found.

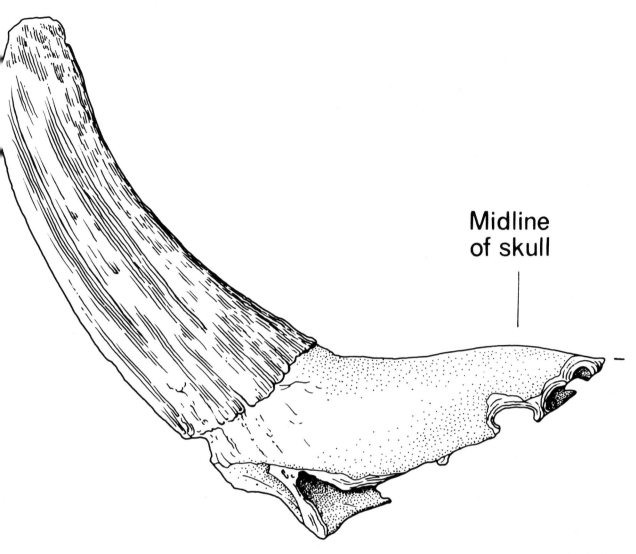

Midline of skull

Fig. 70. Fragment of an ox skull showing shape of intercornual ridge and horn core, posterior aspect, from DM I 65. (Scale 1:1)

The bones from the military period, and indeed from all the other Roman periods at Cirencester, give a good idea of the sizes of the animals. Cattle and sheep seem to have been consistently small, compared with later breeds (e.g. Mediaeval), but the pigs are much the same as those found on sites of all ages. In size, the cattle seem very much like the diminutive "Celtic shorthorn" originally described by Owen (1846) as *Bos longifrons*, and whose size has more recently been discussed by Jewell (1963). There is only one specimen which includes part of the frontal, shown in fig. 70, and this has a low single arch on the intercornual ridge according to the plan of bovine craniology proposed by Grigson (1976). All the skulls found were those of horned animals, with no evidence of polling. There was some variation in the horn cores, such as general length and cross-section, but only as much as one would expect to occur between the two sexes and castrates.

There were no hornless Sheep found on this site, as opposed to those from Portchester (Grant, 1975), and from other parts of Roman Cirencester.

An abbreviated form of the measurements is set out below, Table 10. Full details of the measurements are available from the writer.

Acknowledgements. I woud like to thank Leicestershire Museums for allowing me to make use of their comparative osteological collections for the preparation of this report.

TABLE 10: MEASUREMENTS OF THE ANIMAL BONES

Abbreviations used: AP – anteroposterior, DV – dorsoventral, ML – mediolateral, P – proximal, D – distal, LDW – least diaphyseal width ML
All measurements expressed in millimetres, giving the range where possible.

Long bones	Length DV	MLP	LDW	MLD
Ox				
Humerus			25.6 – 26.0	
Radius		60.0 – 69.9	29.5 – 35.0	28.0 – 32.0
Metarcarpus	167.3 – 177.2	48.0 – 53.3	26.4 – 31.0	49.6 – 57.2
1st phalanx	51.3 – 63.2	23.0 – 33.0	14.5 – 27.0	17.9 – 30.5
2nd phalanx	35.0 – 42.0	32.3	26.0	28.0
3rd phalanx	(AP 55.6 – 70.5)			
Tibia			29.5 – 41.1	48.1 – 54.0
Calcaneus	121.0			
Astragalus	57.5			
Cuboid		maximum ML 46		
Metatarsus	198.0	39.9 – 45.0	22.2 – 24.0	45.0 – 54.7
Sheep				
Humerus	96.0	28.0	9.6 – 15.2	21.2 – 27.0
Radius	102.0	24.2 – 29.2	12.5 – 16.4	16.5 – 28.0
Metacarpus	122.0	19.0 – 23.0	10.5 – 13.4	22.0
1st phalanx	32.4 – 33.5	13.1	8.0 – 9.4	9.8
Femur			10.0 – 17.5	36.0
Tibia	147.3	27.5 – 35.0	10.1 – 13.8	17.7 – 24.9
Calcaneus	56.8			
Metatarsus	111.8	16.6 – 17.1	9.5 – 11.6	19.5 – 20.5
Pig				
Humerus			13.9 – 14.7	33.2 – 35.5
Radius	102.0	25.8 – 26.3	14.8 – 20.2	28.8 – 30.0
Femur			12.6 – 19.5	
Tibia		34.1	14.8 – 19.2	25.7
Calcaneus	76.0			
Astragalus	36.5 – 40.0		16.0 – 16.5	
Metatarsus II			17.5	
Metatarsus III			11.0	
Metatarsus IV			10.0	
Roe deer				
Metatarsus	188.9	19.0	12.0	21.4
Dog				
Tibia			8.9	15.8
Horse				
Radius		77.3		
Chicken				
Femur	70.0		5.3	
Tibia				20.1

Scapula	Shaft LDW (AP)		Proximal end (maximum) AP	
Ox	43.0 – 50.0		47.0 – 51.6	
Sheep	11.9 – 18.4		18.6 – 28.4	
Pig	21.5 – 25.8		33.0 – 41.0	

| Pelvis | Acetabulum (internal face) | | Shafts DV minimum | | Pubis shaft minimum |
	ML	AP	Ilium	Ischium	AP
Pig	27.5 – 30.8	28.0 – 31.0	20.0 – 24.0		9.2
Sheep	20.0 – 24.8	20.0 – 29.0	12.4 – 13.9	12.8 – 14.6	
Ox	51.0	58.0	37.0		17.0 – 19.5
Horse	61.4	64.0	39.0	25.5	25.7

REPORT ON THE PLANT MACROREMAINS FROM CIRENCESTER
by
Ann Connolly

The three samples from Cirencester: SS 10 (AX II 58); SS 11 (AY I 26); and SS 16 (BC I 47) were softened in water, sieved and sorted using a stereo microscope. All three samples contained very small (less than 5 mm. diameter) fragments of carbonized wood, some tissue debris, a few moss leaves as well as seeds and fruits. Over 30 species have been identified and these are tabulated in Table 11 indicating their frequency and the nature of the part determined.

TABLE 11: PLANT MACROREMAINS FROM CIRENCESTER

1. Flowering plants (Angiospermae)		SS 10	SS 11	SS 16
Aphanes arvensis L. (Parsley Piert)		—	—	14
Arenaria serpyllifolia L. (Thyme-leaved Sandwort)		—	—	7
Avena sp. (a wild Oat)	Awn	—	—	1 frag
Cares sp. (or Scirpus)		—	—	1
Caryophyllaceae (undet.)				c. 5
Chenopodium album L. (Fat Hen)		—	—	2
Cirsium cf arvense (L.)Scop. (Creeping Thistle)		—	—	3+
C. cf palustre (L.)Scop. (Marsh Thistle)		—	—	1+
Corylus avellana L. (Hazel)	Nut	—	—	frag
Eleocharis palustris (L.) Roem. & Schult subsp. palustris (Common Spike-rush)		—	—	1
Hypericum maculatum Crantz (Imperforate St. John's Wort)		—	—	3 + frag
Hypochaeris radicata L. (Cat's Ear)		—	—	2
Isolepis (Scirpus) setacea (L.)R.Br. (Bristle Scirpus)		—	—	2
Juncus cf acutiformis Ehrh.ex Hoffm. (Sharp-flowered Rush)		—	—	1
J. cf bufonis L. (Toad Rush)		—	—	2
J. effusus-type (a Rush)		—	)cf	c. 4
Juncus spp.		4	)7	
			total	c. 4
Leontodon autumnalis L. (Autumnal Hawkbit)		—	—	1
Linum catharticum L. (Purging Flax)		—	—	1
Linum cf usitatissimum L. (Cultivated Flax)	Seed	—	—	1 +
Linum cf usitatissimum L. (Cultivated Flax)	Capsule	—	—	1
Mentha aquatica/arvensis L. (a mint)		—	—	1
Montia fontana subsp. chondrosperma (Fenzl)Walters (Blinks)		—	—	6+44 frag
Polygonum aviculare agg. (Knotgrass)		—	—	2 frags +
Polygonum convolvulus L. (Black Bindweed)		—	—	3 frags
Potentilla cf reptans L. (Creeping cinquefoil)		—	—	4+3 frags
Prunella vulgaris L. (Self-heal)		—	—	2
Ranunculus repens/acris L. (Buttercup).		—	—	3+ frags
Rumex acetosa L. (Sorrel)		—	—	1
Sagina spp. (Pearlwort)		—	—	47
Sheradia arvensis L. (Field Madder)	Mericarp	—	2★	—
Sonchus asper (L.) Hill (Spiny Sow-thistle)		—	—	3
Stellaria media (L.)Vill. (Chickweed)		—	—	c. 4+
Torilis nodosa (L.)Gaertn. (Knotted Hedge-parsley)		—	—	1
Urtica dioica L. (Stinging Nettle)		—	—	1
Valerianella dentata (L.)Poll. (a Cornsalad)		—	—	1
Graminae-non Cereal (Grasses)	Leaf	Lfrag†	—	—
Graminae-non Cereal (Grasses)		—	1★+2	—
Graminae – Cereal		—	—	1★
2. Mosses, Ferns or other non-seed plants				
Sphagnum	L	2	—	—
Pteridium aquilinum L. (Bracken)	F	—	—	4 frag
Dryopteris-type	Spm	1	—	—
Endogonaceae (a fungus)†		+	—	+

3. *Wood**
? *Salix* (Willow)   −   +   −
undetermined fragments   +   +   +

Abbreviations: * = carbonized
              † = possible modern contaminant
              S = Seed
              F = frond/pinnule
              Spm = Sporangium
              L = Leaf
              unmarked entries refer to seed, fruit or fruitstone

AX II 58 (SS 10)   *From a pit outside the fort*

This sample was very poor in identifiable plant remains. It contained some minute pieces of carbonized wood, a variety of plant tissue debris, many rootlets (probably modern penetration). A dehisced fern sporangium was not identifiable but belongs to one of the orders to which most of the common British species belong. The *Juncus* seeds had lost their diagonistically important outer layer. The leaf of a *Sphagnum* moss could well have blown in and not grown on site.

AY I 26 (SS 11)   *From beneath a street in the vicus*

This sample was also very poor in seeds and plant remains. Amongst tissue debris were a carbonized grain of a wild grass and the remains of two smaller uncarbonized ones, some tiny bits of bark, and some carbonized wood fragments too small to determine accurately, but some at least were diffuse-porous and possibly willow *(Salix)*. They were not Oak. Of the seven seeds of *Juncus* some suggest *J.effusus*-type, i.e. Rushes of damp pasture and meadows. The two separate mericarps of a carbonized fruit of *Sheradia arvensis* fitted together. The size, the oval not circular shape in outline, and the oval shape and incurved rim of the ventral hollow as well as the dorsal rugosity forming longitudinal furrows all agree well with this species rather than any *Galium* of appropriate size; a determination supported by the less regular cell pattern. This species is typical of dry banks and well-drained arable fields. It has been used as a source of dye, (Godwin, 1976).

BC I 47 (SS 16)   *From the old ground surface outside the fort in Chester Street*

This comparatively rich sample contained, besides insects, mite and other animal remains, a few mosses and seeds and fruits of about 30 species of flowering plants. There were a number of plant tissue fragments, including part of a dicotyledonous leaf, three or so fragments of a fern frond-pinnule, a broken piece of Hazel nut, a single distorted carbonized cereal grain, a short length of a spirally twisted grass awn (wild Oat *Avena* sp.) and the remains of one – perhaps two – seeds of Flax, which closely resemble the cultivated Flax *Linum usitatissimum*. There was also a broken piece of what is most likely to be a capsule segment from the same species.

COMMENTS ON THE SPECIES IN SAMPLE SS 16

Aphanes arvensis   14 seeds, though a little small for this species were too big for *A. microcarpa*. Frequent as an arable weed, this species also favours dry banks and well-drained open soils.

Hypericum maculatum   3 seeds conform in dimensions with this species (1.0 mm. x 0.375 mm.) giving a length-breadth ratio of over 2.5 whereas in the somewhat broader *H. perforatum* (1.0 x 0.45 to 0.5 mm.) the ratio is nearer 2.0 and not over 2.2. It is not possible to say to which sub-species they belong, but sub-species *obtusiusculum* is the most likely.

Juncus   Using Körber-Grohne (1964), one seed must belong to the *J.acutiformis* group because of the spiculate projections; despite the difficulty of distinguishing their forking, the large size of the seed indicates *J.acutiformis*.

Mentha aquatica or *arvensis*   A single nutlet agrees in size with both these species which are not easily distinguished.

Montia fontana subspecies chondrosperma   A number of seeds and numerous fragments agree with this subspecies. Scanning electron micrographs show the typical papillae around the base of the major raised areas.

Pteridium aquilinum   3 or 4 minute pieces of pinnule with inrolled margins showed venation typical of Bracken and the hairs on the lower surface characteristic of this species.

DISCUSSION AND ASSIGNMENT OF SPECIES TO PLANT COMMUNITIES

All the species from samples SS 10 and SS 11, with the exception of *Sheradia arvensis* and perhaps the grass 'seeds', were also found in sample SS 16. Hence discussion of these three samples can be considered jointly.

The general impression inferred from the plant species identified is of rather mundane community of common plants several of which have wide tolerances and could have grown in any of a number of communities; there are few species of narrowly defined, precise habitats. Moreover, there are very few species represented by more than a single or couple of specimens so that chance incorporation from elsewhere rather than autochthonous *(in situ)* growth cannot be precluded.

Despite the paucity of species determined the majority is consistent with lowland grassland communities and waste places with disturbed ground. There is little or no direct evidence of woodland in the immediate vicinity: the wood and bark specimens of trees or bushes and the broken hazel nut could well have been brought in, and do not imply local (on site) growth. The bracken fragments, perhaps used for litter, could equally well have blown in. Many species listed require open, unshaded (i.e. no tree-cover) conditions; *Hypericum maculatum* and *Anthriscus caucalis* are commonly hedgebank denizens, but not obligatory so.

1. **Grassland communities**

Pasture and/or meadowland are indicated by many of the species: e.g. *Prunella vulgaris, Rumex acetosa*, the buttercups, thistles, and the composites *Leontodon autumnalis* and *Hypochaeris radicata*.

Damp, ill-drained pasture is indicated by the *Juncus* species, especially *J.acutiformis* and *J.bufonius; Isolepis setacea* and *Eleocharis palustris* demand even greater wetness. *Isolepis* could grow in trampled muddy patches with at least periodically filled hollows such as ruts or hoof-prints, but *Eleocharis palustris* suggests the presence of a wet ditch if not a streamside. *Prunella vulgaris, Linum catharticum* and certain species of *Sagina* (cf. *S.procumbens*) and even *Cerastium* (cf. *holosteoides*) could well grow in such a damp pasture, though they could equally occur in dry grassland. *Montia fontana* normally characteristic of springs and wet pool margins can also be found on hummocks of drier soil, especially the subspecies *chondrosperma* represented here. *Mentha aquatica* suggests a wet ditch or stream, the alternative *M.arvensis,* would imply somewhat drier conditions.

Other species, in contrast, such as *Torilis nodosa, Sherardia arvensis* and *Arenaria serpyllifolia* point to a well-drained slope or bank, or even on a wall, while the last two can grow on isolated hummocks such as ant-hills. *Aphanes arvensis* and *Linum catharticum* too are typical of these habitats though occurring in others.

2. **Weedy species of wasteground, wayside and disturbed ground; and places associated with human habitation; arable fields.**

Trampling by large (grazing) animals is suggested by *Polygonum aviculare, Potentilla reptans* and *Sagina* (if *procumbens*) and might besides provide the disturbed ground required by many of the weedy species. Several of these – *Chenopodium album, Stellaria media, Sonchus asper, Urtica dioica* – are plants of well-manured and fertile soil rich in nitrate and phosphate; the margin of an old dung-heap or midden would be a likely place. A number of these weedy species are, in addition, commonly found as arable crop-plant weeds: *Chenopodium album, Stellaria media, Polygonum aviculare, Sonchus asper.*

Polygonum convolvulus occurs most frequently as an arable weed, *Aphanes arvensis* and *Arenaria serpyllifolia* commonly so, and *Torilis nodosa* occasionally. *Sherardia arvensis* is a typical cornfield species, but of all the weed species listed, *Valerianella dentata* is the most closely tied to a cornfield habitat. Perhaps it is significant that *Aphanes arvensis, Montia fontana* ssp *chondrosperma* and *Sagina* sp alone occur in numbers that can be taken as relatively high.

3. Cultivated and man-collected species

Remains of cultivated species or of those collected and utilized by man are sparse, and could have been accidentally dropped on the site. A single carbonized cereal grain, a seed or perhaps two and part of a capsule segment of the Flax cf *Linum usitatissimum* and a broken bit of Hazel nut is all there is. There are no representatives of those species with medicinal properties and of culinary and herbal usage so often found associated with human habitation sites – for example in Roman wells – there are no seeds of Poppies (*Papaver* spp.) nor of Hemlock *(Conium maculatum)*, Henbane *(Hyoscyamus)*, Mallow *(Malva sylvestris)* or of *Coronopus squamatus* (Swine's cress). Nor, more surprisingly, are there any stones of Elder *(Sambucus nigra)*.

In summary, the species listed suggest a lowland, probably grazed, pasture or meadow, on neutral to weakly alkaline soil with both ill-drained and water-logged areas or a wet ditch as well as well-drained dry places. In addition some waste ground, probably well-manured, on which the weeds could have grown. Cultivation of crop plants is hinted at, though not necessarily in the immediate vicinity. There are no indications of very acid conditions, no heath nor mire species. Tree-shade was probably lacking. All the species identified have previously been recorded from archaeological or quaternary sites (Godwin, 1976). All occur today in the Cirencester area.

I am indebted to Mrs Gay Wilson and to Dr. Frances Davies for help with critical identifications.

REPORT ON THE INSECT REMAINS FROM CIRENCESTER
by
P.J. Osborne

The sample examined was very small and many of the insects of which it was composed were so fragmentary as to be unidentifiable. Thus the following notes on the ecology of the site are based on only thirteen taxa which is not a large enough number to enable anything but a tentative picture to be drawn.

Insects recognised

DERMAPTERA
Forficula ?auricularia L.
COLEOPTERA
Calathus fuscipes (Goeze)
Calathus melanocephalus (L.)
Cercyon sp.
Hister sp.
Aphodius sp.
Onthophagus ovatus (L.)
Byrrhus sp.
Adalia bipunctata (L.)
Apion sp.
Barynotus sp.
Mecinus pyraster (Hbst.)
HYMENOPTERA
Formicidae, probably *Lasius flavus* (F.)

Implications of the fauna

Calathus fuscipes and *C. melanocephalus* are predators which are both found in moderately dry grassland and *Aphodius* and *Onthophagus ovatus* are dung beetles which live in the droppings of grazing animals such as cattle, horses and sheep. *Cercyon* and *Hister* are found in decaying vegetable refuse of various kinds although again dung is probably their most frequent habitat. The weevil *Mecinus pyraster* is also found in meadowland where its larvae live at the roots of *Plantago lanceolata*. Ants were only represented by two heads devoid of any appendages whatever so that their identification is no more than tentative. If, however, they are *Lasius flavus* this species, too, is found on dry, open grassy ground.

There is, therefore, a strong suggestion that the local environment consisted of grassland on which large herbivorous mammals were grazing. The common earwig, *Forficula auricularia* and the two spotted ladybird *Adalia bipunctata* are both so common and widespread as to have little significance at all. Members of the genus *Byrrhus* are usually associated with moss but are widely distributed today, while *Apion* and *Barynotus*, though both plant feeders, cannot supply any further ecological information as neither was specifically identified.

On the negative side it is noteworthy that no insects suggesting the presence of trees were found, nor any aquatic species.

All the insects identified could be caught in the neighbourhood of Cirencester today and there is no reason to suppose that the climate of the area was different from that of the present day.

ABBREVIATIONS

Antiq. J.	Antiquaries' Journal
Archaeol. Aeliana	Archaeologia Aeliana
Archaeol. Cambrensis	Archaeologia Cambrensis
Archaeol. J.	Archaeological Journal
Brit. Archaeol. Rep.	British Archaeological Reports
Brit. Numis. J.	British Numismatic Journal
Bull. Geol. Surv. of Gt. Br.	Bulletin of the Geological Survey of Great Britain
Geol. Mag.	Geological Magazine
J. Archaeol. Sci.	Journal of Archaeological Science
J. Roman Stud.	Journal of Roman Studies
Medieval Archaeol.	Medieval Archaeology
Mem. Geol. Surv. England and Wales	Memoirs of the Geological Survey England and Wales
Monmouthshire Antiq.	Monmouthshire Antiquary
O.R.L.	Der Obergemanisch – Raetische Limes des Römerreichs
Primer Congreso Geol.Chileno	Primer Congreso Geologia Chileno
Proc. Cambridge Antiq. Soc.	Proceedings of the Cambridge Antiquarian Society
Proc. Chelt. Natur. Sci. Soc. N.S.	Proceedings of the Cheltenham Natural Science Society (New Series)
Proc. Cotteswold Natur. Fld. Club	Proceedings of the Cotteswold Naturalists' Field Club
Proc. Devon Archaeol.	Proceedings of the Devon Archaeological Society
Proc. Geol. Assoc.	Proceedings of the Geological Association
Proc. Prehist. Soc.	Proceedings of the Prehistoric Society
Proc. Soc. Antiq.	Proceedings of the Society of Antiquaries
Proc. Soc. Antiq. Scot.	Proceedings of the Society of Antiquaries of Scotland
Proc. Somerset Archaeol. Soc.	Proceedings of the Somerset Archaeological Society
Quart. Journ. Geol. Soc.	Quarterly Journal of the Geological Society
Rept. Brit. Assoc. Adv. Sci.	Report of the British Association for the Advancement of Science
Soc. Bibliography Nat. Hist. London	Society for the Bibliography of Natural History, London
Trans. Birmingham Archaeol. Soc.	Transactions of the Birmingham Archaeological Society
Trans. Birmingham Warwickshire Archaeol. Soc.	Transactions of the Birmingham and Warwickshire Archaeological Society
Trans. Bristol Gloucestershire Archaeol. Soc.	Transactions of the Bristol and Gloucestershire Archaeological Society
Trans. Essex Archaeol. Soc.	Transactions of the Essex Archaeological Society
Trans. Leicester Lit. Phil. Soc.	Transactions of the Leicester Literary and Philosophical Society
Trans. London Middlesex Archaeol. Soc.	Transactions of the London and Middlesex Archaeological Society
Trans. Norfolk Norwich Nat. Society	Transactions of the Norfolk and Norwich Naturalists' Society
Wiltshire Archaeol. Natur. Hist. Mag.	Wiltshire Archaeological and Natural History Magazine
Yorkshire Archaeol. J.	Yorkshire Archaeological Journal

BIBLIOGRAPHY

Alföldy, G., 1968
Die Hilfstuppen der romischen Provinz Germania Inferior, *Epigraphische Studien*, 6, 19-21

Allen, D. F., 1961
A Study of the Dobunnic Coinage, in *Bagendon : A Belgic Oppidum*, (ed. E. M. Clifford), 75-149

Allen, D. F., 1967
Celtic Coins from the Romano-British Temple at Harlow, *Brit. Numis. J.*, xxxvi, 1-7

Allen, J. R., 1896
Notes on "Late-Celtic" Art, *Archaeol. Cambrensis*[5], XIII, 321-36

Anderson, A. S., 1977
The Roman Pottery Industry of North Wiltshire, unpublished M.A. thesis, Univ. of Leicester

Andrews, A. H., and Noddle, B. A., 1975
Absence of premolar teeth from ruminant mandibles found at archaeological sites, *J. Archaeol. Sci.*, 2, 137-144

Annable, F. K., 1961
A Romano-British Pottery in Savernake Forest, Kilns 1-2, *Wiltshire Archaeol. Natur. Hist. Mag.*, 58, 1961 (1963), 142-155

Annable, F. K., 1966
A late first-century well at *Cunetio*, *Wiltshire Archaeol. Natur. Hist. Mag.*, 61, 9-24

Arkell, W. J., 1933
On a boring into the Great Oolite at Latton near Cricklade, Wilts, *Proc. Cotteswold Natur. Fld. Club.*, 24, 181-183

Arkell, W. J., 1941
The Upper Oxford Clay at Purton, Wilts., and the zones of the Lower Oxfordian, *Geol. Mag.*, 78, 161-172, 316

Arkell, W. J., and Donovan, D. T., 1952
The Fullers Earth of the Cotswold and its relation to the Great Oolite, *Quart. Journ. Geol. Soc.*, 107, 227-253

Arkell, W. J., and Tomkereff, S. I., 1953
English Rock Terms chiefly as used by Miners and Quarry men, Oxford University Press

Armitage, P. L., 1975
The extraction and identification of opal phytoliths from the teeth of ungulates, *J. Archaeol. Sci.*, 2, 187-198

Atkinson, D., 1914
A hoard of samian ware from Pompeii, *J. Roman Stud.*, iv, 26-64.

Atkinson, D., 1957
A fragment of a diploma from Cirencester, *J. Roman Stud.*, 47, 196-7

Barker, M., 1976
A stratigraphical, palaeoecological and biometrical study of some English Bathonian Gastropoda (especially Nerineacea), Ph.D. Thesis, Univ. of Keele

Baring-Gould, S., and Burnard, R., 1904
An exploration of some of the Cytiau in Tre'r Ceiri, *Archaeol. Cambrensis*[6], IV, 1-16

Behre, K. E., 1977
Acker, Grünland und natürliche Vegetation während der römischen Kaiserzeit im Gebiet der Marshensiedlung Bentumersiel/Unterems, in *Probleme der Kustenforshung im südlichen Nordseegebeite*. Bd. 12

Boesterd, M. H. P. den, 1956
Description of the Collections in the Rijksmuseum G. M. Kam at Nijmegen V : The Bronze Vessels, Nijmegen

Bogaers, J. E., 1974
Troupes Auxiliaires Thraces dans la partie Néerlandaise de la Germania Inferior, in *Actes du Ixe Congrés International d'Etudes dur les frontieres Romaines*, Bucharest, 1974 = *idem* Thracische Hulptroepen in Germania Inferior, *Oudheidkundige Medeelingen*, 55, 198-220, with English summary 217-219

Boon, G. C., 1962
Remarks on Roman Usk, *Monmouthshire Antiq.*, I, 28-33

Boon, G. C., 1967
Micaceous sigillata from Lezoux at Silchester, Caerleon,

and other sites, *Antiq. J.*, 47, 27–42

Brailsford, J. W., 1962 — *Antiquities from Hod Hill in the Durden Collection*, Vol. I, London

British Museum, 1951 — *The British Museum Guide to the Antiquities of Roman Britain*

Brown, A., 1894 — On the structure and affinities of the genus *Solenopera* together with descriptions of new species, *Geol. Mag.*, (4), 1, 145–151

Buchem, H. J. J. van, 1941 — *De Fibulae van Nijmegen*, Acad. Proefschrift, Univ. te Nijmegen

Buckman, J., 1850 — Substances employed in forming the tessellae of the Cirencester Pavement and on their chrometic arrangement, *Archaeol. J.*, 7, 347–354

Buckman, J., 1853 — On the structure and arrangement of the Tesserae in a Roman Pavement discovered at Cirencester in August 1849, *Proc. Cotteswold Natur. Fld. Club*, 1, 47–51

Buckman, J., 1858 — On the Oolite Rocks of Gloucestershire and North Wilts., *Quart. Journ. Geol. Soc.*, 14, 98–130

Buckman, J., 1860 — On some fossil reptilian eggs from the Great Oolite of Cirencester, *Quart. Journ. Geol. Soc.*, 16, 107–110

Buckman, J., and Newmarch, C. H., 1850 — *Illustrations of the Remains of Roman Art in Cirencester*, G. Bell, London.

Buckman, S. S., 1895 — The Bajocian of the mid-Cotteswolds, *Quart. Journ. Geol. Soc.*, 51, 388–462

Buckman, S. S., 1897 — Deposits of the Bajocian Age in the Northern Cotteswolds: the Cleeve Hill Plateau, *Quart. Journ. Geol. Soc.*, 53, 607–629

Buckman, S. S., 1901 — Bajocian and contiguous deposits in the North Cotteswolds: the main Hill Mass, *Quart. Journ. Geol. Soc.*, 57, 126–155

Buckman, S. S., 1903 — The Cotteswold Hills: a Geographical Enquiry, *Proc. Cotteswold Natur. Fld. Club*, 14, 205–250

Bushe-Fox, J. P., 1913 and 1914 — *First and Second Reports on the Excavations on the site of the Roman Town at Wroxeter, Shropshire, 1913 and 1914*, Soc. Antiquaries of London, I and II

Bushe-Fox, J. P., 1925 — *Excavation of the Late Celtic Urn-Field at Swarling, Kent*, Soc. Antiquaries of London, 5

Bushe-Fox, J. P., 1926 — *First Report on the Excavatons of the Roman Fort at Richborough, Kent*, Soc. of Antiquaries of London, 6

Bushe-Fox, J. P., 1928 — *Second Report on the Excavations of the Roman Fort at Richborough, Kent*, Soc. of Antiquaries of London, 7

Bushe-Fox, J. P., 1932 — *Third Report on the Excavations of the Roman Fort at Richborough, Kent*, Soc. of Antiquaries of London, 10

Bushe-Fox, J. P., 1949 — *Fourth Report on the Excavations of the Roman Fort at Richborough, Kent*, Soc. of Antiquaries of London, 16

Callender, M. H., 1965 — *Roman Amphorae*, London

Cave, R., and Cox., B. M., 1975 — The Kellaways Beds of the area between Chippenham and Malmesbury, Wilts., *Bull. Geol. Surv. of Great Britain*, 54, 41–66

Channon, P. J., 1951 — A new section at Cowcombe Hill, near Chalford Station, Glos., *Proc. Geol. Assoc.*, 62, 174–176

Chaplin, R. E., 1971 — *The Study of Animal Bones from Archaeological Sites*, London, (Seminar Press)

Clifford, E., 1961 — *Bagendon : A Belgic Oppidum*, Cambridge

Collingwood, R. G., 1923 — *The Archaeology of Roman Britain*, London

Cotton, M. A., 1947 — Excavations at Silchester, *Archaeologia*, 92, 121-167

Cunliffe, B. W., 1964 — *Winchester Excavations 1949-1960*, Vol. I

Cunliffe, B. W., 1968 (ed.) — *Fifth Report on the Excavations of the Roman Fort at Richborough Kent*, Soc. of Antiquaries of London, 23

Cunliffe, B. W., 1971 — *Excavations at Fishbourne, 1961-69*, Soc. of Antiquaries of London, 26, 27

Curle, J., 1911 — *A Roman Frontier Post and its People : The Fort of Newstead in the Parish of Melrose*, Glasgow

Cripps, W. J., 1898 — Notes on the Roman Basilica at Cirencester, lately discovered by Wilfred J. Cripps, *Trans. Bristol Gloucestershire Archaeol. Soc.*, XXI, 70-8

Cripps, W. J., 1897-99 — Roman Basilica of *Corinium*, at Cirencester, *Proc. Soc. Antiq.*, 2nd series, xvii, (1897-1899), 201-208

Dannell, G. B., 1964 — The Potter *Petrecus* and his connections, *Antiq. J.*, XLIV, 147-52

Dannell, G. B., 1971 — The Samian Pottery, in *Excavations at Fishbourne, 1961-69*, (ed. B. W. Cunliffe), 260-316

Darling, M. J., 1977 — Pottery from Early Military Sites in Western Britain, in *Roman Pottery Studies from Britain and Beyond* (ed. J. Dore and K. Greene),

Davies, R. W., 1971 — The Roman Military Diet, *Britannia*, II, 122-142

Déchelette, J., 1904 — *Les Vases céramiques ornés de la Gaule romaine*, tome II, Paris

Douglas, J., 1793 — *Nenia Britannica : or A sepulchral history of Great Britain, from the earliest period to its general conversion to Christianity*, London

Douglas, J. A., and Arkell, W. J., 1928 — The Stratigraphical Distribution of the Cornbrash – the South-Western area, *Quart. Journ. Geol. Soc.*, 84, 117-178

Down, A., 1978 — *Chichester Excavations*, Vol. III, Chichester

Down, A, and Rule, M., 1971 — *Chichester Excavations Vol. I*, Chichester Civic Society Excavation Committee, Oxford

Dunnett, B. R. K., 1971 — Excavations in Colchester, 1964-8. The Telephone Exchange Site, *Trans. Essex Archaeol. Soc.*, 3, 15-38

Elliott, G. F., 1973 — A Palaeoecological Study of a Cotswold Great Oolite fossil-bed (English Jurassic), *Proc. Geol. Assoc.*, 84, 43-51

Elliott, G. F., 1975 — Transported Algae as indicators of different marine habitats in the English Middle Jurassic, *Palaeontology*, 18, 351-366

Ettlinger, E., and Simonett, C., 1952 — Romische Veramik aus dem Schuttligel von Vindonissa, *Verottent lichungen der Gesellshcaft pro Vindonissa*, Band 3

Eyles, V. A., 1973 — John Woodward's Brief Instructions in all Parts of the World, 1696, *Soc. Bibliography Nat. Hist. London*

Farrar, R. A. H., 1973 — The Techniques and sources of Romano-British Black Burnished-Ware, in *Current Research in Romano-British Coarse Pottery*, (ed. A. Detsicas), Counc. Brit. Archaeol. Res. Rep. 10, 67-103

Farrar, R. A. H., 1977 — A Romano-British black-burnished ware industry at Ower in the Isle of Purbeck, Dorset, in *Roman Pottery Studies in Britain and Beyond* (ed. J. Dore & K. Greene) BAR 30, 199-227

Fell, C., 1936 — The Hunsbury Hill-Fort, Northants. : a new survey of the material, *Archaeol. J.*, XCIII, 57-100

Fell, C., 1951 — An openwork bronze disc from Haslingfield, *Proc. Cambridge Antiq. Soc.*, XLV, 1951 (1952), 65-6

Forster, R. H., and Knowles, — *Corstopitum* : Report on the excavations in 1910, *Archaeol.*

W. H., 1910

Aeliana³, vii, 143-268

Fowler, E., 1960

The origins and development of the pennanular brooch in Europe, *Proc. Prehist. Soc.,* xxvi, 149-77

Fox, A., 1940

The Legionary Fortress at Caerleon, Mons., Excavations in Myrtle Cottage Orchard, 1939, *Archaeol. Cambrensis,* 95, 101-153

Fox, A., 1951

Roman Discoveries in Exeter in 1951-2, *Proc. Devon Archaeol.,* IV, 106-113

Frere, S. S., 1967

Britannia : A History of Roman Britain

Frere, S. S., 1972

Verulamium Excavations, Vol. I, Soc. of Antiquaries of London, XXVIII

Frere, S. S., and St. Joseph, J. K, 1974

The Roman Fortress at Longthorpe, *Britannia,* v, 1-129

Fursich, F. T., and Palmer, T. J., 1975

Open crustacean burrows associated with hardgrounds in the Jurassic of the Cotswolds, England, *Proc. Geol. Assoc.,* 86, 171-181

Garrod, P., 1975

in H. Hurst, Excavations at Gloucester : Third Interim Report : Kingsholm, 1966-1975, *Antiq. J.* lv, 267-294

Gerster, E. W., 1938

Mittelrheinische Bildhauerwerkstatten im I Jahrhundert n. Chr., Bonn

Gillam, J. P., 1957

Types of North British Coarse Ware, *Archaeol. Aeliana⁴,* 35, 180-251

Gillam, J. P., 1960

The Coarse Pottery, in Excavations at Mumrills Roman Fort 1958-60, (ed. K. A. Steer), *Proc. Soc. Antiq. Soc.,* 94 (1960-1), 86-132

Gillam, J. P., 1968

Types of Roman Coarse Pottery Vessels in Northern Britain, 2nd ser.

Gillam, J. P., and Mann, J. C., 1970

The northern British Frontier from Antoninus Pius to Caracalla, *Archaeol. Aeliana⁴,* 48, 1-44

Glasbergen, W., 1944

Versierde Claudisch-Neronische Terra Sigillata van Valkenburg ZH, *Jaarverslay van de vereeniging voor Terpenendock,* 1944 (1940-44), 206-236

Glasbergen, W., and Groenman-van-Waateringe, W., 1974

The Pre-Flavian Garrisons of Valkenburg ZH, *Cingula,* II

Godwin, H., 1976

History of the British Flora, Cambridge, 2nd edition

Grant, A., 1975

The Animal Bones, in *Excavations at Portchester Castle, Vol. I, Roman,* (ed. B. W. Cunliffe), 378-408

Gray, H. St. G., 1924

Excavations at Ham Hill, South Somerset (Part I), *Proc. Somerset Archaeol. Soc.,* lxx, 104-116

Green, G. W., and Donovan, D. T., 1969

The Great Oolite of the Bath area, *Bull. Geol. Surv. of Great Britain,* 30, 1-63

Green, G. W. and Melville, R. V., 1956

The Stratigraphy of the Stowell Park Borehole, 1949-1951 *Bull. Geol. Surv. of Great Britain,* 11, 1-33

Greene, K. T., 1972

Guide to Pre-Flavian Fine Wares, c. AD 40-70, Cardiff

Greene, K. T., 1973

The Pottery from Usk, in *Current Research in Romano-British Coarse Pottery,* (ed. A. Detsicas), Counc. Brit. Archaeol. Res. Rep. 10, 25-37

Greene, K. T., 1974

A Group of Roman Pottery from Wanborough, Wilts., *Wiltshire Archaeol. Natur. Hist. Mag.,* 69, 51-66

Griffiths, N. A., 1978

A fragment of a Roman cavalry tombstone from Cirencester, *Britannia,* IX, 396-7, fig. 5.

Grigson, C., 1976

The craniology and relationships of four species of Bos. 3. Basic Craniology : *Bos taurus L.* Sagittal profiles and other non-measurable characters *J. Archaeol. Sci,* 3,

115-136

Groot, J. de, 1960 — *Masculus* von La Graufesenque, *Germania*, 38, 55-65

Haevernick, T. E., 1967 — Die Verbreitung der "Zarten Rippenschalen", *Jahrbruch des Romisch-Germanischen Zentralmuseums Mainz*, 14, 153-166

Hanson, W. S., 1978 — The Organisation of Roman Military Timber-Supply *Britannia*, IX, 293-305

Harker, A., 1886 — On a remarkable exposure of the Kellaways Beds in a recent cutting near Cirencester, *Proc. Cotteswold Natur. Fld. Club*, 8, 175-187

Harker, A., 1891 — On the Geology of Cirencester Town and a recent discovery of the Oxford (Kellaways) Clay in a deep well boring, *Proc. Cotteswold Natur. Fld. Club*, 18, 178-191

Harland, T., and Torrens, H. S., in press — A redescription of the Red Alga *Solenopora jurassica* Brown from Chedworth, Gloucestershire, with remarks on its preservation, *Paleontology* (in press)

Hartley, B. R., 1972 — The Samian Ware, in *Verulamium Excavations, Vol. I*, (ed. S. S. Frere), Soc. of Antiquaries of London, 28

Hartley, K. F., 1973 — The Marketing and Distribution of Mortaria, in *Current Research in Romano-British Coarse Pottery*, (ed. A. Detsicas), Counc. Brit. Archaeol. Res. Rep. 10, 38-51

Hartley, K. F., 1977 — Two major potteries producing mortaria in the first century A.D., in *Roman Pottery Studies in Britain and Beyond*, (ed. J. Dore and L. Greene), 5-17

Harvey, R. A., 1971 — *The Life of Henry Cavendish, 1731-1810*, Ph.D. Thesis, Univ. of Sheffield

Hassall, M. W. C., and Rhodes, J., 1974 — Excavations at the New Market Hall, Gloucester, 1966-7, *Trans. Bristol Gloucestershire Archaeol. Soc.*, XCIII, 1974 (1975), 15-100

Hassall, M. W. C., and Tomlin, R. S. D., 1977 — Roman Britain in 1976 : II Inscriptions, *Britannia*, VIII, 440

Hatt, J-J., 1953 — Les Fouilles de la Ruelle Saint-Médard à Strasbourg *Gallia*, XI, 225-248

Hawkes, C. F. C., 1961 — The Western Third C Culture and the Belgic Dobunni, in *Bagendon : A Belgic Oppidum*, (ed. E. M. Clifford), 43-67

Hawkes, C. F. C., and Dunning, G. C., 1930 — The Belgae of Gaul and Britain, *Archaeol J.*, 88, 1930 (1931), 150-335

Hawkes, C. F. C., and Hull, M. R., 1947 — *First Report on the Excavations at Colchester, 1930-39*, Soc. of Antiquaries of London, 14

Hawkes, S. C., and Dunning, C. C., 1961 — Soldiers and Settlers in Britain, fourth to fifth century, *Medieval Archaeol.*, 5, 1-70

Hénault, 1934-6 — *Pro Nervia*, VI

Hermet, F., 1934 — *La Graufesenque (Condatomago)*, Paris

Hildyard, E. J. W., 1955 — Roman Fibulae from Chichester, Sussex, *Sussex Notes and Queries*, XIV (1955) 109-122

Hobley, B., 1971 — Excavations at 'The Lunt' Roman Military Site, Baginton, Warwicks.,1968-71. Second Interim Report. *Trans. Birmingham Warwickshire Archaeol. Soc.*, 85, 1971-3 (1973), 7-92

Hodder, I., 1974 — The Distribution of Savernake Ware, *Wiltshire Archaeol. Natur. Hist. Mag.*, 69, 67-84

Holder, A., 1896-1907 — *AltCeltischer sprachschatz*, 3 vols, Leipzig

Holwerda, J. H., 1913 — Een Vondst uit den Rijn Bij Doorwerth, *Oudheidkundige Mededeelingen, Leiden*, Supplement XII, 1-26

Holwerda, J. H., 1941 — *De Belgischer Waar in Nijmegen*, Nijmegen

Household, H., 1969 — *The Thames and Severn Canal*, David & Charles

Hull, M. R., 1958 — *Roman Colchester*, Soc. of Antiquaries of London, 20

Ibbetson, L. L. B., 1847 — On three sections of the Oolitic Formations on the Great Western Railway at the west end of Sapperton Tunnel, *Rept. Brit. Assoc. Adv. Sci. Transactions of Sections*, 61

Jacobs, J., 1913 — Sigillatafunde aus einem romischen Keller zu Bregenz *Jahrbruch fur Altertumskunde*, 6td Band 1912, Wien 1913

Jarrett, M. G., 1969 — Thracian Units in the Roman Army, *Israel Exploration Journal*, 19, no. 4, 215-224

Jewell, P. A., 1963 — Cattle from British Archaeological Sites, in *Man and Cattle*, (eds. A. E. Mourant, and F. E. Zeuner), Royal Anthrop. Inst. Occasional Papers, no. 18, London

Jones, M. J., 1975 — Roman Fort Defences to AD 117, *Brit. Archaeol. Rep.*, 21

Kenyon, K. M., 1948 — *Excavations at the Jewry Wall Site, Leicester*, Soc. of Antiquaries of London, 15

Kilbride-Jones, H. E., 1937-38 — Glass armlets in Britain, *Proc. Soc. Antiq. Scot.*, lxxii, 366-396

King, A. C., 1975 — The animal bones in *Animal Bones in Romano-British Archaeology with particular reference to Cirencester and its region*, unpublished B.A. thesis, Univ. of London

Knorr, R., 1912 — *Die Terra-sigillata Gefässe von Aislingen*, Dillingen

Knorr, R., 1919 — *Topfer und Fabriken verzierter Terra-sigillata ersten Jahrunderts*, Stuttgart

Knorr, R., 1952 — *Terra-sigillata Gefässe des ersten Jahrhunderts mit Topfernamen*, Stuttgart

Koethe, H., 1938 — Zur gestempelten belgischen Keramik aus Trier, in *Festaschrift fur Augutt Oxé*, Dormstadt

Korber-Grohne, U., 1964 — Bestimmungschlüssel für subfossile *Juncus*-Samen und Gramineen Früchte, *Probleme der Küstenforschung in südlichen Nordseegebiet. Bd. 7*

Lehner, H., 1904 — Die Einzelfunde von Novaesium, *Bonner Jahrbücher*, 111/112, Taf. XXXIV, 243-418

Lucy, W. C., 1888 — *The Origin of the Cotteswold Club and an epitome of the proceedings*, Jon Bellows, Gloucester

Lysons, S., 1797 — *An Account of Roman Antiquities discovered at Woodchester in the County of Gloucester*, London

McWhirr, A. D., 1973 — Cirencester, 1969-1972 : Ninth Interim Report, *Antiq. J.*, LIII, 191-218

Macgregor, M., 1976 — *Early Celtic Art in North Britain*, 2 vols. Leicester Univ. Press

Manning, W. H., 1972 — The Iron Work, in *Verulamium Excavations, Vol. I*, (ed. S. S. Frere), Soc. of Antiquaries of London, 28, 163-195

Manning, W. H., 1976 — *Catalogue of Romano-British Ironwork in the Museum of Antiquities, Newcastle-upon-Tyne*, Dept. of Archaeology, The University of Newcastle-upon-Tyne

Margary, I. D., 1973 — *Roman Roads in Britain*, 3rd. ed., London

Marsh, G., and Tyers, P., 1976 — Roman Pottery from the City of London, *Trans. London Middlesex Archaeol. Soc.*, 27, 228-255

May, T., 1916 — *The Pottery found at Silchester*, Reading

May, T., 1930 — *Catalogue of the Pottery in the Colchester and Essex Museum*, Cambridge

Munro, R., 1882 — *Notice of Excavations made on an Ancient Fort at Seamill, Ayrshire*, Archaeological and Historical Collections relating to the Counties of Ayr and Wigtown, III, 1882, 59-65

Myres, J. N. L., *et al*, 1959 — The Defences of *Isurium Brigantum* (Aldborough), *Yorkshire Archaeol. J.*, XL, 1-78

Nash-Williams, V. E., 1932 — The Roman Legionary Fortress at Caerleon, Mons.. Report on the Excavations carried out in the Prysg Field, 1927-9, *Archaeol. Cambrensis*, 87, 48-105

Negus, P. E., and Beauvais, L., 1975 — The Fairford Coral Bed (English Bathonian) Gloucestershire, *Proc. Geol. Assoc.*, 86, 183-199

O'Neil, H. E., 1965 — Excavations in the King's School Gardens, Gloucester, *Trans. Bristol Gloucestershire Archaeol. Soc.*, 84, 1965 (1966), 15-27

O'Rahilly, T. F., 1946 — *Early Irish History and Mythology*

O.R.L. 14, 1901, Nr. 73 — Das Kastell Pfunz, Streckenkomissar : Gutsbesitzer Fr. Winkelmann

Oswald, A., 1939 — A Roman skillet from Broxtowe, Nottingham, *Antiq. J.*, 19, 441

Oswald, F., 1948 — *The Commandant's House at Margidunum*, Nottingham

Oswald, F., 1952 — The Volute in late-Arretine Ware, and its adoption in early South Gaulish Terra Sigillata in the Tiberius-Claudius period, *Antiq. J.*, XXXI, 149-153

Oswald, F., and Pryce, T. D., 1920 — *An Introduction to the Study of Terra Sigillata*, London

Owen, R., 1846 — *A History of British Mammals and Birds,* London

Palmer, T.J., 1979 — The Hampen Marly and White Limestone formations, *Paleontology*, 22, 189-228

Palmer, T. J., and Fursich, F. T., 1974 — The ecology of a Middle Jurassic hardground and crevice fauna, *Palaeontology*, 17, 507-524

Parsons, C. F., 1976 — Ammonite evidence for dating some Inferior Oolite sections in the north Cotswolds, *Proc. Geol. Assoc.*, 87, 45-64

Payne, S., 1972 — Partial recovery and sample bias : the results of some sieving experiments, in *Papers in Economic Prehistory*, (ed. E. S. Higgs), Cambridge

Peacock, D. P. S., 1967 — The heavy mineral analysis of pottery : a preliminary report, *Archaeometry*, 10, 97-100

Peacock, D. P. S., 1968 — A petrological study of certain Iron Age pottery from Western England, *Proc. Prehist. Soc.* 34, 414-426

Peacock, D. P. S., 1977 — Pompeian Red Ware, in *Pottery and Early Commerce*, (ed. D. P. S. Peacock), 147-162

Petrikovits, H. von, 1961 — Die Ansgrabungen in Neuss (Stand der Ausgrabungen Ende 1961), *Bonner Jahrbücher*, 161, 449-485

Pfeffer, W. von, and Haevernick, T. E., 1958 — Zarte Rippenschale, *Saalburg Jahrbuch*, XVII, 76-88

Phillips, J., 1844 — *Memoirs of William Smith LL.D.*, John Murray, London

Rawes, B., 1972 — Roman Pottery Kilns at Gloucester, *Trans. Bristol Gloucestershire Archaeol. Soc.*, XCI, 1972 (1973), 18-59

Reece, R., 1977 — The Ashcroft Site, Cirencester, *Trans. Bristol Gloucestershire Archaeol. Soc.*, xciv, 92-100

Rennie, D. M., 1959 — The Excavation of an Earthwork on Rodborough Common in 1954-55, *Trans. Bristol Gloucestershire Archaeol. Soc.*, 1959 (1960), LXXVIII, 24-43

Rennie, D. M., 1971 — Excavatons in the Parsonage Field, Cirencester, *Trans. Bristol Gloucestershire Archaeol. Soc.*, XC, 1971 (1972), 64-94

Richardson, K. M., 1962 — Excavations in Parsonage Field, Cirencester, 1959, *Antiq.*

J., XLII, 167

Richardson, L., 1904   *A handbook to the Geology of Cheltenham and neighbourhood*, Norman, Sawyer and Co., Cheltenham reprinted 1972

Richardson, L., 1911   On the sections of Forest Marble and Great Oolite on the Railway between Cirencester and Chedworth, Gloucestershire, *Proc. Geol. Assoc.*, 22, 95-115

Richardson, L., 1922   A boring at Calcutt, near Cricklade, Wiltshire, *Geol. Mag.*, 59, 354-355

Richardson, L., 1925   Excursion to Cirencester and District, *Proc. Geol. Assoc.*, 36, 80-99

Richardson, L., 1933   The Country around Cirencester, *Mem. Geol. Surv. England and Wales*, (sheet 235)

Richardson, L., and Webb, R. J., Brickearths, pottery and brickmaking in Gloucestershire,
1910   *Proc. Chelt. Natur. Sci. Soc. N. S.*, 1, 222-282

Richmond, I., 1968   *Hod Hill : Excavations carried out between 1951 and 1958 for the Trustees of the British Museum*, Vol. II, London

Ricken, H., 1939   Die Bildschüsseln der Kastelle Saalburg und Zugmantel II. Teil, *Saalburg Jahrbuch*, IX, 87-96

Ritterling, E., 1913   *Das frührömische Lager bei Hofheim, im Taunus*, Annalen des Vereins fur Nassauische Altertumskunde, XL

Rivet, A. L. F., (ed.) 1969   *The Roman Villa in Britain*, London

Rodwell, W., 1976   Coinage, Oppida and the rise of Belgic Power in South-Eastern Britain, in *Oppida : the beginnings of Urbanisation in Barbarian Europe*, (ed. B. W. Cunliffe and T. Rowley), *Brit. Archaeol. Rep.* Supplementary Series II, 1976, 181-367

Rogers, G. B., 1974   *Poteries sigillées de la Gaule Centrale, I : les motifs non figurés*, Gallia, Suppl. 28.

RIB   Collingwood, R. G., and Wright, R. P., *The Roman Inscriptions of Britain*, I, 1965

RCHM(Eng), 1962   *Eburacum : Roman York, Vol. I*, Royal Commission on Historical Monuments, England

Rouvier-Jeanlin, M., 1972   *Les Figurines Gallo-Romaines en Terre-cuite au Musée des Antiquités Nationales*, Gallia, Suppl. 24

Savory, H. N., 1966   A Find of Early Iron Age Metalwork from the Lesser Garth, Pentyrch (Glam.), *Archaeol. Cambrensis*, CXV, 27-44

Sieveking, G., de G., *et al*, 1976   *Problems in Economic and Social Archaeology*, London

Silvan, P. L. I, 1976   Litofacies del Bathoniano en el area de Cirencestre (Gloucester) Inglaterra, *Primes Congress Geol. Chilerp 1*, C41-56

Silver, I. A., 1963   The ageing of domestic animals, in *Science in Archaeology*, (eds. D. Brothwell, and E. Higgs), 283-302

Smith, D. J., 1973   *The Great Pavement and Roman Villa at Woodchester, Gloucestershire*, F. Bailey, Dursley

Smith, W., 1816-1819   *Strata identified by Organised Fossils*, Part 1-4, London

Smith, W., 1817   *Stratigraphical System of Organised Fossils*, Part 1, London, F. Williams

Stanfield, J. A., 1937   Romano-British decorated jugs and the work of the potter *Sabinus*, *J. Roman Stud.*, XXVII, 168-79

Stanfield, J. A., and Simpson,   *Central Gaulish Potters*, London
G., 1958

Stead, I. M., 1965   *The La Tène Cultures of Eastern Yorkshire*

Stead, I. M., 1976   *Excavations at Winterton Roman Villa*, Dept. of the

	Environment Archaeological Reports, no. 9
Stein, E., 1932	*Romische Beamte und Truppenkorper in Deutschland*, Vienna
Stevenson, R. B. K., 1954–56	Native Bangles and Roman Glass, *Proc. Soc. Antiq. Soc.*, lxxxviii, 208-221
Swan, V. G., 1975	Oare reconsidered and the origins of Savernake Ware in Wiltshire, *Britannia*, VI, 39-61
Tacitus, *Annales*, xii, 31	
Thawley, C. R., in preparation	*The animal bones from Roman Cirencester*
Thill, G., 1969	Fibeln vom Titelberg aus den Beständen des Luxemburger Museums, *Trierer Zeitschrift*, 32, 133-172
Todd, M., 1968	*The Roman Fort at Great Casterton*, Nottingham
Torrens, H. S., 1969	*Guides to Field Excursions from London*, International Field Symposium on the British Jurassic, Keele University
Torrens, H. S., 1978	Geological Communications in the Bath area in the last half of the Eighteenth Century, in Jordanova, L. J., and Porter, R. S. (eds.) *Images of the Earth*, British Society for the History of Science, Monograph 1, 215-247
Torrens, H. S., 1980	Bathonian correlation chart, in Cope, J. C. W., (ed.) *A correlation of Jurassic rocks in the British Isles : Part 2* Geological Society of London Special Report, 15
Ulbert, G., 1959	Die Römischen Donau-Kastelle Aislingen und Burghöfe, *Limesforschungen*, I, Berlin
Ulbert, G., 1969	Das Fruhromische Kastell Rheingönheim, Limesforschungen, 9, Berlin
Wacher, J. S., 1969	*Excavations at Brough-on-Humber, 1958-61*, Soc. of Antiquaries of London
Wacher, J. S., 1975	*The Towns of Roman Britain*, London
Waugh, H., and Goodburn, R., 1972	The non-ferrous objects, in *Verulamium Excavations, Vol. I*, (ed. S. S. Frere), Soc. of Antiquaries of London, 28, 115-162
Webster, G., 1959	Cirencester, Dyer Court Excavation, 1957, *Trans. Bristol Gloucestershire Archaeol. Soc.*, LXXVIII, 1959 (1960), 44-85
Webster, G., 1960	The Roman Military Advance under Ostorius Scapula, *Archaeol. J.*, 115, 1958 (1960), 49-98
Webster, G., 1963-4	A Roman bronze saucepan from Caves Inn, *Trans. Birmingham Archaeol. Soc.*, 81, 1963-4 (1966), 143-4
Webster, P. V., 1976	Severn Valley Ware : A Preliminary Study, *Trans. Bristol Gloucestershire Archaeol. Soc.*, XCIV 18-46
Wheeler, R. E. M., 1930	*London in Roman Times*, London Museum Catalogue, no. 3
Wheeler, R. E. M. and Wheeler, T. V., 1936	*Verulamium : A Belgic and Two Roman Cities*, Soc. of Antiquaries of London, 11
White, K. D., 1970	*Roman Farming*, London
Williams, D. F., 1977	The Romano-British Black-Burnished Industry : An essay on characterization by heavy mineral analysis, in *Pottery and Early Commerce*, (ed. D. P. S. Peacock), 163-220
Wilson, D. R., 1966	Roman Britain in 1965, *J. Roman Stud.*, lvi (1966), 203-4
Wilson, M. G., 1972	The Coarse Pottery, in *Verulamium Excavations, Vol I*, (ed. S. S. Frere), 263-370
Woodward, H. B., 1884	A memoir of Dr. S. P. Woodward ALS, FGS., *Trans. Norfolk Norwich Nat. Soc.*, 3, 279-312
Woodward, H. B., 1894	The Jurassic Rocks of Britain, vol. 4, The Lower Oolite

Rocks of England, *Mem. Geol. Surv. U.K.*

Woodward, S. P., 1848

On the geology of the district explored by the Cotteswold Club and more particularly the clay subsoil of the (Royal Agricultural) College Farm, *Proc. Cotteswold Natur. Fld. Club*, 1, 2-8

Wright, R. P., and Hassall, M. W. C., 1974

Roman Britain in 1973 : Inscriptions, *Britannia*, V, 461

INDEX